Direct Investment and Joint Ventures in China

Direct Investment and Joint Ventures in China

A HANDBOOK FOR CORPORATE NEGOTIATORS

James E. Shapiro, Jack N. Behrman,
William A. Fischer,
and
Simon G. Powell

QUORUM BOOKS

New York • Westport, Connecticut • London

Library of Congress Cataloging-in-Publication Data

Direct investment and joint ventures in China : a handbook for
    corporate negotiators / James E. Shapiro . . . [et al.].
        p.   cm.
    Includes bibliographical references and index.
    ISBN 0–89930–646–2 (alk. paper)
        1. Investments, Foreign—China.   2. Joint ventures—China.
    3. Technology transfer—China.   I. Shapiro, James E.
    HG5782.D57   1991
    658′.044–dc20   91–15

British Library Cataloguing in Publication Data is available.

Library of Congress Catalog Card Number: 91–15
ISBN: 0–89930–646–2

First published in 1991

Quorum Books, One Madison Avenue, New York, NY 10010
An imprint of Greenwood Publishing Group, Inc.

Printed in the United States of America

The paper used in this book complies with the
Permanent Paper Standard issued by the National
Information Standards Organization (Z39.48–1984).

10 9 8 7 6 5 4 3 2 1

Copyright Acknowledgments

The authors and publisher gratefully acknowledge permission to reprint material
from the following sources:

Documents on Xerox joint venture negotiations with China.

William A. Fischer, "The Structure and Organization of Chinese Industrial
R&D Activities." *R&D Management* 13, no. 2, 1983.

Contents

Illustrations

FIGURES

Preface

On a trip to China for one of his many negotiation sessions with Chinese officials and for seminar dialogues with them and academics on issues of foreign direct investment and technology transfer, Jim Shapiro commented to me that someday he wanted to write a book about his experiences in forming the Xerox equity joint venture in Shanghai. He wanted to provide some guidance to newcomers so that their learning curve could be shortened. Out of this conversation has come this book; because the subject is so vast and changing, it expanded into much more than originally envisioned. The focus is on the foreign direct investment route to "doing business," with technology transfers as a secondary topic; trade issues are not included, nor are military transactions.

The reason for another volume on China is that nothing in the existing literature combines in one place an appreciation of the nuances faced in negotiation of joint ventures with an examination of the investment environment in China and an assessment of its past traditions, current policies, and emerging problems. To encompass these aspects has required the talents of all four of the co-authors.

James Shapiro, who traveled frequently to China during the mid-1980s, is the source of major company experiences included—not only those arising from the Xerox joint ventures he negotiated, but also those from cases of various other companies, plus the effects on joint ventures of shifts in China's policies. These show the direct relevance of the arguments and theses of the book. Jim brought experience of joint venture negotiation with Xerox in the South Pacific, as well as from his current role as chief executive officer of a DuPont-Xerox venture in the United States. He also provided a mass of materials on the development of China's policy to foreign direct investment and joint ventures, without which the chapters would be much less complete.

William Fischer is an academic "China hand," having spent substantial time

teaching Chinese enterprise-managers and ministerial officials about manufacturing management and technology transfers; out of these experiences and much
empirical research he has written a number of case-oriented analyses, and has
been called on by many groups to guide their education on China's new business
development policies.

Simon Powell has a Ph.D. in economic geography, with a concentration on
China. He has contributed to several studies of China's development and was,
fortunately, ''on the scene'' when this book was initiated. As with the others,
his major contribution stemmed directly from his background, but none of the
co-authors restricted themselves to one specific topic. Dr. Powell also made a
major contribution in editing and arranging the arguments of the entire work,
plus providing empirical support for them.

I am the only one without professional experience in China, though I have
had the good fortune to visit and lecture there on occasion during the past four
years. My listeners were intrigued by my ''broad knowledge'' of China. My
reply was that ''I know little of China, but I have studied economic development
and governmental policies toward foreign direct investment and technology transfers around the world, and China faces problems similar to those of other countries in similar stages of development.'' In my explanations to various Chinese
groups of the orientations of transnational companies, I learned quite a bit about
their expectations. In addition, I have spent many years studying cross-cultural
aspects of management, and China was part of that research.

Although one often finds substantial difficulties in meshing the views and
styles of several authors, this has not been the case in this effort. Each author
made substantial contributions to the work of the others, so that we all learned
as we worked together. It has been a distinct pleasure to work with such professionals and to be able to bring this book to fruition. I trust that it serves well
the purpose for which it was written.

One of the objectives of the book is to help transnational enterprises to explain
their contributions to Chinese officials more completely. Few Americans have
had significant experience with the Chinese, and few Chinese have had much
experience with Western-type enterprises.

The audience addressed is not only business managers, for whom the book is
principally written, but also government officials both in the United States and
China and in other foreign countries (which are seeking to obtain more preferred
positions through direct negotiations). In addition, graduate students in business
schools will find the volume useful, as will a general public seeking to understand
the conflicts arising in a country that is trying to accelerate its economic growth
by moving out of a centrally planned into a market-driven economy.

The opening of the Chinese economy to activities of transnational corporations
(TNCs) is a historic act, significantly altering the makeup and direction of the
Chinese economy. It will take decades to sort out the implications for China's
position in the world. Although the outcome is principally in China's hands, it
is not wholly so. The response of TNCs also is critical, and the necessity to find

an accommodation between TNCs and the Chinese government is a new experience for both parties.

It is too soon to tell whether the "opening" will succeed. But so much has been committed already that any rupture of the current initiatives will set back China's progress for years to come—much more than the mere delay of lost time. Nor is the shape of new developments clear. All that can be said is that a new road has been taken, that the condition of the road is not fully known, nor its direction; it also is not clear how long it will be before significant mileposts are passed. It appears evident, however, that China cannot reach current levels of living standards in the West until the middle of the twenty-first century.

This book was prepared for publication just as the events in Tiananmen Square broke the strides China was making toward a more open economy. It was decided to hold off for a while to assess the probable changes. We have since updated the materials, assessed the impacts, and modified our views as was thought necessary. Two sections were added on the aftermath of Tiananmen and its impacts on attitudes of foreign investors, as well as specific changes throughout each chapter.

But both China and many Western (and Eastern) companies have placed sizable bets on a successful entry of China into the world economy. It is important for any major company to assess the impacts of China's opening on its international business strategy and to make appropriate modifications. It is hoped that this book will significantly assist in that endeavor.

Jack N. Behrman
Chapel Hill, N.C.

1

Introduction and Overview

The opening of the Chinese economy offers two opportunities to the West: an expansion of the world economy with wider industrial integration, and the opening of new opportunities for business in China, including the upgrading of China's labor and management. It also creates substantial challenges as the Chinese are likely to evolve into formidable competitors in a number of industries.

Although political and economic developments at the macrolevel in China will directly affect the activities of companies attempting to do business there, of more immediate concern to Western business are the opportunities to invest in China to serve either the local or export market. Indeed, corporate expectations regarding the potential profits in the short or long term may be one of the most critical factors for the success of Western investments. The social, political, and economic implications of such long-term investment are so important that the succeeding chapters focus on the investment opportunities and skirt the problems of direct exports and imports, except as tied into a direct reinvestment of technology transfer. Rather, the emphasis is on why and how Western business should consider entering the Chinese economy, the obstacles that can be expected, the methods of negotiation, the alternatives offered, and the future environment for business. This environment has been changing rapidly in the past ten years, and it can be expected to do so in the future, though not at the same rate or in the same ways.

The general trend in the reforms that the Chinese government has embarked on over the past twelve years or so constitute a full-scale restructuring not only of the economy, but also of the institution of property, the patterns and sources of decision-making, the role of the market, the position of financial institutions, and the role of government. The objective is to raise the standard of living of its people, numbering roughly 1.1 billion, so as to begin to match that in developing countries, most of which are ahead of China. With a per capita gross national product (GNP) of $250 to $300, China averages only one-tenth that of Taiwan and only one-fiftieth that of the United States. It will take fifty to seventy years for the Chinese to reach the U.S. levels of today, and maybe longer. The high rates of economic growth that China has enjoyed for the pase decade, and that can be expected for several more years, will undoubtedly decline as much of the easy growth is achieved and the harder problems remain. But even if China can grow at the rate of 5 percent per year (a respectable rate by the recent standards of the OECD [Organization for Economic Cooperation and Development] nations), GNP will double every fifteen years or so, which will mean an increasingly attractive market plus increasing abilities to become competitive internationally.

Sustained Chinese economic growth will have profound consequences both inside and outside the region. As the Chinese economy develops, foreign firms will increasingly have to learn to establish themselves in this market and to do business there. Similarly, the domestic markets of many foreign countries will experience Chinese competition at home. In many cases in fact the situation will turn out to be a zero-sum game; exports from China will mean less production at home or in another source country. Companies will have to integrate China into their long-term sourcing strategies as well as their marketing plans.

For its part, China by then will have completed substantial movement toward the accomplishment of the "four modernizations" of agriculture, industry, political and military, and science and technology; the goals were to achieve 1980s world class status in each of these fields by the end of the century. None of these will come easily, and each requires substantial redirection of institutional structures and the formation of new justifications to support such radical changes. China currently is embracing an ideology of pragmatism, asserting that what works is what is appropriate and good. The "working" is toward an advanced economic system, which most immediately raises living standards throughout the populace. Yet China is not likely to give up its orientation to socialism, which emphasizes a distribution of wealth that is more equitable than exists in the current capitalist countries. Although it is now said that "to get rich is glorious," the glory will quickly fade if there is not a reasonably broad participation in the benefits of the reforms through an improved standard of living. The perks of officials (special stores to shop in, vacations, autos, and many other sanctioned and unsanctioned privileges of the elite) and their favoritism to family and friends were major complaints in the 1989 occupation of Tiananmen Square by students and workers. Despite the trappings of modernity, the confusion over market influences, and the native entrepreneurial talents of those whose fates lie outside the formal economic system, China still retains a large degree of sympathy toward communal objectives, egalitarianism, and socialist goals.

Along with this shift toward pragmatism, new political institutions and relations will have to be developed to support an economy freed from central planning. This implies a repositioning of the privilege and security of the old guard toward the young and expert. But the primary significance of the opening to Western business is outwardly a complete shift in attitudes from indifference, suspicion, and even antagonism toward foreign companies to friendliness and welcome.

This is not to suggest that the future role of foreign business within the Chinese economy is necessarily clear-cut. In its turn to pragmatism the Chinese government has sought to learn lessons from the experience of other developing countries with foreign direct investment (FDI). It commissioned a number of studies by U.N. organizations and examined the record of many other countries. The lessons it has learned were the same as those recognized in the 1950s in the many studies of the "climate for foreign investment" made both within the United States and elsewhere as a means of determining how to use private investment to stimulate growth in less developed countries. The characteristics identified included the establishment of a "welcoming attitude," which seeks to accommodate the needs of companies basing their decisions mostly on free-market criteria; the establishment of legal institutions and regulations that would permit freedom of decision-making and protect proprietary rights; even-handed application of statutes and regulations; willingness to negotiate the implementation of regulations to fit the specific needs in a given sector or for different company conditions and orientations; a recognition that the general treatment of business in the country is more important than specific incentives to individual foreign investors or to foreign investors as a whole; and the necessity to maintain general economic health as an attraction to FDI.

Even if China can offer these prerequisites and supporting conditions, there will remain a number of problems in FDI. China has recognized some of them and has sought to ameliorate them through continued dialogues with both public and private officials in foreign countries. A number of seminars have been conducted both in and outside of China on the new open-door policy and what it means to foreign investment. These seminars have critiqued the existing policies of the Chinese government and proposed modifications to make them more attractive and effective.

A major attraction to all outsiders is the size of the potential Chinese market, causing them to be eager to get in during the early phases. This eagerness has bolstered the bargaining strengths of the various levels of Chinese government, each of which has responded differently to its relative bargaining positions vis-a-vis the foreign investor. In many instances (contrary to the experience in other less developed countries) the local (provincial and municipal) governments have been more recalcitrant, at least in the implementation of agreements with foreign investors, than has the central government. In other cases (those in the South—Guangdong and Guangzhou) the local governments have moved far beyond the original pace and intentions of the central government in working with foreigners. Each government level is seeking to maintain a balance between attracting the foreigner, giving him greater leeway than has existed in the past for domestic enterprise, and at the same time protecting the community's interest, including the power and position of officials in the government. Each government is aware of the "zero-sum" nature of foreign investment location in China, and of the potential domestic political consequences associated with being "too close to foreigners." Delicate balancing of changes is required, which obviously will never be "just right." To achieve even an acceptable balance will require a continuous negotiating stance on the part of foreign investors, which is not the way they usually like to operate. Going in with this expectation will prepare the foreign investor, but it also will make others in the company nervous. Corporations like stability, but this is not available in any country completely, and in China stability in the Western sense of doing business goes out the window almost immediately. With the realization that conditions need to be negotiated, investors have the opportunity to bargain for a degree of permanence on some key issues important to them.

CHINA'S CURRENT OPEN-DOOR ATTITUDE

To help in achieving the necessary understanding of the situation in China, as well as to develop a flexible approach to entry, it is necessary to begin with a characterization of China's current attitudes toward opening up to the outside world and to foreign business in particular. It is not enough to know what the current policies are; it also is necessary to know why they have been developed and, therefore, what their likely direction will be as conditions change competitively throughout Southeast Asia and around the world in major industrial sectors. The question arises—after years of endorsing the benefits of relative economic autarky and "self-reliance"—as to whether China is more likely to accept a degree of interdependence through trade, or will it eventually welcome a durable and competitive foreign investment presence within its domestic market?

The overall environment for private investment—whether local or foreign—is in many ways more important to the foreign investor than any special incentives or attractions offered to him in negotiation. It is, therefore, desirable to examine the geographical location of economic activity and the special incentives for private enterprise throughout the economy. Priority attention has been given to Special Economic Zones, the coastal cities, various open economic zones, and open inland cities. A serious problem of balance in economic development has arisen, however, and continuous attention will be given to that among the various levels of government, frequently changing the environment for the foreign investor. The organizational structures open to foreign investors will be a matter of negotiation, and the emphasis placed on one form or another (e.g., wholly owned foreign ventures, joint ventures, compensation trade, licensing) will shift according to the policy objectives of the various levels of government.

China has, however, in its quest for foreign technology and investment, continuously (if sometimes awkwardly) extended itself to create a hospitable climate for foreign investment. China's record over the past decade or more in fashioning a legal environment for doing business displays great efforts, given the distance it has had to come to equal the position in other developing countries. To give stability and a higher degree of certainty plus freedom to the foreign investor, more than 100 laws have been passed relative to private enterprise and the foreign investor during the past ten years, and each of them is in varying degrees of implementation through a variety of regulations. China, however, often has announced new policies, such as the "22 Articles" on foreign investment in November 1986, without any published guidelines for implementation. This moves the process along more quickly but causes more confusion and uncertainty, while lower levels of government attempt to interpret and implement the changes.

Despite these efforts at hospitality, China has had only differential success in attracting foreign investors; the primary sources are Hong Kong and Macao, with Taiwan, the United States, and Japan among the next most active (the United States the next largest and Japan the third). The differences and the timing of the various national investments are significant, with Hong Kong alone representing nearly 65 percent of financial investments during the years of initial opening in 1979–1985, with only 13 percent from the United States and just under 10 percent from Japan during the same period. The remainder was spread over a number of countries, including West Germany, France, Britain, and even some developing countries. After the economic slump of 1986, foreign investment in China began to pick up again, peaking in a boom during 1988 and up through the first quarter of 1989, but abruptly brought to a halt by events after the killings in Tiananmen Square in June of 1989. During this boom period, "foreign investors committed US $5,297.06 million in direct investment to a total of 5,945 projects in China. These figures were 42.9 percent and 166.2 percent higher than the $3,708.84 million invested in 2,233 projects the previous year."[1] At this point in time, 65.6 percent of the foreign investment came from Hong Kong and Macao, 16.1 percent from Japan, and 7.4 percent from the United States. In the post-Tiananmen period, Taiwan has become the single largest foreign investor in China: By the end of 1989, Taiwanese investment represented 60 percent of all new foreign investment in China made after the events of June 1989. Primarily located in Fujian Province, most of the investment has been in low-technology, labor-intensive operations. Despite this fact, the average Taiwanese investment has risen from US $2 million in 1989 to $3.6 million in 1990.[2]

In the wake of the Tiananmen incident, foreign investment in China dropped precipitously. Even official Chinese figures showed a 43 percent drop, relative to the year before, in newly approved contracts during the fourth quarter of 1989 and a 42 percent drop, also against year-earlier figures, in the first quarter of 1990.[3] By the fourth quarter of 1990, these figures once again began to show some signs of a reverse, albeit at a much slower rate of growth than nearly any time in the previous decade.

Throughout much of the 1980s, the major foreign investments were in the resource and service sectors (hotels), and they were located primarily in the major metropolitan and coastal areas, taking advantage of the concentration of labor, transport, and customers.

China is not a society in which information is readily gathered or disseminated. As one "China-hand" has commented many times, "what you are about to hear is true; it just may not be terribly reliable."[4] Thus, given the enormity of both the country and the economic experimentation that has been taking place, almost anything is true of China somewhere, sometime. The problem is determining relevance to particular decisions. Even so, some generalities hold, and some general insights can be generated for decision-making by foreign investors with regard to the nature of its market, the process of decision-making, the demographic structure of the peoples, the relative significance of the cities and the rural areas as buyers and suppliers, and the role of government as a consumer.

It is equally difficult to determine the characteristics of China as a production base, again because of the scarcity of information. Even so, some information is available on the resource base of the economy, its infrastructure in terms of transportation, communication, and education, the skill of its labor force, and its managerial capacities. The production process in China has long been guided by central planning, but presumably it will now move toward freer decision-making. This movement will begin to alter the nature of the enterprise itself, which has historically been a cultural and social center within Chinese industrial society. The freer movement of labor into and out of enterprise could reduce that orientation. Further, it is equally likely that management styles will shift from merely achieving production quotas to full-scale enterprise decision-making on investment, production, marketing research, sales and distribution, and research and development technology innovation. This will entail a greater concern for cost and tax accounting and personnel responsibilities (including recruiting, amenities, training, firing, and relocation). It also will raise issues concerning the potential failure of factories, the application of bankruptcy law, and the general division of responsibility between government and corporate officials.

In any negotiation on entry or operation of foreign investment projects, the different levels of Chinese government will be primarily concerned with the contributions that foreign investors can make to the interests of the community to which they are responsible. The Chinese government, as with most developing countries, is primarily concerned with contributions to employment, technology inflow, export opportunities, and, specifically, industrial advance and foreign exchange earnings. It also is concerned with the location of economic activity and contribution to the development of managerial skills and the infrastructure of China for further industrial development. These priorities are reflected in the degree to which incentives are offered for each of these and the extent to which freedom of decision-making is permitted the foreign investor.

A major concern of China is to increase the local content of products manufactured in the country, reducing the import content and enhancing the ability of local vendors to supply the foreign investor. Although there have been some success stories, such as Volkswagen's reaching 50 percent local content in the production of the Santana automobile in Shanghai, the difficulty of finding such potential suppliers and negotiating firm arrangements with them remains a serious obstacle to FDI. Although suppliers in China range from very poor (almost back to the 1930s) to excellent (as advanced as any other suppliers), the task of upgrading the poorer factories is so great that the Chinese government wants foreign investors to undertake it.

Given the potential problems and opportunities, an understanding of the economic, commercial, and financial networks, before negotiation, becomes critical. Multiple levels of negotiation are necessary, and each party has its own attitudes toward the foreign investor and the way negotiation should take place. Negotiations may be required with the vendors and suppliers, with central ministries, and with provincial and city bureaus. Each of them expects a certain amount of delineation of roles in the feasibility studies offered as the basis of the project. Early understanding of their differences will eliminate a number of errors that need to be reviewed by a potential foreign investor. Of significance also to the foreign investor is the fact that Chinese custom permits a request for renegotiation of contracts almost from the moment of signing and virtually any time within the duration of the agreement. But this does not mean that China will not honor contracts. Only in extremis will contracts be broken, and even then some restitution is likely.

A major guideline for success, therefore, is a degree of flexibility on the part of the foreigner, yet also firmness as to the limits beyond which he cannot be expected to go. The negotiator needs to identify early on the fundamental, critical elements for the success of the venture and hold fast to them.

Finally, given that the situation in China and its open policy are highly dynamic, changing not only from lack of experience, but also from success and failures in various directions, an assessment of likely future problems is desirable. For both China and potential investors the negative experiences of some investors in the recent past are a serious obstacle. Some understanding by both sides of the reasons for these experiences is desirable to assist in future negotiations.

Governmental policies at all levels will undoubtedly shift in the future, and foreign investors need to be involved in dialogues concerning the process of change. Foreign investors also can expect that the competitive situation in China will change significantly because local companies will become more autonomous and sensitive to market signals and other foreigners will enter to serve the Chinese market or create a base for international production. The development of domestic suppliers will remain a high priority for the Chinese government, and attention will need to be paid to training, developing high-quality products, financing these operations, and helping them find markets so as to expand their scale of production and reduce their costs. Foreign investors should reach firm agreements with domestic suppliers and government agencies before undertaking any development activities. The real growth of opportunities in China will be a function of the evolution of the domestic market, which is itself a function of marketing activities and distribution facilities. Responsibility for developing these will fall on the enterprises rather than on the Chinese government.

Conceptually, China's master plan is to pay for technology transfers with incremental exports. In the simplest form, China would import foreign equipment to develop exportable products from Chinese material and labor. AMF did this for some years with leather balls. The lack of a large supplier base in China makes this considerably more difficult, if not impossible, with more advanced products such as automobiles and copiers. How to overcome this gap is the challenge facing foreign investors.

The push to export also will remain for quite some time, despite the fact that the largest market opportunities are within China (comparatively), since world markets are already well served from other sources. Therefore, a great deal of thought will be required to determine how to fit Chinese production into existing channels of distribution. The scarcity of foreign exchange will continue for a decade or more, given the high demand for capital equipment, components, and even some raw materials. This will require some imaginative financing and exchange of currencies to maintain access to funds both for acquisition of technology and for repatriation of profits, as required by foreign investors.

There also will undoubtedly be a future emphasis within China on the development of local research and development institutes, both those that are tied to companies and those that are independent, serving all members of an industrial sector. Support for these will be sought at all government levels, and therefore the foreign investor who is able to think ahead in this direction and provide early support will garner considerable gratitude, if not economic advantage.

The opening of China should be seen as a major opportunity to expand freedom both economically and politically, and for either Chinese or foreigners to miss or to corrupt this opportunity is itself a disservice to humanity. The aftermath of Tianamen (June 1989) appears as a reversion to central planning, but the reforms have taken hold sufficiently so they cannot be eliminated. They will be tabled for a while or weakened, but the passing of the current leadership will be followed by more openings. Even with some reversion toward planning, China is open to FDI and continues to prepare Special Economic Zones.

China seems to move in cycles of change, but the sequencing will alter with new leadership. In his *Search for Modern China*, the historian Jonathan Spence records repetitions of anti-imperial, antigovernmental plots and revolts; the impression is left that such is the very nature of China. The country repeatedly seems to require centralization, but not of the types of authority that arise within it. One cycle that has rather long waves is that of opening to the world and then turning inward again. Spence notes Hegel's views in the 1820s that China seemed incapable of joining the world and repeated insistence by the West (the latest by Nixon in the 1970s) that it do so. This sequence has been repeated over the past 400 years.[5] So one must take the long view.

The current economic imperatives are recognized as requiring liberalization, even though the political system will remain centralized. The openings in the 1980s are, therefore, to be seen as harbingers of a more liberal future. And this is as it should be, for the world is ill-served by economies that cannot become modernized because of the weakness of individuals or officials in being unable to serve causes larger than themselves. Both China and the foreign business community will be ill-served if there is a repeat of the pattern of the eighteenth- and nineteenth-century corruption of the government and of Chinese society, sometimes through foreign influence.

Historically, China has held a view of itself that is elevated beyond that of being a mere member of the world community to one through which the earth is tied to heaven. Its name as "the Middle Kingdom" (Zhong meaning "middle" and Kuo meaning "kingdom") reinforces this concept of its destiny, and it is matched on the Western side (United States and Western Europe) by the concept of liberalism, democracy, and market-driven economies. These two philosophical traditions now appear to have an unprecedented opportunity to join in setting the atmosphere of cooperation and collaboration, as well as competition, within a world economy that is being more closely integrated and that needs a greater sense of a worldwide community of interest.

NOTES

1. China-North Asia Section, JETRO, "Direct Investments in China Losing Momentum," *Jetro China Newsletter*, January–February 1990, pp. 17–20.

2. Peter Wickenden, "Taiwan in Two Minds on Trade with China," *Financial Times*, June 6, 1990, p. 8.

3. Julia Leung, "China's Lure for Foreign Investors Fades," *Wall Street Journal/ Europe*, August 20, 1990, p. 10.

4. John Frankenstein, personal communication.

5. Jonathan D. Spence, *The Search for Modern China* (New York: W. W. Norton, 1990). *Christian Science Monitor* (May 23, 1989, p. 1) records eight major shifts and significant changes in China during each of the decades of the twentieth century: 1900—Boxer Revolt; 1911—Qing dynasty overthrown and May 4 Movement's demands for democracy; 1920s—rise of Kuomintang and massacre of Communists; 1930s—Communist Long March and Japanese invasion; 1940s—war with Japan and civil war; 1950s—Communist purges and "Great Leap Forward"; 1960s—Cultural Revolution for ten years; 1970s—sweeping economic reforms; 1980s—protests and Tiananmen.

2

China's Open Policy

For thirty years China was the world's most vociferous defender of central economic planning and economic autarky. China's opening of its economy, during the decade of the 1980s, to market influences in production and consumption, in distribution of goods and income, and in acquisition of private property and to individual motivation was a historic reversal of its political and social objectives and economic policies. Adding the initiatives in the Soviet Union under Gorbachev to open and restructure the Soviet economy, and the recent economic and political revolutions in Central Europe, there has been a nearly universal recognition of the severe limitations of central planning and its underlying ideology.

Though it may take some years for the Chinese to abandon that system entirely—if they do in fact—it would be a missed opportunity for the nations of the West, as well as Western business, not to take advantage of these openings. There are many reasons why it should be grasped, but to do so successfully requires an understanding of the new policies, as well as the background from which they have emerged.

OFFICIAL WELCOME BY CHINA

China effectively isolated itself and was, in turn, isolated by other powers from interacting with the world economy in the late 1950s, and has only recently looked toward the West for the technology required to modernize its antiquated industrial sector. Although China has identified priority sectors in which it wants foreign businesses to invest, the timing of China's welcoming of foreign investment and the environment in which that investment has been made suggest that China may not benefit as much as it had hoped from what foreign investment has occurred.

From Liberation to the Open Door

China's economic history over the past century has been turbulent, especially so during the Maoist period from 1949 to 1978. After an initial period of economic rehabilitation in the early 1950s, China's policymakers looked to the Soviet Union as a model for their own economic development. China's first five-year plan was promulgated in 1953, relying on the importation of whole factories and basic technology from the Soviet Union (plants and technology that will remain at the heart of China's industrial capability at least into the 1990s).

Beginning in the late 1950s with the disastrous attempt at controlled socialization of the economy (characterized by the small-scale industrialization in the Great Leap Forward) and continuing through the 1960s and early 1970s with the even more disastrous Cultural Revolution, China moved sharply away from trade with the Soviet Union in particular and the Eastern bloc countries in general. But despite this move, China did not significantly increase its dealings with the West until 1972, and even then contact was limited to massive imports of grain to bolster faltering domestic agricultural performance. Not until 1978, with the declaration of the open-door policy, did China's dealings with the West firmly move into the ascendancy, and only then were Western companies officially welcomed to invest directly in the Chinese economy.

In comparison with the paucity of foreign business interests in China between 1949 and 1978, the decade of the 1980s witnessed a reversal of isolationist policies and centralized control. New legislation was passed both to stimulate foreign investment in China and to strictly control its influence. Despite this, China remains a highly protected economy and is still "feeling its way" in dealing with the foreign influences that accompany inflows of foreign direct investment (FDI). Even today China continues to desire self-reliance as far as is possible; but it also faces the reality that without complementary foreign technology, know-how, and management development, the future growth it desires would be too slow.

These competing desires have caused some confusion in policymaking over the past decade. Furthermore, Chinese policymakers lack experience in dealing with the West after years of isolation, and this is reflected in the plethora of legislation concerned with foreign investment that the state has promulgated since 1978. Each new statute or regulation was a "welcome"—an open door— yet each also was a screen, reflecting both hesitancy in allowing too much of a foreign presence and an incomplete understanding of the objectives of foreigners.

China's Need for Foreign Investment

China recognizes the need to be flexible in its attempts to attract foreign investors because the potential benefits of each investor vary.[1] The Chinese realize that FDI in China can promote domestic technological growth and the development of managerial abilities—which, in turn, foster higher domestic standards of living and increase China's national security—through the provision of access to modern management methods, advanced production techniques, and industrial know-how. China's industrial sector is antiquated; one general rule of thumb is that 55 to 60 percent needs replacement, 20 to 25 percent is backward but serviceable, with only 20 percent being post–1960s technology.[2] And its managerial skills remain backward. These are both legacies of China's isolation from the world economy during the Cultural Revolution. They require immediate attention if China is going to be able to fulfill its goals of broad modernization. Perhaps only China's military sector is an exception, as witnessed by China's contracting with the United States to launch satellites after the Challenger disaster and the fact that these factories are in high demand to do nonmilitary work because of their technical capability.

China's self-imposed exile from the world economy also has left it out of the networks of global trade that have been established in the past twenty years. Thus FDI offers China some access to foreign export markets through the distribution channels of the foreign corporations.

The Chinese government also sees FDI as a way to make optimal use of its limited foreign exchange resources by encouraging ventures that will promote import substitution, export promotion, and resource exploitation—without having to spend its scarce foreign exchange. A policy of import substitution continues to be seen as important in allowing China to obtain relevant technology that it can then feed to China's domestic industrial market relatively inexpensively, without exposing the domestic industrial base to foreign competition. Similarly, the Chinese want to develop value-added export industries, which requires the transformation of their export sector from the labor-intensive products that dominate today to more high-tech, capital-intensive products. At the same time, the Chinese believe that, for the moment at least, their comparative advantage lies with low-cost labor. So they have been encouraging foreigners to invest so as to utilize this most abundant resource. Finally, the Chinese also have been quick to allow foreign investors to utilize those natural resources that China itself has not been able to exploit because of a lack of capital and technology. They have adopted this attitude, most noticeably in the development of its oil industry, to earn foreign exchange from the resulting exports, which, in turn, is used to import foreign technology.

Channeling FDI and the Seventh Five-Year Plan

To maximize the benefits to China of foreign investment, the Chinese government has made it clear to foreign investors (both in official statements and in the application of the law on foreign investment) that investment in certain sectors has priority—and consequently will be more readily permitted. These priority sectors were presented in the seventh five-year plan (1986–1990) and include

energy, transport and communications, raw and semifinished materials, and agriculture.

Specifically, opportunites for FDI will be found in such areas as the following:

- Equipment for thermal and hydroelectric power stations
- Extraction of oil, gas, and coal
- Modern telecommunications networks
- The automotive industry
- The railway industry
- Iron and steel products
- Non-ferrous metals
- Chemical industries
- Construction materials industries

Emphasis also has been laid on technological transformation of China's existing enterprises. Between 1983 and 1985 the State Economic Commission identified 3,000 technology import projects that were designed to renovate small and medium-sized projects. Under the seventh five-year plan, this renovation process is being intensified. Again, key sectors for renovation have been identified: machinery, electronics, textiles, food processing, packaging, metallurgical, chemical, pharmaceutical, and construction materials. Within these sectors, the Chinese are looking for technology, know-how, and equipment that will help them to reduce wasteful consumption of energy and raw materials, upgrade product quality (preferably to a level where they can begin to export products), and improve management skills.

Prospects for the Eighth Five-Year Plan

During mid-1990, China was preparing a new five-year plan (the eighth), to run from 1990 to 1995. The underlying strategy, as enunciated by Deng Xiaoping, was to double the gross national product (GNP) between 1980 and 1990 and again from 1990 to 2000. Achieving this second doubling of the GNP during the decade of the nineties is to be based on the following principles:

1. Learn from the lessons and experiences of the past forty years. In today's political and economic environment in China, this first principle is primarily a concern over losing control over the economy and reinitiating the inflationary pressures that surged nearly out of control in the middle and late 1980s. It also is a not-so-subtle reaffirmation of the virtues of some central planning and the dangers associated with too much reliance on market influences.

2. Planning should not be too tight, but should leave some room for flexibility. Given that China has always had the most flexible of central plans, the emphasis here is on the fact that planning will remain, not on the flexibility.

3. Continue to stick to reform and open-door policies. According to a very senior official who shared these principles, and who usually is counted among the so-called economic conservatives in China, "the past ten years argues against isolation and closing [the] door."

4. The development of the five- and ten-year plans should take self-reliance into consideration. A comment by a Chinese official in conversation is illustrative: "If we fail to rely on the Chinese people, our economy cannot develop. This is not contradictory with the open door policy. It allows us to open better. One complements the other."

With these four principles as a guide, the following priority areas will play an integral part in developing the next five-year plan:

Agriculture. The Chinese population will reach 1.25 billion by the year 2000 (or even as high as 1.3 billion). Increased agricultural productivity is a necessity.

Population. For the same reasons, family planning will continue to play a critical role in Chinese development policies.

Water conservation. China has a severe water shortage and a problem of unbalanced availability—there is considerably less water available in the north than there is in the south.

Industry. Energy and transportation will be the first two priorities for industry. Increased use of petroleum and nuclear energy is being planned. Raw materials and process industries also will receive more attention.

These sectors are the most likely priorities for FDI inflows.

During 1990, Chinese officials announced that they did not want FDI in certain areas, for example maintenance of automotive products and household appliances, cotton textiles, food products for domestic consumption, and elevator manufacturing. Yet, for the most part, emphasis continues to be on attracting investment in energy, transportation and infrastructure, raw materials development, and any technology-intensive industry that promotes economic efficiency, upgrades product quality, and increases production capacity.[3] Even with incentives for FDI, however, constraints will remain on access to the domestic market and the emphasis will be on assimilation of technology to permit the Chinese to achieve self-reliance.

The Timing of China's Welcome

China's emergence as a world player has been both dramatic and difficult. China is now more accessible to Western business than at any time since 1949. Yet its opening has not been as easy as perhaps it had anticipated. Although China's goal on foreign investment inflows by the year 2000 seems certain to be exceeded, the amount of FDI in China to this date remains smaller than earlier expected—by both the Chinese and the West. The reluctance shown by foreign businesses toward investment in China illustrates the difficulties China is having creating an environment attractive to FDI. The events of June 1989, and the subsequent erosion of confidence in the vision and even durability of the Chinese government, have not helped to overcome these difficulties. Indeed, these problems have been exacerbated by the opening up of Eastern Europe and the Soviet Union, and their consequential competition with China in challenging investment opportunities.

China's opening also has come at a time of increasing global competition. As a result, many foreign businesses, notably in those areas where innovation and technical advance is slow, are reluctant to "arm" potential competitors with technology, equipment, and know-how that could be used against them in international markets. Japan, for example, is much more ready to export yen to China, through financing arrangements, than it is to transfer technology. Similarly, China has encountered growing protectionist sentiment against its low-cost, labor-intensive exports to the developed world—for example in textiles. By the late 1980s, nearly sixty anti-dumping actions had already been taken in developed countries against such Chinese imports as natural bristle paintbrushes, cast iron products, iron nails, paraffin candles, small-diameter standard welded steel pipe, and enamel cookware.[4]

China's Welcome Compared with That of Other Developing Countries

China has sought to learn from the experience of other developing countries, which have presented a wide range of policies toward international trade and investment.[5] Although the "four dragons" of Southeast Asia have been the most open, others, like Bulgaria and Burma, have been virtually isolationist. Yet all have sought to contain the impacts of foreign investors on their economy and society. Each has had to encourage some degree of nationalism to consolidate their desired economic growth and political stability. China has the same objectives, under different circumstances, and these circumstances make the same policy prescriptions less applicable.

One of the circumstances is that other developing countries have traversed a road that is now well traveled and not as rewarding to late voyagers. Earlier and present less developed countries have attempted to follow the Japanese model of setting priorities for investment inflows aimed at substitution for imports and high-tech sectors. They have played on their low-cost labor and provided protection for new projects, and they opened their domestic markets to FDI affiliates. What they did not recognize was that these markets were potentially not as large as Japan's. Thus they were not able to attract sufficient volumes of investment to meet their needs. Nor have they been willing to permit the transnational corporations (TNCs) to benefit from industrialization among members of a regional association, or been willing to use the TNCs to gain the regional integration avowedly desired.[6] China is following the same path with less favorable results, simply because so many countries still offer similar or greater attractions in both growth and stability. The major comparative advantage that China holds is its potentially large domestic market; others have low-cost labor, as it does. To make China's welcome most enticing requires access to that market. China will offer this attraction to the foreigner in exchange for technology transfer arrangements or for foreign ventures that will earn foreign exchange. But often China's time schedule for balancing foreign exchange within the venture is unrealistically short.

Thus lessons of the experience of other less developed countries have not been fully learned—only the superficial policies and objectives, not the results and alternatives available.

WHY WESTERN COMPANIES SHOULD RESPOND

China offers the attractions of both a large domestic market for capital goods, intermediate products, and final goods and services, and a base of operations from which to eventually serve not only the domestic market, but also the world market. The size of the potential domestic market offers economies of scale in both production and distribution and, ultimately, low enough costs to manufacture products at competitive prices. Yet the manufacture of products at competitive costs and quality will require substantial education of workers and managers and assistance to Chinese factories and to those staffing foreign-owned enterprises. This is the role of FDI in any developing country, and the opportunity in China is too great to be passed over.

From the standpoint of corporate strategy, it is important for virtually every major company to assess the significance of consolidating a position within the Chinese market so as to present when demand accelerates and competition becomes more extensive. As the chief executive officer of a major international company said, "with 22 percent of the world's population in China, we cannot afford not to be there." He followed by asserting that the investment should be minimal until it was clear that the joint venture could successfully sell into the domestic market and could successfully source locally, preparing to manufacture for export. Today imports into China come predominantly from Hong Kong and Japan, and Japan is ranked third in supplying goods through affiliates in China. It is, therefore, the dominant outside supplier in the Chinese market. Japan has achieved this status through a savvy strategy of initially pricing products low enough to obtain a foothold in the market and then raising the price after securing a market position; it also makes substantial profits on spare parts and services. This is recognized by the Chinese and will cause them to favor European and U.S. investors if other aspects of the investment are comparable, the main one being financial arrangements.

Japan has saturated the potential buyers in China with some 300 corporate offices in Beijing alone, compared with one-third that number of offices of U.S. companies, and the staffs of its salesmen, engineers, and support personnel are several times the number of people in an average U.S. office, which frequently number only one or two professionals. In addition, Japanese branch offices are located in dozens of Chinese cities, such as the port city of Dalian, where many Japanese trading companies have offices, compared with only a handful of Western representatives. In supplying the needs to modernize a plant in China, for example, ten to twenty American companies would be required to provide the various machines needed; a Japanese trading company would be able to put all of the requirements together in a single package, including financing, shipping, insurance, and any special engineering.

Japan also have an advantage over the West in that it better understands Chinese culture, and is quick to respond to the cultural niceties both in business and socially. Another, somewhat related advantage of the Japanese stems from their work culture at home, where workers often endure long hours and live in dormitories. It is much easier for Japanese expatriates to live for extended periods in areas outside the major cities because living conditions are frequently dormitory-like, with few other foreigners around (especially Westerners) for socializing. Many more Japanese speak Chinese and can read it because of the sharing of characters, and thus are able to manage quite well in non-urban areas, where fluent English seldom is found. But this should not be interpreted to mean that the Japanese and Chinese are culturally close. They are in fact quite different—as different as the French are from the Germans.

Although the Chinese remember quite clearly the Japanese invasion of China and are wary of the aggressiveness of Japanese suppliers, they will do business with the Japanese quite readily and often have no other alternative. This, however, is not their preferred position, and Western visitors to China often are struck by the number of times they are asked, "Why isn't your country interested in doing business with us?" It is embarrassing under such circumstances to reply "Because the companies are not interested."

The Japanese also have greater familiarity with and in fact themselves use the system known as "guanxi," under which one person becomes obligated to another, essentially through appropriate and (eventually) supporting behavior and actions. In addition, the Japanese government has given billions of dollars in low-cost loans to China, which become funds for purchases from Japanese companies. In this way Japanese companies won nearly 75 percent of China's $1 billion-dollar-plus investments in telecommunications equipment in the mid-1980s. Although China began the decade of the 1990s with an apparent trade surplus vis-a-vis Japan, the persistent imbalance of trade between China and Japan in the 1980s is likely to remain one of Japan's handicaps in its growing business with China, but Japan does not let up. The meshing of business and corporate interests in Japan shows the extent to which Western governments and business need to work together to help consolidate a strong position within the Chinese economy.[7]

The opportunities for doing business in China extend across the entire range of industrial, commercial, and financial activities. China is rich in resources that have yet to be developed, extending from offshore petroleum to minerals in the interior. The government is seeking technology, managerial expertise, and opportunities to use the distribution channels of international resource companies. Some of the first joint ventures were established in the resource field, and many of them are quite profitable because of the easier task of balancing foreign exchange. American companies have been relatively successful in obtaining the bids to exploit offshore petroleum, but much more can be done. The Chinese government also has set a high priority on the development of appropriate infrastructure and is quite willing for foreign investors to add to these facilities—in transportation and communication, in energy capacity, and even in education.

The major thrust, however, is in industrial manufacturing, so as to provide employment, acquire technology to raise the skills of labor, and gain higher wages in the urban areas. Although the government would strongly prefer that new manufacturing have an export capability, it also is quite willing for the manufacturers to substitute for imports, thereby cutting foreign exchange needs. Such import substitution often will place the foreign investor in competition with existing Chinese enterprises. In fact, with higher quality and despite higher costs owing to importation of parts, it is not inconceivable that the competition can drive out the Chinese enterprise, leaving China dependent on foreign investment, technology, and inflow of parts. Such a result would raise a myriad of other problems, to be discussed later.

An alternative approach is to rationalize the foreign investment so as to fit within the needs of the economy but to produce items not as yet supplied to local customers. This means the introduction of new products or differentiated items in which there would not be face-to-face competition with existing products, a potentially difficult, if not impossible, political situation if the Chinese people viewed this as preferential treatment. The Chinese prefer quality, which is a major weakness of all Chinese civilian products. But quality is costly, and the small internal market for quality products (at higher costs) means that markets must be sought in a larger market outside of China, and this would clearly be to the interest of the Chinese government, which is seeking exports to earn foreign exchange. Sourcing components from China should be the strategy of most major companies, but it is a rather difficult task because of the shortage, irregular supply, and frequent high cost of raw materials, deficiency in quality control, and poor transportation for delivery. The use of China as a foreign source of components is one action that each major company should, however, assess as part of its international strategy. It is an excellent way to build relations, learn the investment environment, and establish a flow of foreign exchange before selling into the Chinese market. Achieving quality will be the biggest task in sourcing from China, but it can be done successfully. Chinese leadership knows that quality is the Achilles heel of the industrial reform, but pushing it down to the worker level is a long and difficult task, as the United States has learned.

To do business in China only through production, letting local enterprises do the marketing, is likely to lead to frustration on the part of the foreign investor. He also must participate in marketing and either seek or develop the channels of distribution. It is, therefore, potentially necessary that the foreign investor include within his investment plans the creation of or some additions to the distribution facilities in the country. Finally, there are a number of ancillary services that support businesses in their normal day-to-day operations—marketing, insurance, shipping, warehousing, short hauls and deliveries, repair and maintenance, credit and finance, and technical services to customers or suppliers. Western companies take these services for granted, but they often are nonexistent in China. Marketing is not part of the Chinese system, a fact often overlooked by foreign investors seeking domestic distribution. Each of these services will require additional investment by the foreign investor, and should be included in an overall strategy.

Finally, China eventually will develop significant competitors, who will be strong enough not only to displace FDI affiliates, but also to penetrate foreign markets. A presence in China would provide a better understanding of the competition and also a means of keeping up with the application of various innovations in that market. Western business should now expand the scope of its strategic planning to include the Chinese economy—at least to the extent of forming its responses to emerging competition, if not entry into the market itself through investment or trade. In the not too distant future, it will be difficult to be an international corporation without being in China; the question is not if, but when and how to invest.

WHY WESTERN GOVERNMENTS SHOULD RESPOND

The opening of the Chinese economy is a recognition that the growth of China is tied to that of the world economy and that economic isolation is no longer beneficial. Given the policy of most Western governments to encourage international integration, this is an opportunity that they also should seize. To date, however, it has appeared to be more passive than active. Although the United States has passed legislation that permits the extension of economic aid to China, the volumes are small and do not significantly support U.S. FDI initiatives. The political impasses reached after Tiananmen (and only gradually relaxed after China's siding with the West in opposition to the Iraqi invasion of Kuwait) considerably altered FDI inflow, both delaying planned investments and cautioning prospective investors.

Economic advance among the Western nations must export to prosper long term. Japan, China, and others have learned this already. The West needs China as an export customer to help balance its trade accounts. Western governments should help China succeed so that they can have it as a significant importer of their goods and services. Although other countries, especially Japan and Europe, recognize this long-term opportunity in China, Americans in particular must match or exceed Japan in providing low financing, technology transfer, and management know-how such as initiated under the U.S. Department of Commerce's program in Dalian to educate high-level Chinese managers.

One close observer of China saw in the mid-1980s that the opening might not be uninterrupted. Still, he argued, the United States should not try to second-guess China's commitment to capitalism or a reformed socialism. Rather, it should foster China's adjustment to participation in the world economy through technology transfers and scientific and cultural exchanges on a long-term basis.[8]

Both politically and militarily, it is important for Western policy that China be drawn into a network of Southeast Asian countries, most of which are more free market–oriented than China and more closely related to the West. It also is desirable for the West to help pull China into the world economy so as to broaden and deepen it, making it more competitive, more efficient, more integrated, and potentially more peaceful. Too many countries attempt to use the world economy without participating significantly in it. It is only through joining in the world economy and accepting a number of trade-offs and adjustments that the rate of world progress can be accelerated and the resources of the world used more efficiently.

In addition, the concept that one can achieve "world peace through world trade" must be modified by experience, which shows that closer ties than trade are necessary to reduce belligerency among nations. The phrase should be changed to "world peace through world investment," which ties national economies together through integration of the operations of international companies. This integration of companies provides a greater understanding of peoples, cultures, and modes of doing business and expands personal contacts through business dealings and negotiations. It is this mutual understanding of objectives and institutions that reduces the drive to settle disputes by war. Thus Western governments should welcome the addition of the Chinese economy to the worldwide network.

Commensurate with its welcome, the West should avoid moves that make Chinese entry into the world market more difficult. Thus it should ameliorate or eliminate all but the most necessary of controls over technology flowing to China. China should be treated as an ally, or at least as an independent country, not as a potential enemy. The post-Tiananmen period is an exception to such advice. For its part, China must recognize that acceptance into the world's marketplace is not merely an economic phenomenon. There also are globally accepted means of behavior, and when nations step outside of such conventions, the other nations have the legitimate right to rescind the privilege of membership.

Another example of frustration is that caused by the U.S. government in its continued adherence to and strengthening of the Multi-Fiber Agreement, through which Chinese exports to the United States are held back. They see this as a one-sided attempt to choke the products of a low-technology industry and to stimulate the export of high-tech products from the United States. The resulting trade imbalance will give China pause as to the amount of imports it can take from the United States.

FOREIGN RESPONSE TO CHINA'S OFFICIAL WELCOME

The response to China's opening to the world economy can be seen in both its growing trade activity and its foreign capital inflows.

Table 2.1
China's Exports, Imports, and Balance of Trade, Selected Years, 1950–1988
(US$ billion)

	Total	Exports	Imports	Balance of trade
1950	1.13	0.55	0.58	-0.03
1952	1.94	0.82	1.12	-0.30
1957	3.11	1.60	1.50	0.10
1962	2.66	1.49	1.17	0.32
1965	4.25	2.23	2.02	0.21
1970	4.59	2.26	2.33	-0.07
1975	14.75	7.26	7.49	-0.23
1976	13.44	6.86	6.58	0.28
1977	14.80	7.59	7.21	0.38
1978	20.64	9.75	10.89	-1.14
1979	29.33	13.66	15.67	-2.01
1980	37.82	18.27	19.55	-1.28
1981	40.37	20.89	19.48	1.41
1982	39.30	21.82	17.48	4.34
1983	40.73	22.20	18.53	3.67
1984	49.77	24.41	25.36	-0.95
1985	66.70	26.46	40.24	-13.78
1986	73.83	30.93	42.90	-11.97
1987	82.70	39.50	43.20	-3.70
1988	102.90	47.60	55.30	-7.
1989	111.50	52.50	59.00	-6.50

Source: Statistical Yearbook of China, 1986; except for 1987, from the State Statistical Bureau, as reported in China Business Review May-June 1988; for 1988-89; Journal of Commerce, Jan. 31, 1990.

Trade

China's isolation from the world economy before the mid-1970s is reflected in its limited foreign trade to that point, as shown in Table 2.1.

Reflecting its isolationist policy, the People's Republic of China's trade until 1978 was both minimal and balanced. Trade volumes increased in the mid-1970s with the necessity to import significant quantities of grain after the poor performance of China's agricultural sector during the Cultural Revolution, and an increase in exports to pay for those grain imports. In 1978, with the beginnings of the open-door policy, imports and exports began a rapid expansion; imports rose from $10.89 billion in 1978 to $55.3 billion in 1987, while exports increased from \$9.75 billion to \$47.6 billion over these ten years. In just one decade, China's total trade increased more than 500 percent, from \$20.64 billion in 1978 to \$111.5 in 1989. Although total trade continued to grow during 1989, the impact of economic sanctions after Tiananmen combined with an austerity program and the devaluation of the renminbi to reduce overall trade during 1990. In particular, although exports continued to rise, imports were cut sharply; consequently Chinese officials were predicting a balance-of-trade surplus for the first time in seven years.[9]

Despite the decline in imports during 1990, the overall growth in China's imports are a recognition that it must import both foreign technology and key raw materials to modernize its economy. China still imports significant amounts of wheat, refined sugar, timber, and chemical fertilizer (domestic production of which remains inadequate, despite the attention paid to the need to build up the domestic fertilizer industry). The bulk of its imports, however, are related to shortages in the industrial sector, such as iron ore, rolled steel, trucks and truck parts, and complete sets of capital equipment. Synthetic fibers also are imported for the production of garments that are subsequently exported. These import needs signal the sectors in which the People's Republic of China wants foreign investment.

China's exports are predominantly agricultural goods (rice, tea, and various canned produce), textiles, and petroleum products. Although accepting that these products will continue to be important exports, Chinese officials also are committed to developing export capability in the high-quality machinery and equipment sectors. This goal remains unrealized, signaling the problems of earning foreign exchange.

Until 1985, China was effectively able to balance its trade. In 1985, however, a combination of factors caused its imports to dramatically exceed its exports. First, oil prices slumped, reducing the significant revenues China was earning from its oil exports and also undermining its attempt to attract foreign investment to further exploit its oil reserves. At the same time, other mineral and agricultural prices were falling, exacerbating problems caused by declining oil prices. Second, China began to face hostility from the United States and the European Economic Community over the amount of cheap textile products it exported. This growing protectionism reduced potential growth in China's exports and indicates future problems as China succeeds in raising its exports. Third, the pent-up demand for foreign consumer products was released after a reduction in exchange controls, and imports of consumer products—cameras, televisions, radios, wristwatches—rose dramatically. Factories were directed in the 1984 economic reforms to earn a profit; consequently they began importing products to sell on the domestic market rather than the capital equipment needed to produce for export. At the extreme was the importation of thirty-five stretch Cadillac limousines for transporting foreign guests; most of the time these sat idly outside Beijing's Great Wall Hotel. Similarly, fleets of taxis were imported, only to sit idle on the sides of streets for lack of competent drivers. The lack of planning for implementation of these reforms resulted in the freeze on imports during the second half of 1985. This freeze hurt investment flows into China because many investors perceived it as a partial closing of the Chinese market, when actually it was a necessary interim step for the long-term health of the economy.

This increase in consumer imports was compounded by a domestic price structure that encouraged such imports, even though they could have been produced at lower real-cost domestically.

Finally, the Chinese government lost control over its foreign trade balances, as a result of its decentralizing foreign trade decision-making that proliferated local bodies with the authority to utilize foreign exchange, making it easier to get foreign exchange for imports. After recentralization and renewed restrictions on the use of foreign exchange in 1987, plus growth in Chinese exports, trade became more balanced. In 1988 and early 1989, however, the economy was once again out of control and the government struggled to reimpose control over foreign trade activities. Given China's concern to maintain balanced trade, one can anticipate such restrictions to recur periodically in the future whenever trade balances result in serious deficits. Hence the austerity program of 1990.

Foreign Capital Inflows

Foreign capital inflows into China are of two kinds: FDI and loans. An analysis of FDI by country of origin reveals the significant role played by overseas Chinese, in particular those based in Hong Kong. Table 2.2 shows Hong Kong as the largest source by far.

Investment in the first half of 1989, the last "burst" of investment in the pre-Tiananmen era, revealed a number of interesting things about who was investing in China, where these investments were taking place, and for what reason. On the basis of contracts signed, Hong Kong continued to lead all investors, with US $1.6 billion, for the first half of that year. The United States was second, with investments of $380 million, and Japan was third, with $230 million. Taiwanese investments were fourth, with more than $200 million, and European investment trailed.[10] After June 1989, Taiwan moved into first place, with roughly 60 percent of the new investment value.

In terms of implemented investment, between the beginning of 1988 and the end of the first half of 1989, 65.6 percent came from Hong Kong and Macao, whereas Japan accounted for a 16.1 percent share and the United States, 7.4 percent (see Table 2.3).

Complete figures detailing how much capital committed has actually been utilized are not available, but it is unlikely that they would differ significantly percentagewise from commitments. If anything, investments from Hong Kong and Taiwan would probably be more quickly utilized because of the small size of each project. Indeed, during the first half of 1980, when the opportunities first opened up, the overseas Chinese established more than 600 of the 750 equity

Table 2.2
Sources of FDI Commitments in China, 1979–1985

Country	Amount (US$Million)	Per cent of Total
Hong Kong	10628.96	63.8
United States	2177.01	13.1
Japan	1628.63	9.8
Great Britain	378.3	2.3
France	262.5	1.6
Sweden	202.4	1.2
Singapore	192.5	1.2
West Germany	162.1	1.0
Italy	137.4	0.8
Australia	105.2	0.6
Others	765.46	4.6

Source: U.S. Joint Ventures in China: A Progress Report, National Council for U.S. China Trade, 1986, p.186.

joint ventures approved,[11] and the *number* of Hong Kong and Taiwanese investments has grown more rapidly than those of other countries.

Similarly, the relative importance of other countries as a source of foreign investment commitments can be expected to remain on the order of that shown in Table 2.2. However, although the data for *utilized* foreign capital (1979–1985) that do exist indicate that the Japanese had invested more funds in China than the United States to that point, by 1985 the United States was beginning to turn contracted agreements into actual foreign investment.

Indeed, China has found it much easier to attract foreign loans than foreign investment. Between 1979 and 1989 the Chinese contracted for $46.5 billion (U.S.) worth of foreign debt, ranging from concessionary loans from governments and major lending organizations to bond issues by major cities (see Table 2.4). Foreign lending dropped dramatically in 1989 because of Tiananmen and remained low through 1990, despite some indication from major lending institutions that they might be willing to resume lending. China historically has utilized about three-quarters of these loans and faced a debt repayment peak of US $12 billion to 13 billion in the first half of 1990. Although this brings China dangerously close to the debt service rule of 20 percent, by 1992, this ratio should fall to a securer 10 to 15 percent.[12] In the wake of the precipitous tourism decline after the Tiananmen massacre, one of the most interesting debt-related issues concerns the borrowing of hotel joint ventures in China. An estimated 40 percent of all foreign hotel loans in China will have to be renegotiated, raising

Table 2.3

Foreign Direct Investment in China, by Country, 1986–1988 (in $ thousands and percentage)

Country/ Region	1986 Value	%	1987 Value	%	1988 Value	%
HK/Nacao	1,329	59.2	1,598	69.1	2,095	65.6
Japan	263	11.7	219	9.5	514	16.1
U.S.A.	326	14.5	263	1.4	236	7.4
U.K.	35	1.6	5	0.2	34	1.1
Norway	na	na	2	0.1	32	1.0
Italy	29	1.3	16	0.7	30	0.9
Singapore	14	0.6	22	0.9	28	0.9
France	44	1.9	16	0.7	23	0.7
Netherlands	2	0.1	-	0.0	21	0.6
Denmark	1	0.1	2	0.1	20	0.6
Totals	2,244	100.0	2,314	100.0	3,194	100.0

Source: China Statistics Yearbook, 1989, as quoted in China-North Asia Section, JETRO, "Direct Investments in China Losing Momentum," JETRO China Newsletter, Jan-Feb 1990, pp. 17-22.

the intriguing question of who stands behind the loans of local governments and Chinese agencies?[13]

Commercial borrowing, which represented some two-thirds of China's utilized foreign capital loans between 1979 and 1983, shrank to only one-quarter of utilized foreign capital loans in the period 1984–1986. China's emphasis switched to concessionary loans, as indicated by a 1983 loan of $2 billion from Japan's Overseas Economic Cooperation Fund, a 1984 loan of $3 billion from the Import-Export Bank of Japan, and commitments of $1.9 billion from the World Bank. This changed emphasis reflects the desire of the Chinese leadership not to become overindebted through high debt repayments.

The individual country response to China's search for concessionary loans varies considerably. Japan, for example, has loaned large amounts to China, while being less inclined to undertake FDI projects. The United States, on the other hand, has tended not to make concessionary loans to China, but U.S. companies have invested quite significantly in joint and cooperative ventures. It is possible to characterize the competitive struggle of the United States and Japan in the Chinese market as one of capital versus technology transfer. The Japanese weakness in China is their reticence in transferring current or advanced technology for fear of future Chinese competition. The United States is willing to transfer technology if China can become a cheaper source of supply to help keep

Table 2.4
Foreign Capital in China, from All Sources, Contracted and Utilized, 1979–1988
(in U.S. $billions)

	Loans		FDI		Totals	
	Contr-	Util-	Contr-	Util-	Contr-	Util-
Year	acted	ized	acted	ized	acted	ized
1979-82	13.5	10.7	7.0	1.8	20.5	12.5
1983	1.5	1.1	1.9	0.9	3.4	2.0
1984	1.9	1.3	2.9	1.4	4.8	2.7
1985	3.5	2.7	6.3	2.0	9.9	4.6
1986	8.4	5.0	3.3	2.2	11.7	7.3
1987	7.8	5.8	4.3	2.6	12.1	8.5
1988	9.8	6.5	6.2	3.7	16.0	10.2
Totals	46.5	33.0	32.0	14.7	78.5	47.7

Note: Figures may not add to totals because of rounding; also, figures in totals may be less than the sum of each year because a single loan may involve several contracts but is counted only once in the final total.

Source: China Statistical Abstract, 1988, p. 75 (adapted). Series Ed. William T. Liu, N.Y.: Praeger, 1989.

the United States competitive. Others, such as France, have adopted more of a middle ground approach. The magnitude of China's development plans will, however, clearly outstrip the potential concessionary finance that is available to it. Once these sources are exhausted, China will need to contemplate entering the commercial money markets on a much greater scale or, alternatively, be in a position to attract far greater amounts of FDI.

Certainly, the steady promulgation of laws pertaining to FDI inflows and the growing confidence of foreign investors in China's stability have enabled FDI to play a growing role in the Chinese economy. However, China's economic difficulties in 1985 and 1988 and its political difficulties in 1989 indicate the fragility of that foreign confidence in the Chinese economy, as these difficulties caused a leveling off of FDI at the same time that Chinese borrowing from abroad jumped sharply.

Thus, in the short term, concessionary loans will continue to be an important part of China's foreign capital sourcing (as well as part of larger trade packages with individual countries). But in the longer term, Chinese officials clearly want to create an environment in which FDI becomes the major source of foreign capital.

CHINA'S ASSESSMENT OF THE RESPONSE

The importance of FDI to China's future was stated clearly by the former Chinese premier Zhao Ziyang at the National People's Congress in 1987:

Using foreign funds and attracting foreign businessmen to launch joint ventures, cooperative enterprises or wholly foreign-owned ones is a major component of our open policy. It is also an important means to make up for the shortage of domestic funds, enhance our capacity to earn foreign exchange through export and raise China's technological and managerial levels.

Even though Zhao Ziyang is no longer in a position of authority in the Chinese government, the sentiment of his remarks remains a valid reflection of Chinese thinking. Foreign investment is being counted on to play an important part in the renovation and modernization of key Chinese industries. It has already been important in the exploitation of China's natural resources, notably oil and coal. For example, the largest Sino-U.S. joint venture is that of the Antaibao coal mine in Shanxi Province, with Occidental, the foreign partner, investing $175 million.

Despite all of this financial activity, the Chinese have remained disappointed with several aspects of foreign investment. Chief among their complaints has been the relatively small-scale nature of the foreign investment outside of contracted oil ventures. In a sample of 1,449 of the earliest joint ventures in China, only 103 (7.1 percent) had an investment of more than $10 million, and more than half (825, or 56.9 percent) had investment running below $1 million. A simple average of utilized investment and operational venture numbers between 1979 and 1987 (10,279 ventures and $8.47 billion of utilized FDI) reveals a foreign investment of only $825,000 per venture. Furthermore, this figure of $825,000 is skewed by the amount of investment in contractual oil ventures, without which average foreign investment per venture would be only $610,000. A comparison of the size of contractual oil ventures to other FDI organizations in China is given in Table 2.5.

There are three reasons for the relatively modest amounts of foreign capital invested in Sino-foreign non-oil ventures to date. First, it must be expected that after thirty years of virtual isolation from the West, China's overtures to foreign investors would be received with caution. Only a few foreign companies have entered China with large investments. The negotiation process in China, for example, is acknowledged to be lengthy, costly, and difficult, thereby limiting the potential investors essentially to the large TNCs and Hong Kong. China has recognized this at the senior levels and has tried to find ways to attract small U.S. firms to China. The State Economic Commission made several specific attempts in 1987 but found the initiatives difficult in both the United States and China. When Zhu Rongji left the vice-chairmanship of the State Economic Commission to become the mayor of Shanghai, this effort faded. As in U.S. organizations, every program needs a sponsor.

Table 2.5
China's Average Foreign Partner Equity, 1979–1987

	1979-83	1984	1985	1986	1987	1979-87
Equity JVs	0.91	0.34	0.45	0.91	0.65	0.60
Contractual JVs	0.67	0.43	0.39	n/a	n/a	
Wholly foreign-owned ventures	1.81	1.23	0.28	n/a	n/a	n/a
Contractual oil ventures	25.42	n/a	n/a	n/a	n/a	50.79

Source: Derived from Chen, Nai-Ruenn, "Foreign Investment in China: Current Trends", in China Business Review, May-June 1988 p.57, and Intertrade, February 1988, p.27-29.

Although the Chinese accept that large Sino-foreign investment projects have been "difficult to realize," they claim that with "persistent negotiations," successful large ventures can be developed, as evidenced by the Sino-American ventures at the Antaibao coal mine in Shanxi Province ($175 million by Occidental) and the Beijing Jeep Company ($16 million by American Motors), the West German Shanghai Volkswagen automobile factory ($90 million by Volkswagen), and the British Shanghai Yaohua-Pilkington Glass Company ($15 million each by Pilkington and United Development, Inc.).[14] A second reason usually cited for the small scale of foreign investments in Sino-foreign joint ventures is the fact that so much of the foreign investment comes from Hong Kong and Taiwan. Most of the ventures that result from Hong Kong and Taiwanese participation tend to be small scale and labor-intensive. These ventures typically are located in Guangdong Province, which borders Hong Kong, or Fujian Province, which is across the Straits of Formosa from Taiwan, and rely on family connections. The Hong Kong businesses in particular prefer these small-scale ventures because they are easy to set-up (avoiding expensive and lengthy negotiations), involve quick returns, and can be readily terminated. Although the Chinese would prefer to attract larger-scale investment, most Hong Kong–based firms have shown little inclination to move in this direction.

By way of contrast, a study of the investment patterns in China from the United States, Japan, Britain, France, and West Germany indicates that the average investment per venture for the period 1979–1985 (excluding oil ventures) was $8 million, $2.5 million, $3.3 million, $3 million, and $13.4 million respectively.[15]

Closer investigation reveals that these averages also tend to be skewed significantly by one or two major investments. Great Britain's average commitment of $3.3 million per manufacturing venture arises from a heavy concentration in one venture (the Shanghai Yaohua-Pilkington Company), accounting for $15 million of the $20 million invested by British companies in manufacturing joint ventures (leaving the remaining six ventures averaging less than $1 million per venture). Similarly, $21.6 million of France's total investment in manufacturing investment is in one plant, the Guangzhou Biaozhi Automobile Company. The remaining eleven Sino-French manufacturing ventures average only $1.33 million per venture, much less than the $3 million average investment for all French partnerships in manufacturing ventures. Similar patterns are found for the United States, Japan, and West Germany.

Thus, despite the fact that the number of large-scale, "high-visibility" ventures in China is increasing, small-scale ventures—especially those that involve Hong Kong companies, but also the bulk of ventures with Western and Japanese partners—remain dominant.

In addition to the small-scale nature of many of the Sino-foreign ventures, the Chinese complain that the technological levels of many of the ventures are unsophisticated, contributing little or nothing to China's modernization program, simply seeking quick returns to investment by utilizing cheap Chinese labor.[16] This is to be expected in a legal and economic environment that is still unfolding. Until foreign investors are more confident in the stability of that environment, large-scale investments that involve the transfer of sophisticated technology will remain the exception rather than the rule. They will be pioneered by the very large, truly international companies who believe that China is too large not to be there. But even these investments will be small, $15 million to $20 million, from a large corporation's portfolio perspective. They also have been typically directed out of the corporate chairman's office because the investments in China have a hard time surviving against other corporate priorities in terms of profits, risks, and rank within long-range plans. In many U.S. companies, it takes the chairman's vision to sustain interest in a Chinese joint venture.

NOTES

1. See J. N. Behrman and R. E. Grosse, *International Business/Government Relations* (Columbia: University of South Carolina Press, 1989), especially Chapters 1 and 2, for an assessment of different company expectations.

2. A more empirical evaluation, resulting from a 1987 study by the China Research Centre for Science and Technology for Development, surveying 1,200 kinds of industrial facilities in 19,000 important enterprises, concludes that "only 12.9% reached ordinary world levels applicable to the early 1980's. . . . Another 21.8% were classified as advanced domestic level, 47% ordinary level, and 18.3% were backward." Wang Dontai, "Industry Still Reliant on Handwork," *China Daily Business Weekly*, March 6, 1989, p. 2.

3. *Journal of Commerce*, July 31, 1990.

4. Xue Rongjiu, "The Causes of Protectionism and How to Deal with It," *Guoji Maoyi Wenti* 3:1–9, 1987, as translated in FBIS, JPRS Report, JPRS CAR-87–050, October 7, 1987, pp. 30–43.

5. See Behrman and Grosse, *International Business/Government Relations*, Chapters 6–9.

6. See J. N. Behrman, *Industrial Policies: International Restructuring and Trans-nationals* (Lexington, Mass.: Lexington Books, 1984), especially Chapters 8 and 9.

7. For an assessment of "How Japan Beat the U.S. in China," see *Billion*, July 1990, pp. 54–56.

8. Michel C. Oksenberg, "China Joins the World: Prospects and Implications," *Issues in Science and Technology*, Spring 1985, pp. 113–127.

9. *Journal of Commerce*, July 25, 1990.

10. China–North Asia Section, JETRO, "Direct Investments in China Losing Momentum," *JETRO China Newsletter*, January-February 1990, pp. 17–22.

11. Nai-Ruenn Chen, "Foreign Investment in China: Current Trends," *China Business Review*, May-June 1986, p. 77.

12. Masaki Igarashi, "Chinese Bonds in the Introduction of Foreign Capital," *JETRO China Newsletter*, September-October 1989, pp. 9–15.

13. Sheryl WuDunn, "Hotel Debts Mount as China's Tourism Industry Fails to Bounce Back," *International Herald Tribune*, May 29, 1990, p. 17.

14. Data on 840 joint ventures through 1984, by region, source, industry sector, total investment, equity participation, and duration are recorded by P. W. Beamish and Hiu Y. Wang, "Investing in China Via Joint Ventures," *Management International Review* 29:57–64, 1989.

15. Yang Mu, "U.S. Investment in China" (Paper presented at the Conference on Sino-U.S. Economic Cooperation, Fudan University, Shanghai, April 1987), p. 5.

16. William A. Fischer, "China as a Player in the Global Economy," *China Economic Review* (no. 1), 1989, pp. 9–21.

3

Why the New Policy?

Although the economic reforms of Deng Xiaoping and his colleagues have been more successful than almost anyone anticipated, in retrospect, the specific reasons behind each reform often remain obscure or contradictory. In the mid-1960s, before the chaos of the Great Proletariat Cultural Revolution, Deng was associated with ideas of economic pragmatism and reform under the leadership of Zhou Enlai. Their objective apparently was to shed some of the ideology in economic policymaking and to restore China to the progress that it had experienced for most of the decade after the formation of the People's Republic. Those ideas were suppressed during the Cultural Revolution and were a reason for Deng's isolation during those years. Nonetheless, on his reascension to power in 1978, Deng almost immediately authorized experiments in Sichuan's agricultural sector, reflecting his earlier ideas for establishing a more efficient and more pragmatic economy. (These experiments were conducted under the direction of Deng's protégé, Zhou Ziyang, then provincial governor; Zhou later became premier and, ultimately, general secretary of the party and, until 1989, the potential successor to Deng, before being dismissed in the middle of the Tiananmen crisis.) The general economic situation in China in the late 1970s was sufficiently bad that virtually all observers, including the Chinese leadership itself, recognized that some radical change was needed to get the economy moving again. China's industrial productivity was stagnating, its products were falling increasingly further behind world standards, and the volume of its foreign trade was minimal. The prior system simply did not work and was failing to provide the Chinese people with a satisfactory quality of life, even by third world standards. The failings of the system were compounded by rapid population growth. The total Chinese population rose from 550 million in 1950 to 1.1 billion in 1989.

Despite these pervasive arguments for change, just what to change was not clear, and not all Chinese leaders agreed even on a general direction. Many officials had a significant commitment to past institutions and were in power because of them. Deng Xiaoping needed their political support, especially in the turbulence after the passing of Mao Zedong.[1] Political survival became a stronger motive than economic necessity in the economic reforms.[2] With such broad pressures, compromises were necesssary and specifics were less important than movement itself.

PRIOR STAGNATION

The economic record of the People's Republic has been one of wide cyclical changes, reflecting several political upheavals over its four decades of history. Chronic problems have persisted throughout these cycles—a rigid bureaucracy, an inadequate institutional base for science and technology, the chronically mistaken belief that there is a large permanent market for all that can be produced, the predominance of politics over economics, the segmentation of industry, continuing pressure of egalitarianism, and an absolute lack of managerial skills. These problems are among the principal targets of the recent economic reforms.

Omnipresent Bureaucracy

Among their many historical accomplishments, the Chinese people have been credited with the early perfection, if not actual origination, of bureaucratic control. The geographical dispersion of China's peoples required a mechanism for control. This bureaucracy was developed in the Confucian and neo-Confucian periods,[3] supported by Confucian ethics and vested in tradition; it allowed the dynastic rulers to maintain control in volatile situations. Like some corporate bureaucracies that are risk-averse, it suppressed change and suffocated creativity for the preservation of the system and protection of the people in power. Preservation of the system became more important than the well-being of the people. The historian Joseph Needham has attributed the decline of Chinese science and technology, from its predominance in the Middle Ages to scientific poverty by the late eighteenth century, to the stagnating and stultifying effects of an omnipresent bureaucracy.

Despite the anti-establishment origins of the Communist government in China, the burdens of governing a nation as diverse as China quickly led to the re-institution of a bureaucratic government that eventually grew to be as rigid and unresponsive as its historical predecessors. It was to eliminate this "monster" that Mao Zedong launched the Cultural Revolution in 1966.

A primary characteristic of the Chinese system was the existence of parallel (party and state) and often over-lapping decision hierarchies; these required even the simplest request to be repeatedly applied for and scrutinized by authorities at several levels. The long time for approvals, even when they were clearly to be given, frustrated industrial change. Further, a system of personal political files, kept on every major official, biased decisions toward conservatism—no decision or "no change," was less risky than any new initiative.

The managers of industrial enterprises were responsible only for quantity of product output and management of labor. Few managers were willing to risk new decisions, for the penalties for making the wrong decision far outweighed the rewards associated with a good one. There was little opportunity for personal advancement and no concept of a career path. Every action was subject to review and repeal by higher authorities, who typically knew far less about the situation than the person being monitored and were, therefore, even more risk-averse.

Inadequate Civilian Science and Technology

Bureaucratic rigidity was in fact one of the reasons for the low level of investment in civilian science and technology during the 1960s and 1970s. The Chinese government publicly extolled the rewards of enhanced science and technology, but the funds went mainly to military science and technology and "showpiece" projects such as the synthesis of insulin, leaving meager funds for industrial research and development (R&D).[4]

In addition to the lack of initiative on the part of the bureaucracy, the lack of management skills was accentuated by a Maoist preference for relying on "the people" as a primary source of invention and change and by the absence of competition in industrial markets to serve as an inducement for improvements.

Neglect of Domestic Engineering

Most of the Chinese industrial work force have little formal education, being trained largely through on-the-job experience. In addition, the task of reaching international standards has been made more difficult by past economic and technical embargoes by Western countries. Nor did the short-lived reliance on Soviet engineering (1949–1959) sufficiently advance China's industrial know-how. The engineer's task was made even more difficult by the inability of the planners to optimize resource allocations, deliver supplies on reliable schedules, or generate the new products and capital investment required in a modern economy. Chinese engineers had to use ingenuity and skill in "making do" with what was available just to keep the system working. One positive result of all this is that Chinese enterprises value highly the input of skilled workers and technicians and appoint technically trained people to positions of responsibility at the enterprise level.[5]

Today the predominant source of new scientific and technical ideas is from foreign countries. This reliance provides some shortcuts in the innovation process but will cause China to lag in its ability to create world-class technology. There also is a risk of atrophy among China's indigenous scientific and technical personnel, who focus on adaptation rather than on invention.[6] Before a new technology is ready for product development, it has typically been in research for a minimum of five years, often ten to fifteen years, and two to three years in product development. Thus, when a foreign-developed product is adopted in China for local manufacturing, the technology is already seven to eight years old and the product often obsolete when compared with similar products under development outside of China. The only way to break this cycle is to develop a technology base in China.

"Big Market" Mentality

A continuing impediment to innovation in China has been the widely accepted view that "the Chinese market is a big market; demand always outstrips supply; anything we make will sell." Until the 1980s, China was a seller's market, in which chronic scarcities and no competitive options left the buyer with little choice but to accept what was offered. For their part, industrial enterprises accepted both supplies and equipment as they arrived (late and unuseful), re-pairing or modifying them to meet their needs rather than rejecting them and risking a loss of supply. Consumers also had to repair defective items, since the availability of alternatives could not be counted on.

As long as the seller's market continued, it made no sense to acquire a competitive advantage through innovation, so Chinese enterprise managers were uninterested in promoting R&D and rejected change. Market-oriented reforms have introduced some competition, which, in turn, has shifted some markets from "seller's" to "buyer's." Consequently Chinese managers are adjusting their perspectives. But such shifts are difficult, and the rate of innovation and productivity increases within Chinese industry is slowed by the persistence of this long-lived, but increasingly obsolete "big market" view. Even in the 1980s, enterprises continued to receive orders from the industrial bureaus that controlled them and to deliver the product to another set of bureaus, often without any contact with the ultimate user of the product. Consequently, many enterprises remain unresponsive, almost arrogant, in the face of consumer needs, and little or no product innovation is generated.[7]

Under conditions in which producers face no market competition, performance is based on cost minimization.[8] In the past, therefore, managerial and enterprise performance were predominantly focused on some combination of the "eight great factors": production volume, quality, profit, costs, labor efficiency, con-sumption of resources, capital utilization, and production value. The only reason for product innovation in such circumstances, other than at the initiation of higher-level authorities, was to produce a "new" product that would not fall under the existing price regulations, and thus the government might allow a new price to be set at a more profitable level. In fact, almost all requests for new products were granted by the authorities, with a review of whether or not a new price could be set often taking place years later.

The "big market" mentality has been so pervasive that even when military factories, producing technically advanced products, shifted to the production of civilian items, quality instantly fell. Officials had to tell the workers that high quality was to be expected for civilian products also.

Politics over Economics

During the Cultural Revolution, the guide was "Politics in Command." This followed an earlier experiment in subordinating technical elites to those with political connections ("Red" versus "Expert"). Former managers were badly treated, often physically abused and sometimes killed, and unprepared workers placed in managerial positions. Such extremes were caricatures of the preeminence of politics over economic rationality reflected in the People's Republic from its beginning, relying on ideological credentials for positions of power and responsibility. (Only in extremis was there a return to some form of economic discipline, such as the adoption of "one-man management" philosophy in the early 1950s.[9] Consequently many ill-prepared people have held key decision-making positions throughout the life of the People's Republic.)

Today some of the factory managers do have responsibility for profit and loss, but many of these do not have appropriate managerial skills. Their lack of training reinforces their reluctance to entertain decisions that involve any risk of failure. Further, the party representatives in the factory still make major inputs into all policy decisions, creating ambiguity over who is actually in charge and slowing the decision process.

Vertical Segmentation of Chinese Industry

The organizational structure of Chinese industry, copying that of the Soviet Union, has been one of vertical sectors, segmented from one another under specific industrial ministries. These groups gradually insulated themselves from most of the other sectors, often becoming virtually self-contained, to ease the planning process by encompassing all stages of production. Duplication and fragmentation across sectors resulted, reducing efficiency. This ministerial independence was reinforced by inadequate communications and distribution linkages, as well as by conflicts between national and local governments. Dependability of supply was so low that most Chinese ministries and enterprises found it more expeditious and safer to create their own supply sources. This insulation, in turn, reduced the economies of scale available to specialist firms able to serve several ministries, delaying the emergence of manufacturing and technical specialization and recognition of a national Chinese market, which would have encouraged technological initiatives. The "turf warfare" between industrial ministries, each seeking to enhance its position by staking claims to new technologies (usually from abroad), also had the effect of slowing the adoption and creation of new technologies. These ministries also run their own universities, further reducing the cross-flow of information.

Legacy of Egalitarianism

One of the legacies of Confucian influence in China (see Chapter 5) has been a preference for group advancement rather than individual achievement, unless the latter comes through a high degree of social isolation. Furthermore, under Communist administrations, it has been prudent to meld into the group and to maintain a low profile, thus also reducing tendencies toward individualism. The major campaigns—the "antirightist" campaign of the mid–1950s, the Cultural Revolution of 1966–1976, and the campaigns against "spiritual pollution" and "bourgeois liberalism" in the 1980s—have victimized any who stand out from the masses, for whatever reason. Consequently reforms that encourage differentiation of incomes, wealth, career directions, and individual decisions are looked on as being risky. Even today it is not unusual for factory managers in successful foreign direct investment (FDI) joint ventures to refuse bonuses for fear of being viewed as wealthy or as an exploiter of the workers. A preference persists for equalization in all forms of organizations, but this is based more on fear of disapproval than on any lack of desire for individual advancement.

Egalitarianism has blunted many attempts at establishing differential pay and reward systems for exceptional performance and, as a result, has reduced the Chinese manager's capacity to encourage innovation and productivity. Egalitarianism was reinforced by the lack of opportunity for improvement in one's personal situation. Whether it be in housing, schooling, income, or career, the individual was a captive of the system, assigned under bureaucratic control to school, to work, to housing, and to a position on the basis of factors that were unknown, uncertain, invisible, and often dominated by favoritism to those in power. The individual's responses to such assignments have been recorded in personal dossiers, held by the work unit, and used to influence his or her career opportunities.[10]

In sum, the Chinese have labored under a system that has penalized more than it has rewarded, and rewarded political and personal loyalties more than technical or economic accomplishment. The recent reforms seek a shift of 180 degrees.

COMPETITIVE SUCCESSES IN ASIA

China has been pressed from the east and south by models of successful economic development in Japan and the "four dragons"—Korea, Taiwan, and the city-states of Hong Kong and Singapore. Each of these has close cultural and historical ties to China, resulting in competitive as well as collaborative relations. Despite the relative isolation of China, it has witnessed these successes and feels their competitive pressures as it opens into the world market. The success of neighbors has been a significant encouragement to China's opening.

The success of Japan and the "four dragons" has involved modification of the traditional oriental governmental control over economic activity and a relaxation of centralized authority toward more open economies. They have not fully adopted the Western model of development, but have relied on a stimulus to exports (rather than import substitution), on the free market and technology and private enterprise, and on FDI inflows. In doing so, each of these countries has relied extensively on government guidance, regulation, and support.

Whatever the policies, the results have been extremely successful, raising each of these countries to high living standards within the past two generations. All five have experienced rapid rates of growth of real gross national product (GNP) and of exports during the 1970s and 1980s—considerably higher than those in other developing countries and in many advanced countries as well. They are all characterized by the willingness of workers to put in long hours of dedicated effort, by high savings (sometimes legislated, as in Singapore) and investment rates, by the maintenance of low wages, by a drive to export markets, and by pragmatic assistance by government. No small part is the historic, almost cultural understanding by the people themselves of the need to export to survive. But the specific routes to development taken by each are somewhat different, offering diverse models for China to assess, despite the similar movement away from centralized planning to free market decisions. All five countries also are much smaller in size and population than China and, therefore, easier to manage, and each has an excellent educational system.

Japan

A model of Japanese development would be a complex one, covering virtually every facet of the society, simply because Japanese society is highly integrated. Yet, for purposes of comparison, it is possible to delineate characteristics that have played the most significant roles.

During the Meiji reformation of the mid-nineteenth century, Japan decided that it needed to industrialize, abandoning its feudal society. It did so through governmental supports to the landlords and the samurai to become industrialists and merchants. It encouraged private-sector development, but with continued guidance and support of the government. It also determined that there were three requisites for success: reliance on market signals to achieve efficiency and appropriate competition; development of honest communication and promise, so as to facilitate market performance; and a stable currency, so as to encourage savings and investment. These requisites were urged and supported by the government itself, centered on the Imperial Palace. These characteristics have remained singular threads through Japanese development over the past century and a quarter.

After its failure to gain secure access to raw materials through commercial and military conquest in the form of a "Greater Asia Co-Prosperity Sphere," Japan turned after World War II to industrial development for exports, to pay for imported raw materials needed for that industrial development. At the same time, it imposed protection against industrial imports and against random foreign

investment while establishing priorities for acquisition of certain foreign industrial technologies.

Since the departure of the post–World War II occupation, Japan has maintained
a policy of industrial targeting, aimed at rapid development of export sectors
and creating a competitive domestic industrial base. Working with and through
the large conglomerates (Keiretsu), the government provided support for mergers,
R&D, export promotion, and capital investment, as well as restricting entry of
foreign companies. The lack of antitrust laws and the existence of MITI (Ministry
of International Trade and Industry) to focus on international activities have been
key enablers in Japan's export strategy. MITI currently has targeted the computer
industry, with a strategy for developing the fifth-generation computer; it hopes
to thrust Japan into a dominant role in this sector. When foreign investors were
permitted in, it was principally in the form of joint ventures with Japanese
partners—IBM-Japan being one of the few major wholly owned companies.
Even technology agreements were scrutinized by the government and were limited as to the terms that it deemed appropriate. By the 1960s, Japan was able
to dictate the terms of foreign entry because of the size and rate of growth of
its domestic market, which was highly attractive to foreigners.

The government also has maintained stability in the monetary system, encouraging high rates of savings (around 30 percent) and of domestic investment.
It has encouraged aggressive domestic competition among the large companies,[11]
though the existence of a protected market has permitted the raising of domestic
prices above international levels, offering profits to the companies for future
expansion. It has encouraged the gathering and dissemination of information
required for industrial development and market decisions, and it encourages the
transfer of information (particularly technological) among the Keiretsu. The
purpose is to make Japan competitive with the rest of the world more than to
help any one company gain a competitive advantage. Information plays a key
role in development of open economies; Japan recognized this early and promoted
an information-based society.

All of these developments have occurred within a culture that places each
individual within a group to which he or she has obligations and an extended
loyalty. Companies are societies, responsible for the individuals attached to the
companies in return for the obligation of individuals to make the company
successful. Each individual has his or her place, and though there is some
competition for positions of advancement, there is little mobility between companies to enhance one's career. The motivation of individual managers and
workers, therefore, is service to the company and to his or her group within the
company and through the company to Japan as a nation. This hierarchy of
loyalties extends all the way from the family itself to the nation, but not beyond.
Japan is not a member of any regional common market, though it is a member
of the Organization for Economic Cooperation and Development. It has not
assumed significant international obligations and in fact still sees itself as buffeted
by international competitive forces.

Japan has achieved an economic miracle of advancement out of devastation. It has risen to one of the premier positions, perhaps the strongest country financially, in the world economy within two generations—a phenomenon unmatched in history. It has, therefore, far outstripped China, which has a much greater resource base, an aggressive population, and some of the same cultural traits as Japan. China, however, has virtually no history of significant industrialization under private enterprise or market signals. This is what it now faces, and it is looking for appropriate models from outside.

The "Four Dragons"

Although the "four dragons" have not achieved the same levels of advancement that Japan has, their rise within the past three decades also has been phenomenal. They also have relied principally on market signals and private enterprise. Yet they are not copies of the Japanese model, nor are they identical among themselves.[12]

Each has a relatively small population compared with Japan or China, and though their per capita incomes are rising and are significantly higher than those of other developing countries, they remain modest compared with Japan. They have shown an increasing competitiveness in global markets and have been able to restrain domestic inflation so as not to undercut that competitiveness.

From 1983 to 1987, Korea's GNP grew at an annual rate of more than 10 percent (in 1986 at 12.5 percent), fueled largely by an even higher increase in merchandise exports (in 1986 at 28 percent). Despite such growth rates, inflation has remained relatively low (in 1986 only at 2.3 percent), whereas China saw rates in double digits in the late 1980s. Much of its industrial expansion has been financed by foreign borrowing for capital-producing goods, leaving Korea in the mid–1980s as one of the larger net debtors internationally (at roughly $45 billion). It has now reached a substantial current account surplus (more than one-tenth the size of its debt) and is beginning to pay off its external debt. China is beginning to consider as acceptable foreign debt spent on capital-producing equipment versus consumer goods, as part of successful economic reform.

The success of private enterprise is indicated by the development of a significant stock market, the increasing liberalization of imports, an upgrading of the technological base, diversification and deregulation of industry, and improvements in the social welfare system.

Taiwan shows similar success, with low inflation, but more like Japan with perennial balance-of-payments surpluses, high international monetary reserves second only to Japan, the virtual absence of significant international debt, and high rates of GNP growth (averaging more than 9 percent annually during 1983–1987). In 1986, exports rose nearly 30 percent; the export surplus was nearly 40 percent of total exports in 1986. Taiwan also has an active stock market, to which foreign investors have limited access, and it has recently liberalized the outflow of investment capital to other countries. It proposed a free trade arrangement with the United States in the late 1980s, since more than 80 percent of its trade surplus is with the United States.

Despite its prospective absorption into the People's Republic (in 1997), Hong Kong continues to grow at substantial real rates of increase (more than 7 percent GNP growth annually during 1983–1987), based on a significant current-account surplus (estimated at $4 billion in 1987). In addition, the Hong Kong government had a huge budget surplus in both 1987 and 1988. The major stimulus to growth in Hong Kong has been exports of its own domestic production, which rose nearly 20 percent in 1986. Its reexports also are quite significant in terms of the flow of trade and, therefore, its knowledge of world markets. It remains attractive to foreign investors, offering a favorable climate, including good communications, transportation, and technical infrastructure. The combined exports of domestic product and reexports actually exceed GNP annually.

Singapore grew more than 5 percent annually during 1983–1987, achieving one of the highest per capita incomes among the "four dragons," again based on a high percentage of exports out of Gross Domestic Product. It has done this through highly productive low-cost labor and a niche strategy in industrialization. It has maintained an openness to FDI, never having adopted an attitude of hostility to foreign investors, which are officially seen as bringing packages of capital, technology, production and management know-how, and access to the world market. This inflow is extremely important to Singapore, which has developed a bureaucracy capable of negotiating with the foreign investors and thereby ameliorating or eliminating some of the concerns that other countries had voiced toward foreign investment. The Singapore government officially rejected the six accusations commonly made against multinational corporations: excessive profits from transfer pricing; exploitation of cheap labor; corruption of the government and bureaucracy; undue influence and control over local politicians; ignoring the interests of the host country; and possession of tremendous economic power, making it impossible to negotiate fair or equitable bargains for pursuit of mutual interests. These accusations have not represented the concerns of Singapore; and when any such concern did arise, it was easily handled through direct negotiations between the government and prospective investors. Singapore also did not find that its interests and those of the transnational corporations (TNCs) were antagonistic, and the major problem of corruption was handled simply by internal surveillance and controls. Singapore did not find that TNCs resorted to corruption, bribery, or exercise of undue influence over local politicians when there was no *need* to do so. Removal of corruption within the country itself and the election and appointment of men and women of integrity eliminated the problem within, and therefore removed the enticements of foreign investors. All those who were found to be involved on either side of such activities had to be summarily punished. Even if Singapore has not been able to eradicate all such corruption, the high attention given to it has paid significant dividends in making market operations more honest. In this stance, it has been similar to Japan, at least until the recruit scandal in 1989, which implicated many in the ruling

Liberal Democrat Party in accepting questionable campaign donations of stock in the company. It is a lesson China has yet to learn (see Chapter 11).

The governmental policies that have supported the success of the "four dragons" have not been wholly free market. On the contrary, governments have played critical and substantial roles in all aspects of development in these four economies. In Korea and Taiwan in particular strong absolutist regimes have characterized most of the post–World War II era. The differences in their policies are critically related to the ways in which each needs to rely on the international market to stimulate its growth. Each of them has adopted policies of stimulating exports, but not all have been "export-led" in their development. On the contrary, Taiwan, Korea, and Japan have used import-substitution tactics to stimulate their internal industrial advance. Singapore and Hong Kong, much more reliant on the international market, have used few, if any, barriers to trade or investment; for example, Hong Kong uniquely has no tariffs or duties on imports.

In Korea, less than a third of manufacturing production is exported, whereas 50 percent of Taiwanese industrial output is exported. In contrast, Hong Kong and Singapore export a much higher percentage, though in each case the figure includes re-exported products. Both Korea and Taiwan have historically imposed high tariffs, selective quotas, and even prohibitions (banning cigarette imports into Korea and Japanese cars into Taiwan). Nor are internal markets wholly free, with price controls and subsidies in agriculture, government marketing monopolies, wage controls, and direct intervention in the private financial sector. In Singapore, the government owns 75 percent of the land and 80 percent of the housing of the populace.

Private enterprise also is not the sole means of organizing economic activity in these countries, with government departments owning most of the infrastructure, utilities, and energy supplies and regulating activities in finance, industry, and agriculture. In addition, there are state-owned enterprises in heavy industry, in resource extraction and petroleum, and in petrochemicals, either having a monopoly or a dominant position in several of these countries. Furthermore, each provides incentives and disincentives—support in the form of subsidies, selected protection and tax exemption, guaranteed grants, assistance in labor training, low-cost capital, and so forth—to stimulate or guide industrial development.

Although foreign investment is highly visible in each of these countries, it has played a relatively minor role in accelerating economic growth, except in Singapore, where some 75 percent of manufactures for export are from foreign-owned affiliates. Manufacturing exports out of Hong Kong, South Korea, and Taiwan originating from foreign-owned firms amount only to 10, 15, and 20 percent, respectively. In the majority of cases of foreign investment, the form is that of joint venture, so that even in the case of foreign-owned manufacturing of exports, there is a significant local input. Only Hong Kong has not retained restrictions on foreign investment in some form or other. Investment by China in Hong Kong has grown significantly, and by 1997 could reach 25 to 30 percent of total foreign investment. A majority of local ownership (frequently the state) often is required in foreign investment projects exploring domestic resources or manufacturing or the domestic market. Even Singapore and Hong Kong permit 100 percent foreign ownership only when total output is to be exported.

The opening of these economies to international competition, which has required wide dissemination of economic and commercial information, has lead to pressure for more democracy politically; although the four countries are not democratic, they have moved toward Western-style parliaments. Korea and Taiwan retain a type of authoritarian democracy, with a current unwillingness to move much further because of the apparent necessity of a strong state in guiding economic development in these countries. The state is needed to bring about the necessary compromises in the sacrifice of current consumption for future growth and stability of the country.

These patterns of government and business relations and government policy in surrounding countries contain elements that China hopes to adopt or adapt; and in fact, it has done so fairly extensively. The reasons for success of each in the "four dragons" differ significantly. Barriers to trade and investment are successful *only* if they lead to the development sought, which also includes the generation of local capital, a local entrepreneurial group, and eventual orientation to world markets. These policies also are aimed at maintaining an acceptable distribution of income, so as to reduce tensions and dissent within the society. This distribution of income also is matched by an attempt to balance power between agriculture and industry, between labor and capital, and to maintain an acceptance of deferred consumption to increase current investment. The state also has played an active role in stimulating projects that were not initially profitable but that it could assist in becoming so, thereby stimulating the flow of private investment into longer-term projects. This was particularly the case in the heavy industries and those that were capital-intensive, but that later produced the high export growth precedent to higher per capita incomes. The state also has been a means of generating managerial capabilities through development of bureaucratic techniques of decision-making.

As the "four dragons" continue to succeed in their economic growth, it is likely that they will move even further toward the relaxation of constraints, but it is unlikely that they will remove their state-directed orientation to development. It may well be mitigated, but not eliminated. It is this balance between state control and state guidance that China is searching for. If it goes too far toward import substitution, it risks the inefficiencies that arise from such protection, including continued government control, opportunities for corruption, and eventual high resistance of those protected to the removal of barriers to competition.

Efforts in each of these countries to move toward greater liberalization, privatization, and democratization face vested interests generated through protection and government guidance—both in terms of monopolized private enterprise and those privileged to exercise bureaucratic authority. Even so, Taiwan is continuing to reduce its average tariff rate, as is Korea, and Korea has removed all restrictions on the repatriation of funds from FDI—either principal or earnings.

Privatization also is opposed in the "four dragons" by some who see the power of overseas Chinese becoming even more important. And democratization is opposed by some who see it opening the door for greater influence by citizens working with and oriented to foreign enterprise. Yet the continuation of state-owned enterprises or state-subsidized companies, which often make it difficult for small entrepreneurial companies to arise, eventually could lead to a lack of competitiveness. Many of these same concerns are evident now or will become more evident in the Chinese picture. Those looking to do business in China are forewarned of future problems by examining the experiences of other Asian countries, and they are admonished to beware of potentially misleading analogies.

WORLDWIDE TECHNOLOGICAL ADVANCE

The technological advancement of the world is well known—as is the relative technological stagnation of China. China's backwardness in technology is the result of a number of different actions and events. It is partly due to the Cultural Revolution, when most universities were shut down and the educated were sent to the countryside for "rustification," but also partly due to the stultifying nature of its centrally planned economy and the way in which intellectuals were discriminated against for much of the People's Republic's history, and to its isolation from the world since 1949, which, in turn, was the result of both foreign economic blockades and internal Chinese policy preferences for economic autarky. China was left with few technological resources, mostly dedicated to the military sector. It has, therefore, sought to open its economy to be able to attract foreign technology, and it is concerned that the U.S. government—directly and in concert with the Coordinating Committee (COCOM), which collectively restricts export of high-technology items by Western European, American, and Japanese corporations to "prohibited destinations"—is not more forthcoming in permitting the transfer of defense technology to China. This policy will remain a contention between China and the West.

Further, the Chinese government has recognized that the longer it waits to begin catching up on technology, the harder it will be. It cannot simply leap into the latest technology by turning over all technological development to wholly owned foreign enterprises. So it is attempting to accelerate its mastery of technology by opening up to companies that will bring technology in, as well as to engineers and other experts who will help in the educational process. Any such opening to technology will itself become a pressure to open up in other ways as well. This is recognized and accepted, at least in principle.

A third pressure arising from technology is that it is no longer the preserve of even the advanced countries. For a time after World War II, the United States was a single center of technological advance, transferring it to other industrial countries as they became ready for it, albeit with a significant lag. Now few countries are able to obtain a significant advance in any technological field without standing on the shoulders of researchers in other countries. A network of R&D and of innovation is arising through links in research institutes, licensing agreements that transfer technology almost automatically, and the necessity to know what others are doing. A worldwide technology network is developing that China must enter or be passed by—as the USSR has recognized in its own case.

These ties mean that China will have to accept a higher level of dependence, or at least interdependence. Thus far, China has not yet shown itself willing to integrate economically with outsiders. It seems interested in acquiring and then cutting loose. China could, however, truly take a "great leap forward," with positive results, if it were willing to accept a high degree of integration in technology R&D activities and markets of countries of the West. This would mean the development of cooperative activities, collaborating institutes, and even joint ventures in research, leading to a network of innovation and commercialization. As of the end of the decade of the 1980s, China was not politically ready to take such a step.[13] On the contrary, its priorities in the "four modernizations" show how it expects to enter the modern world.

THE FOUR MODERNIZATIONS

The program of "four modernizations" was conceived by Zhou Enlai in 1975. He envisaged the modernization of agriculture, industry, science and technology, and national defense, after an initial phase in which an independent, industrially oriented economic system would be created through the reform of management and control systems.

Little came of Zhou's vision until the ten-year plan for 1976–1985 (the fifth and sixth five-year plans, ironically, after his death in 1976). These included the construction of 120 large-scale projects centered on improvements in the basic industries (steel, coal, petroleum, electricity generation, and nonferrous metals), including 10 iron and steel complexes, 9 nonferrous metal projects, 8 coal extraction projects, 10 new oil and gas fields, 30 hydroelectric power stations, and improvements in transportation facilities (including construction of 6 new trunk railways and 5 harbors). Gross industrial output was expected to increase 125 percent by value during the ten-year period.

Agricultural modernization was centered around increased mechanization of production, including increased production of tractors and farm machinery, and the improvement of China's cultivable land through improved irrigation and drainage and increased production of chemical fertilizer. Food production was expected to rise by 50 percent in the course of the plan.

Modernization of China's military was to be built on the incremental strengthening of the armed forces begun before 1978. Military equipment was to be upgraded, as was the education of Chinese officers in modern warfare theory and tactics. Yet equally important was the accepted reality that defense was the fourth modernization, holding a lower priority than the others.

Strengthening China's scientific and technical capability was acknowledged as the basis for the other three modernizations. Nine broad areas for scientific and technical modernization were identified: energy resources, natural resources (including iron ore, copper, aluminum, and nickel), computers, lasers, space science (satellites, skylabs, and space probes), high-energy physics (proton accelerator development), genetics, agricultural technology, and anti-pollution technology. To achieve this strengthening would require the re-creation of a science and technology sector that had been decimated by the Cultural Revolution.

This would involve the creation of an appropriate research environment, the training of a new generation of technicians, and the establishment of research centers. Immediate improvements in the research environment would be made by replacing the emphasis on political work with scientific and technical activities. In addition, more theoretical research was to be encouraged rather than the production-oriented work that had previously dominated.

The need for skilled research technicians was acute. Proposals to improve this situation included improving domestic education, sending thousands of Chinese students to Western universities, rehabilitating technicians displaced in the Cultural Revolution, and improving technical competence in the science and technology bureaucracy. It also was acknowledged that China should seek advanced Western technology on which to base its development—an indication of the opening up that was to follow.

As early as 1979 it became clear that the goals set for the four modernizations program were unrealistic. Projected annual growth rates were too high, too much capital was being invested in too few projects, and poor planning was resulting in wasted resources. A major steel plant was built in Shanghai (Baoshan) with imported Japanese technology, but the Chinese later learned that the plant would require literally half of the power in Shanghai, the largest city in China. This event made the Chinese cautious of foreign advice. The capitalization program was scaled down in 1979, although it remained large, with capital investment for the period 1978–1985 still scheduled to equal total capital investment for 1949–1977. Overseas orders were frozen, and the construction of new large-scale projects was cut back.

Other important shifts in direction included a movement away from heavy investment in basic industries. Steel production, for example, which had been scheduled to double to 60 million tons per annum by 1985, was cut back. Greater emphasis was laid on light industries and export-oriented industries from which China could earn the foreign exchange needed to finance its modernization plans and that would produce badly needed consumer products to stimulate greater productivity in China's domestic economy. Agricultural production also was accorded a higher priority.

In the seventh five-year-plan (for 1986–1990), the lofty aspirations of the four modernizations were further scaled down under a more pragmatic assessment of China's needs and capabilities. The plan emphasized the need to renovate and renew existing industrial capacity, rather than to construct new projects. The need to tackle pressing problems rather than long-term goals was reflected in priorities addressing a lack of capital availability, poor technical absorptive capacity, inefficient use of energy, shortfalls in the energy sector, inadequate transportation and telecommunication facilities, bureaucratic inertia, and use of incentives to increase labor productivity.

This five-year plan also included better and more realistic planning of foreign investment. In the critical computer sector, selected major TNCs (technology leaders) were identified as the preferred partners in joint ventures or technology agreements. China did not rule out arrangements with other companies, but the implication was that those selected would receive primary support from Beijing. Provinces or cities may structure agreements with other companies, but funding would have to be supplied locally.

Concentration of resources with a few companies in a sector is a prudent decision for China, but it is difficult for the foreign investor to ascertain whether the factory partner and local government officials have the support of the central government for the proposed venture. As is characteristic of bureaucratic organizations, government or corporate, everyone appears to have broad responsibilities and authority but in reality few do. Obtaining central government support for a foreign investment project often is essential for its success, but determining whether that support exists is difficult without offending the local government and factory managers because this may necessitate going over or around them.

Concentration into a few ventures has advantages for both China and the foreign investor, but it also entails risks for China and reduces opportunities for companies not selected. For China, it narrows the range of technologies to be transferred and assimilated, and if the foreign investor is a technology leader, with worldwide distribution, the opportunity for future exports is enhanced. The local sourcing of parts is made easier because of fewer products, which is part of the five-year plan for key industries. The computer industry was projected to move from about 30 percent of internal sourcing to some 60 percent during the seventh five-year plan. This is a realistic goal, if China does not have to deal with a dozen product lines in the same industry. The limited number of such investors in a sector, however, puts China at risk arising from changing priorities in the plans of the foreign investors. This risk is heightened by the spread of acquisitions, mergers, and leveraged buyouts in the United States during the late 1980s among major corporations, and by the increased vulnerability that ensues when the country becomes dependent on one or two key suppliers at a time of great political uncertainty—such as what happened after June 1989.

China remains determined to achieve the status of a front-line industrial nation. The modernization of its agricultural, industrial, defense, and scientific and technical capability remains its goal. But the challenges and risks China is facing, and will face in the future, are now more readily understood by the Chinese planners than in 1978, and visions of a modern, industrial society by the year 2000 have been replaced by a step-by-step, pragmatic approach to reform for which there is no specific time frame and few details that are locked in as unmodifiable.

China's development objectives have in fact become quite modest, with the stated goals of achieving $800 (1980 U.S. dollars) per capita GNP by the year 2000, which would place it in the middle ranks of the developing countries; becoming an "intermediately developed country" by the year 2020; and reaching "close to the level of the economically developed countries" by the year 2050. Modest as such goals may appear, they require a 5.5 to 6 percent per annum growth in GNP over sixty years, a feat that is clearly not modest.

NOTES

1. Roger Garside, *Coming Alive: China After Mao* (New York: Mentor, 1981).

2. Harry Harding, *China's Second Revolution* (Washington, D.C.: Brookings Institution, 1988).

3. Etienne Balazas, *Chinese Civilization and Bureaucracy*, trans. H. W. Wright (New Haven, Conn.: Yale University Press, 1964).

4. Tony Saich, *The Evolution of Science and Technology Policy in the People's Republic of China Since the Death of Mao Zedong*, Sinologisch Institute (Netherlands: Leiden University, December 1984).

5. William A. Fischer, "The Chief Engineer," *China Business Review*, November-December 1983, pp. 30–34.

6. William A. Fischer, "Follow-up Strategies for Technological Growth," *California Management Review*, Fall 1978, pp. 10–20.

7. Peter N. S. Lee, *Industrial Management and Economic Reform in China, 1949–1984* (Hong Kong: Oxford University Press, 1987), pp. 26–29.

8. William A. Fischer, "Chinese Industrial Management: Outlook for the Eighties," in Joint Economic Committee of the Congress of the United States, *China's Economy Looks Toward the Year 2000* (Washington, D.C.: U.S. Government Printing Office, 1986), p. 557.

9. Ibid.

10. Fox Butterfield, *China Alive in the Bitter Sea* (New York: Times Books, 1982), p. 323.

11. James Abegglen and George Stalk, Jr., *Kaisha: The Japanese Corporation* (New York: Basic Books, 1985).

12. There are many studies of these countries' development—for example the early one by Ted Geiger, *Tales of Two City-States: The Development Progress of Hong Kong and Singapore* (Washington, D.C.: National Planning Association, 1973); also Lawrence A. Viet, "Time of the New Asian Tigers," *Challenge*, July-August 1987, pp. 49–55; Peter L. Berger and Hsin-Huany Michael Hsiao, *In Search of an East-Asian Development Model* (New Brunswick, N.J.: Transaction Books, 1988); and Joel Kotkin and Yoriko Kishimoto, *The Third Century* (New York: Crown, 1988).

13. William A. Fischer, "China as a Player in the World Economy," *China Economic Review* no. 1 (1989): 9–21.

4

The Investment Environment

The major determinant of foreign direct investment (FDI) flows around the world since World War II has been the existence of a "favorable climate," which means economic potential, political stability, cultural receptivity, a high degree of conformity in the rules, a substantial role for private enterprise (local and foreign), freedom of movement of goods, money, and peoples, and autonomy in decision-making by private management. China is selectively trying to provide such an environment for FDI and technology transfers.

ALTERNATIVE ORGANIZATIONAL STRUCTURES

The various forms of "foreign investment" included in China's open-door policy encompass organizational arrangements wider than those usually termed as "foreign direct investment." Not only are there wholly owned foreign enterprises (WOFEs) and equity joint ventures with a range of equity participation, but China also has welcomed the structuring of cooperative or contractual ventures that involve coproduction or cooperative development of oil or other extractive resources. Compensation trade (for example, technology exchanged for some of the output produced by it), bartering, plus some manufacturing and assembling contracts that do not take on the nature of "ventures" also have been widely encouraged by the Chinese in an extremely flexible approach to facilitating technology transfer. The flexibility is such that sometimes these different forms are melded or linked so as to defy precise categorization.

In addition, licensing contracts have been sought—both the longer-termed contracts and continuing ("dynamic") arrangements as well as the one-shot ("static") licensing agreement, under which a stock of technology is transferred and paid for either in lump sum or through a continuing royalty. Finally, loans and company borrowing also are considered "foreign investment." Data on "foreign investment" must, therefore, be carefully examined to see what forms of capital flow and asset contributions are actually included. The relative importance of each of these arrangements has changed during the past decade and can be expected to receive differing welcomes during the next ten years.

The objectives of the Chinese government in opening to foreign investment were principally to supplement the capital investment requirements of modernization and to obtain management skills and access to advanced science and technology and export channels.

The alternative organizational forms reflect the pragmatic orientation of the Chinese. "Bottom-line profitability" is not the first concern of the Chinese government in promoting joint ventures, though enterprise managers eventually may become so concerned. Conversely, the "reasonable profits" orientation of the Chinese usually is not the same concept held by foreign investors, who see profits and repatriated earnings derived from participation in sales by the joint venture, royalties on licensing, fees for training and other services, and income from sales to the joint venture as the primary objective. The last often is the primary reason for establishing the joint venture because the foreign company had no real intention of exporting from China in the first place. The sales also are seen as unique opportunities to enter the Chinese market, which is otherwise not open to them, and only sometimes to create low-cost foreign sourcing for manufacture and export into their worldwide operations. In addition, some enterprises are seeking access to raw materials.

The initial pattern of investment in China is principally of the resource-seeking type, looking for low-cost inputs of materials or labor. This is consistent with China's own policy, and those foreign investors who primarily seek to establish a position in the Chinese market are seen by some Chinese as welcome only for the period of time necessary for the hosts to gain adequate familiarity with the operations and technology so that they can take over the activities completely. The various contractual forms reflect this orientation, as with the initial requirement, a limitation that has since been relaxed. This would be a further indication of China's increased understanding of an ever-changing investment environment.

Wholly Owned Foreign Enterprises

In the world's experience with FDI since World War II, WOFEs are by far the most significant form of cross-national direct investment. They are the preferred form on the part of the foreign investor, though many host countries prefer joint ventures. The wholly owned venture has not been given a high priority in China, which has sought to limit the incursion of the foreigner in terms of control. It is precisely this control that the foreign investor seeks to make certain that the operations of the affiliate fit with the parent's worldwide strategy. Wholly owned affiliates are particularly important in the strategies of transnational corporations (TNCs) that are seeking to integrate their international activities so as to reduce cost, raise efficiency, and achieve high levels of competitiveness with other TNCs.

China has tended to limit the use of WOFEs to situations in which the technology desired is significant or the total output of the affiliate is to be exported. However, wholly owned ventures jumped eightfold to some 400 new entities formed during 1988. One U.S. firm has been in this category for five years, being formed in 1985 after four years of negotiation; the experience of 3M in Shanghai is of interest, especially from the standpoint of supply of local materials. 3M obtained approval because it offered high technology and exportable products.[1] In China's case, the desire on the part of foreign investors to transfer quite sophisticated technology is relatively small, and those who are eager to integrate the entire output of a plant in China with their other operations are relatively few. Where this form has been used in China, it is set up by smaller investors who are familiar enough with the situation in China to feel comfortable managing the operation completely and who know how to use the opportunity to the mutual benefit of themselves and China.

The tendency to limit WOFEs also was motivated by China's desire to understand their benefits and disadvantages before a significant number were established. Joint ventures appeared to offer a better structure to transfer technology and management know-how to China, but they also required use of foreign exchange by China. As China's experience with foreign investment has increased, the Chinese have learned that joint ventures also restrict investment by some companies because of corporate policy; they learned also that WOFEs employ Chinese, who will become technically trained and experienced in management know-how. Consequently, China has become more open to the establishment of WOFEs.[2]

Joint Ventures

The form of FDI preferred by China is the equity joint venture, usually with a fifty-fifty equity split or a minority for the foreigner.[3] Yet, among TNCs that accept joint ventures, the fifty-fifty split is the least desired. The advantages that China sees in joint ventures are the attraction of foreign technology, the addition to foreign exchange of capital resources, the contribution from foreign management and training of Chinese management, the development of skilled labor, and a potential outlet to foreign markets.[4] Some of these advantages are likely to be attenuated by the reluctance of the foreign partner to integrate into its long-term planning an organization over which it does not have clear control, or to release technology to a venture that it cannot direct. This is obviously true for the minority venture. The fifty-fifty venture will need to build into the joint venture agreement some controls or limits to provide the foreign partner with enough control to ensure the predictability and dependability of the joint venture in meeting its commitments to the foreign investor. A joint venture owned in the majority by the foreign investor may not, however, receive a complete flow of the latest technology as readily as a WOFE would. After all, in either a wholly or minority-owned venture, the foreign investor is providing technology that will reside in a country that nationalized foreign companies after 1949. Thus there is a perceived risk. Any of these ventures will be manned by nationals, and a leakage of information to a state-owned competitor is a further risk. Therefore, any venture is likely to have a restricted flow of information in the early stages. This is particularly the case when the joint venture is for a fixed (relatively short) term. Under a more permanent arrangement, and with increased familiarity among the partners, the flow of information tends to increase.

The disadvantages of any joint venture to the foreign investor include not only the absence of total control, and therefore the inability to manage as seen fit, but also the potential development of a competitor in the future through the transfer of technology, the inability to hire and fire workers as the foreign parent sees fit, the time consumed in arriving at consensus decisions, and potential disagreements over the financial matters of pricing, dividends, borrowing, cost accounting procedures, expatriate salaries, and so on. It is much more difficult to establish "standard operating procedures" in a joint venture than in a WOFE.

The disadvantages of minority and fifty-fifty joint ventures to the host country are apparently not perceived as significant in the views of Chinese officials, but they can in fact be significant. Every foreign investor will make trade-offs in various activities of an international arrangement so as to achieve its longer-term objectives as closely as possible, including reasonable profit. This means that if, in negotiating the arrangement, the foreigners must give up some desired provisions, which reduce the joint venture's profit contribution, they will be more adamant on others, which act to restore their targeted profit objectives. Anything less than a majority ownership in a joint venture will lead to constraints in the incorporation of the venture into the long-term plan, and on the types and amounts of technology that will be offered, the training and support arrangements for the flow of technology and its adaptation in the joint venture, the priority that headquarters will give the venture, the support through funding and inter-company accounts that would be forthcoming, cooperation in common purchasing and in marketing distribution that will be offered, the availability of export markets served by the TNC, information on new products or processes being developed (in which the joint venture might have a later interest), and so on. Virtually every aspect of a joint venture negotiation is subject to being traded-off for any other, so as to balance the costs and benefits in the minds of the negotiators. Thus the benefits that accrue to the host country are principally determined by its ability to bargain with the foreign investor, since, in a foreign majority or WOFE, the foreign investor is looking after the interest of the affiliate and the total company, which may or may not be coincident with that of the host country. Even so, with careful assessment of the project being proposed, a host country can impose constraints on a WOFE or foreign majority venture that enhance the host country's ability to gain desired benefits. China has, therefore, by becoming more open to WOFEs, significantly increased the viable investment options of the foreigners and thereby increased its own benefits coming out of FDI.

There are distinct advantages to the foreign investor of a fifty-fifty and even minority venture, and these should be considered when determining the most appropriate strategy. Three major elements are crucial to joint venture success: foreign exchange, import licenses, and marketing. If the output of the joint venture is sold in the domestic market, the sales will be limited to organizations that have foreign exchange, unless the local currency (renminbi) revenues can be converted into foreign exchange for imports of materials and components or repatriation of profits. (In China, foreign currencies are exchanged for "foreign exchange certificates," which commonly must be used to buy any goods that are imported [ranging from photographic film to capital equipment] as well as for payments in hotels catering to foreigners. Local currency—renmenbi literally meaning "people's money"—cannot be used to purchase imported goods or be converted to foreign exchange certificates; neither can foreign exchange certificates nor foreign currency be officially exchanged for renminbi. This "dual-currency" system is due to be phased out at some undetermined date.) Generally, only foreign enterprises, hotels, and government agencies have foreign exchange, and unless there is a sufficiently large market, the joint venture will need to sell also for renminbi. The Chinese government manages the majority of conversions of renminbi to foreign exchange, and having them as a partner can be important, since there is more demand for renminbi conversion than there is foreign exchange (see Chapter 11). It is, however, also possible for a foreign joint venture to "swap" renminbi for the "excess" foreign exchange earnings of other joint ventures to repatriate a portion of earnings. This works because there are limits on the amount of foreign exchange that any joint venture can repatriate. However, because some joint ventures, such as tourist hotels in particular, deal almost exclusively with foreign exchange, they typically have an excess above what they can repatriate. This excess can be swapped for renminbi from other foreign exchange–poor joint ventures through mechanisms called "swap markets."

Similarly, China controls imports through requiring licenses, thereby restricting the volume. If a foreign enterprise is competing against a Chinese factory that produces an item requiring imported parts or sets (complete knocked-down or semi–knocked-down kits) and the foreign enterprise is wholly owned, the logical tendency of the government is to favor the Chinese factory, so that it is profitable.

Marketing is the third critical factor. Unless the foreign investor is familiar with China, he will have difficulty in the marketing and distributing of the product both locally and nationally. Locally, it may be difficult or impossible to achieve success if there is a local Chinese competitor, or if the local distributors have alliances with Chinese factories. National distribution in China is just emerging, since under the previous system each region had its own factories to fulfill its needs, with none of the factories marketing outside their regions. With such conditions, it would be difficult for even an established Chinese enterprise to achieve national distribution, let alone a foreign venture.

Regardless of which arrangement is preferred by China, foreign investment will continue to take place in China simply because it is a potential source of low-cost production; it provides an opening into the domestic market of China that eventually can become quite attractive; and it can provide an opportunity for returns on technology transfers. Therefore, there is a long-term profit potential.

In the Western experience, international or domestic joint ventures have, until recently, been reluctantly used or agreed to; they arise mainly when the host government requires it or when the other party has assets or capabilities that one cannot readily attain, so that the joint venture becomes a competitive necessity. For example, sufficient attraction exists in special capabilities of a potential partner, such as a unique position in the home market, a unique technology of its own, or close, critical relations with the host government. By and large, few of the Western TNCs (Xerox being an exception) have sought to establish a global network of joint ventures, but this is changing. Joint ventures and network arrangements are becoming a more pervasive part of corporate strategy, driven by a variety of reasons, such as low-cost sourcing, the high cost of new technologies and innovations, the high cost of innovative failures, the expense of generating higher market share, and the high cost of independently acquiring management know-how, which was rationale for the GM-Toyota joint venture in California.

Contractual Ventures

The contractual venture, sometimes confusingly called, in China, a "contractual joint venture," has offered much more flexibility in negotiation than the equity joint venture. The name covers a variety of arrangements leading to long-term cooperation in ventures in China that set forth contractually specific responsibilities and rights on the part of both parties. It commonly is simply a contract between two entities to perform specified tasks, with resources provided by each and managed by a joint team. Because there is no separate entity, this contractual venture is not strictly a joint venture and is not taxable itself, but the results will be taxable through the contracting parties. The distinction between the contractual venture and the joint venture is blurred by the fact that *at times* the contractual venture is a new legal entity with its own board of directors and bylaws (rather than being a contract between two formerly existing entities).

The Chinese government has not seen fit to regulate the contractual venture in the manner in which it does the joint venture, and thus almost any arrangement can be made between the two parties, ranging from virtually all the sales going to the domestic market or to the export market, and with the output or the profit being shared in whatever proportion the parties agree. The duration of such agreements usually is one to five years, based on the search for a secured supply of materials or components coming out of China, or a market penetration by a foreign supplier. The contractual ventures have been formed mostly with Hong Kong firms and have been based in the neighboring Guangdong Province.

United States and Western investors, for various reasons, have not found the contractual venture as attractive as have the Southeast Asian investors. This is because a lengthy search is required to find appropriate partners, which the overseas Chinese are more adept at or more patient in doing. In addition, the U.S. and Western legally documented contractual negotiations and approval processes can be lengthy and costly for short-term commitments, making the contractual venture potentially less attractive to the Western TNC. The Southeast Asian investor is likely to be moving in and out of contractual venture arrangements because of his advantages in know-how, patience, flexibility, and proximity to China.

Xerox formed a contractual venture arrangement with the Ministry of the Electronics Industry of the central government to operate an electronic printing service bureau, with Xerox supplying the equipment and the ministry underwriting any losses. The Chinese got advanced technology and Xerox electronic printers. Xerox gained reputation and potential customers for the time when marketing of electronic printers would begin in China.

Cooperative Development Contracts

In the area of exploration and mineral resources, particularly petroleum, still another form of contract has been used for cooperative projects. In these contracts, foreign companies undertake the up-front costs of exploration, with the Chinese partner entering during the developmental stage and sharing the capital costs and risks of that stage with the foreign partner. If there is a commercially significant output, it will be divided between the parties according to a pre-agreed formula, applicable throughout the duration of the project. This arrangement is not strictly a joint venture, and it does not have the same limitation of duration that is imposed on joint ventures in China, though it is expected to terminate at the end of commercial production. It usually is restricted to development of specific sites and is, therefore, not a permanent joint venture relationship.

Compensation Arrangements

There are several types of compensation arrangements that are considered by the Chinese as foreign investment, which normally would not be so categorized in business literature. Regardless, the continued trade deficits and the need for foreign financing will support continued use of such agreements. These arrangements may involve direct trade or imports of components and materials to be processed or assembled for local use and sale, or for sale only to the foreigner and compensated by various returns from China.

Under compensation trade, a TNC supplies equipment, technology, or components to a Chinese enterprise, which then combines them with its own labor, materials, and plant facilities to produce goods that are exported over a fixed term to repay the foreign contributions. Eastman Kodak, as an example, had an arrangement in Shanghai in which it supplied the equipment and know-how necessary to assemble carousel projectors for the Asian market. To assure quality, Kodak also renovated the space, which then looked like part of its U.S. facility transplanted to an old Shanghai factory. Kodak receives 40 percent of the output as payment for its investment. Shanghai was free to sell the remaining production locally, but not for export. The repayment obviously includes a profit and a return for waiting on the part of the foreigner. This arrangement provides for delayed trade, and therefore clearly involves an investment on the part of the foreigner in the form of the loan of assets to the Chinese enterprise. It also provides the foreigner with market entry and presumably offers advantages in future Chinese purchases, as the foreigner's technology is already in use. The Chinese gain the opportunity to acquire advanced technology without spending scarce foreign exchange.

Similarly, the foreign ''investor'' can supply machinery, technology, or components to a Chinese firm that repays *not* in the final product manufactured out of these assets, but in commodities or manufactured goods of another type that are desired by the foreign supplier. This is close to straight barter, though delivery may be delayed over time. Bausch and Lomb has an unusual arrangement, in that it established a joint venture for the production of contact lenses in one province and will export microscopes from a factory in a different province; what is unusual is that two provinces are involved. PepsiCo supplies Pepsi concentrate and is repaid in Chinese mushrooms, which it uses in its Pizza Hut operations worldwide. Thus mushrooms become the real mechanism for the repatriation of the profits earned in the sales of concentrate.

The contracts that involve processing and assembly arrangements are ones in which the foreign party supplies materials or components for processing or assembly *solely* for the benefit of the foreign supplier, who then will pay a fee for the service with deductions for whatever value he may have contributed in terms of machinery and technology. These arrangements are essentially manufacturing contracts, but they do involve a period of waiting on the part of the foreign party and, therefore, are considered ''investment'' by the Chinese.

Service, Repair, and Maintenance Arrangements

Because the network of repair and maintenance facilities is not adequate in China, any opening into that market, including direct trade, may necessitate the establishment of a service network. Virtually any one of the arrangements mentioned above can be used in the formation of such a network, and there also is a transfer of technology, with commensurate training of mechanics and other technicians. After-sales service centers have been established in cooperation with Chinese enterprises, in stand-alone repair and maintenance centers, in cooperation with parts warehouses, and so on.

Among such centers are those owned and managed 100 percent by Chinese, joint ventures of Chinese and foreigners, and contractual ventures. There are few, if any, foreign-owned and -managed service centers, owing to the extremely high operating costs, complicated and unreasonable taxation, and the extreme difficulties in setting up such centers. Because most companies involved are interested in having a service network that eventually is Chinese-owned and -managed, many companies have provided Chinese organizations with maintenance tools, instruments, spare parts, and training of personnel, who will be capable of servicing their sales in China. Once such a network is formed, a single maintenance center could service the equipment of a number of enterprises in the same industrial sector or product line. In some instances, a contract is negotiated with a government ministry having the appropriate facilities; it then undertakes the responsibility for establishing the service network for several companies in that sector. Although sometimes the establishment of such centers is separate from the direct investment itself, it is a necessary part of the investment and should be considered one aspect of doing business in China.

Relative Significance of FDI Forms

The actual use of the alternative forms for foreign investment in China is reflected in rather sparse data—see Table 4.1. There is, further, a considerable difference between projects agreed on and actual utilization of funds.

Although China had contracted for at least $27 billion of foreign investment, by the end of 1988, less than 40 percent of this investment had been committed. The figure becomes even lower if oil ventures are excluded (in any discussion of total foreign investment in China since 1978, it must be remembered that the extent of investment in contractual oil ventures skews the data). On occasion, preliminary agreements signed by high-level delegations ultimately bear little fruit; with others, initial enthusiasm for investment often cools as the details are hammered out in long, drawn-out negotiations, with projects being heavily scaled down, especially as the foreign exchange requirements become more precisely identified.

Although China had declared a preference for equity joint ventures, the initial response of investors from advanced countries to investment in such arrangements was only lukewarm. The uncertain nature of doing business in China immediately after the opening of the Chinese economy to investment encouraged the adoption of the contractual joint venture organizational form—project-specific and short-term in nature—as opposed to the more long-term and wide-ranging equity joint venture. Furthermore, the implementing regulations accompanying the joint ven-

Table 4.1
Contracted FDI in China by Form, 1979–1987 (U.S. $Millions)

Type	1979-1983	1984	1985	1986	1987	1988	1979-88
Equity Joint Ventures	308	1060	2027	1375	1920	3134	9824
Contractual Jt. Ventures	3230	3752	2189	1358	1286	1624	13439
Wholly-owned affiliates	4	99	32	20	470	481	1106
Contractual oil ventures	2313	n/a	n/a	77	4	58	2888
TOTALS*	5855	n/a	n/a	2830	3680	5297	27257

*Totals are for those forms of FDI shown in Table 4.1. Actual FDI totals will be higher because of compensation trade and other forms of FDI for which data are incomplete.

Note: Even after funds are "contracted", they cannot be "utilized" until a project is approved; utilization rates range from 10 to 50 percent of contracted. Lack of utilization is less a matter of inability to use than of indecision or delay on the part of officials.

Source: Chen, Nai-Ruenn, "Foreign Investment in China: Current Trends", in China Business Review, May-June 1988, p.57; Intertrade, February 1988, p.27-9; China Statistical Abstract, 1988, p. 83 (Series Ed. William T. Liu, N.Y.: Praeger, 1989).

ture law were not immediately published, leaving potential investors somewhat uneasy about what the law actually required or permitted.

It was not until 1984 that foreign attitudes toward equity joint ventures warmed; then this form surpassed contractual joint ventures (which included the popular technology transfer agreement). The shift to the equity joint venture was an indication of investor confidence in the emerging investment environment within China, an environment that was being tailored toward that form of FDI. Since then, investor confidence has waxed and waned, shifting with political currents, China's progress in dealing with investor concerns, and the presence of attractive investment opportunities. Thus, during the first half of 1989, foreign investment contracts increased in number more than 40 percent and in dollar amounts nearly 50 percent. But for the three months after Tiananmen, the number of contracts fell by 20 percent and amounts by 23 percent.[5] Similarly, technology transfer contracts declined markedly in later 1989. Investments during the first six months of 1990 continued down compared with the first half of 1989. Chinese officials argued that by the middle of 1990, some recovery was occurring in the inflows, but major investments seldom were visible.[6]

To date, licensing agreements have not formed a significant part of the foreign capital invested in China. This situation may change with the passing of a new patent law designed to ease the worries of foreign companies licensing technology to Chinese firms, but early indications are that it has not. In many cases, potential choice licensees are not fully capable of presenting the licensed product in its best light.

WOFEs are even less significant, accounting for only 3 percent of utilized foreign investment and a little more than 4 percent of contracted investment. Contracted foreign investment during 1987 and 1988 suggested that wholly owned foreign ventures may become more acceptable in China, especially after the promulgation in April 1986 of the "Law of the People's Republic on Wholly Foreign-Owned Enterprises," the first of its kind in any socialist country. But the capital amounts are still less significant than those under equity and contractual joint ventures. Foreign investment in joint and wholly foreign ventures in China is shown in Table 4.2 by number of contracted ventures.

These data underscore the rising importance of equity joint ventures over contractual joint ventures, the slowing-down of enterprise start-up after the economic difficulties of 1985, and the relatively minor role of wholly owned foreign ventures to this point. The relative importance of foreign investment in contracted oil ventures is, however, diminished in this picture, since the relatively small number of ventures (less than 1 percent) accounts for more than 10 percent of contracted foreign investment and almost 25 percent of the foreign investment utilized in China.

GEOGRAPHICAL LOCATION

Since the opening up of China to foreign investment, numerous localities have received authority from Beijing to seek foreign investment. The foreign company

Table 4.2
FDI in China by Enterprise Type, 1979–1988 (Numbers of Ventures)

Source	1979	1980	1981	1982	1983	1984	1985	1986	1987	1988	1979-88
Equity Joint Ventures	6	20	28	29	107	741	1300	892	1399	3909	8431
Contractual Jt. Ventures	0	320	70	402	331	1089	1500	582	786	1621	6701
Wholly-Owned Ventures	33*	15	26	46	18	45	410	455			
Contracted oil ventures	8	4	0	1	18	0	4	6	3	5	49
TOTALS	14	344	98	465	471	1856	3300	1498	2233	5945	15636

* Cumulative 1979-82 figure.

Source: Chen, Nai-Ruenn, "Foreign Investment in China: Current Trends", in China Business Review, May-June 1988, p.57; Intertrade, February 1988, p.27-9; China Statistical Abstract, 1988, p. 83 (Series Ed. William T. Liu, N.Y.: Praeger, 1989).

is enticed by various incentives and opportunities to locate either in Special Economic Zones (SEZs), coastal cities (and their Economic and Technological Development Zones), inland cities, or Open Economic Zones.

The Special Economic Zones

China's first four SEZs were established in 1979. Three (Shenzhen, Shantou, and Zhuhai) are in Guangdong Province, while the fourth (Xiamen) is in Fujian. The island of Hainan was made a province in April 1988 and an SEZ. Although it is hoped that Hainan will become the "Hawaii" of China, it will take significant amounts of capital—officially estimated at $50 million over twenty years—to realize such hopes. All of the original four are close to Hong Kong (see Table 4.1), and have strong ties to its overseas Chinese community. These zones also are in locations on the periphery of China, so as to limit the inflow of negative foreign influences that the Chinese leadership expects to accompany Western technology and know-how. (In this sense, "enclaves" become "catchments.") Because Guangdong and Fujian provinces had previously been given some independence in decision-making in foreign trade planning and management, they already had some commercial experience considered invaluable for the successful establishment of the SEZs. SEZs also have been sources of entrepreneurial talents, creating or spinning off new enterprises.

Official attitudes on the SEZs were that they should be seen as experimental, that is, as an initial attempt by the Chinese Communist Party to create an economic environment conducive to FDI inflows. But the bold nature of this move, especially in the wake of the Cultural Revolution, and the size of FDI inflows quickly made the SEZs an important testing ground for the new open policies. Their future in the immediate post-Tiananmen period will be more subdued; but ultimately they will probably return to the aggressive experimentation that has characterized them to date.

The proposed growth of the original four SEZs as initially conceived is tabulated in Table 4.3. Clearly, of all the SEZs, Shenzhen was intended to be the most important.

The Shenzhen SEZ

In the initial formulation of SEZs, only Shenzhen was designed to be a large-scale, comprehensive zone, with a primary focus on industrial development (high-tech, advanced technology sectors), as well as on agriculture, tourism, and trade. The other three zones were to be more limited in scale. Bordering on the new territories of Hong Kong, Shenzhen was designed as a gateway to Hong Kong. This involved the transformation of the rural landscape surrounding the small township of Shenzhen into what would be the largest economic zone of its type in the world. To do so required the injection of large sums—more than US $2.24 billion between 1979 and 1986—for basic infrastructure.

The SEZ is permitted to offer incentives above and beyond national investment

Table 4.3

China's SEZ Program Projected at Year 2000

	Shenzhen	Zhuhai	Shantou[*]	Xiamen[*]
Area (km^2)	327.6	.8	3.3	2.5
Industrial area (km^2)	15.0	2.3	1.6	2.0
Urban Population:				
1981	30,000	25,000	neg.	neg.
1985	250,000	n/a	n/a	n/a
1990	400,000	n/a	28,000	35,000
1995	n/a	87,900	n/a	n/a
2000	1,000,000	175,000	52,000	65,000
Employment	145,000	41,700	29,200	36,500
Factory number	1,500	227	160	200
Export Value ($m'n)	3,750	568	400	500
Investment (RMB m'n):				
Urban facilities	1,670	273	88	110
Infrastructure	2,000	400	45	70
Foreign Investment ($million)	1,500	227	280	350

[*] As originally conceived, Shantou and Xiamen SEZs were more limited, respectively, to the Longhu and the Huli industrial zones. In 1984, the size and scope of both SEZs was substantially extended at the same time that China afforded the 14 coastal cities and other areas a wider role in foreign investment.

Source: Adapted from V.C. Falkenheim, "China's SEZs", China's Economy Looks Toward the Year 2000, U.S. Congress Joint Economic Committee Report, May 1986, p.356.

incentives.[7] It can authorize FDI projects without approval of higher authorities at levels of capital investment—some $17 million for heavy industry, $10 million for light industry, and $33 million for nonindustrial projects such as hotels— considerably higher than commonly permitted to local authorities. These limits are designed to eliminate some bureaucratic red tape by reducing the number of approvals that are required for the establishment of ventures within Shenzhen. Other incentives include complete exemption from Enterprise Income Tax for high-tech ventures for the first five years, reductions and exemptions on import and export duties, exemption from Profit Remittance Tax, and longer land lease periods and lower land use fees as compared with other regions of China.

Essentially, the attraction of Shenzhen lies in its proximity to Hong Kong, cheap land, cheap labor (by Western standards), and the discretionary incentives it can offer in addition to the standard national package. These attractions, the Chinese hoped, would offset the inevitable major difficulties that would accompany the transformation of Shenzhen into an industrial base and would make it competitive with incentives offered in other countries.

The most obvious difficulty faced was the lack of infrastructure—roads, buildings, sewer lines, power supplies, telecommunications, and so on. Supply of electricity remains problematic throughout China. Although some areas of Shenzhen have their power supplies guaranteed by the Hong Kong China Power and Light Company, and certain high-tech and export-oriented enterprises also are guaranteed supplies, other enterprises regularly suffer day-long cuts and adjust their production schedule accordingly. Meanwhile Shenzhen authorities continue to construct new power stations. Although Shenzhen transportation and communication facilities are now considered advanced by Chinese standards, they remain inadequate for FDI affiliates, and improvements—such as the development of Shenzhen's Yantan Harbor into an international center for containerized and conventional cargoes—are continuing.

Other improvements necessary for the success of the SEZ appear harder to solve. Labor, for example, although cheap by Western standards, is more expensive in Shenzhen than elsewhere in China, thereby diminishing one of the key attractions to foreign investors of investing in Shenzhen. Furthermore, the nature of Shenzhen's labor imposes limitations: First, it is predominantly rural-based labor, lacking the experience and discipline of factory-based employment. Training of new workers for periods of three months to a year is necessary, depending on the complexity of the production operations to be established. Second, technical and skilled workers are difficult to find. In 1986 alone, for example, the Chinese reported a need for an additional 2,000 to 3,000 technicians and engineers, and another 1,000 skilled workers in Shenzhen's various textile concerns. Shenzhen itself has only a limited supply of technical talent coming out of its newly established higher educational institutions.

Almost all of the projects in Shenzhen are export-oriented. Shenzhen has the advantage of utilizing imported raw materials, compared with the inland cities. Domestically sourced raw materials are in short supply, irregular in delivery, and deficient in quality, and have unreasonably high prices. There is, however, a disadvantage in relying heavily on imported raw materials. Although the price paid for those raw materials is largely competitive with that paid for domestic materials, payments must be in foreign exchange rather than in renminbi (local currency), re-emphasizing the need to gain foreign exchange through exports.

Because Shenzhen has no established industrial base, enterprises that depend on a network of suppliers are less likely to be attracted to locate there. This is a major shortfall in the development of Shenzhen and other SEZs, and perpetuates the attractiveness of Shanghai, which has a strong industrial base but is already overcrowded. Enterprises that produce a finished product for the consumer market find conditions more favorable, but these are likely to involve simple assembly of low-tech products, which is not the SEZ's top priority.

Finally, zone officials were drawn from other pursuits or directly from universities and have had to learn on the job about dealing with foreign investors. Their development has not always been smooth. For example, foreign investors have been indiscriminately charged with up to fifty operating fees beyond such things as wages, welfare subsidies, factory rent, and electricity supply. Companies have complained, and the Shenzhen government has announced plans to standardize the various operating fees throughout the SEZ and reduce the amounts charged by individual districts within the zone.

Shenzhen's record, like that of the SEZ initiative in general, is a mixed one. Although the total value of goods and services produced in Shenzhen has risen by 50 percent per year for the past ten years,[8] foreign investment exceeding $2 billion U.S. and the population increasing from 50,000 to 1.6 million, the entire story is not wholly satisfactory. Instead of the manufacturing and technology that the Chinese leaders envisioned being produced in such SEZs, the zones, especially Shenzhen, have become service-oriented and entrepôts. Corruption and illicit activities are more prevalent in the "wild West" atmosphere of the zones than elsewhere in China, and the child labor abuses and other illegal labor practices are written about frequently.

Because of the initial problems that Shenzhen—like China in general—has encountered in its establishment, the results in attracting FDI have been somewhat disappointing. Investment in Shenzhen through 1984 amounted to $580 million (about one-quarter of the amount that was actually pledged). Moreover, of 3,495 agreements signed, only 460 (18 percent) were Sino-foreign joint ventures or wholly foreign-owned ventures. The other 3,035 were small processing and assembly agreements, the majority established by the Shenzhen and other provincial authorities in search of export earnings, with a significant number involving Hong Kong firms moving to Shenzhen to get away from rising wage and land use cost in Hong Kong.

Only a small proportion (10 percent in 1984) of the manufacturing enterprises established in Shenzhen are classified as high-tech. (The level of some of the technology received must be questioned, since the definition of high-tech at that time was anything that was slightly more advanced than Chinese technology. As mentioned earlier, much of China's industry uses pre-1960s technology.) The bulk of the manufacturing enterprises established in Shenzhen were essentially rather crude, labor-intensive ventures that produced such products as cheap radios, knitwear, and plastic flowers.

This was hardly what Beijing had envisioned when it had announced the formation of the SEZs, especially Shenzhen, but neither was it particularly surprising. As Li Guofu, president of the Shenzhen Industrial and Trading Center, commented: "We are naive if we think this industrial desert can go high-tech in just a few years"—a statement describing Shenzhen, but equally applicable to China in general.[9]

In place of the advanced industrial economy sought by Beijing, Shenzhen developed an economy based on a flourishing tourist industry and a speculative property market. In 1984, for example, 34 percent of Shenzhen's business profits were derived from tourism and shopping and 18 percent from construction, with only 25 percent from industry. Furthermore, exports from Shenzhen in 1984 accounted for only 20 percent of its $450 million gross industrial output (a figure that rises only to 35 percent when domestic sales of import substitutes are added).

For Beijing, which identifies strong export performance with technological advancement, this last figure was especially displeasing. Shenzhen was told to increase the export percentage of its gross annual industrial output to 60 percent. An early-1986 criticism of all the SEZs (pointedly at Shenzhen) complained that the SEZs were not earning foreign exchange commensurate with the massive state investment they had received. In particular, too many projects were being developed in the service sector, with too little attention paid to the technologically advanced manufacturing ventures that were the prime motivation for establishing the SEZs. Improvement was demanded.

Shenzhen attempted to respond, and has attracted a growing number of sophisticated joint ventures, indicating that foreign investors were becoming more confident about the environment created in Shenzhen and that the zone might be able to support the high-tech, capital-intensive projects for which it was originally established. Joint venture contracts, which only amounted to 460 through 1983, have increased (454 in 1986 and 334 in 1987 and by the end of 1989 totalling 2,571). Similarly, foreign investment in Shenzhen, which amounted to $580 million through 1984, rose to a cumulative $2.8 billion by the end of 1989. Exports in 1986 accounted for 51 percent of gross industrial output, and this figure increased to 53 percent in 1987. Tourism still accounted for as much as 20 to 30 percent of the zone's foreign exchange earnings in the late 1980s, and it continued to develop assembly operations to meet the demand from Hong Kong manufacturers that produce electronics, textiles, and leather goods.

The Shenzhen experience is typical of that of the other three SEZs. Each has received substantial amounts of investment to establish the infrastructure necessary to attract foreign investment. Each has been given some authority to set regulations to attract foreign investment beyond those established for China nationally. After slow beginnings—and sharp rebukes—it was only in 1987 that these SEZs began to realize their potential. In 1989, after the Tiananmen events and the restoration of an economically and politically conservative government in Beijing, much of the autonomy that had been granted the SEZs was withdrawn. Of particular importance was the withdrawal of the SEZs' privilege of retaining all of the foreign exchange earned within the zones. Since 1989 the zones must now turn over 20 percent of their foreign exchange earnings to the central authorities and, in return, receive renminbi. Although this rule does not apply to joint ventures with foreign investment, it does limit the attractiveness of the SEZs as ports of entry for shipping the exports of inland domestic producers.

In addition, Beijing bestowed preferential advantages on an industry rather than on a geographical basis, which eliminated the differential advantage given the SEZs.

The results of the diminished attractiveness of the SEZs to foreigners and to the new central government are obvious from the numbers. In Hainan pledged foreign investments in 1989 fell 26 percent against the previous year and by 90 percent in the first half of 1990. Shenzhen's US $489 million of new investment in 1989 was roughly at the level of that in 1988. Only Xiamen grew in 1989, with foreign contracts both signed and utilized increasing by 300 percent each in 1989 (to US $385 million and US $238 million, respectively), largely because of surging Taiwanese investment.[10]

Ironically, through the central government policies of granting other areas of China the authority to offer incentives and subsidies to foreign investors, the SEZs now face greater internal competition in their attempts to attract foreign investment. The SEZs illustrate an underlying problem in China's economic reform: Service businesses, such as hotels, have low entry barriers, especially in terms of foreign exchange investment and the time to reach profitability; and high-technology businesses require significant investments of foreign exchange by China and take four to six years to earn a profit and to develop products that are competitive on international markets so as to earn foreign exchange.

Cities as Development Centers

Chinese industry has historically developed around a few coastal cities, largely as a result of foreign industrial activities in what were formerly "treaty ports," cities that had been forced open by the Western powers as ports of entry for trading into China and as coal and maintenance stations for their fleets. This pattern of coastal rim development—responding to a need of foreign interlopers from more than a century ago—has raised serious problems of balance,[11] as occurred in Brazil and other nations dependent on international trade. China has sought to build on the existing strengths on the coast, yet also redress the imbalances. Consequently Shanghai clearly remains the dominant industrial center, and will be in the future unless specific steps are taken to encourage growth elsewhere, and even then the change will be a long-term one. Foreign ventures aimed at exporting will tend to locate where there is an adequate infrastructure of suppliers and skilled labor, such as in Shanghai.

The Fourteen Coastal Cities

In April 1984, China announced the opening to foreign investment of fourteen coastal cities plus Hainan Island off the South China coast. These fourteen cities—Dalian, Qinhuangdao, Tianjin, Yantai, Qingdảo, Lianyungang, Nantong, Shanghai, Ningbo, Wenzhou, Fuzhou, Guangshou, Zhanjiang, and Beihai—plus Hainan were able to offer incentives similar to those in the SEZs: attractive tax rates, flexible application of customs duties, negotiation of charges such as land use fees, and simplified administrative procedures. The specific incentives varied from city to city. Shanghai and Tianjin municipal authorities were allowed to approve investment up to $30 million; Dalian and Guangzhou, $10 million; and the others were limited to approvals of only $5 million.

In addition, each coastal city was allowed to establish an Economic and Technical Development Zone (ETDZ) outside the city, where uniform income tax rates of 15 percent were offered and the 10 percent profit remittance tax also was waived.[12]

This move by Beijing to open up some of the more well-established coastal cities to foreign investment was, in part, a reaction to the demands of these cities that they be allowed more latitude in pursuing foreign investment. But it also was an acknowledgment by the central authorities that it made sense to exploit the existing infrastructure in these cities, given the relatively poor return on its investment in the capital construction of the SEZs. These coastal cities were among those most able to take advantage of Western technology and know-how to *upgrade* their industrial base and stimulate regional economic development. *Thus the thrust of the coastal cities was much more one of technological renovation rather than technological importation for exports.*

Indeed, the attractions of these coastal cities to foreign investors were essentially those that the SEZs are criticized for not having: a relatively strong industrial base, a skilled work force, established higher educational institutions (providing a local supply of skilled labor and also an element of research and development support), and existing port facilities.

These cities are not without their own problems. Many are already over-crowded, with pressure on land and building space pushing up land use fees and costs in general. This is particularly true of the larger cities, such as Shanghai, and this overcrowding is not likely to be relieved in this century because demands on city resources are great. In the case of Shanghai, where 250 large enterprises are running at a loss, municipal revenues (which are drawn heavily from industrial taxes) have fallen since 1986, cutting funds for much-needed housing, improved transportation, sewage systems, and so forth. Yet Shanghai still earns the pre-dominant portion of China's foreign exchange each year, a position it intends to solidify with the proposed development of the Pudokng Industrial Complex.[13]

As with Shanghai, the coastal cities hold a dominant position in China in that they collectively

- produce about one-quarter of China's gross value of industrial output;

- generate one-quarter of its taxes and profits;

- provide two-fifths of its exports;

- have productivity levels two-thirds above the national average; and

- handle one-fifth of all China's freight and virtually all of the port cargo.

By responding to the pressure of these cities to be allowed to open up to foreign investment, Beijing effectively institutionalized the advantages offered by the cities to foreign investors and thereby retained an element of control over them.

This control was demonstrated in 1986 when Beijing rescinded the approval ceiling of $5 million for ten municipal governments—Qinhuangdao, Yantai, Qingdao, Lianyungang, Nantong, Ningbo, Wenzhou, Fuzhou, Zhanjiang, and Beihai—and reinstated provincial government approval of such decisions. This move was a reaction to several well-publicized cases of corruption (the most visible involving several ranking Communist Party officials on Hainan Island) and to the foreign exchange crisis faced that year. Central authorities in Beijing believed that a partial recentralization of decision-making authority was necessary to curb what they saw as excessive corruption and free spending by the coastal cities. In addition, this move probably reflected the distaste Beijing authorities experienced in surrendering part of their authority in the first place; the corruption and foreign exchange issue presented them with an ideal opportunity to reclaim some of that authority. This situation reflects a continuing struggle for decision-making authority between central and local authorities in the new open policies.

Tianjin and the Tianjin Economic and Technological Development Zone

Tianjin lies some seventy miles to the southeast of Beijing. It is China's third largest city, with 8.8 million people, and North China's major container port. It is a key industrial center, with a gross industrial output ranking twelfth among China's provinces and provincial-ranked municipalities (besides Beijing and Shanghai municipalities, Tianjin lagged behind Guangdong, Heilongjiang, Henan, Hubei, Jiangsu, Liaoning, Shandong, Sichuan, and Zhejiang). And it is a former German "treaty port." As shown in Table 4.4, Tianjin has received considerable interest from foreign investors.

Among the 64 ventures actually operating in Tianjin (out of the 164 in Table 4.4), economic returns were said to be good and foreign exchange earnings also were favorable. Yet, of these sixty-four, service enterprises outnumbered industrial enterprises almost two to one (forty to twenty-four).

Tianjin's ETDZ was established in December of 1984. It has considerable development potential: a relatively abundant supply of cheap, easily developable land; access to port, rail, and road facilities; solid local industrial base; and a good supply of technical workers from a variety of higher educational institutions nearby. The initial development is in an area of three square kilometers. This "starting zone" is scheduled to accommodate 100 to 150 enterprises and employ 20,000 workers by 1990. If there is sufficient demand, the zone will expand to ten square kilometers by 2000. Planners envisage the ETDZ's industrial output in thirty years being equivalent to current industrial output for all of Tianjin.

The Tianjin ETDZ offers a wide range of incentives and subsidies to foreign investors similar to those noted for the SEZs. A selection includes the reduction of enterprise income tax to 10 percent (instead of 15 percent); further exemptions

Table 4.4
Tianjin's Sino-Foreign Investment Agreements, 1979-June 1986

	Number	Percent of number	Percent of value
Investment:			
by foreign investors			49
by Chinese investors			51
Agreements by Origin:			
Hong Kong/Macao	76	46	53
United States	25	15	31
Japan	41	25	8
Singapore	6	4	7
Others	16	10	1
Agreements by sector:			
Industry	102	62	
Services	49	30	
Other	13	8	

Source: Chen Guofeng and Zheng Ning, "Patterns of Opening to the World and TNCs", Paper presented to the International Symposium on the Role of TNCs and China's Open Policy, Nankai University, Tianjin, October 1986.

from enterprise income tax to long-term Sino-foreign ventures and also to high-tech ventures; waiver of local enterprise income taxes until 1990; swift approval processes; lower charges for water, electricity, and fuel; standard charges for land; and the establishment of management and technology service centers to serve potential foreign investors. Furthermore, foreign banks have been allowed to establish branch offices in Tianjin to ease financing procedures.

Initial response to the Tianjin ETDZ was marked. By the beginning of 1987, for example, twenty industrial projects, including several technologically advanced enterprises (concerned with telecommunications facilities, computers, and medical supplies) and other export-oriented ventures (for example, in building ceramics, food processing, and the processing of marble), were under way. Foreign investment levels, however, have not reached those expected by Tianjin officials, who conceded that foreign reluctance to invest in China after Tiananmen and subsequent austerity measures combined to restrict the growth of the ETDZ.[14]

Interior Cities

The designation of the fourteen coastal cities and Hainan Island as priority areas for foreign investment predictably met with a cool reaction in China's interior cities. In the middle of 1984, under pressure from various provincial authorities, Beijing (through the Bank of China) announced certain foreign exchange privileges for a number of interior cities: Urumqi, Harbin, Changchun, Shenyang, Hohhot, Yinchuan, Xining, Lanzhou, Xian, Taiyuan, Shijiazhuang, Nanjing, Hefei, Hangzhou, Wuhan, Nanchang, Changsha, Nanning, Guiyang, Kunming, Chongqing, and Chengdu.

This list effectively means that at least one city in every province has some special privileges in attracting foreign investment. However, this has not been of much assistance to the interior provinces. With the exception of one or two large mineral projects, little interest has been shown by foreign companies in investment in the interior.

The major disadvantages of the interior are that it lacks an adequate infrastructure, despite heavy government investment and the emergence of individual industrial bases (at Wuhan, Chongqing, Chengdu among others); there is no coordination between individual industrial departments; the supply of raw materials and parts is poor; its incentives to foreign businesses usually are below those offered by the coastal regions; its ability to raise foreign exchange is similarly weak; and transportation inadequacies pose a grave problem to any foreign investor who has to import equipment and export finished products.

Open Economic Zones: The Three River Deltas

In 1985, China continued to expand the areas that were able to offer incentives to foreign investors, establishing three Open Economic Zones (OEZs) stretching from Guangzhou to Shanghai. In many respects, these zones expand the previously established priority investment areas to include their natural hinterlands. The aim was to encourage the general integration of local raw materials and components (beyond the confines of the SEZ or coastal cities) into regional foreign investment planning. The most significant of these zones is the Yangzi River Delta OEZ adjacent to Shanghai. This zone encompasses the important industrial cities of Suzhou, Wuxi, and Changzhou in Jiangsu Province, as well Jiaxing and Huzhou in Zhejiang Province. Spreading across 27,000 square kilometers with more than 18 million persons, this zone is one of the wealthiest in China, with a relatively developed infrastructure and a skilled work force.

The Pearl River Delta OEZ surrounding Guangzhou also is a wealthy region of China. With an area of 23,500 square kilometers and more than 11 million inhabitants, this zone essentially encompasses that portion of the mainland with the closest links to Hong Kong and Macao. Numerous parts in this region have direct links to the two colonies.

The smallest and perhaps least attractive of the three OEZs is the Southern

Fujian Delta OEZ. Surrounding Xiamen and including the cities of Quanzhou and Zhangzhou, this zone has a population of about 10 million.[15]

SOURCES OF FDI IN CHINA

Other Asian countries—notably Hong Kong and Japan—have been the most important investors in China. American businessmen, although initially enthusiastic about China's move toward openness, were reluctant to enter into investment agreements. Only in the late 1980s did American firms rekindle their initial enthusiasm and begin to invest more heavily in China. The responses of each source of FDI reveal differing attitudes toward China's opening to foreign investment and reflect diverse competitive positions, displayed in the sectors and location of their investment.

Asia

Although China has developed quite significant ties with many Asian countries, its relations with Hong Kong and Japan are clearly dominant.

Hong Kong

With only a little more than 400 square miles in land to support more than 5 million inhabitants, Hong Kong has long relied on imports from the People's Republic for its supplies of basic foodstuffs, water, energy and fuel, and raw materials (from metals to textiles) for its thriving manufacturing industry. China enjoys a large trading surplus—roughly $465 million per month for the first three quarters of 1989—with Hong Kong. Only in 1985, when Hong Kong consumer goods flooded into China, was this position reversed.

Hong Kong is one of the most important financial centers in the world. There is considerable wealth among Hong Kong Chinese, and a number of entrepreneurs control a variety of small and mid-sized companies worldwide. Their knowledge and understanding of China, personal relations and patriotic ties to the "motherland," ability to respond quickly and flexibly, and ability to earn trust are major reasons for their successful investment in China. The inevitability of Hong Kong's merger with the mainland no doubt also adds a touch of pragmatism to the romance of China for most Hong Kong investors. With their future tied to that of China, it makes considerable sense to invest there, gaining favor and influence with the various governments.

Hong Kong also is one of the finest deep-water ports on the South China coast, housing one of the largest container terminals in the world. It has long been a major gateway for China's imports and exports as well as a channel for China's trade with Asian countries, including Taiwan and South Korea, for example, with whom Beijing has had little official contact in the past. Thus FDI ties by Hong Kong investors can enhance China's informal integration into the world economy.

Hong Kong is the largest and most frequent foreign investor in China, having invested more capital and being in more ventures than any country. Most of these ventures are small-scale (capitalization under $1 million) and export-oriented, involving low levels of technology and yielding quick returns. Contractual joint ventures are most popular with Hong Kong businessmen, fitting their project-specific, fixed-duration orientation to doing business in China. Further, these ventures are predominantly located in Guangdong Province, with family ties undoubtedly playing a major role in the specific location of Hong Kong business ventures. Many investments are channeled through Hong Kong by both Taiwanese and other overseas Chinese, as well as by Western companies. This pattern might be expected, given Hong Kong's character as an economy of relatively small businesses and multiple-representation offices of companies throughout the world. The magnitude of the resulting relationship is somewhat overwhelming, however. It is estimated that in 1990, between 1.5 and 2 million people in the Pearl Delta in Guangdong work in Hong Kong–linked processing factories, and that probably as many again are employed in related activities; it also is estimated that as much as 20 percent of Hong Kong's currency is circulating in Guangdong.[16]

Although a number of Hong Kong's larger companies (and divisions of overseas companies based in Hong Kong) are making substantial investments that involve more advanced technology, small-scale, low-tech ventures continue to be the most important portion of Hong Kong's investment in China, reflecting the importance of small-scale, family-operated businesses in Hong Kong itself. Accordingly, China will probably remain disappointed with the level of technology it acquires from its ventures with Hong Kong businesses, but it will seek to maintain these ties nonetheless for the international contacts that they carry with them.

The potential future role of Hong Kong investment in China is different from that of Japan or the United States simply by the fact that the British colony will return to the control of Beijing in 1997. The major concerns of people in Hong Kong are over China's stability and ability to carry out the 1997 transfer agreement. China is now faced with an exodus from Hong Kong that is gaining momentum; according to Hong Kong government figures, 19,000 residents left in 1986, 30,000 in 1987, 45,000 in 1988, and an estimated 60,000 in 1989.[17] Hong Kong is losing an essential nucleus of professionals and middle managers, despite the fact that the Chinese have agreed to maintain the current economic system in Hong Kong for at least fifty years after 1997.[18] There are many in Hong Kong who are not certain of this guarantee and are concerned about becoming People's Republic citizens. It is increasingly apparent, however, that Hong Kong will play a critical role in China's economic reform, so the guarantee is seen as more likely to be carried out, especially since any reneging on the part of China would set back its goal of reunification with Taiwan. The events in Tiananmen Square, however, have appeared to confirm the worst fears of

Hong Kong's citizens and clearly will lead to a rearrangement of Hong Kong's government before 1997.

In many respects, the extent of further investment in China by Hong Kong businesses (with contracts extending beyond 1997) may prove to be the best indication of the future role of Hong Kong itself. Given the importance of Hong Kong investment in the past decade, it must be expected that China will continue to encourage such investors in the next decade as well as beyond 1997.

Japan

Japan strengthened its relationship with the current Chinese leadership with its signing of the Sino-Japanese Treaty of Peace and Friendship in 1978. Since that time, Japan has played a wide-ranging role in China's drive for modernization through the provision of advanced technology (embodied in new plants and equipment for the renovation of existing Chinese plants), technical assistance to key industries (particularly steel, petrochemicals, textiles, chemical fertilizers, and consumer electronics products), loans and development assistance, FDI, and various training programs.

The depth of Japanese involvement in China is an indication of the compatibility—geographical, economic, and cultural—between the two countries. Japan's proximity to China does more than simply make travel to China easier and less costly. Since the nineteenth-century, Japan has viewed interaction with China as crucial to its long-term economic prospects. This view contributes significantly to the aggressive and persistent approach shown by Japanese businessmen to doing business in China.

The composition of trade between the two countries illustrates these ties. Japan's imports from China are predominantly of basic foodstuffs (especially fish and shellfish), energy resources (especially coal and oil), and light manufacturing goods. Its exports to China are dominated by heavy industrial and high-tech products. The Japanese prize this mix, and China finds it suitable to its current needs.

China's chief concern about its trading relations with Japan since the early 1980s has been its consistent trade deficits ($860 million in 1987, down from $6 billion in 1985). In 1988, however, after record two-way trade between the two countries of $19 billion (19 percent of China's total trade), China had a trading surplus of $380 million, its first since 1983, and another surplus in 1989. These trade surpluses were largely a result of substantial Chinese government pressure to reduce imports from Japan. This trading surplus will undoubtedly temper what had been increasing concern among the Chinese about the Japanese presence in China, a presence that had been perceived by some as an "economic occupation" paralleling Japan's earlier military occupation of China, and that had resulted in such strong adverse popular reactions as the tearing down of billboards advertising Japanese products and student protests criticizing the "second Japanese occupation."

Finally, although the cultures of Japan and China do differ, they also share common roots. The Japanese, for example, fully understand the concept of "saving face" and recognize when it is and is not appropriate to bring up points of contention. In contrast, most Western businessmen remain unclear about basic Chinese customs and norms of social behavior and make little effort to learn.

The Japanese have made great efforts to cultivate their relationship with China, an effort that makes it both more difficult and easier for Western companies in their efforts to enter China—more difficult because of Japan's competitiveness and cultural affinity and easier because of China's desire not to let Japanese relations dominate. Even the Japanese government has strived to develop a political atmosphere conducive to trade, strengthening personal ties with their Chinese counterparts—both political leadership and bureaucratic officials. These personal ties also have been strongly cultivated by nongovernment officials such as trade unionists and corporate leaders and by businesses, through representative offices both in Beijing and in twenty other major cities (compared with two or three by other countries' companies). In this way, the Japanese are much more able to tie into the networks of personal relations—*guanxi*—which are so important to ensuring a relatively smooth ride through China's bureaucracy. The Japanese government has offered direct and indirect financial incentives to encourage business with China: preferential tariff rates, most-favored-nation status, *yen* credits from its Overseas Economic Cooperative Fund, and low-interest loans from its Export-Import Bank.

The Japanese trading company has particular advantages in doing business with China. Chinese officials admire the ability of these companies to coordinate all aspects of a project: finance, shipping, construction, insurance, and even management training. The trading companies are better able to include financial incentives, such as low-interest loans in a project, even linking one set of negotiations with one venture to another set with a different venture. Western countries find it difficult to match this "package" of services. The U.S. companies going to China almost always expect the Chinese to do business the U.S. way, without trying to learn the Chinese way.

Conceding

While negotiating a contract for the sale of 10,000 Xerox copiers to be delivered over a fifteen-month period, the Chinese requested a penalty clause for late delivery. The U.S. lawyer wrote the clause in the standard U.S. style—the penalties went into effect only if there were losses suffered because of the late deliveries. The Chinese argued that penalties should be paid regardless of whether they suffered losses. This debate went on for three hours; finally, the Chinese conceded. At lunch, the English-speaking Chinese lawyer quietly indicated that the Chinese manager, an experienced negotiator for Shanghai, had made a major concession. He explained that all Chinese factories, in spite of being state-owned, made penalty payments regardless of whether damage was sustained from late delivery. In an economic system that is not profit-driven, the penalty payments for late deliveries or other contractual failures are a measure of factory performance. Thus an American company selling to a Chinese factory, but not subject to the same penalty payments, unless damages were demonstrated, was clearly an exception, and some would have probably argued that it constituted favoritism.

Yet, for all the interaction between the countries, Japan's loans to China far outweigh its direct investment. Japanese loans to China first became important in 1979 after Beijing's scaling down of its ambitious "four modernizations" and the canceling of contracts involving $2.5 billion signed with Japanese plant equipment manufacturers. More loans followed in 1981 when Beijing proposed to cancel a further $1.5 billion in contracts with Japanese companies for steel and petrochemical plants, including the much publicized Baoshan steel mill just outside Shanghai.

After a number of years of lagging behind the United States in direct foreign investment, Japan finally surpassed the United States in this regard in 1988, when it invested US $515 million compared with the U.S. direct foreign investment of $236 million. In 1989 this lead continued, with Japan investing US $356 million compared with the United States $284 million. Interestingly, Taiwan surpassed both nations in 1989 with direct foreign investment of US $400 million.[19]

China remains dissatisfied not only with the amount of Japanese foreign investment, but also with the nature of that investment. Like their Sino–Hong Kong counterparts, Sino-Japanese ventures are characterized as being small-scale and low-tech and yielding quick returns, for example light processing projects. But, although Japan continues to make loans to China, it has failed to increase its direct investment accordingly. Indeed, Japan now ranks behind the United States as well as Hong Kong as a source of direct investment in China. Furthermore, a substantial amount of Japanese direct investment comes in the form of property development, which, for reasons discussed below, is considered less risky for the foreign investor but also has fewer benefits for the Chinese.

Japan's reluctance to make large direct investments in China can be illustrated by its dealings with China's coal industry. A basic assumption of trade agreements between the two countries has been that Japan would buy coal from China in exchange for manufactured goods. However, China's coal industry was unable to supply the amounts of coal agreed to. Japan decided to help China develop its coal output capacity, thereby increasing China's ability to generate foreign exchange through exports of this greater coal output to Japan.

Rather than set up joint ventures, the Japanese provided loans to the Chinese for the development of coal mines in addition to yen credits to build up rail and port facilities to help ensure the delivery of that coal. Compare this with the massive U.S. investment at Antaibao, where Occidental, with a 25 percent equity share of the Pingshuo coal mine, invested $175 million directly in the venture.

The Japanese cite numerous difficulties as reasons for their hesitancy to become more directly involved in China, including irregular supply of raw materials, foreign exchange shortages, vague labor and wage agreements, low levels of Chinese training and education, a weak infrastructure, and a lack of venture profitability. These difficulties are those commonly expressed by foreigners, causing all but a handful of companies to be reticent about committing substantial resources to China.

Yet there is a further reason why the Japanese may remain more reluctant than others. Although the Japanese certainly are not afraid of taking risks, they are reticent about sacrificing control over their investments. In a survey of seventy-one Japanese joint ventures, nearly half expressed dissatisfaction about not being able to run their factories along the lines agreed to in joint venture contracts, that is, along the lines they were comfortable with.[20] This reticence to relinquish management control creates obvious conflicts in the Chinese system, where local bureaucracies and the factory's Communist Party manager can have more say in the running of a plant than its own management. The Japanese are not comfortable in such systems; they may be able to develop wholly owned and managed enterprises in China, but it remains to be seen how eager they are to enter into larger joint venture agreements.

Europe

The pattern of European direct investment in China has been dominated by resource exploitation ventures, in particular offshore oil drilling in the South China Sea. Britain, for example, in the period from 1979 to 1985, had contracted investment of $270 million pledged to the cooperative development of offshore oil, some 70 percent of its total contracted investment in China. (However, even by 1989, Britain's total of utilized FDI stood at only $31,800,000.) The French figure for oil was only a little lower at $210 million, more than 72 percent of its contracted investment.

With the exception of West Germany (with large investments of $90 million at the Shanghai Volkswagen Auto Factory and $12.5 million in the Xiamen Beer Company, Ltd.), European direct investment in manufacturing has been more modest. As with the joint ventures of other countries, the Europeans have kept their investments relatively small. However, although the Chinese acknowledge that many of the European ventures have been small-scale, they are more pleased by the number of these ventures that have been capital-intensive, involving quite sophisticated levels of technology.

The United States

U.S. investments in China principally have been in joint ventures, as seen in Table 4.5.

Of the $2.6 billion investment contracted between the United States and China, about half has actually been utilized. As with the European investment, the bulk of U.S. investment has been in offshore oil contracts.

In contrast to investors from other countries, U.S. investors have strongly favored the formation of equity joint ventures over the more popular—to this

Table 4.5
U.S. Investment in China, 1979–1986*

	Number of Contracts	Percent of Total Contracts	Contracted Investment ($millions)	Percent of Total contracted investment
Equity JVs	219	7.0	528.08	11.1
Contractual JVs	53	1.2	1,070.00	14.8
Wholly-owned enterprises	7	5.1	6.27	4.0
Oil contracts	25	61.0	1,028.00	40.5
TOTAL	304		2,632.35	

* The figures for US contracted investment do not include $54,540,000 in compensation trade.

Source: National Council for U.S. China Trade, U.S. Joint Ventures in China: A Progress Report, Washington, D.C., March 1987; and Tables 4.1 and 4.2 above.

point at least—contractual joint ventures. U.S. businessmen argue that the costly and difficult partner search, negotiations, and approval process render short-term ventures (one to five years) uneconomic.

A number of large, project-specific Sino–U.S. contractual ventures have, however, been successfully negotiated, including the ARCO $170 million, thirty-year investment to develop the gas fields of Hainan Island, and the Occidental project at Antaibao. Such large-scale ventures serve to explain why U.S. contractual joint ventures, despite being heavily outnumbered by equity joint ventures, represent such a large percentage of total U.S. investment in China. Similarly, together with substantial oil contracts, these large-scale ventures explain why the United States ranks only behind Hong Kong in total direct foreign investment in China, despite numerically small participations by the United States.

The scope of U.S. involvement in China has risen dramatically in the late 1980s. After having signed only 99 venture contracts through 1984, U.S. companies signed 101 contracts in 1985 and 102 in 1986 (despite the fact that total contracts signed in 1986 dropped sharply after China's economic problems in 1985). U.S. firms entered into joint ventures in such diverse areas as electronics, food processing, textiles, machinery, agriculture, mining, oil, and tourism. Although actual dollar commitments followed the general trend and fell from $1.1 billion in 1985 to only $528 million in 1986, this fall was exaggerated through the bolstering of 1985 investment commitments by substantial oil contracts as well as by the ARCO and Occidental contractual ventures.

Although U.S. companies are taking a more active role in direct investment in China, the U.S. government continues to provide only minimal loans to the Chinese government. Through 1985, the U.S. government had extended only about $60 million in low-interest, general-purpose loans, insignificant compared with Japan's concessionary loan policy. Still, U.S. businessmen see these as "government supporting national industry" and working to the detriment of their own competitive funding ability.[21]

The U.S. position on loans (which it considers foreign aid) is weaker even than that of Canada, for example. The Canadian International Development Agency (CIDA) currently gives $40 million (Canadian) annually to China in foreign development aid. Although this aid is ostensibly to further economic development in China, and not to boost directly Canadian business opportunities in China, a recent feasibility study for the proposed Three Gorges hydroelectric dam was funded by CIDA and carried out by Canadian hydroelectric and engineering companies. This came after a $7 million feasibility study was prepared by Swedish companies and given to the Chinese gratis. This kind of assistance, combined with acknowledged Canadian expertise in the hydroelectric power field, may prove to be crucial in the negotiation of future contracts (worth as much as $30 billion, if the project is realized).

Such CIDA involvement can be added to other programs, such as the Canadian Project Preparation Facility (CPPF). The CPPF funds feasibility studies to increase the awareness among Canadian firms of business opportunities in large-scale development projects in China, which are to be funded by the World Bank and other international financial institutions. Similarly, funds for feasibility studies have been used to promote Sino-Canadian joint ventures, although few had come to fruition in the late 1980s.

The Canadians also have established the Technology Cooperation Fund (TCF) with $5 million (Canadian) in 1987 for feasibility studies for projects designed to encourage technology upgrading in China by Canadian companies. Under the TCF, projects would be first nominated by MOFERT (Ministry of Foreign Economic Relations and Trade) and then tendered to Canadian companies. In this way, it is hoped to translate feasibility studies into actual projects.

The United States remains reticent in its foreign loan program and continues to refuse China the status of a beneficiary developing country (BDC). China has received most-favored-nation status from Congress and is a member of the International Monetary Fund, but it has yet to be admitted to the General Agreement on Tariffs and Trade, which is the third prerequisite for BDC status.

China's positive reaction to U.S. investment is coupled with a Chinese feeling that there is room for improvement in the relations between the two countries. Up to 1985, China had received only 4 percent of total U.S. direct investment overseas; the Chinese would like to see this proportion rise significantly. U.S. firms have been unwilling to make major investments of capital and technology without a clear understanding of how profits were repatriated or, more important, how to export profitably. Companies that have found feasible projects include

American Motors (Beijing Jeep), Wang, Hilton, Foxboro, Gillete, Xerox, Nike, Boeing, DuPont, Eastman Kodak, and McDonnell-Douglas, to name a few. How much improvement takes place will be determined by the success of high-visibility projects, such as Occidental's at Antaibao (though not a manufacturing project) and Xerox-Shanghai's joint venture in copier development and production, which is one of the largest manufacturing joint ventures. Again, continued improvement depends on China's ability to create an economic environment into which American companies want to venture.

SECTORAL CONCENTRATION

China's priorities for FDI inflows were stated in its last five-year plan. However, difficulties experienced by some of the pioneer joint ventures, the uncertain Chinese economic and legal environment, and the differences between the goals of China for FDI and those of foreign investors have limited investment in most sectors. An exception to this pattern of investment has been offshore oil exploration.

Offshore Oil

Chinese officials clearly envisage a major role for FDI in the exploitation of its oil reserves, although the extent to which the oil industry has dominated current levels of foreign investment is more an indication of disappointing levels of FDI in other key sectors. As noted earlier in this chapter, oil contracts accounted for less than 1 percent of total contracts in number but represented almost 25 percent of utilized foreign investment in China by value. Thus China's welcome to foreign exploration throughout the Yellow and South China seas stemmed from its urgent need to develop offshore resources. This urgency reflected a declining onshore oil production and a scarcity of foreign exchange for imports.

For foreign oil companies, China represents an important opportunity in two respects: the area available for exploration represented the largest (estimated) untapped reserves in the world, ranging from 30 to 100 billion barrels;[22] and it is a non-OPEC (Organization of Petroleum Exporting Countries) source.

In January 1982 the "Regulations of the People's Republic of China on the Exploitation of Offshore Petroleum Resources in Cooperation with Foreign Enterprises" were promulgated, followed by establishment of the China National Offshore Oil Corporation (CNOOC). CNOOC was made responsible for the activities of Sino-foreign ventures in the offshore oil fields. The first round of bidding for exploration areas began in late 1982. Before the bidding, interested foreign investors were handed a "model contract" to ease the negotiation process. The model contract—a hybrid of a joint venture contract, production-sharing agreement, and cooperative offshore agreements found elsewhere in the world—outlined three points around which negotiation could take place: the work program, including the schedule and extent of exploration; a factor bid, determining the percentage of production the foreign investor would receive as profit; and a bid of other contributions, detailing what else the foreign company would offer.

Negotiation on these elements showed differences of objectives, and other aspects of the contract gave foreign investors pause: their lack of control over daily operations as well as long-term strategic decisions; the urging to use locally sourced materials, when possible; high wage rates for Chinese workers; the extent of technology transfer expected; and the issues of repatriation of profits. The broad nature of some of these concerns caused negotiations to drag on beyond the time table established by the Chinese, who had hoped for final contracts to be signed by the end of 1982. Only one contract of the nineteen signed in the first round of bidding was signed in 1982, the other eighteen signed in 1983.

The second round of bidding was much less successful, with less than half the number of contracts signed in this round as compared with the first. The initial enthusiasm of having gained access to the anticipated huge reserves had been tempered by the absence of a truly viable discovery. Moreover the drop in international oil prices prompted oil companies to cut back on exploration investment and staff, since lower oil prices made many Chinese resources commercially less attractive. Of the $2.2 billion invested in oil exploration, less than 10 percent was from the second round of bidding.

Declining oil prices threatened to halt the exploitation of the offshore oil fields on which China was depending for future supplies of export earnings and domestic energy. In response to this situation, the Chinese have developed some of the smaller fields themselves for domestic consumption.

To gain further foreign investment, which is crucial to the development of the larger offshore fields, China has had to offer better contract terms. Large companies, such as Exxon, Shell, British Petroleum, and Texaco, stated intentions of continuing their oil exploration, whereas others cut the scale of their operations in China in 1988. To maintain the attractiveness of even the small and medium-sized oil fields, the royalties on fields with annual production of less than 1 million metric tons have been waived. This waiver also may be negotiated for marginal fields under prior contract. The Chinese have indicated a willingness to reduce the cost of production through reducing bureaucratic procedures and improving the training of Chinese personnel and the conduct of feasibility studies.

Along with the halt on the development in offshore drilling came a concomitant slowing down of the development of related service industries. CNOOC has been involved in establishing the necessary support services to offshore oil exploration, forming joint ventures in such fields as geophysical surveying, drilling, electric logging, core analysis, and helicopter services. Cable and Wireless, for example, entered into a joint venture—the Huaying Nanhai Oil Telecommunication Service Company—with the Guangdong Posts and Telecommunications Administrative Bureau to develop an onshore-offshore telecommunications network for the oil industry over a period of fifteen years. Because the market has failed to develop as anticipated, the venture has thus far been a disappointment to Cable and Wireless.

Manufacturing and Services

Joint ventures in manufacturing outnumbered those in services by almost two to one in the listing shown in Table 4.6. For the most part, these investments have been small-scale (more than 57 percent represent an investment of less than $1 million, with only 12 percent being over $5 million) and limited in duration, averaging around thirteen years, with few exceeding twenty years. Both conditions indicate tentativeness on the part of both the Chinese government and foreign investors.

During the major part of the 1980s, equity joint ventures were predominantly in property (by value), but the larger number of such ventures were in servicing and technical services projects. Property investment was mainly in hotels and office space for expatriate accommodation. Other sectors were considered a higher risk and showed much smaller investment sums compared with hotels.

Investment in hotels, for example, is relatively attractive to the foreign investor because of the high demand for hotel accommodations and the ease of balancing foreign exchange. These foreign investor hotels are new and Western-like, appealing to the foreign travelers, who can pay only in foreign exchange certificates. In fact, sometimes Chinese who pay in local currency are frowned on by these hotels. The major operating items include land rental, labor, utilities, and food, which do not require imports.

The growth of foreign exchange earnings from tourism have been dramatic, as shown in Table 4.7. This growth continued through 1988, but tourist dollars fell dramatically in 1989 and 1990—perhaps by as much as $1 billion per year— because of the uneasiness associated with the student movement in China. Before Tiananmen, most major hotels enjoyed a year-round occupancy rate of 80 percent, at room rates averaging $80. Immediately afterward, occupancy dropped to break-even rates at 50 percent and room rates to $50 per night.[23] In addition to the growth in tourism, the number of foreign businessmen traveling to China rose with the opening. Indeed, in the larger cities at peak periods of the year, demand for hotel rooms is so acute that it often is difficult to find rooms without early reservations—which are not easy to make. For the businessman, this is yet another problem in doing business in China.

A second attraction to investment in hotels is their profitability, and the third is the prestige involved. For a foreign investor like Sheraton, for example, image is important. Although a hotel in Guilin or Xian may not be a major money-maker in comparison with its other hotels, there is an "image pay-off." Similarly, local governments like large hotel developments because of the prestige they see them bringing the locality, not to mention the foreign exchange. Thus local

Table 4.6
Classification of 1,410 Sino-Foreign Ventures

Category	Number	% of total
Raw materials/energy production:	14	1
Oil industry	12	
Electricity generation	2	
Labor intensive:	91	6
Construction	91	
Process manufacturing:	570	40
Light industry	326	
Building materials	75	
Food processing	62	
Textiles	58	
Metallurgy	21	
Chemicals	15	
Pharmaceuticals	12	
Petrochemicals	1	
Assembly manufacturing:	270	19
Electronics	168	
Machinery	49	
Vehicle and vehicle part production	29	
Magnetic tape	24	
Services:	465	33
Hotels and restaurants	112	
Daily services	53	
Commerce	50	
Tourism	42	
Technical services	39	
Photographic processing	39	
Taxis	34	
Technology development	31	
Car repairs and maintenance	29	
Leasing	11	
Publishing and printing	10	
Ship repairs	7	
Telecommunications	4	
Miscellaneous	4	

Source: Chu Baotai, "A Few Things to Know about an Investment in China", Intertrade, March 1986, p.47

Note: Omissions in this table compared to a categorization of 840 sino-foreign equity joint ventures in Chapter 9 reflect the broader categorization of industries in the source material.

Table 4.7
Tourism in China, 1978–1985

Year	Total Number of Tourists (million)	Foreign Exchange Income from Tourism ($million)
1978	1.81	263
1980	5.70	617
1981	7.77	785
1982	7.92	843
1983	9.48	941
1984	12.85	1,131
1985	17.83	1,250

Source: Statistical Yearbook of China, 1986, Beijing, p. 504.

financing, access to local inputs, and guidance through the local bureaucracy are made easier.

Still, hotel ventures have their problems. The advantage of high local input at low cost, for example, also can mean low quality. Local levels of service often are not what is expected from prestigious and expensive hotels. As an example, the Shanghai Hilton had one of its staff detained by the Public Security Bureau, and the hotel was fined for sanitary lapses. The hotel also raised hackles by insisting on managing in its own way, bringing in more than 100 foreign staff, discharging locals, and setting up their own procedures.[24] Moreover, in the major cities—Beijing, Shanghai, and Guangzhou—there has been overexpansion in hotel construction. The fall of tourism and business travel generally in late 1989 exacerbated the problems and contributed to the delay in the opening of the China Trade Center in Beijing, for example.

This center is a combination of apartments, hotels, conference hall, exhibition rooms, office, and retail space; it was scheduled to open in September 1989, but did so only in August 1990, with considerable cost overruns (some owing to damage during Tiananmen). Debt repayments on the center have been postponed until 1992, and tenants have been hard to find, though officials claim that hotel occupancy is 50 percent, office space at 80 percent, residential at 70 percent, and retail at 65 percent. The rates charged at the center, however, have been markedly under those originally projected (up to 40 percent discount).

EMERGING ISSUES

The geographical location of Sino-foreign joint ventures reflects the government's interests in pushing development in key regions and cities, as shown in Table 4.8. Guangdong's dominance reflects its proximity to Hong Kong and the major role Hong Kong investment has played since 1978. Fujian also is directly

Table 4.8
Geographical Location of Joint Ventures

Location	Contracts (percent)
Guangdong	45
(Shenzhen SEZ)	(27)
Fujian	15
Beijing	5
Tianjin	5
Shanghai	4
Other coastal areas	13
Inland provinces	13

Source: <u>South China Morning Post</u>, November 8, 1986, based upon a survey of 841 equity joint ventures, representing all ventures formed 1979-83 and 651 of 741 formed in 1984.

across the straits from Formosa (Taiwan) and benefits from that location; it also is the home of a large number of émigrés, providing strong ties to that province. The Chinese government has built on the links (cultural, economic, and geographical) between its southern coastal provinces and Hong Kong through the establishment of the SEZs in those provinces.

The coastal cities and provinces also are the location of many of China's more modern industries, making them logical choices for contracts with Hong Kong in serving its foreign markets. Also, the pressure placed on Sino-foreign joint ventures to export final products makes access to port facilities (either in China or through Hong Kong) an important consideration and adds to the appeal of a coastal location. These advantages also exist in the port cities of Shanghai and Tianjin; in addition, these cities have greater decision-making autonomy in attracting foreign investment.

Beijing also has been an important location of foreign business. Location near the central bureaucracy is considered a major advantage. Furthermore, Beijing has received much investment in the form of hotels, office development, and services, reflecting its role as both modern capital and historical center.

In contrast, the interior seemingly has little to offer the potential foreign investor, being isolated and with poor infrastructure facilities. Table 4.9 gives the percentage distribution of foreign investment between 1979 and 1987, reemphasizing the difference between the coastal areas and the interior depicted in Table 4.8.

Even when the Sino–Hong Kong ventures are excluded from consideration, the coastal regions still receive the bulk of foreign investment, although different geographical patterns of investment are discernible among foreign investors, as shown in Table 4.10. First, the number of contracts and value of U.S. com-

Table 4.9
Geographical Distribution of Foreign Investment, 1979–1987 (Percentage)

Municipalities:		8.0
	Beijing	2.4
	Tianjin	2.6
	Shanghai	3.0
Coastal Provinces:		82.0
	Guangdong	61.0
	Fujian	10.0
Interior Provinces		10.0
TOTAL		100.0

Source: Intertrade, August 1988, as cited by China Business Review, March-April 1989, p.50.

Table 4.10
FDI in China, by Source and Location, 1979–1985

Source	Number of contracts by region (%)			Value of commitments by region (%)		
	Inland	Coastal	Metropolitan*	Inland	Coastal	Metropolitan
U.S.A.	25.7	32.0	43.3	11.0	30.7	58.2
Japan	7.0	59.3	33.7	1.4	66.3	32.3
Other Western#	12.1	57.6	30.3	12.9	77.7	9.4
Asia**	23.0	63.5	13.5	9.3	70.8	19.9

* Beijing, Tianjin, Shanghai
# Europe, Canada, Australia, and New Zealand
** Singapore, Thailand, and the Philippines

Source: "US Joint Ventures in China: A Progress Report", The National Council for US-China Trade, Washington, March 1987, p.129, based on a sample of 301 Sino-foreign equity joint ventures established between 1979-85.

mitments in the interior are seen as quite large, in sharp contrast to the Japanese, who have virtually ignored the interior. The value of dollar commitments from the United States, however, is heavily skewed by the Occidental Antaibao coal mine project. This project alone represents some 75 percent of total U.S. commitments in the interior. Even so, American companies have other investments in the interior besides the Antaibao project.

Second, the U.S. companies have shown a preference for the metropolitan areas over the coastal provinces, a preference that is not matched by other countries. The reasons behind this pattern of investment include the importance of U.S. hotel development in Shanghai and Beijing, the strong Japanese and Asian ties with the coastal provinces (Japan, for example, has strong historical links in Manchuria and, consequently, dominates investment in Liaoning Province and Dalian in particular), and the relatively late arrival of American companies into China (especially after 1985), which has thus far limited them to the more obvious targets of Beijing and Shanghai.

Although the coastal areas remain a favorite target for foreign investment, the decision of Chinese policymakers to strongly emphasize the development of the coast at the expense of the interior may present them with long-term problems. The biggest problem will be that of unequal development among the coastal and interior provinces.

Inequality between the coast and the interior is longstanding, but it has been a high priority of the Communist Party to correct it. At Liberation in 1949, the coastal areas, by virtue of their natural advantages as well as the treaty port system, were clearly the more urban and industrial and wealthier. The Communists tried to reduce the disparity between the coastal and interior provinces before 1978 and, to some extent, succeeded. But the initial differences between the two regions (coupled with a desire to extract the maximum economic benefit from existing industrial facilities) were more than enough to maintain a marked degree of inequality.

Since 1978, by choosing to concentrate the economic growth generated by FDI in a network of SEZs, Regional Economic Zones, and coastal cities (for the most part established centers of economic activity), Chinese leaders have acknowledged that the inequality between the coastal regions and the interior will intensify.

Although the current regime has moved away from the Maoist policy of egalitarianism, increased inequality within China remains difficult for the state to countenance openly. The Chinese leadership, while acknowledging that in the short-term inequalities are inevitable, believes that eventually such inequalities will disappear. It argues that the coastal regions, into which it has channeled foreign investment, will become the catalyst for economic development in the interior, acting as a ''double window,'' absorbing foreign technology and know-how from the West and transferring it into the interior. Initially, the coast will develop and prosper ahead of the interior, but eventually (so it is argued) the interior will catch up.

To encourage such catching up, various *internal* technology transfer arrangements are envisioned, for example raw materials from the interior exchanged for technology, training, or investment from the coast; profit-sharing arrangements established between interior and coastal enterprises, with a percentage of the interior enterprise profits exchanged for coastal technical assistance; and coastal enterprises reselling foreign technology or patent rights to interior enterprises (although current experience with such an arrangement has shown that coastal enterprises are not averse to overcharging for this technology); and the "spark" plan, designed to stimulate technological change in the Chinese interior. In all of these cases, the existence of "third-line" factories, placed by Mao Zedong in the Chinese countryside as part of the dispersion of industry for national security reasons, provides an institutional and political basis for technology transfers. These types of domestic transfer are small-scale and limited in scope and have had little impact.

Other government actions have added to this inequality. The facilitation of foreign investment, for example, requires considerable domestic investment. If foreign investment continues to be concentrated in the coastal regions, domestic investment for infrastructure also must be concentrated there. Much needed investment in interior construction projects will be limited.

Indeed, the need to upgrade basic infrastructure in the coastal cities becomes more pressing as the extent of FDI increases. The appeal of many of these cities was the preexisting infrastructure that would immediately support investment projects. All too often, however, the infrastructure in these cities is inadequate and overloaded, with domestic investment seemingly able only to ameliorate problems that have already become more serious through even greater needs. This situation will worsen if potential foreign partners insist, as they have done, that they be located near other Sino-foreign ventures already engaged in similar activities to facilitate access to materials, labor skills, and components. Sino-foreign ventures also see choice of location as an opportunity to supply one another with high-quality components that they cannot source from local Chinese suppliers.

Finally, there is the issue of competition between the various zones and cities as each tries to capture foreign investment to stimulate local economic development. There is little doubt that the size of the Chinese economy has warranted the expansion of efforts to attract FDI beyond the SEZs to the fourteen coastal cities and other areas. The attraction of the SEZs, however, has been greatly diminished by the opening of the fourteen coastal cities and the creation of the ETDZs.

For the SEZs, this competition could be beneficial by stimulating the zone authorities to create an even more attractive environment for potential foreign investors. However, it also could serve to substantially reduce the development goals held by Beijing for the SEZs. Shenzhen, for example, ultimately may succeed not as a high-tech zone, but as a trade and commercial center, as it has shown signs of becoming. Alternatively, it might accelerate its existing relations with Hong Kong, with Shenzhen supplying cheap labor to Hong Kong manufacturing companies through simple subcontracting and export-processing arrangements.

The ever-changing role of the SEZs, with the emergence of the coastal cities as competitors for foreign investment and the fluctuations in the autonomy of decision-making passed on to the coastal cities themselves, illustrates China's evolutionary state with regard to foreign investment and the absence of a set of detailed policies as compared with general guidelines for development. China's experience with the SEZs has taught it that it cannot predict FDI responses or even establish specific attractions that will achieve desired results. Further modification in its development strategy will undoubtedly occur as new situations and responses arise.

NOTES

1. See Nigel Adam, "Doing Business in China," *Billion*, Inaugural Issue, 1989, pp. 36–42.

2. For an assessment of the advantages of WOFEs in China, see Lucille A. Barale, "Wholly Foreign-Owned Enterprises," *China Business Review*, January-February 1990, pp. 30–35.

3. Agreement was reached, however, in early 1989 to form the first joint venture with multiple and majority foreign ownership. After three and a half years of negotiation, one Hong Kong and two U.S. corporations have set up a polyurethane operation in Sanshui, employing about fifty Chinese. *Pacific Rim Business Digest*, February 1989, p. 22.

4. One China-watcher has concluded that joint ventures with China are unlikely to become a major factor in American foreign economic activities. Marshall I. Goldman, "Joint Ventures Return to Communist China and the Soviet Union," *Business in the Contemporary World*, Winter 1989, pp. 84–92.

5. Richard Brecher, "The End of Investment's Wonder Years," *China Business Review*, January-February 1990, pp. 27–29.

6. See *Journal of Commerce*, January 23, 1990, and July 19, 1990.

7. A selection of investment incentives offered by various Chinese entities since 1978 include the following: for joint venture contracts of ten years and above, Joint Venture Enterprise Income Tax exemption for the first two profit-making years and a 50 percent reduction in the subsequent three profit-making years; for approved joint ventures involved in long-term capital recovery projects, a 15 to 30 percent tax reduction after ten years in addition to the above provisions plus a 40 percent refund on income reinvested in China for five-plus years; for wholly foreign-owned ventures, complete tax exemption in the first profit-making year and 50 percent reduction for the subsequent two years, with further reduction on approval; exemption from Customs Duties/Industrial and Commercial Consolidated Tax on materials used for processing, assembly, or subsequent exports; and approved high-tech joint ventures are exempt from a range of labor subsidies, excess utility charges, and tax on reinvestment. It should be noted that all of these incentives are subject to change in some way and that individual locations may have the authority

to set their own incentives. Further, these incentives often are not clear-cut and may be open to negotiation.

8. John Burgess, "In a Chinese Economic Zone, It Isn't Business as Usual," *The Washington Post Weekly Edition*, July 10–16, 1989, p. 17.

9. *Wall Street Journal*, July 9, 1985.

10. Elizabeth Cheng, "No Fireworks for SEZ Birthday," *Far Eastern Economic Review*, August 23, 1990, pp. 43–44.

11. Thomas Rawski, *China's Road to Industrialism* (Ann Arbor: University of Michigan Press, 1980).

12. More detailed information about each city and ETDZ is available from their respective administrative offices.

13. *Journal of Commerce*, October 1, 1990.

14. Ibid.

15. The Southern Fujian Delta OEZ and the Yangzi Delta OEZ also form part of an even larger comprehensive economic zone established in 1982 and known as the Shanghai Economic Zone. With Shanghai as its focus, it encompasses Jiangsu, Zhejiang, Anhui, Jiangxi, and Fujian (and the open coastal cities and Xiamen SEZ within them) and one-quarter of China's population. The aim of this larger spatial grouping is to foster still further the integration of the economies contained within its boundaries through ties between enterprises of all sizes. However, just as conflicts exist between central and local decision-makers, so they exist among local decision-makers, and little has been made of this grouping to this point. In what was a most controversial proposal, former premier and general secretary of the Communist Party, Zhou Ziyang, proposed to open the entire "coastal rim" as some form of economic zone. In the wake of his dismissal in 1989, it is too early to judge if this proposal retains any support. It probably will be shelved until a more liberal or confident government appears.

16. John Elliott, "A Wealth of Low Wages," *Financial Times, Survey-China*, December 12, 1989, p. v.

17. Michael Selwyn, "Sober Realities of Migration," *Asian Business*, September 1989, p. 26.

18. Other key planks of the agreement include the following: (a) the designation of Hong Kong as a special administrative region in China under Article 31 of the Chinese constitution; (b) the retention of the basic legal structure, although the highest court of appeals would be based in Hong Kong rather than in London; (c) local and expatriate civil servants, including members of the police force and administrators, would be allowed to continue in their posts; (d) Hong King's status as a free port and international financial center would be continued, with the Hong Kong dollar remaining a separate and freely convertible currency, and the economic interests in Hong Kong of all nations respected; (e) Hong Kong residents would continue to enjoy free speech, assembly, and press and freedom to travel.

19. Elizabeth Cheng, "Taiwan Money One Bright Spot," *Far Eastern Economic Review*, August 23, 1990, pp. 42–43.

20. *Japan Economic Journal*, November 15, 1986.

21. "Master Merchants," *Wall Street Journal*, November 18, 1989, p. 24.

22. Chris Brown, "Tough Terms for Offshore Oil," *China Business Review*, July-August 1989, pp. 34–37.

23. *Journal of Commerce*, October 1, 1990.

24. Nicholas D. Kristof, "At China Hilton, Subject Was Butter," *New York Times*, December 15, 1988, pp. 1–6.

5

Cultural Environment

Both Chinese and foreigners recognize that cultural aspects are critical influences on the success or failure of business negotiations and operations in China. Culture is the "collective programming" that leads to differential behavior of peoples of different societies; it is deep-rooted and difficult to change. The Chinese themselves observe that most foreigners are simply unfamiliar with Chinese culture, and therefore do not relate well to the Chinese mind, management style, or ways of doing things. The Japanese and Koreans are exceptions in some ways, since their cultures are similar in many respects. Although the Japanese, Koreans, and Chinese have similar customs as peoples, they are no more similar than the English, French, and Germans—a distinction that should be kept in mind. A common Asian heritage does not mean that an understanding of either Japan or Korea is a sound basis for dealing with the Chinese. Americans recognize the differences among European countries and should learn to do the same in Asia. Some similarities make Japan a more attractive partner to the Chinese, but there is still a considerable reticence on the part of the Chinese to become too closely tied to Japanese enterprise—a result of World War II and other, earlier conflicts. The Chinese would prefer more ties with Western Europe and the United States, though these appear more difficult to consummate for a variety of reasons, ranging from a lack of familiarity with China to doubts about the long-term success of the reforms.

A further important understanding for the foreigner is that there are significant cultural differences and conflicts within China itself, as well as between Chinese and other cultures. These are reflected in the fact that although there is one major written language, there are two *major* spoken dialects (Mandarin and Cantonese) plus many minor dialects, of which one of the most widely spoken is Shanghainese. Such major cities and provinces tend to have their own dialects, as does Nanjing, only 250 miles from Shanghai. Significant differences exist in language as between the coast and the interior. Different ethnic groups live in distinct regions of the country, and the mountains of central China have long marked a singular difference between North and South. In addition, there are several major cuisines (Mandarin, Cantonese, Shanghainese, Sichuan, and Hunan), each with different manifestations in various regions. For example, the world-famous Peking duck has its counterparts, which are quite different, in Shanghai duck and Guangzhou (Canton) duck.

These differences were exacerbated by a history of conflict between the North and the South, between the interior and the coastal regions, among the warlords and emperors, and between Chinese and foreigners for hundreds of years. This history produced strong currents and crosscurrents with diverse loyalties extending beyond the family. At any one time, loyalties could shift according to the ebb and flow of power and influence.

Not the least of the difficulties in understanding China is its own choice of words to describe its culture or value base. Thus the goal of the current regime of creating a "spiritual socialist civilization" would seem to harken back to some of the ancient sages of China; but in fact, it is seen by its leaders as an affirmation of pragmatism, without influence from the ancients.

SOURCES OF CHINESE CULTURE

There are three major roots to Chinese culture: the ancient or "traditional" culture, modifications under Sun Yat-Sen and Mao Zedong (1912–1978), and efforts to modify again under the current regime.

Traditional Culture

The most dominant of the three sources is the traditional culture, rooted in ancient wisdom and reflecting Confucianism, Buddhism, and Daoism (Taoism), plus a number of other spiritual and philosophical teachings and practices. Within this tradition is a reverence for the past, which is seen as glorious (compared with the present) and which should be reinstituted either through acts of will or the mere passage of time. The concept of time itself is a singular indicator of the nature of and differences between cultures; China's concept is that time is circular and repetitive over millennia; situations in past periods will be repeated and those in the present will come again in the long-term future. The high periods of the past, therefore, as with the dynasty of Emperor Chou, are seen as those that should be sought again in the future.

All of the *revered* ancient periods are those of strong emperors ruling through personal authority and practicing personal virtues, which also are elicited from others. Virtue was considered so important that Emperor Yao passed the throne onto a low-born but virtuous man (Emperor Shun) rather than give the position to his own son, whom he saw as disputive and abusive. In turn, Shun selected the virtuous Yii to succeed him.[1]

The ancient Chinese writings centered on noble figures as models to inspire virtuous behavior by the reader, and Chinese scholars studied these classics to learn the virtues that would presumably qualify them for high position.

Though today the Confucian *Analects* are no longer formally studied on the mainland, they and other sources of ancient wisdom continue to permeate the society, affecting thinking and behavior, particularly with reference to the family and the organizations to which they belong, plus demanding respect for their leaders. The basic concepts arising from Confucian values are expressed in the following seven Chinese words:

Kunja—the perfection of man, which will lead to perfection of society

Ren—consideration of others

Yi—sacrificing one's own interest for that of others

Li—right, proper, or normal conduct plus ritual

Xin—being true to one's word

Qi—pursuit of knowledge that enlightens the person

Xiao—filial piety and the family as the central relationship and social institution

Unlike societies based on the Judeo-Christian traditions, Confucian societies begin with the belief that "man is good" and that he and society can be perfected. But the perfect society would be developed only with men achieving their own personal perfection. Confucius stated: "Govern the people by laws, and regulate them by penalties, and they will try to do no wrong but they will lose the sense of shame. Govern the people by virtue and restrain them by rules of propriety and the people will have a sense of shame and be reformed by themselves."

As shown in Chapter 6 with reference to legal orientations, traditional Chinese values contain a distrust of laws through which criminals are restrained and punished, preferring the teaching of good behavior and a reeducation of those behaving improperly. The Confucian values stress acceptance of place and reverence for social harmony under an absolute ruler who is himself an exemplar of virtue. There is a disdain for partisan politics and popular elections, since leaders were chosen because of the quality of their character and clarity of their thought, rather than through campaign popularity. These values have little support for the nineteenth-century concept of progress in that wisdom lay in copying the past and perpetuating the status quo to achieve peace and harmony. But both the past and the present are to be based on virtuous behavior, particularly of leaders and their officials. Confucianism is not a religion (having no convenanting God, though a deity is recognized), but a set of behavioral ethics, leading to a perfect life and perfect society. The key aspects of such a society are (a) its hierarchical nature, based on five basic relations with unequal but mutual obligations among members of the society—ruler/subject, father/son, older/younger brother, friend to friend, and husband/wife; respect and obedience is given in return for protection and consideration; (b) primacy of the family as the prototype of all social relations; individualism is subsumed within the family, requiring restraint to act honorably and save "face" (meaning not to lose one's dignity); one should "give face" to others, providing them dignity; this behavior is learned in the family and practiced to all in the "societal family"; (c) virtuous behavior toward others, meaning to behave as you would like others to behave toward you; and (d) virtuous life and work, meaning to work hard, be frugal, be patient and persevering, acquire knowledge and skills necessary for improvement, plus moderation in all acts of work and consumption.

Confucianism is a way of living both for individuals within a society and for the total society; there is no concept of an individual apart from society; life *is* relations with others. Therefore, virtue is the key concept; through it, stability and order will be achieved and both individuals and society will be able to progress, however slowly. Progress is more a matter of pursuit of Truth than of material progress, but that pursuit lies in personal and societal behavior, not in scientific inquiry. The society is, therefore, people-oriented, rather than things-oriented; it is other-oriented, but not materially oriented.

Some aspects of Confucianism are potential obstacles to material progress—the lack of scientific empiricism, protecting "face," "reciprocity," respect for ancestors and traditions, and personal place and stability. Science was pursued in ancient and "old" China (as noted later in this chapter), but it was not carried into industrial application, since material advance was not as important as improvement of personal relations. Face means that difficult personnel decisions to achieve efficiency would be avoided. Reciprocity in gifts and favors, in consideration and obligations removes the arm's-length dealing of markets. Respect for tradition interferes with technological change, and acceptance of place dampens career ambitions.

Contrarily, the Confucian tradition has recently been credited with being the basic reason why the countries of Asia have "taken off" so rapidly in terms of economic growth. Given the opening of markets and greater political stability and openness, the Confucian ethic is seen as a key initiator of industrial and competitive activity.[2] These traits are called by Hofstede and Bond "Confucian dynamism"—based on the value of "ordering relationships by status and observing this order," which makes entrepreneurial roles easier (and less risky) to play. Having a "sense of shame" supports fulfillment of contracts; "thrift" and "frugality" lead to savings for investment; and "perserverance" leads to dedication and commitment to enterprise goals. The Asian economies, as well publicized in Japan and China, are dominated by long-term relations between companies, such as manufacturer and supplier, rather than arm's-length dealings.

Culture in Negotiations

Initially, in its negotiations with Shanghai, Xerox was seeking definitive agreements for each and every issue because it was thought that future risk could be reduced through such an orderly process. It sought agreement that if a certain situation occurred, the Chinese would respond in a certain way and Xerox's response was to be stipulated also. With all of the provisions of such an agreement in place, Xerox thought that it could forecast the potential future paths for the venture and convince the corporate staffs at home that the negotiators had identified all the future risks and planned for them. Meanwhile the Chinese were assessing the potential long-term relationship, particularly the sincerity and long-term commitment of this prospective partner.

It is easy, in hindsight, to see how the historic Confucianism of the Chinese and the U.S. corporate style of contingency planning were butting against each other even though both negotiators were anxious to move ahead. An experienced U.S. vice-president from AMF's Asian operations provided some extremely valuable advice that proved to continue to be wise: "Friendly negotiations and mutual agreement," he said, "is the Chinese approach for resolving issues, and it works."

It is impossible to describe in advance, and especially in contractual language, all of the conditions that may exist in future disagreements. Therefore, by agreeing to friendly negotiations and resolution by mutual agreement, both sides are protected and days of protracted discussions about possible problems in the future are eliminated. In reality, if arbitration or courts are ever needed, the joint venture has a questionable future. One could say that the real issue from the Chinese perspective is whether both parties have acted in an honorable (virtuous) manner in regard to the disputed incident or activity.

The distinctive difference between Confucian dynamism and Western orientations lies in the communitarian basis of Chinese culture versus the individualistic basis of American culture.[3] These bases lead to different concepts of life itself and the requisites for its improvement or evolution. Given its grounding on individual desires and drives, the West requires "order" for the achievement of social progress; without order, anarchy results. Furthermore, for individuals to make rational decisions, a high degree of certainty must exist. Therefore, a high priority is placed on "order and certainty," with managers having a high interest in "uncertainty avoidance." Consequently Western managers tend to be monochronic (seeing time as a linear flow), pursuing one issue at a time and thinking and acting in a linear (cause and effect) pattern.

Eastern managers assume that the world is not orderly (it has seldom been in their experience), and find stability instead in personal and organizational relations. Order comes from hierarchy and authority and mutual obligations; it is not achieved by institutions of law or government, but by people (in and out of government). Thus certainty is achieved by personal and social means, complex and unwritten. Given the ever-changing world, managers are polychronic in decision-making; that is, they are able to pursue several issues simultaneously, readily accepting interruptions and "detours," since they are all part of a larger scheme that is in continuous change, which is better represented by the yin-yang symbol than the linearity of mechanical physics.

This acceptance of uncertainty is the result of the view that man cannot know *The* Truth, at least not objectively; *The* Truth is not pursuable through examining detailed manifestations in nature created by the One Creative Source. The idea of the existence of an absolute Truth is a Western concept, leading to empirical, detailed, and objective research, seeking to find *The* Origins in every microcosm. Confucius left open the question of Truth, as does Lao-Tsu (Taoism); instead, man is to seek Absolute Virtue. It is by living a complete and perfect life that man progresses, not by "knowing" the Truth objectively.

Western religions and science are both imbued with the search for Truth, leading to certainty and prediction (even to the concept of "the calling" in Calvinism). Not seeking One Truth through their religions, Easterners can simultaneously follow several "religions" or concepts of life—in Hinduism, Buddhism, Taoism (and in Japan, Shintoism)—focusing on each at different stages of life or for different needs. Behavior is more important than belief; beliefs can separate people; behavior must integrate. Western thinking is analytical and objective; Eastern thinking is synthesizing and subjective in the sense of person-related.

Because management and governance the world over are increasingly based on the *art* of systematizing, rather than the *science* of manipulation and prediction, the East has an advantage in rapid growth in the modern world.[4]

The primacy of Confucian dynamism rests in placing art over science and behavior over techniques in organizational dynamics. Hofstede and Bond conclude that there is a "strategic advantage in . . . Eastern cultures that practice virtue without a concern for truth."[5] (One can reconcile these opposites. Both are concerned with Truth and Virtue, but virtuous behavior to the West is derived from truth [religion], whereas in the East, truth is approached through a virtuous life. Because truth covers the whole of the universe, it is too complex to understand and can only be "experienced" through proper behavior; truth in the East is seen as behavioral [emotional and spiritual], rather than as empirical [intellectual and material].)

In a study of *The Chinese Heritage*, K. C. Wu found a recommendation in an ancient *Book of the Worthy and the Capable* that the ruler select *worthy* men who "may be entrusted with leadership positions externally" and *capable* men who "may be charged with business management internally."[6] Leadership (and management), in the view of the sages, does not arise from skills and detailed knowledge, but from "strength of conviction and moral character." This concept of "goodness and perfectibility" of man has given China its mark of a high culture and its claim to be the "Middle Kingdom"—resting halfway between earth and heaven. (The Chinese character for "China" includes a square with rounded corners having a vertical line through it; this symbol, indicating centrality, shows China's middle position in the universe.) The current period is especially difficult for China as a developing country because it has historically seen itself as elevated above other nations in the world. In earlier centuries, all foreign diplomats had to "bend the knee" (kowtow) before the emperor, but the first American ambassador refused, and forced an eventual change in the custom.

China's level of economic development places it in the awkward position of having to rely on the West for technology, capital, management expertise, and markets for economic growth. This relationship constitutes a dependence contrary to China's historical view of itself and one that it will seek to eliminate as soon as possible. Consequently joint ventures with the West are set for specific duration, with the hope that China will be able to move on its own thereafter. Contradictions abound in China's attitude toward the rest of the world. On the one hand, there is some disdain for the "newness" and cultural "crudity" of outsiders, compared with the ancient lineage of China, and therefore a strain of disinterest that often is misinterpreted by foreigners as "xenophobia." Yet, as a consequence of ancient philosophy, there also is a felt responsibility for the world, to elevate it to the higher position held by China. It is difficult to be estranged from yet responsible for others; China has yet to focus on how it will reconcile these views. (This problem is discussed further in Chapter 12.)

Maoist Period

Mao Zedong attempted to change traditional Chinese culture through the "collective programming" of the people, through propagation of the "Thoughts of Mao Zedong," reinforced by the extensive group learning sessions during the period 1949 through 1978, culminating with the trauma of the Cultural Revolution (1966–1976). Modification of "traditional place" had begun with the overthrow of the emperor in 1911 and the effort of Sun Yat-Sen to unify China under a more democratic government. The Kuomintang (literally, "National Party"), under Generalissimo Chiang Kai-shek,[7] sought to centralize authority, but without the "virtuous" quality of Confucianism; it was in fact a highly corrupt government whose policies created disastrous inflation.

Mao attempted to substitute loyalty to the commune, brigade, and team for traditional family loyalty, establishing a hierarchy from the central government to the individual (now literally torn from family). He wanted to reconstruct "correct behavior" by establishing a new set of rules in defining the ideal Communist—a person who would sacrifice his or her own well-being for the good of the whole proletariat or for the commune.[8] This collective group was itself to define the specifics of proper behavior and any deviant or criminal action would be corrected or punished by the group, relying primarily on reeducation. This approach is reminiscent of the ancient Chinese office of neighborhood "rescuer," who was assigned to supervise recalcitrants, persuading them to correct their ways and teaching them how. Virtue lay in cooperation at the *local* level, through the dictatorship of the proletariat. Such cooperation (proper behavior) would lead to the removal of poverty through greater opportunities for all and greater equality. Security for individuals would be achieved through the success of collective activities.

Security and egalitarianism apparently reduced material temptations. The People's Republic of China was known (until the mid–1980s) as a country in which a foreigner could leave his hotel room unlocked and know that his belongings were safe, where lost articles would be returned if possible, and where the people did not expect and would refuse tips. Despite this orientation, crime remained throughout the Maoist period, not so much in the form of violence or outright theft, but through a number of methods of circumventing the system (including corruption) and avoiding one's responsibilities to the collective. There also were swindlers and racketeers, using a number of tactics, including bribing officials, defrauding the state with phony receipts, forging official seals, hoarding scarce materials to resell at high black market prices, illegally recruiting workers, operating underground factories, and directing goods through black markets in several locales. In addition, there are many cynical stories of high officials in the government and in the party who abused their positions to live plush lives and accumulate privileges to themselves. A former bodyguard of Mao Zedong (Wang Dongxing) reportedly appropriated $4.2 million in public funds to build a palatial home even more elaborate than Chairman Mao's, able to accommodate seventeen relatives, with a gymnasium and a cinema.

Although such behavior is criticized, the Chinese have continued the ancient system of "going in the back door," which involves pulling strings and trading favors on a personal or familial basis to gain advantages. The children of emperors and noblemen often were granted high posts and salaries to maintain their security and positions, and Communist officials were able to get their children into schools and universities overseas, despite their lack of educational preparedness. As in an old Chinese saying, "when you get to the top, even your chickens and your dogs go to heaven." Corruption, favoritism, and "going in the back door" were basic complaints that prompted the 1989 student marches, leading to the occupation of Tienanmen Square. In many ways, correction of these abuses were the essence of the "democracy" the students called for, not a fundamental change in the party structure or the government. These observations are not to criticize or condemn, but merely to display the fundamental aspects of Chinese culture, which are more personal than institutional.

Current Regime

The Deng regime is seeking to modify both traditional and Maoist influences. "Proper behavior" is seen as (virtually) anything that promotes economic growth (i.e., anything that "works"). The concept of service, which is an essential part of socialism, has been made indirect through acceptance of the trickle-down approach—"to get rich is glorious" and the benefits of riches are to flow down subsequently to others in the system. Both the hierarchy of place and the security of equality are being thrown out for individual initiative and responsibility, neither of which are part of China's past. The collectivist concept is being replaced by a commodity orientation with the law of value, private ownership, and shareholding—calling forth individualistic desires and goals to achieve efficiency before security. Material bonuses, for example, had the highest ranking out of twenty possible "factors influencing work motivation in China" among a casual sample of twenty-five workers in twelve industrial enterprises in China in 1984.[9] This finding gives credence to Welder's contention that Mao's true legacy may have been an increased desire for material incentives rather than a perpetuation of moral suasion for the building of a socialist society.[10] A mid-1988 slogan on billboards proclaimed that "efficiency is life—time is money." The purpose is to raise living standards and achieve prosperity. The fear has arisen, however, that freeing the people from group constraints—either of hierarchy or of collective—will release corrupting influences from the primary pursuit of material goals; the evidence of an increase in theft, rape, bribery, and prostitution feeds such fears. Some Chinese studies by the Shanghai Academy of Social Sciences (1986–1988) have found that religious and moral teachings in some communities were instrumental in lowering crime rates and maintaining traditional family values. But party officials have not sanctioned religious groups for this purpose, rather only if they can and will make a contribution to China's modernization and economic development.[11]

Though religion is not officially sanctioned, churches have been permitted to reopen and to rebuild.[12] Religious precepts (especially Taoism) do consciously or unconsciously continue to influence the thinking and behavior of the Chinese. The removal of guaranteed employment, price controls, and "place" also reduces security, stability, and loyalty. The average Chinese intellectual in early 1989 appeared quite concerned about the destabilizing consequences of these losses, despite the intoxication of deifying economic growth and vastly improved quality of material life. For these reasons, the reappearance of Mao Zedong badges and posters among the "democracy" movement supporters should have come as no surprise. Mao gave relatively little in the material sense, but under his leadership, security, stability, and loyalty prevailed. China has not yet mastered the lessons of Confucian dynamism that keep traditional values but modernize without "Westernizing." But it will probably adjust. Up until 1989, the Chinese tended to respect any internal authority and had learned to accept almost any change to survive, but the widespread support given the student marchers in 1989 by workers and journalists, especially, may now cause substantive changes in China.

CHINESE CHARACTERISTICS

A number of major characteristics of Chinese people can be summarized in contrasting traits and ideals and in a number of constant themes.

Contrasts

There is both a highly spiritual orientation, reflected in the concern for virtue, and a quite pragmatic orientation of finding "what works." These are both societal and personal qualities, affecting both strategies and tactics.

The Chinese are both reserved and open. The Chinese have a saying that "the first visit you meet a stranger; the second visit you meet an old friend." This reflects the desire for relationships over arms-length dealing. But the Chinese also are reserved, in that they will not press themselves on another, and their family life is private.

The Chinese seek contacts with foreigners, yet have characterized them as "foreign devils." There is much in the history of relations with foreigners to indicate that the West acted devilishly, including the Opium Wars, in which European countries insisted on the ability to sell opium in China to balance trade deficits, despite its damaging effects on Chinese. A centuries-old conflict remains between holding fast to what is "Chinese" and acquiring the advancements seen in other countries. The conflict surfaces most pointedly in the desire to retain centralized political authority (often extended to "decentralized" hierarchical units at the local level) but the necessity to decentralize economic affairs. These traits are shown by Graeme Browning, in her book on *American Capitalism in Communist China*, to be unreconciled through any recent century of Chinese history. The resolution so far has always been on the side of conservatism and control, putting "China first" over its foreign relations and thereby maintaining an omnipotent bureaucracy that stifles risk-taking or the assumption of personal responsibility.[13] To avoid risks from the daily oppression of their economic and political system, the Chinese wear a variety of masks.[14]

The Chinese take the "long view," seeing history as repetitive and guided by "the Will of Heaven," yet they are quite concerned with what is occurring now, and consider it their right and duty to struggle against the Will of Heaven if it is seen as bringing adverse conditions.

A dichotomy arises here similar to that in the Western concepts of predestination and free will. The Chinese accept their fate as the "Will of Heaven," and yet struggle to survive or change "Heaven's Will" more in accordance with the group's desire. There is a unity of all things but a place for man to make a difference, if he wills to do so. Therefore, man is both shaped by and able to shape the world in which he lives. There is a constant push-pull relationship that it is man's destiny to live in but never to understand fully. The purpose of life is the search for this understanding.

The Chinese are serious but also have a sense of humor. The humor of China is, however, different from that of the West; in many cases it is subtle—often a play on words or a situation pushed to an extreme that becomes funny in its ridiculousness. In no way would Chinese humor affront an individual or a group, or ever be at the expense of someone else. This raises a caution to the foreigner as to the transference of jokes or humor from his own society into a Chinese setting.

One of the most difficult conflicts in China is the pull of the ancient—toward stability and harmony—and the necessity to move into the modern world, which requires continuous change in technology, types of products produced, institutions of control, motivation, personal relations, and even family ties. A major concern is the impact of industrialization on traditional culture. The traditional culture is not experimental in the sense of social change, though it was somewhat scientific in inquiry, including medicine, and there were changes in the art forms of China historically. But science was not pursued to the extent of causing significant social change, with both the clock and gunpowder seen as curiosities rather than as bringing major changes in economic or social activity.

There is a strong, underlying desire for peaceful relations, yet also strong currents of violence both within and among regions of China—historically more recurrent than with foreigners.

Despite a high concern for virtue and morality, the Chinese are not a religious people in an institutional sense. There is no church, such as found in the West, and no separate God who is distinct from mankind and nature. They are a spiritual and ceremonial people, however, recognizing the place of man within nature and as part of the universe, and relying on shamanism in many rural areas to divine the spirits and guide behavior.

Constants

Apart from these contrasts, there are a number of characteristics that are constant throughout China and are important in a foreigner's understanding of how to communicate and operate. The first is the strong family orientation. The family is the survival unit and commands the highest loyalty. The family remains the central organizational unit in China and establishes order. The role of parents is revered, and even popular songs are sung in praise of mother, including the desire of the soldier or separated son to return to his mother's arms. Sometimes family ties go beyond two generations (the nuclear family) to include the parents, children, and a son and his wife and any of their children (the stem family) or the parents, children, and several sons with wives and children (the joint family). There have even been some enlarged joint families encompassing four and even five generations. Given that there is a limited space allocated to the family, this means that living is fairly communal, with several people in a bedroom or even one single-family bedroom. Despite the vastness of China—a region almost equal in size to the United States plus Alaska—the concentration of about 95 percent of China's 1.2 billion inhabitants into only one-half of its land resources has put a premium on space. With the costs of space and construction, many couples with young children live in apartments of less than 600 square feet.

Related to the family is an agrarian society's strong tie to the land, from which the family gains its security. Identification with the land is so strong that at least some member of the family will retain and use the family's allocated land, if at all possible, so that all members have a place to go in an emergency. A person's "hometown" may be a place he or she has never visited but where the family name resides.

The ties to family and land are reflective of the high value placed on security. Traditionally, the individual obtained security through the family, which obtained its security from the land. Only the armies of the emperor provided overall security, and these, at times, were used to oppress the peasants, throwing them back on the land itself for security. Security is such a high value in China that the Communists had to find a means of providing security to obtain followers. They attempted to do this through the guarantee of a job, when they moved the people off of their land into collectives and into industry. There is a saying in China that "once you have your job, you love your job." The guarantee of state employment became known as the "iron rice bowl," which signaled that the bowl out of which one gained one's survival could not be broken and could not be empty (jobs being passed from one family member to another in the event of retirement or death, for example). This meant a guarantee of at least subsistence for life. The current attempt to remove the "iron rice bowl" is injecting insecurity back into the system, more so in urban areas, and for this reason has engendered resistance, or at least hesitancy, among even the better-educated Chinese citizens. Throughout rural China the return to systems of essentially family farming has meant a return to security of control over the land.

These value characteristics are complemented by an orientation toward hierarchy, with each layer above having some responsibility for those below and the ones below having responsibility to those above. This interdependence not only exemplifies the familial relationship, but establishes organizational ties and loyalties and provides security as well. It also provides order and place, for which one is to be thankful and accept the position without complaint. This hierarchy leads to a series of relationships, which produce the second major loyalty of the Chinese, to the network that supplements that of the family. In China this second structure is the government—essentially the central government, though the intermediate levels (such as the factory) linking the localities to the center are included. The Chinese, therefore, are loyal to family and the state, reflecting a high degree of patriotism when it is needed. Loyalty to the country was personified in the leader rather than to an abstract concept, or to the nation.

The value of loyalty is high and in Chinese culture, with a clear definition that those *inside* receive loyalty and those *outside* are to be treated differently. The Chinese refer to themselves as "Zhongguo ren," or people of the kingdom, and foreigners are collectively called "Waiguo ren," or people *outside* the kingdom. Not only does this insider-outsider attitude exist toward the foreigner, but it also exists between the dominant Chinese Han (which constitute 95 percent of the population) and various minorities, who frequently have been discriminated against in the past. On the other hand, the outsider, who is a guest, will be treated with great hospitality, not only in terms of the rooms offered, but also the meals and other amenities. Even an insider (Chinese) guest may not be treated so lavishly.

One possible implication of this orientation to the foreigner is that an expatriate Chinese may be a better negotiator than the foreigner himself, knowing the culture and being received as an insider. However, many non-Chinese may feel that the expatriate Chinese himself may consider that he owes loyalty to China and the party with whom he is negotiating. But, since most expatriate Chinese are no different than Hong Kong Chinese or other Asian Chinese in conducting business negotiations for their respective employers, the expatriate Chinese who is confident will act without such biases. The less confident ones are sensitive to their special situation and would go to the extreme to show their loyalty to their foreign employers. However, the expatriate Chinese may not be treated as lavishly by the Chinese hosts as the foreigner, setting up a differentiation within the negotiating team that may be uncomfortable.

The Chinese expatriate working for the foreigner will be more sensitive to Chinese cultural nuances and may be regarded as an insider, receiving some differential advantages as a result. The foreigner, however, although seen as "less than Chinese" (even a "barbarian" at the extreme), will probably receive greater symbolic courtesies and may be taken more seriously. Although expatriate Chinese may be given more insider access and advantage, it will be expected that they retain an underlying fealty to China; thus greater pressure can be put on them to remember their essential "Chineseness" and to act accordingly.

The Chinese value loyalty so highly that there has been little tradition of dissidence compared with that found in the USSR and the West. Although there is a tradition of student demonstration (for example, the May 4 movement of 1919, the student uprisings at the death of Zhou Enlai, discontent after the more recent death of Hu Yaobang, plus the most significant hunger strikes in Tienanmen Square in Beijing during May 1989—the anniversary of the 1919 uprisings), there are few "dissidents" in China expressing their dissatisfaction in art or literature. These student protests notwithstanding, the traditional orientation for Chinese who find themselves out of line with existing events is to withdraw until a more propitious time.

Jonathan Spence, in *The Search for Modern China*, observes that the role of the intellectuals (particularly students) has historically been to monitor the government as to its moral behavior—not its authority or its centralized nature. It is principally through the approval of the intellectuals that Chinese governments have obtained their legitimacy, since most of them were recruited into the bureaucracy, which would serve so long as the ruler remained relatively honorable. Along with this intellectual elitism arose secret societies and popular uprising when the system became unacceptable. These arose because, in the words of another China observer, "Chinese political culture does not abide pluralism and lacks a means of peacefully making democratic change."[15]

CONFLICTS AND DIFFERENCES

The mind-sets that arise in Chinese culture are so different from those of the West that it is virtually impossible for a Chinese to view questions on fundamental relations in the same way an American would. For example, the intensity of family loyalty and the scope of the extended family are much greater than in the United States. But, at the same time, Chinese peasants see nothing wrong with selling their (or buying others') children or buying a wife—even one who has been kidnapped for such sale. Reports from China's official press early in 1990 described tens of thousands of abductions, in the coastal province of Shandung, some 30,000 women and 1,000 children were reported stolen and sold in recent years. Police efforts to break the practice have been met with resistance from buyers and sellers (even parents) alike, who consider that they are doing a "good deed" by helping out others. Historically, wives have been mortgaged (given as security to lenders for their use during the debt) and children sold into "slavery."[16] The Chinese see multiple relationships, interweaving and intertwining and requiring a balancing of forces to maintain stability and harmony, despite complex and continuing change. Americans see a more linear world of cause and effect moving toward a positive and desirable result—progress. The Chinese do not see current relationships as necessarily continuing or permanent, recognizing that things move from positive to negative and vice versa over time; Americans tend to consider new relationships more in terms of the tasks at hand than in terms of the people involved. These attitudes are affected by the basic concept of the sweep of time, illustrated in an imaginary conversation between an American and a Chinese in which the American asks, "How long has corn been planted in China?" The Chinese answers, "Four hundred years." The American responds, "Oh, it's been here for quite a long time." The answer: "No!"

The American should recognize that the 200 years of the U.S. existence as a nation is shorter than the average Chinese dynasty (rule by a single family lineage), of which there were twenty-two. Archeological evidence shows settlements in China going back 6,000 years B.C., with "high civilization" being reached centuries before Christ, and the first emperor to unify China at 200 B.C. (Emperor Qin, who was buried at Xian surrounded by thousands of life-sized terra-cotta soldiers.) The implication for the foreigner is not to get excessively caught up in detailed planning over short- and intermediate-term periods, since the Chinese see a necessity for flexibility to adjust to uncontrollable changes. The Chinese do little in haste, and change direction when circumstances change. This can probably be attributed to the Chinese long-term view of time, but no doubt the lack of profit motivation before 1980 and the "iron rice bowl" have entrenched the no-haste approach to work.

Consequently a move toward openness will lead to building international relations; if it does not work out favorably, the Chinese will simply move on to another potential partner. Cooperation with the United States will be seen as tactical by some Chinese—not even a strategy, and much less a permanent association. The United States is not seen by all Chinese as a country on which one can rely over a long term simply because this has not been the pattern of the past, despite the friendly relations of the nineteenth and early twentieth centuries. In addition, some of the extremes in American life are rejected by those seeking to guide Chinese development, including the high materialism, extreme divergence of incomes, high stress and anxiety, drug cultures, religious cults, unemployment, and the existence of nuclear families.

Inconstancy

At a time when Xerox negotiations were winding down and friendships were strengthening, the chief Xerox negotiator asked a senior Shanghai official, who had dealt with foreign corporations for years, both inside and outside of China, what were his greatest concerns about joint ventures. Despite the many issues involved in developing a joint venture, he said simply, "Earning foreign exchange and the changing priorities of the foreign partners."

Most who have read the U.S. financial pages for any length of time would readily agree. Corporations have moved through periods of diversification and now back to a "stick to your business" approach. This is an example of changing corporate direction in the past. Domestically and internationally, U.S. corporations today are entering joint ventures at an impressive rate, but there is certainly no guarantee that these alliances will meet expectations and survive long term. This also is apparent to Chinese observers of the United States. Thus they may think that their relations with U.S. companies cannot go beyond the tactical because of changes in corporate strategies or attitudes in the United States itself.

LANGUAGE

Besides the concept of time, there is probably no single aspect of culture that is more characteristic of the differences among peoples than language. The legend of the Tower of Babel signals the key role of language in binding and separating people. Language both reflects the mode of thinking and forms it. It reflects the relations among those using the language and is formed to reflect those relations. It leads either toward logic and scientific methods in thinking, or toward emotion, intuition, and ambiguity. Cavalierly, English can be characterized as a language of science, German as that of philosophy, French as that of diplomacy, Italian as that of lovers, Spanish as that of conversation, Sanskrit (and Hindi) as that of spirituality, Russian as that of emotions, Japanese as that of ambiguity (circumlocution) or delicacy, Arabic as that of poetry, and Chinese as that of tangible things and events.

Compared with the Indo-European languages, Chinese is deficient in notations of number, tense, gender, and relationships. It is relatively poor in expressing abstractions or general classes or qualities, such as truth or hope; when such ideas are expressed, they are applied to specific things or events, such as the truth of the current situation or the hope in a new structure of government. Therefore, foreign translations into Chinese frequently lose their original style of expression and even the purpose of the message, especially if it is somewhat abstract (for example, spiritual truth or scientific understanding). Each of the Chinese characters has many meanings of itself, separately and in different contexts or phrases or coupled with other characters. To a Chinese, an expression can mean many other things, depending on the context of the rest of the sentence. Despite the many meanings attached to each character, each of these meanings standing alone is weightier in providing meaning than a single syllable of Indo-European language, which has meaning only when combined into words. The combination of characters in Chinese will produce different meanings even from those of the individual characters.

Each of the characters has been given additional meanings through history, and each of these have changed through time. Translations, therefore, pick up the "historical baggage" of the Chinese character, losing the foreign connotation intended, sometimes completely. In translation, the foreign idea has to be inseminated through acceptable Chinese concepts, which may not be even close to a literal interpretation. For example, the Chinese concept of "father" is so different from that of a "father" in the West that the use of "Our Father" to signify God would stimulate a completely different image in the Chinese listener than intended. Or, because the place of honor in a Chinese diplomatic setting is on the left of the host, to insist that the spiritual standing of Jesus is exemplified by his sitting at the right hand of God also provides less than a full understanding. Conversely, whereas the West saw the "socialist struggle" in China as the class struggle enunciated by Western socialism, in China the concept has held connotations of the *inner* struggle to develop individual personality through self-cultivation and socialization.[17]

Because of the lack of standardization of characters for given terms, the translation of scientific terms into Chinese often leads to a misunderstanding through multiple meanings. In addition, rather than writing all of the characters necessary for full translation, the Chinese often abbreviate an expression, so as to cut the number of characters, leaving only the essential thought. For a casual reader, the meaning may well be altered when he accepts what is written or attempts to read between the lines. "Wu qi," for example, may be "5" or "7" or "May 5th," or it may stand for the "May 7th Cadre Corps," used for reeducation during the Cultural Revolution.

Given the fact that there are no characters for some Western concepts, sometimes phonetic transliteration is used rather than translation (i.e., reproduction of a similar sound in Chinese through using a character or set of characters that produces the same aural sound as in the foreign language). This leads to what is recognized by linguists as a "barbaric and inhuman result," with the words themselves being obscured and phonetics producing a new Chinese word with different meaning from the character used. This is a frequent route taken in translating foreign names into Chinese, but it leads to the problem that the same complicated name may be spelled quite differently in Chinese characters by different translators, depending on how they hear the phonetics of the foreign word. Foreigners need to understand clearly the Chinese meaning of the words (characters) used to approximate the sound of their non-Chinese name. Sometimes the translation has been an embarrassment to the foreigner and humorous to the Chinese, until someone quietly points out the Chinese meaning. Western names can be phonetically represented by quite different characters, so one is not stuck with an embarrassment.

Finally, the mere fact that the message is written down alters the meaning of words in Chinese culture. As one linguist has observed, written symbols become "endowed with efficacy that makes them more than mere notations and gives them a semi-magical control over the phenomena symbolized."[18]

In the experience of one American company, the Chinese workers in the joint venture responded indifferently to oral instructions but precisely to written instructions. Thus they were instructed, in writing, to no longer place mirrors on the fenders of the cars that were being produced, since customers thought that this made them look like taxis rather than passenger cars. However, cars continued to come through the line with the two screw holes bored in the fenders, since it was not explicitly stated that this was not to be done.

Given that all joint venture agreements are to be in Chinese and the foreign language, and that the Chinese text is the "official" one, the process of translation itself can make a difference to the understanding of the venture and its operation. Yet the foreigner is at a disadvantage in knowing what the Chinese version states and even more so as to how it will be understood, especially by those who were not at the negotiating sessions. Efforts on the part of the foreign partner to stick to the letter of the agreement may produce wholly unwanted results. One solution is to agree that both the English and the Chinese versions of the contract are binding, which provides the foreigner with a better legal base for negotiation.

SCIENCE AND MEDICINE

Chinese science and medicine are double-tracked: traditional and Western. Western science and medicine have been learned to be able to communicate with the rest of the world and to learn its advances. But traditional Chinese science and medicine start from a different viewpoint of the world and proceed to their understanding quite differently. The process is not understood by most Westerners and even rejected in many circles.

Western science starts from the concepts of disaggregative investigation developed by Aristotle, which were to take things apart progressively to find out what the components were and, therefore, how they worked together. Both Chinese and Islamic science start from the other end of the continuum; that is, they seek to understand the whole and how elements therein are meshed and guided. The Chinese view is that all things are part of other things in making up the whole—which eventually extends to the universe.

Underlying this holistic orientation to both science and medicine is the concept of yin and yang, which is the first duality coming out of the One Creative Source of the universe (Qi). Yin and yang are the two aspects of anything that distinguish them from the one fundamental energy in the universe. They represent characteristics that are found in everything, such as the positive and negative poles in magnetism, the hot and the cold in water, the moist and the dry in air, the hard and the soft in wood, the flexible and the brittle in metal, and so on. Yet the yin and yang are not opposites, for, as we know from biology, though there is a male and a female, there are female characteristics in the male and male characteristics in the female; the turn of the genes in the fetus to one or the other sex develops out of an actual struggle of one set to dominate.

Because there is yin in the yang and yang in the yin, there is a constant pulsing flow between the yin and the yang as to the predominant expression of the moment. These shifts cause or represent vibratory energy that pervades everything that exists. This energy is Qi; thus everything has a basic similarity. It is more important to understand the integrating, binding, balancing, and unifying forces than to try to take apart the various things in which these forces are manifested. In fact, to take things apart removes the very essence of their being. As one observer commented with reference to this problem of reductionist versus holistic science, "you can either have cat or know something about cat: if you dissect cat, you know something about cat but you no longer have cat; to understand cat you must have cat." The two approaches, therefore, start at different ends of the continuum, but traditional Chinese science avers that it is impossible to understand the whole from trying to examine innumerable disaggregated manifestations; such a search will take one off of the road to understanding.

This integration of things also is represented by the concept of colors. In the Chinese viewpoint, there is no such set of opposites as black and white, or red and green. There is no absolute black or absolute white; rather, there is black in white and white in black; there is red in green and green in red; there is blue in red and red in blue; and there is black in red and red in black. Therefore, all colors are manifestations of all other colors; they are simply reflections of a dominant vibration at a given time or situation. The Chinese, therefore, are not given to absolutes; rather, everything is attenuated by its existence along with everything else and the necessity to interact with other elements.

The same approach is taken in traditional Chinese medicine, which has as its objective the maintenance of health in the whole body, including the emotions and the mind. The allopathic approach of Western medicine seeks to remove the symptoms of a disease or attack the disease itself, rather than to strengthen the body so that it can eradicate the disease through its own strength. Once again, the Western approach is particularistic, whereas the Chinese approach is holistic.

Chinese traditional medicines are aimed at strengthening a body that has become weak in certain ways. Herbal medicine and acupuncture are directed at strengthening the body through stimulating energy centers that will rebalance the body and thereby remove the disease (imbalance) that exists at some place in the body. The point to be strengthened is not necessarily the point within which the symptoms are located. A weakness in one of the energy centers may be manifested in many places in the body; if a symptom is removed through invasionary medicine, although the basic weakness is not, then a different illness will crop up elsewhere in the body as a manifestation of the weakness. Thus the objective is to regain health in the body's basic energy flows and then let the body heal itself.

Both herbal medicine and acupuncture are based on the concepts of energy meridians that flow through the body in patterns that can be used to repair particular parts, since these energy lines feed the various elements of the body. They feed it through subtle vibrations that are stimulated by eating, drinking, breathing, and thinking. Each of these produce a particular level of energy, with the subtler being that of the impressions of the mind, going down through air, water, and solids. Each of the higher levels directs the lower and maintains integrity of the whole, while the lower provide substance for all above. There is no clear demarcation between them, since they all flow into making the whole. Any imbalance among them or inadequacy within any one of them will be manifested in any of the several levels, leading either to physical, psychological, or mental illness. Thus an imbalance in eating can lead to mental illness, or ill thoughts can lead to physical infirmity.

The purpose of the doctor in Chinese medicine is to maintain health; in some practices, the doctor pays for any illness or hospitalization that the patient sustains, and the patient supports the doctor through regular payments to maintain health. Thus the payment to the doctor is for health promotion and disease prevention (HPDP in Western concepts) rather than for illness removal.

Health, therefore, is a result of balance among the elements of man's nature and between him and his environment. Each person is responsible for maintaining that balance, with the assistance of those who can show him the way to do so.

These comments on Chinese culture and thought show the distance that must be bridged in coming to a "meeting of the minds." Too frequently concepts that should be readily understood are instead misinterpreted and misapplied, despite the best of good will. Even thinking and communicating clearly and logically does not achieve harmony in action, for the mind-sets and logic systems are different. The opening by China, thus, requires an equal "opening" by foreigners to "see and understand" the positions and approaches of their Chinese counterparts, officials, and consumers.

In this regard, a former editor of *The Beijing Review* (Dr. Duan Lian Cheng) gave the following advice to a group of Americans looking at business in China:

- Adopt patience—it is a virtue learned by Chinese in the family, which requires closeness and forbearance.

- Respect formalities—these show place and acceptance, as in ceremonies and toasts.

- Be sensitive to differences—social and political relations are hierarchical; democracy has few roots in the culture; there is little tradition of dissent; Chinese suffer through catastrophe to survive; authority is respected; and business will be affected by each of these attitudes.

• Understand China's national pride—Chinese are quite sensitive to criticism; proud of their culture, history, and destiny; and resent condescension.

These are good starting points, but a fuller appreciation of cross-cultural adjustments is required to be an effective negotiator and manager in China.

NOTES

1. Herrlee G. Creel, *Chinese Thought* (Chicago: University of Chicago Press, 1953), p. 50.

2. See Herman Kahn, *World Economic Development: 1979 and Beyond* (London: Croom-Helm, 1979); also George Lodge and Ezra Vogel, *Ideology and National Competitiveness* (Boston: Harvard Business School, 1987).

3. Geert Hofstede and Michael H. Bond found this through surveys of Eastern and Western managers. See "The Confucius Connection: From Cultural Roots to Economic Growth," *Organizational Dynamics* (Summer 1987), pp. 5–21.

4. See the argument to this end made from an analysis of nine countries by George C. Lodge and Ezra F. Vogel, *Ideology and National Competitiveness* (Boston: Harvard Business School Press, 1987).

5. Hofstede and Bond, *Organizational Dynamics*, p. 20.

6. K. C. Wu, *The Chinese Heritage* (New York: Crown, 1982), p. 417.

7. The Kuomintang was created by Sun Yat-Sen, who was later succeeded by Chiang Kai-shek. The party was explicitly Leninist in its organizational design and major objectives; it was supported by the Soviet Union over the Chinese Communist Party of Mao Zedong until the late 1940s, when Mao ran Chiang out of the mainland into refuge in Taiwan.

8. Liu Shaoqi, former president of the People's Republic of China and among the leaders of the party, titled his best-known book *How to Be a Good Communist*.

9. John S. Henley and Nyaw Mee-Kau, "The Development of Work Incentives in Chinese Industrial Enterprises—Material Versus Non-Material Incentives," in Malcolm Warner, ed., *Management Reforms in China* (London: Frances Pinter, 1987), pp. 127–148.

10. Andrew G. Walder, "Some Ironies of the Maoist Legacy in Industry," in Mark Selden and Victor Lippit, eds., *The Transition to Socialism in China* (Armonk, N.Y.: M. E. Sharpe, 1982), pp. 215–237. See also Mark Selden, *Remaking the Economic Institutions of Socialism: China and Eastern Europe* (Stanford, Calif.: Stanford University Press, 1989).

11. *Christian Science Monitor*, August 9, 1988, p. 7.

12. The regime has long attempted to put Christian churches under government control and has continued to harass both Catholic and Protestant leaders. (*Christian Science Monitor*, July 19, 1989, p. 18.)

13. See Graeme Browning, *If Everybody Bought One Shoe* (New York: Hill and Wang, 1989).

14. See the many vignettes by Bette Boa Lord, *Legacies: A Chinese Mosaic* (New York: Alfred A. Knopf, 1990).

15. William P. Alford, "The Roots of Repression," *Christian Science Monitor*, June 9, 1989, p. 19.

16. Ann Scott Tyson, "Chinese 'People Mongers' Prey on Women and Children," *Christian Science Monitor*, March 29, 1990, p. 1.

17. Arthur F. Wright, "The Chinese Language and Foreign Ideas," in Wright, ed., *Studies in Chinese Thought* (Chicago: University of Chicago Press, Phoenix Edition, 1967), p. 300.

18. Ibid., p. 299.

6

Legal Environment

The legal environment for foreign investment in China is composed of two major aspects: the legal orientation and framework of Chinese society, out of which legal decisions will be made, and the specific laws and regulations concerning foreign direct investments (FDI) inflows and operations. Both are changing as China opens to Western ways of doing business.

CONCEPT OF GOVERNANCE

The ideal of governance in China is that emanating from the man of merit, ruled by a virtuous elite, which is presumed to be educated to governing. It is a rule *by* (or through) law emanating out of a meritorious, virtuous leader. It is not the Western concept of rule *of* law, made out of political compromise. The Chinese concept is like that of the Platonic philosopher-king rising to that position through merit and intelligence. The hurly-burly of backroom politics is anathema to the Chinese. Power is not to be sought for the sake of its exercise, but is to be assumed as a responsibility. It is more akin to the Jeffersonian concept of the servant-leader, without a democratic electorate. The leader would be educated to understand the holistic concepts in Chinese philosophy under which everything depends on everything else, each has his or her place, and status is conferred on all through the dignity of each individual.

The ideal having been stated, it remains to observe that the ideal has seldom been reached in Chinese history. Many emperors and warlords achieved their positions by many non-virtuous means, though some emperors were seen after the fact as virtuous leaders. Despite this sparse record of success, the Chinese continue to prefer governance by men rather than by laws.

The purpose of governance is to maintain social harmony and political stability.

This priority of purpose stems from the fact that China has faced, throughout its history, upheavals from nature (on one year losing half of its population through natural disasters), wars, disease, pestilence, rebellions and uprisings, plus the more recent revolutions.

To achieve the purposes of government, Deng Xiaoping in 1979 enunciated four "cardinal principles of government" that were *not* to be questioned. They were as follows:

1. The role of the party—which was to achieve unity of the country through a single-party system

2. The structure of the state—which was to represent and protect the national interest through representations of individuals from the various regions or groups

3. The commitment to Marxism—which requires continued loyalty of the people to socialism and to China

4. The socialist development strategy—which means continuation of the goal of socialist equality

The objective, therefore, is to achieve "socialism with Chinese characteristics," which means that the concept of socialism from the West, or even from other Marxist states, cannot be laid down as a template on China. The cultural characteristics and history of the country as well as its current objectives will instead significantly change the characteristics of socialism, rather than the reverse.

The style of governance is essentially "participative authoritarianism," involving consultation among representatives who have been elected through the party mechanisms and have achieved their position through long service in the party. This participative process is not pluralistic in the sense of melding diverse ideas. Rather, a great similarity in viewpoint is achieved through a person's elevation in the party. The process is not even authoritarian pluralism in the sense of an authority deciding which of many competing ideas are to be followed. It relies instead on consultation around a central theme—the theme being that of achieving material progress with socialist concepts and objectives. The process is rule by regulation, intervention, and law, but not a law of compromise; it is a law of edict. The recent opening to the West, however, is bringing a good bit more compromise in the formation of law, as foreigners are brought into the consultative process both for emulation and for accommodation.

Government intervention is itself limited in some respects through the concept of "spheres of immunity"; the government in effect says that it will not intervene in certain activities within the country. These spheres are increasing in number as the current regime attempts to relax governmental intervention. There also are "spheres of indifference," within which the government can and will intervene if it desires to do so; otherwise, it is indifferent to the activities taking place and chooses not to intervene.

Given the history and culture of China, it is not likely that the three concepts of legality, freedom, or democracy will be interpreted similarly by the Chinese and the West; nor are they, according to recent developments, seen similarly by many of the Chinese people and the government leaders. The rule of law is seen in the West as an end in itself, curbing the power of the state and of individuals. To curb it further, the structure of the state involves a series of checks and balances, including multiparty systems. These orientations are not found in China.

The concept of freedom in the West deals with choices by individuals in marriage, family, religion, education, market decisions, career, and so forth. Many of these are restricted or circumscribed by custom or governance in China, despite the fact that they are seeking a freer society.

Democracy in the West is a pluralistic process of competing interests out of which comes acceptable compromise. Democracy in China is exercised through a single party and through consultation, and with an understanding that collective benefit to the group or state can outweigh individual rights.

These same three concepts are being used in China to regain political confidence and stability (the use of democracy), to achieve economic and technical advance (through greater freedom of choice), and to enhance certainty and predictability with popular support of the government both by Chinese and foreigners (through emphasis on legalization). Therefore, these concepts are means to other ends, not ends in themselves. The basic system orientations of the United States and China remain different, though not necessarily divergent or in conflict. For the company doing business in China, the issue is simply how to understand and work with the Chinese orientations.

As China's world trade increases, a separate nonideological force also will influence its laws to move them closer to Western concepts. That will be the need for consistency and clarity in treatment. Processing of transactions in the generally accepted manner will prove more impressive to foreigners than expressions of ideology or nonideology.

ORIENTATIONS AND FRAMEWORK

Domestic law in China has different origins and orientations than Western law. It does not begin with the concept of a society ruled by law, but rather that of a society ruled by men using law. The emerging law is based on China's enduring traditions and on more recent experience under the Communist regime. With increasing involvement of joint ventures in domestic activities, the foreign investor will be working within both frameworks, resulting in some confusion, if not conflicts.

Traditional Attitudes

Traditional Chinese attitudes are jaundiced toward law, exemplified by the popular characterization of lawyers as "litigation tricksters" who increase the difficulties of settling disputes.[1] Consequently commercial agreements remain somewhat vague and flexible, so as not to engender disputes over legal niceties.

There is another tradition in the Chinese culture that argues the opposite: the reverence of the written word as compared with the oral. Since Confucian times, the Chinese have been taught to respect the written word, whereas the oral word is changeable and adaptable to the situation and the times. The written word has the respect of both tradition and expertise.

Contracts are seen as an arrangement between partners, similar to a marriage, based on good intentions and mutual interests. Therefore, it is important to recognize the need to balance precision with flexibility; this leads to detailed documentation plus a willingness to adjust. Flexibility also will permit the contract to integrate future unforeseen circumstances without the need for formal changes. Documentation should be meticulous and clear—as clear as possible in two languages—but there also should be flexibility in interpretation and a willingness to adjust to changing circumstances. For example, the breakthrough in Sino-American relations came to the Nixon Administration with the 1972 Shanghai Communique, in which both sides agreed to recognize and live with their differences by resorting to deliberate vagueness through stating their agreements and simply omitting their disagreements, rather than attempting a futile effort to reconcile them. The Chinese, however, can be meticulous when they deem it desirable, so the foreign negotiator should not be drawn into laxness by a desire to be cooperative.

The role of law in China is signalled by the fact that its leaders, both revolutionary and prerevolutionary, have had little or no formal training in the law, whereas many leaders in the West and even in the USSR have been trained in the law. As a result, law has not been seen as the basis of governmental authority or procedures.

Rule by Law

"Rule by men" or "rule *by* men through law" has been the traditional way of guiding human relations in China, with the leader of the group resolving disputes and forming the instructional program by which the group was to learn appropriate behavior. It was seen as better to have a leader ruling with virtue than a set of impersonal laws prescribing proper behavior.

In contrast, the West has long opted for "rule *of* law," considering that power tends to corrupt and that leaders with power will not be virtuous. In China, appeal to law and reliance on legal precedent have not been traditional patterns. Resolution of disputes traditionally occurred through intermediaries who could determine appropriate compromises or solutions. Problems seen in the West as legal matters and appropriately brought before legal institutions will probably continue to be handled by more informal (personal) or socially oriented methods in China.

The regime under Mao sought to institutionalize a legal system, following the

Russian model, which itself was derived from the European. But this effort was abandoned in 1957, and for twenty years there was no significant move toward legalization of the Chinese society, with even criminal acts handled by local groups. This distrust of law and respect for proper behavior reflect the traditional Confucian attitudes and the Communist ideology of collective and communal guidance. The basic concept during this twenty-year period was to move the responsibility for proper behavior down to the masses, who would be best able to determine what was acceptable behavior within the group. Thus a number of interpretations as to what was appropriate would arise, with no attempt to centralize, unify, or codify the rules and regulations or even the processes of prosecution or punishment. Consequently, even today, localities and provincial governments do not look to the central government for the promulgation of appropriate laws or regulations. And when the central government has passed statutes affecting the total populace, implementation and interpretations will be significantly different among locales. This may explain why new laws for joint ventures were never defined in detail; individual cities (such as Shanghai) would later publish its own version with somewhat more detail. These local divergences are reinforced by the fact that China remains a predominantly rural and agricultural society, where formal laws do not permeate. The requisites for dispute settlement before courts shifted from large expenditures of money under the Nationalist regime to large expenditures of time under the Communist regime— the former quick but costly, the latter long-delayed and lengthy but inexpensive.

In the post-Mao reforms, a basic policy has been to develop a series of laws that purportedly would stabilize the society and the means of decision-making. In 1979 alone, seven important laws were promulgated relating to the operations of the People's Congresses and Governments, the electoral process, criminal acts and prosecution, organization and operation on the People's Courts and Procuratorates, and, finally, the incentives and regulations on joint ventures with foreigners. The scope of criminal offenses is significant in showing the orientation in the application of law. Eight categories were covered: counterrevolutionary activities, violation of public security, disruption of the socialist economic system, infringement of the rights of citizens, encroachment on property, disruption of public order, offenses against marriage and the family, and malfeasance.[2] The latter relates to an abuse of power by government officials, which also includes the acceptance of bribes.

The result of these statutes is to institute a "rule by law," which comes from the persona of the government and not from an institutional system of laws guiding society.

Change through Law

The Western concept of law is to codify aspects of the society that should remain stable. Law should buttress that stability. Change is introduced through changes in the law, reflecting changes in values or conditions. Consequently

Western law is "conservative." The slow change in the laws and the legal institutions protect the status quo and allow change to take place only as necessary or desirable to reflect changing conditions or goals.

Conversely, China has, through history, maintained its stability through a cultural attitude of respect for the ancients and reverence of a golden age during the Chou dynasty, several thousand years ago. Until the twentieth century, the Chinese orientation was to achieve at some time this ideal past condition. But with the two revolutions in the twentieth century—those of Sun Yat-Sen and Mao Zedong—change, even revolutionary and destructive change, became regarded as the normal state. Movement—through contradictions and opposites— was expected and fostered.

Given the underlying assumption that man is innately good, the determination of appropriate movement could and should be pushed down to the masses. It was determined that the masses could be trusted with setting the guidelines for proper behavior, and it was there that behavior was determined as proper or not. The Communist orientation is to achieve an acceptable balance in movement, with acceptability or appropriateness determined by those who were involved— the masses.

Because law is to serve the masses, it should be simple (rather than complex) and interpretable by the masses (rather than by legal institutions and the courts). The Maoist principle was that law should be broadly based rather than the exclusive province of professionals. Industrial or commercial disputes were resolved by administrative agencies and tribunals. The courts and the law in fact were avoided as being coercive rather than representing the will of the people.

This orientation made it easy for China to isolate itself and for others to leave it alone, since it lacked Western institutions to permit easy economic and commercial relations. The West requires formal procedures for resolution of legal problems, and China is now trying to move in this direction.

Legal Community

During the early part of the twentieth century, China determined that it would have to modernize its law to deal with Western nations effectively. In the 1920s and 1930s, German and Swiss law were drawn on to form a complete set of criminal and civil codes; in the 1950s, Russian models were used. In both cases, these laws were restricted to major population centers in their primary effect and, in the earlier period, mostly to the commercial centers dealing with foreigners.

Not seeing the law or lawyers as particularly useful, the Communist government abolished the legal profession in 1957. As of June 1957, there were less than 3,000 lawyers in China, and by 1977 still only about 3,500. (Some comparison is instructive: Japan has some 13,000 lawyers with 115 million people and the United States, more than 750,000 lawyers with 245 million people. Thus the United States has thirty times the number of lawyers per capita compared with Japan and more than 600 times the number in China per capita. But many legal functions may be done by other categories of Japanese professionals, whose numbers would enlarge the total. In the United States, the contrary occurs, with nearly half of those trained in the law engaged in other pursuits, such as business and politics.) The role of Chinese lawyers was assumed by party members who were ideologically dependable or who had rendered desirable service to the party. They had no legal training or experience and frequently no formal education. These moves lead to the "peasant courts" and other communal means of handling disputes or deviants. All lawyers are "state legal workers," acting as advisors to all government and people's organizations, undertaking litigation in criminal and civil cases, being responsible to explain legal matters to the public, and drafting legal documents. Thus only major contracts will have a Chinese lawyer involved, but this will not speed up negotiations. The driving force behind every word in the contract will be the Chinese manager with whom you are negotiating, and caution remains a watchword.

To achieve the legalization that is desired in China, the post-Mao regime sought to increase the number of lawyers by more than tenfold as of 1985. This level was not achieved—not least because of the absence of adequate institutions of learning. Yet the government has stated that it needs 1 million college-trained lawyers to achieve the legalization desired. Because the population in the United States is less than one-fourth that of China, this is still well behind the ratio in the United States, even if the comparison is with the approximately 350,000 U.S. lawyers actually practicing before the bar. But by Japanese standards, it would be ample.

The lack of an adequate legal community itself poses a serious problem in establishing a system of economic rules and regulations appropriate for the modernization sought. If appropriate economic legislation is required for an increase in efficiency, there will remain considerable gaps; however, the mere existence of an appropriate legal system does not assure efficiency. One should not expect a great deal out of either the efforts to achieve legalization or the impact of laws promulgated on enhancing economic efficiency. Many difficulties remain in implementing even a series of formal laws that themselves might be highly appropriate. These difficulties stem from the cultural attitudes toward law in China and the traditional flouting of national laws by local authorities, as noted above.

Further, both political and legal theory in China tend to support decisions and actions by the local group, rather than from the center. It is only when the group cannot handle the matter that the decision moves to higher authority. Consequently the need for complex laws and for lawyers to interpret and adjudicate them is reduced within the domestic scene. This is not the case in dealing with the foreigner, for he will be treated in commercial dealings more by Western precepts. The implementation of those rules and regulations, however, is still likely to be done through an orientation that is more Chinese than Western.

China has a long road to travel in moving from the Chinese orientations to law and dispute settlement to Western concepts throughout its entire society. It is likely that such a transition will never take place completely. Traditional Chinese orientations will remain strong in whatever new institutions or laws are promulgated. In the economic and commercial fields, the separation of authority is reflected in the diverse laws that have been passed by the central, provincial, and city governments. Each of these levels has its own incentives to attract FDI and its own regulations as to hiring and firing, competition, pricing, and so forth. This requires separate negotiations at each level and time required to resolve differences or overlapping authority. A negotiation or agreement with one level of government usually will not suffice, since others also are involved and must be satisfied.

The Chinese government, however, has recognized that to achieve the objective of raising the living standards of its people through economic development, it must have Western science and technology, with a Western commercial presence, and this means Western commercial law, as appropriate. The difficulty of negotiating and absorbing large inflows of technology has caused China to recognize the need to establish a legal system to support the opening to Western commerce.

LAWS ON FDI: REGULATIONS AND INCENTIVES

Because private enterprises largely ceased operating in China in 1949, the opening that began in 1978 has required the gradual formation of private commercial law. This has involved the promulgation of a number of laws relating to domestic and foreign commerce. Legal scholars and practitioners from Europe, Asia, and the United States were consulted, and many of their suggestions were incorporated into the new laws. Within the first three years alone, China adopted thirty laws that had a direct effect on foreign investment in the country. In addition to central government regulations, provincial and city governments also have passed their own. Since 1982, the list has grown and been revised and rerevised in the light of the responses of foreign companies.

The concerns of foreign investors over the credibility of Chinese law and assurances of welcome by the Chinese rose to such a level that the Chinese government adopted in late 1982 a Constitutional provision recognizing and protecting foreign direct investment and other mechanisms of economic cooperation:

The People's Republic of China permits foreign enterprises, other foreign economic organizations and individual foreigners to invest in China and to enter into various forms of economic co-operation with Chinese enterprises and other economic organizations in accordance with the law of the People's Republic of China.

All foreign enterprises and other foreign economic organizations in China, as well as joint ventures with Chinese and foreign investment located in China, shall abide by the law of the People's Republic of China. Their lawful rights and interests are protected by the law of the People's Republic of China. (Article 18)

These laws and regulations provide for protection, constraints, guidance, incentives procedures, and required approvals. Five areas of law and regulations are of primary importance to the foreign investor. They are those relating to taxes, the removal of profits and capital from the country, the regulation of domestic business, differential regulation of foreign investors or foreign business, and special incentives given to the foreigner to induce participation in China.

Some of the laws passed to stimulate foreign investment—such as that in 1985 extending comprehensive protection to patents (as it had previously to trademarks)—will, in time, be extended to domestic law.[3] The most important of the laws relating to foreign investment are the 1979 joint venture laws and that promulgated in 1986, commonly known as the Foreign Investment Law, having twenty-two articles relating to a number of facets of foreign investment and providing substantial incentives (see Appendixes A and B). This body of law has been supplemented and amended by a number of other laws and regulations. These include the laws on taxation of individuals and of joint ventures, registration of joint ventures, and labor management and regulations pertaining to the Special Economic Zones and to exchange control. In all, more than a hundred laws and regulations have been promulgated during the 1980s that address foreign commercial and economic relations.

Although China's new laws provide a more modern legal setting for FDI, permitting wholly owned affiliates as well as joint ventures, offering patent protection, supporting licensing agreements, and so on, the various provisions are not consistently implemented or, in many cases, simply cannot be fully implemented because of a lack of facilities or abilities on the part of Chinese production and financial systems. In addition, there is a lack of coordination between the central planning agencies and the provincial or local governments in terms of policy objectives and their implementation. The details of central government policy do not lead to implementation procedures that are adequate for local authorities to administer, and many seek to administer them in ways suitable to their own objectives.

Further, China faces a dilemma in establishing a FDI climate in that it started virtually from zero in forming the legislative and legal framework and will continually have to modify it to accord with responses by the foreign enterprises it seeks to attract. The catch–22 aspect of the situation is that the foreign investors want Western-type laws so as to provide greater certainty and stability in their relations with the Chinese government as well as their partners, suppliers, and vendors, plus financial dealings, pricing, and so forth. At the same time, they would like modifications in the laws that make their operations more flexible and free of government intervention. Repeated changes create uncertainty, even if the changes are in the direction sought, and in many cases, the implementing mechanisms are not yet sufficiently in place to carry them out in the manner sought by the foreign investor. Contracts should be drafted as much as possible so as to capture desirable current law while permitting the parties to take advantage of more liberal laws that are enacted at a later date.

The rapid changes and differences among regulations of provinces and cities, for example, will give rise to disputes over "applicable law." Because the settlement of disputes is a necessary part of commercial activities, China has established economic tribunals with the responsibility not only for handling domestic business conflicts, but also for enforcing contracts and settling disputes within joint ventures. The China Council for the Promotion of International Trade was given authority to arbitrate joint venture disputes, and the 1982 Civil Procedure Law supplemented this arbitration by giving authority to China's courts to resolve disputes involving foreign interests.

Joint Venture Law of 1979

Before 1979, Chinese economic legislation was virtually nil, there being no laws on registration of industrial and commercial enterprises (until July 1982), on notarization of documents (until April 1982), on trademark registration and protection (until August 1982), or on contracts (until December 1982). The Joint Venture Law of July 8, 1979, was a recognition of the need to establish rules overtly. But detailed implementing regulations for the law were not released until September of 1983, showing the difficulties that China faces in understanding the problems of implementation. The priority given to foreign joint ventures and the need expressed by foreigners for an appropriate legal framework are reflected in the enactment of more laws relating to them than to any other economic activity during the 1980s.

During the first three years of the 1980s—until September 1983—a number of rules and regulations concerning joint ventures were promulgated covering the protection of foreign investors' resources and profits, limited liability, percentage of capital contribution (from 25 percent to 100 percent by the foreigner), designation of a Chinese citizen as chairman of the board of directors, repatriation of profit, taxation, duration of joint ventures, technology transfers, and arbitration of disputes. These regulations were an attempt to fill the gaps of the law in terms of detailed operations. In September 1983 a new set of "Regulations for the Implementation of the Law on Joint Ventures using Chinese and Foreign Investment" was promulgated containing 118 articles. It addressed such issues as the geographical and industrial sectors in which a joint venture would be permitted or prohibited, technology transfers, the use of land sites and fees to be paid, preferential treatment in customs duties and industrial and commercial taxes, requirements to maintain balance in foreign exchange receipts and payments, and, with some exceptions, duration of the joint ventures from ten to thirty years.

During the next three years, several more laws were passed, including some concerning joint ventures: the Foreign Economic Contract Law (March 1985), the Accounting Regulations of Joint Ventures (March 1985), the Regulations on Problems of Foreign Exchange Balances of Joint Ventures (January 1986), and the Law on the Wholly-owned Foreign Enterprises (April 1986). These laws helped to bring the Chinese legal structure more in line with that of the West, though the content was not always the same as that existing in advanced countries.

These laws stimulated the inflow of substantial investment, rising in 1984 alone by 33 percent over the previous four years' cumulative total, with a further large increase in 1985 (see Chapter 2). The slowdown in 1986 because of foreign exchange difficulties increased foreigners' exasperation at the continuing problems they faced in China. China reacted with further legislative revisions favorable to foreign investors.

"The 22 Articles"

October 1986 brought "the 22 Articles" for "the encouragement of foreign investment." These articles essentially dropped the prior differentiation between wholly owned or joint ventures, but most important, they provided differential incentives to "productive enterprises" that were principally for export and those that were technologically advanced. These were the enterprises that met the Chinese objectives of earning foreign exchange and gaining advanced technology. "Productive enterprises" without significant technology or exports received only part of the benefits given to those in the first category; the "nonproductive enterprises," meaning essentially hotels and services, received even fewer benefits. These twenty-two articles put the important foreign investor on a relatively equal basis with Chinese enterprise—a major change.

The articles include provision for (a) reduced charges for labor through elimination of some of the state subsidies that enterprises have to pay to staff and workers, cutting labor costs by about 20 percent; (b) reduced land-use fees; (c) reduction or exemption from taxes, including tax holidays, half-rate taxes for another three years, and half-rate taxes on enterprises that export 70 percent or more of their product value, plus exemption from the 10 percent profits remittance tax for some firms; (d) guarantees of some of the supply of services such as water, electricity, transportation, and communication equipment; (e) assurance to joint ventures of greater management autonomy; (f) permission to adjust foreign exchange across joint venture enterprises; and (g) reduction of industrial income and commercial taxes and customs duties.

The twenty-two articles required a number of sets of implementing regulations, including many at the local level that supplemented the national legislation. These conferred still other benefits for certain types of foreign investment projects, including exemption from or reduction of taxes or land use fees for stipulated periods, although some regulations, by design or inadvertence, may have reduced the intended benefit. These additional incentives are provided by provinces and cities seeking to attract foreign investment. In fact, some of these localities were in advance of the national government in promulgating rules governing contracts and investment with foreigners.

In summary, these twenty-two articles formalized the resolution of major issues that were inhibiting the establishment of joint ventures and are an example of how the Chinese will take action when their goals are not being achieved. After the flurry of joint ventures in 1984 and early 1985 from the promulgation of the economic reforms requiring Chinese enterprises to earn a profit, joint venture activity slowed significantly. Foreign investors were not satisfied with vague assurances of receiving priorities for supply of raw materials and energy. They were subject to higher land and materials prices than Chinese factories, with whom they might compete in the future, plus with the ever-expanding taxes, it was unclear that a venture could ever earn a profit, especially if the joint venture management was not permitted to decide its production levels and whom to hire and fire. These articles were the key turning point in establishing joint ventures as equal to Chinese enterprises. Because these issues were stopping the Xerox-Shanghai negotiations, Xerox vice-president Shapiro was invited to Shanghai for dinner with the director of foreign investment. At the dinner, the director explained the new regulations and asked if Xerox would now resume negotiations. Foreign reactions to the changes were important enough that the director skipped a dinner in honor of Britain's Queen Elizabeth that evening to accommodate Shapiro's schedule. The Chinese, especially the Shanghai government, are very businesslike.

Still further changes have been under consideration relating to the removal of a fixed duration for joint ventures, elimination of the requirement that a Chinese be chairman, and dropping all ownership restrictions—more evidence of the Chinese willingness to adapt to necessities.

Taxes

Three laws cover taxes applicable to foreigners: the Joint Venture Income Tax Law, an Individual Income Tax Law, and a Foreign Enterprise Income Tax Law, for which there are implementing regulations as well. Under these laws, joint ventures are given some tax incentives offering a full exemption from income tax in the first year in which it makes profits and a 50 percent reduction in the next two years, rather than the combined national and local tax of 33 percent and the flat 10 percent tax on repatriated profits. Subsequent regulations extended the exemption to two years and a 50 percent reduction to three years. A joint venture that reinvests its profits for five consecutive years will obtain a refund of 40 percent of the income tax on the reinvested funds. Other incentives are offered to non–joint venture foreign investments.

Contracts

A law covering domestic economic contracts was promulgated in 1981, providing guidance also for foreign investors (joint ventures, wholly owned ventures, and certain contractual ventures, as well as state enterprises and collectives). In 1985 the Economic Contract Law on foreign investment provided guidance for all kinds of contracts between foreign companies and Chinese institutions, including foreign investment projects. Regulations governing licensing and other contracts covering importation of technology also were promulgated. And some special tax incentives were offered to encourage foreigners to transfer advanced technology on preferential terms to national security industries.

Commercial Law

In the spring of 1986, the General Principles of Civil Law were promulgated covering agency relations, torts, loan agreements, and other commercial relations. A significant portion of the U.S. uniform commercial code was adopted and incorporated into the commercial sections. This is familiar and reassuring to Western businessmen. China also permitted, in another law, the establishment of wholly owned ventures throughout the country; in still other regulations, it established the terms of product liability.

Legalization, in a Western sense, is not yet complete, requiring further laws on service companies in foreign trade and investment, covering copyrights, mortgages, insurance, and banking, plus a law on negotiable instruments. Additional implementing regulations are yet to come on a number of the laws previously promulgated. That for copyrights was issued in 1990, providing for much of the protection sought by Western interests.[4]

Treaties

China has entered into double taxation treaties with more than fifteen countries, including the United States, reducing the withholding tax on fees, interest, and dividends. It also has some bilateral agreements for the "promotion and protection of foreign investments" against political risks, expropriation, and repatriation of earnings. Consular and other agreements for cooperation in specific industries and among various countries also provide a background for investment decisions. Finally, it has accepted membership in the World Industrial Property Organization, and has accepted the obligations of the Paris Convention and the New York Convention, the latter recognizing enforcement of foreign arbitration awards.

Approvals

None of the provisions of the laws offering incentives to joint ventures or foreign investment enterprises apply without specific approval of the basic contractual agreement between the Chinese enterprise and the foreign investor. Approvals are required at all levels of government that are involved in the enterprise activities, and because virtually all of them are in major enterprises, the U.S. investor can expect approvals to be required by agencies of the local, provincial, and national governments. These approvals relate to individual aspects of the contract as well as to the final contract itself, including land sites, plant facilities, rental fees, employment and wages, hiring and firing, labor benefits, taxes and forgiveness thereof, cost and prices, contractual suppliers, foreign exchange availability, profit repatriation, termination of the agreement, duration, and so forth. Virtually every aspect of the contract will be examined and assessed. In addition to required approvals, it often is desirable to seek the approval or concurrence of Chinese agencies or departments that may in later years be required to process certain aspects of the contract. The experience of several joint venture negotiations is instructive of the approval process, which differs in implementation from one project to another both in intensity of assessment and duration and in the activities approved or disapproved.

Bankruptcy

Article 13 of the 1979 Joint Venture Law made provision for early termination of contracts as a result of "heavy losses," "failure to meet obligations," or "force majeure," with the party responsible (if any) bearing the losses. But the People's Republic had no experience with bankruptcy until the late 1980s, since the enterprise has been seen more as an employer of labor than as a profit or efficiency-seeking organism. There was fundamental opposition to the idea of any enterprise ceasing to exist. It was not a matter of a firm failing, but a matter of the resources being used ineffectively and, therefore, requiring new guidance from central planners. Most inefficiencies were merely absorbed in the system. As the country has moved to an orientation of enterprise, the government recognized that bankruptcy was a necessary corrective, so that resources would be moved completely out of an ineffective or inefficient operation.

In August of 1986, an enterprise in Shenyang (northeastern China) was permitted to go bankrupt. It was a small collective enterprise of only eighty workers, but the event signalled a new willingness on the part of the government to permit such failure. The law covering such events, "the Law on Enterprise Bankruptcy," was passed in December 1986, but even then only for trial implementation—a limitation written into the law itself. The law applies only to state enterprises and was contingent on the later passage of a law regulating enterprises "wholly-owned by the People."

The passage of the bankruptcy law was somewhat traumatic, and its implementation is expected to be also. There was considerable disagreement even within the Standing Committee of the National People's Congress, and Western lawyers were consulted on the experience of bankruptcy laws in their countries before final drafting. As of late 1989, the Shenyang firm appeared to be the only true bankruptcy in China.

As with other commercial legislation, the Chinese also assessed their own prior bankruptcy laws (1906 and 1935) and those of the Soviet Union, Hungary, and Yugoslavia. Although these Socialist states have such laws, the Chinese still questioned whether or not bankruptcy was not contradictory to socialism itself, especially since jobs of citizens would be removed. Others questioned the realism of bankruptcy that would in effect be imposed on a company not having real control over its operations. This questioning led to further arguments over appropriate types of ownership and degrees of control given to management. It was finally agreed that failure was needed as a remedy for inefficiency.

Still, the questions arose as to when bankruptcy should occur in a non-market economy, and who would be bankrupt (bear the losses). Efforts to establish fixed ratios that had to be maintained to prevent a declaration of bankruptcy—for example, debt to assets or losses to capital—were soon seen to be inappropriate for the wide range of enterprise activities in the country. Some of the enterprises in vital or strategic industries were known to be operating inefficiently and would not pass such strict ratios. Finally, the criterion for bankruptcy was determined to be that of heavy losses resulting from poor management and leading to inability to pay debts coming due. Before declaration of bankruptcy, enterprises would be warned about their condition, indicating the likelihood of becoming bankrupt and being given a time for turnaround. If the government wanted the enterprise to continue, it would then help the company to pay its debts or provide other subsidies to relieve the pressures. Relief also was provided in the form of a six-month suspension of the declaration of bankruptcy, if the firm could obtain guarantees that its debts would be repaid within six months.

The bankruptcy law originally was intended to cover all enterprises—joint ventures, wholly owned foreign ventures, Sino-foreign cooperative ventures, and so forth. The determination of appropriate criteria and their application made the consideration of such a law too complex, and the law was restricted to the state enterprises. However, some local bankruptcy regulations have been considered relative to foreign enterprises in the Special Economic Zones.

An unusual feature of Chinese law is the responsibility of the "department in charge," which is the government unit that supervises the daily operation of an enterprise. The department in charge can be considered at fault in the bankruptcy, and if so found, the officials in the department who are responsible will be subject to "administrative sanctions," just as the managers of the enterprise will be. (Criminal penalties would be imposed only if fraudulent acts had been committed in the company.) Otherwise, there are no personal penalties for bankruptcy. The importance of selecting the appropriate department in charge at the outset of negotiations is discussed elsewhere in these chapters.

So as not to leave workers destitute from bankruptcy of a firm, unemployment insurance is provided so that workers so laid off will receive 50 percent to 75 percent of prior wages for two years, the benefits to be funded by employers through contributions of 1 percent of their total wage bill. Despite the attention given to the possibility of bankruptcy, virtually none have been recorded, save the one in Shenyang.

NOTES

1. See V. H. Li, *Law Without Lawyers: A Comparative View of Law in China and the United States* (Boulder, Colo.: Westview, 1978), for a short but cogent review of attitudes.

2. *Beijing Review*, August 17, 1979.

3. See Pitman Potter, ''Bettering Protection for Intellectual Property,'' *China Business Review*, July–August 1989.

4. Peter A. Schloss, ''China's Long-awaited Copyright Law,'' *China Business Review*, September–October 1990.

Appendix A:
Joint Venture Law of July 8, 1979

ARTICLE 1

With a view to expanding international economic cooperation and technological exchange, the People's Republic of China permits foreign companies, enterprises, other economic entities or individuals (hereinafter referred to as foreign participants) to incorporate themselves, within the territory of the People's Republic of China, into joint ventures with Chinese companies, enterprises, or other economic entities (hereinafter referred to as Chinese participants) on the principle of equality and mutual benefit and subject to authorization by the Chinese government.

ARTICLE 2

The Chinese government protects, by the legislation in force, the resources invested by a foreign participant in a joint venture and the profits due him pursuant to the agreements, contracts, and articles of association authorized by the Chinese government as well as his other lawful rights and interests.

All the activities of a joint venture shall be governed by the laws, decrees, and pertinent rules and regulations of the People's Republic of China.

ARTICLE 3

A joint venture shall apply to the Foreign Investment Commission of the People's Republic of China for authorization of the agreements and contracts concluded between the parties to the venture and the articles of association of the venture formulated by them, and the commission shall authorize or reject these documents within three months. When authorized, the joint venture shall register with the General Administration for Industry and Commerce of the People's Republic of China and start operations under license.

ARTICLE 4

A joint venture shall take the form of a limited liability company.

In the registered capital of a joint venture, the proportion of the investment contributed by the foreign participant(s) shall in general not be less than 25 percent.

The profits, risks, and losses of a joint venture shall be shared by the parties to the venture in proportion to their contributions to the registered capital.

The transfer of one party's share in the registered capital shall be effected only with the consent of the other parties to the venture.

ARTICLE 5

Each party to a joint venture may contribute cash, capital goods, industrial property rights, etc., as its investment in the venture.

The technology or equipment contributed by any foreign participant as investment shall be truly advanced and appropriate to China's needs. In cases of losses caused by deception through the intentional provision of outdated equipment or technology, compensation shall be paid for the losses.

The investment contributed by a Chinese participant may include the right to use of a site provided for the joint venture during the period of its operation. In case such a contribution does not constitute a part of the investment from the Chinese participant, the joint venture shall pay the Chinese government for its use.

The various contributions referred to in the present article shall be specified in the contracts concerning the joint venture or in its articles of association, and the value of each contribution (excluding that of the site) shall be ascertained by the parties to the venture through joint assessment.

ARTICLE 6

A joint venture shall have a board of directors with a composition stipulated in the contracts and the articles of association after consultation between the parties to the venture, and each director shall be appointed or removed by his own side. The board of directors shall have a chairman appointed by the Chinese participant and one of two vice chairmen appointed by the foreign participant(s). In handling an important problem, the board of directors shall reach decision through consultation by the participants on the principle of equality and mutual benefit.

The board of directors is empowered to discuss and take action on, pursuant to the provisions of the articles of association of the joint venture, all fundamental issues concerning the venture; namely, expansion projects, production and business programs, the budget, distribution of profits, plans concerning manpower and pay scales, the termination of business, the appointment or hiring of the president, the vice president(s), the chief engineer, the treasurer, and the auditors, as well as their functions and powers and their remuneration, etc. The president and vice president(s) (or the general manager(s) in a factory) shall be chosen from the various parties to the joint venture.

Procedures covering the employment and discharge of the workers and staff members of a joint venture shall be stipulated according to law in the agreement or contract concluded between the parties to the venture.

ARTICLE 7

The net profit of a joint venture shall be distributed between the parties to the venture in proportion to their respective shares in the registered capital after the payment of a joint venture income tax on its gross profit pursuant to the tax laws of the People's Republic of China and after the deductions therefrom as stipulated in the articles of association of the venture for the reserve funds, the bonus and welfare funds for the workers and staff members, and the expansion funds of the venture.

A joint venture equipped with up-to-date technology by world standards may apply for a reduction of, or exemption from, income tax for the first two to three profit-making years.

A foreign participant who reinvests any part of his share of the net profit within Chinese territory may apply for the restitution of a part of the income taxes paid.

ARTICLE 8

A joint venture shall open an account with the Bank of China or a bank approved by the Bank of China.

A joint venture shall conduct its foreign exchange transactions in accordance with the foreign exchange regulations of the People's Republic of China.

A joint venture may, in its business operations, obtain funds from foreign banks directly.

The insurances appropriate to a joint venture shall be furnished by Chinese insurance companies.

ARTICLE 9

The production and business programs of a joint venture shall be filed with the authorities concerned and shall be implemented through business contracts.

In its purchase of required raw and semiprocessed materials, fuels, auxiliary equipment, etc., a joint venture should give first priority to Chinese sources. It may also acquire them directly from the world market with its own foreign-exchange funds.

A joint venture is encouraged to market its products outside China. It may distribute its export products in foreign markets through direct channels or its associated agencies or China's foreign trade establishments. Its products may also be distributed on the Chinese market.

Wherever necessary, a joint venture may set up affiliated agencies outside China.

ARTICLE 10

The net profit which a foreign participant receives as his share after executing his obligations under the pertinent laws and agreements and contracts, the funds he receives at the time when the joint venture terminates or winds up its operations, and his other funds, may be remitted abroad through the Bank of China in accordance with the foreign-exchange regulations and in the currency or currencies specified in the contracts concerning the joint venture.

A foreign participant shall receive encouragements for depositing in the Bank of China any part of the foreign exchange which he is entitled to remit aborad.

ARTICLE 11

The wages, salaries, or other legitimate income earned by a foreign worker or staff member of a joint venture, after payment of the personal income tax under the tax laws of the People's Republic of China, may be remitted abroad through the Bank of China in accordance with the foreign exchange regulations.

ARTICLE 12

The contract period of a joint venture may be agreed upon between the parties to the venture according to its particular line of business and circumstances. The period may be extended upon expiration through agreement between the parties, subject to authorization by the foreign investment commission of the People's Republic of China. Any application for such extension shall be made six months before the expiration of the contract.

ARTICLE 13

In cases of heavy losses, the failure of any party to a joint venture to execute its obligations under the contracts or the articles of association of the venture, force majeure, etc., prior to the expiration of the contract period of a joint venture, the contract may be terminated before the date of expiration by consultation and agreement between the parties and through authorization by the foreign investment commission of the People's Republic of China and registration with the General Administration for Industry and Commerce. In cases of losses caused by breach of the contracts by a party to the venture, the financial responsibility shall be borne by the said party.

ARTICLE 14

Disputes arising between the parties to a joint venture, which the board of directors fails to settle through consultation, may be settled through conciliation or arbitration by an arbitral body of China or through arbitration by an arbitral body agreed upon by the parties.

ARTICLE 15

The present law comes into force on the date of its promulgation. The power of amendment is vested in the National People's Congress.

Appendix B:
Provisions of the State Council for the Encouragement of Foreign Investment

(Promulgated on October 11, 1986)

ARTICLE 1

These Provisions are hereby formulated in order to improve the investment environment, facilitate the absorption of foreign investment, introduce advanced technology, improve product quality, expand exports in order to generate foreign exchange and develop the national economy.

ARTICLE 2

The State encourage foreign companies, enterprises and other economic entities or individuals (hereinafter referred to as "Foreign Investors") to establish Chinese-foreign equity joint ventures, Chinese-foreign cooperative ventures and wholly foreign-owned enterprises (hereinafter referred to as "Enterprises with Foreign Investment") within the territory of China.

The State grants special preferences to the Enterprises with Foreign Investment listed below:

1. Production enterprises whose products are mainly for export, which have a foreign exchange surplus after deducting from their total annual foreign exchange revenues the annual foreign exchange expenditures incurred in production and operation and the foreign exchange needed for the remittance abroad of the profits earned by Foreign Investors (hereinafter referred to as "Export Enterprises").

2. Production enterprises possessing advanced technology supplied by Foreign Investors which are engaged in developing new products, and upgrading and replacing products in order to increase foreign exchange generated by exports or for import substitution (hereinafter referred to as "Technologically Advanced Enterprises").

ARTICLE 3

Export Enterprises and Technologically Advanced Enterprises shall be exempt from payment to the State of all subsidies to staff and workers, except for the payment of or allocation of funds for labor insurance, welfare costs and housing subsidies for Chinese staff and workers in accordance with the provisions of the State.

ARTICLE 4

The site use fees for Export Enterprises and Technologically Advanced Enterprise, except for those located in bury urban sectors of large cities, shall be computed and charged according to the following standards.

1. Five to twenty RMB per square meter per year in areas where the development fee and the site use fee are computed and charged together;

2. Not more than three RMB per square meter per year in site areas where the development fee is computed and charged one a one-time basis or areas which are developed by the above-mentioned enterprises themselves.

Exemptions for specified periods of time from the fees provided in the foregoing provisions may be granted at the discretion of local people's governments.

ARTICLE 5

Export Enterprises and Technologically Advanced Enterprises shall be given priority in obtaining water, electricity and transportation services, and communication facilities needed for their production and operation. Fees shall be computed and charged in accordance with the standards for local state enterprises.

ARTICLE 6

Export Enterprises and Technologically Advanced Enterprises, after examination by the Bank of China, shall be given priority in receiving loans for short-term revolving funds needed for production and distribution, as well as for other needed credit.

ARTICLE 7

When Foreign Investors in Export Enterprises and Technologically Advanced Enterprises remit abroad profits distributed to them by such enterprises, the amount remitted shall be exempt from income tax.

ARTICLE 8

After the expiration of the period for the reduction or exemption of enterprise income tax in accordance with the provisions of the State, Export Enterprises whose value of export products in that year amounts to 70% or more of the value of their products for that year, may pay enterprise income tax at one-half the rate of the present tax.

Export Enterprises in the special economic zones and in the economic and technological development zones and other Export Enterprises that already pay enterprise income tax at a tax rate of 15% anbd that comply with the foregoing conditions, shall pay enterprise income tax at a rate of 10%.

ARTICLE 9

After the expiration of the period or reduction or exemption of enterprixe income tax in accordance with the provisions of the State, Technologically Advanced Enterprises may extend for three years the payment of enterprise income tax at a rate reduced by one-half.

ARTICLE 10

Foreign Investors who reinvest the profits distributed to them by their enterprises in order to establish or expand Export Enterprises or Technologically Advanced Enterprises for a period of operation of not less than five years, after application to and approval by the tax authorities, shall be refunded the total amount of enterprise income tax already paid on the reinvested portion. If the investment is withdrawn before the period of operation reaches five years, the amount of enterprise income tax refunded shall be repaid.

ARTICLE 11

Export products of Enterprises with Foreign Investment, except crude oil, finished oil and other products subject to State provisions, shall be exempt from the Consolidated Industrial and Commercial Tax.

ARTICLE 12

Enterprises with Foreign Investment may arrange the export of their products directly or may also export by consignment to agents in accordance with State provisions, for products that require an export license, in accordance with the annual export plan of the enterprise, and application of an export license may be made every six months.

ARTICLE 13

Machinery and equipment, vehicles used in production, raw materials, fuel, bulk parts, spare parts, machine component parts and fittings, (including imports restricted by the State) which Enterprises with Foreign Investment need to import in order to carry out their export contracts do not require further applications for examination and approval and are exempt from the requirements for import licenses. The customs department shall exercise supervision and control, and shall inspect and release such imports on the basis of the enterprise contract or the export contract.

The imported materials and items mentioned above are restricted to use by the enterprise and may not be sold on the domestic market. If they are used in products to be sold domestically, import procedures shall be handled in accordance with provisions and the taxes shall be made up according to the governing sections.

ARTICLE 14

Under the supervision of the foreign exchange control departments, Enterprises with Foreign Investment may mutually adjust their foreign exchange surpluses and deficiencies among each other.

The Bank of China and other banks designated by the People's Bank of China may provide cash security services and may grant loans in Renminbi to Enterprises with Foreign Investment to Enterprises with Foreign Investment

ARTICLE 15

The people's governments at all levels and relevant departments in charge shall guarantee the right of autonomy of Enterprises with Foreign Investment and shall support Enterprises with Foreign Investment in managing themselves in accordance with international advanced scientific methods.

Within the scope of their approved contracts, Enterprises with Foreign Investment have the right by themselves to determine production and operation plans, to raise funds, to use funds, to purchase production materials and to sell products; and to determine by themselves the wage levels, the forms of wages and bonuses and the allowance system.

Enterprises with Foreign Investment may, in accordance with their production and operation requirements, determine by themselves their organizational structure and personnel system, employ or dismiss senior management personnel, increase or dismiss staff and workers.

They may recruit and employ technical personnel, managerial personnel and workers in their locality. The unit to which such employed personnel belong shall provide its support and shall permit their transfer. Staff and workers who violate the rules and regulations, and thereby cause certain bad consequences may, in accordance with the seriousness of the case, be given differing sanctions, up to that of discharge. Enterprises with Foreign Investment that recruit, employ, dismiss or discharge staff and workers, shall file a report with the local labor and personnel department.

ARTICLE 16

All districts and departments must implement the Circular of the State Council Concerning Firmly Curbing the Indiscriminate Levy of Charges on Enterprises. The people's governments at the provincial level shall formulate specific methods and strengthen supervision and administration.

Enterprises with Foreign Investment that encounter unreasonable charges may refuse to pay and may also appeal to the local economic committees up to the State Economic Commission.

ARTICLE 17

The people's governments at all levels and relevant departments in charge shall strengthen the coordination of their work, improve efficiency in handling matters and shall promptly examine and approve matters reported by Enterprises with Foreign Investment that require response and resolution. The agreement, contract and articles of association of an Enterprise with Foreign Investment shall be examined and approved by the departments in charge under the State Council. The examination and approval authority must within three months from the date of receipt of all documents decide to approve or not to approve them.

ARTICLE 18

Export Enterprises and Technologically Advanced Enterprises mentioned in these Provisions shall be confirmed jointly as such by the foreign economic relations and trade departments where such enterprises are located and the relevant departments in accordance with the enterprise contract, and certification shall be issued.

If the actual results of the annual exports of an Export Enterprise are unable to realize the goal of the surplus in the foreign exchange balance that is stipulated in the enterprise contract, the taxes and fees which have already been reduced or exempted in the previous year shall be made up in the following year.

ARTICLE 19

Except where these Provisions expressly provide that they are to be applicable to Export Enterprises or Technologically Advanced Enterprises, other articles shall be applicable to all Enterprises with Foreign Investment.

These Provisions apply from the date of implementation to those Enterprises with Foreign Investment that have obtained approval for establishment before the date of implementation of these Provisions and that qualify for the preferential terms of these Provisions.

ARTICLE 20

For enterprises invested in and established by companies, enterprises and other economic organizations or individuals from Hong Kong, Macoa, or Taiwan, matters shall be handled by reference to these Provisions.

ARTICLE 21

The Ministry of Foreign Economic Relations and Trade shall be responsible for interpreting these Provisions.

ARTICLE 22

These Provisions shall go into effect on the date of issue.

7

Decision-Making and Markets

The predominant attraction of China for foreign direct investment (FDI) is entry into a potentially huge domestic market of over one billion people. But markets are more than people; otherwise, the developing countries would be the world's largest buyers. China's market is distinctive in the predominant role of the government as both buyer and seller and, therefore, the "maker of the market." Although the government is trying to ease out of this role, it will remain a dominant player in the market for a long time. But more open markets will increase the already existing diversity in consumer patterns throughout China.

CONSUMPTION PATTERNS

Since the opening of China to FDI, Western companies have tried, with only limited success, to break into the potentially huge domestic consumer market. They have been tantalized by the often repeated statement that "our doors are open wide and will be open wider in the future"; yet, when discussions begin, Chinese officials have constantly downplayed the prospect of access to this market, emphasizing their desire for export-oriented, high-technology ventures. The existence of a dual currency system—renminbi (RMB) and foreign exchange certificates—has effectively separated the domestic and foreign markets, permitting the government to select which foreign products are sold domestically and which domestic (or joint venture) products must be exported. This system will probably be retained until the yuan can be made internationally convertible (i.e., when exports exceed imports).

There are, however, indications that China is finally beginning to open its domestic market to Western companies. In the late 1980s, several Western companies—including Coca-Cola, Procter and Gamble, Bausch and Lomb,

Table 7.1
Average Annual Increase in Consumption Levels (Percentages)

Years	Rural	Urban
1953-57	3.2	4.8
1958-62	-3.3	-5.2
1963-65	8.2	12.3
1966-70	2.5	2.1
1971-75	1.3	4.2
1976-80	4.1	4.9
1981-85	10.1	5.6

Source: Statistical Yearbook of China, 1986, (Beijing), p.557.

Johnson & Johnson, Gillette, McCormick, RJR-Nabisco, S. C. Johnson, and Seagram—concluded drawn-out negotiations to establish ventures that are aimed at the domestic market.[1]

For the Western company seeking access to the domestic market, it is important to understand that consumption patterns differ considerably throughout China by region and by income, the latter less significantly than the former.

Regional Differences

The implementation of domestic economic reforms in China between 1978 and 1985 resulted in substantial increases in per capita incomes—15 percent in rural and 9 percent in urban areas after inflation.[2] Chinese statistics show national income per capita increasing (in *current* yuan) from 235 yuan in 1957 to 389 in 1965, to 1,045 in 1978, and to 3,034 in 1988. Peasant income in 1988 was RMB 545 on average, up 6.3 percent from the year before, while per capita disposable income of urban residents was RMB 1,119, up 1.2 percent from the prior year.

Consequently consumption levels have risen to levels not seen since the period immediately after the Great Leap Forward. Table 7.1 shows that urban consumption levels increased significantly more than rural consumption levels. The pattern changed after the introduction of reforms in the rural sector in 1978 (see Table 7.2), but the weakness of distribution channels to the rural areas presents a formidable barrier to gaining access to rural markets and the 80 percent of the Chinese population predominantly served by those markets. Furthermore, as Table 7.2 shows, the gains made by the rural sector have slowed and even reversed relative to the urban sector since 1985, as the pace and vitality of agricultural reforms have lessened.

In 1989, Chinese consumers spent 810 billion yuan on the retail sales of

Table 7.2
Rural and Urban Consumption, Various Years (Yuan per capita, 1988 prices)

Year	Rural	Urban	Ratio Rural:Urban
1952	62	148	1:2.4
1958	83	195	1:2.3
1965	100	237	1:2.4
1978	132	383	1:2.9
1979	152	406	1:2.7
1980	173	468	1:2.7
1981	194	487	1:2.5
1982	212	500	1:2.4
1983	235	523	1:2.2
1984	268	592	1:2.2
1985	324	754	1:2.3
1986	353	851	1:2.4
1987	394	979	1:2.5
1988	482	1238	1:2.6

Source: Statistical Yearbook of China, 1986, (Beijing) p.556; China Statistical Abstract, 1988, p. 90, (adapted) (Series Ed. William T. Liu, N.Y.: Praeger, 1989.)

"social commodities." This level, although actually lower than the figures reported for 1988, still represented the purchasing power (in urban areas) of a country with a per capita income equivalent of US $3,000. By 1990, roughly half of the urban populace in China had television sets and refrigerators, with more than 80 percent possessing these appliances in the cities of Beijing, Tianjin, Shanghai, and Guangzhou.[3] Just as it is important to distinguish between rural and urban markets, it is important to note the different regional markets. First, the municipalities with provincial status (Beijing, Tianjin, and Shanghai) have the highest consumption levels—two to three times those in the poorer regions. Second, the coastal provinces (for example, Liaoning and Jilin in the northeast, the central coastal provinces of Jiangsu and Zhejiang, and the southern coastal province of Guangdong) have levels of consumption even in their rural areas substantially larger than those in interior provinces.[4] This pattern is not surprising, given their relatively high levels of economic performance, their historically strong industrial base, and the differentially favorable treatment by Beijing to enhance economic progress and attract FDI.[5] Third, provinces and autonomous regions (such as Tibet, Quinghai, and Xinjiang, all in the extreme west of China) ostensibly have high consumption levels (particularly in the urban areas) but are in fact areas with very small markets and among the poorest in China.[6]

"Eight Big Things"

The growing importance of material items and their associated consumption patterns also are reflected in changes in major imports. During 1970–1977, consumer products were not among the top ten gainers or in the bottom ten losers in import volume, but among the consumer products that did gain were audiotapes and CDs, books, cameras, clocks, handbags and luggage, toiletries, and watches. This same group was among the major declining categories in 1977–1985. Another group gained throughout the two periods for nearly a decade and a half: autos and taxis, cigarettes, domestic electrical appliances, furniture, radios, televisions, and toys and games. (The last category was probably related to the one-child phenomenon in which there are four grandparents and two parents to dote on one grandchild, raising a common concern that they are being so spoiled that future generations of Chinese will be "grown-up brats.") The change is dramatic from industrial products to sophisticated consumer goods.

Under Chairman Mao, Chinese consumers dreamed of buying the "three big things"—a bicycle, a wristwatch, and a sewing machine. By the early 1980s the "three big things" were a refrigerator, a washing machine, and a television set. By the late 1980s demand had burgeoned to encompass "eight big things"— a refrigerator, a color television, a radio-cassette player, a sewing machine, a bicycle, a washing machine, an electric fan, and a wristwatch, and increasingly, the bicycle is giving way to the motorbike or motorcycle. Different parts of the country show differing demands (e.g., a fan in the south, a videocassette recorder in the north, or a camera instead of a radio-cassette player); the list grows and is different among generations, with the younger generation adding a microwave oven, jewelry (18-karat gold), an apartment, and fine furniture. Clear signs of this consumerism are evident in the major cities of China, but because this development is viewed by many Chinese conservatives as unwanted Western materialism, it may well be tempered in the aftermath of the Tiananmen student marches.

Rural China, although not completely excluded from this consumer boom, remains a difficult market to reach, as Table 7.3 demonstrates. Furthermore, the variations in the volume of consumption and the nature of the products consumed are notable as one goes north from Hong Kong along the coast of China. The southernmost cities are much more open and consume more along patterns of Western styles and entertainment. The more northern cities are more conservative and less flamboyant in their consumer patterns. At all latitudes, moving east to west, one finds greater conservatism as well, with the northwest being the least "modern." Finally, although it is expected that the proportion of Chinese income spent on food will fall by the end of the century, food expenditures will continue to consume about half of a Chinese income.

Western firms can expect to see some increase in consumption levels, though this may not result in the "billion consumer" market originally envisaged (misguidedly) by some firms.[7] Still, the amounts of Western goods (either imports

Table 7.3
Ownership of Durable Consumer Goods per 100 Households

| | 1980/1981 | | 1985 | | 1988 | |
	Rural	Urban	Rural	Urban	Rural	Urban
Bicycles	37	136	81	152	108	178
Sewing mach.	23	70	43	71	52	71
Radios	34	101	54	74	52	49
Wrist watches	38	241	126	275	169	294
TVs (blk/wh.)	1	57	12	67	29	59*
TVs (color)	-	1	-	17	3	44

* Apparent switch into color TVs.

Source: China Statistical Abstract, 1988, p. 95 (adapted) (Series Ed. William T. Liu; N.Y.: Praeger, 1989.)

or domestically produced in joint ventures) being sold on the domestic market will probably increase.

DECISION-MAKING

One of the most frustrating aspects of new market entry is the difficulty of understanding the system of decision-making in purchasing. Such decisions in China are made on both economic and political bases, reflecting not only the influences of culture, but also an institutional structure that is substantially different from that of the West.

Western business people commonly assume that other economic systems make decisions as they do, based on a belief in the virtues of market competition in achieving efficiency and in the desirability of profit as a measure of efficiency and as a means of future growth. These assumptions are ethnocentric, representing the relatively brief experience of Western European nations and the even briefer American experience. Some aspects of the market system also extend into the global marketplace. Even the Chinese, who were not so long ago the most vociferous ideological opponents of this decision-making system, are now partially adopting it.[8] Nonetheless, despite this appearance of "convergence," there remain important and often "invisible" differences in the assumptions underlying decision-making, and in the extent of application of and response to free market signals. These differences, when not understood, make the Chinese system appear illogical or irrational to the foreigner.

In addition, the bureaucratic environment in which Chinese enterprises operate produces a multitude of decision-makers, outside of any enterprises that are still involved in purchase and investment decisions. The involvement of such groups lengthens the negotiation and decision-making process. Even the composition of negotiating teams changes frequently, so that it is never clear who makes what decisions (see Chapter 10). This often is a direct result of the complexity of the Chinese decision-making system, in which many of the "new faces" (who usually are not introduced) on the Chinese team from time to time represent individuals or administrative units that are involved in different phases of operations affected by the supplies sought or the project under consideration.

To appreciate the context in which decision-making and economic rationality are exercised in China, several characteristics and factors need to be understood: China remains a developing country despite its size and power; it places a high premium on security; it seeks self-reliance; it sees the world as a zero-sum game (as do feudalistic or mercantilistic systems); it fails to recognize opportunity costs; and it has a complex mixture of hierarchical, horizontal, and dispersed decision systems.

China as a Developing Country

The fact that China is a developing country is the foremost determinant of economic patterns in the economy. The World Bank ranked China as the eighteenth poorest country in the world in 1987, in terms of per capita gross national product. China also remains a centrally planned socialist economy, and one strongly affected by egalitarian ideals. The drive to equality has, in the past, diverted resources away from investment in the basic infrastructure necessary to provide a foundation for a national market and to foster economic integration of the country.

Despite attempts to take advantage of socialist cooperation, most decisions have remained locally oriented—even those taken centrally. The system of central planning has fractured into planning by diverse ministries and industrial departments. Consequently deficiencies of infrastructure (communications, transportation, and energy) continue to frustrate Chinese development, affecting its ability to absorb new products and technology. Chinese-American businessman C. B. Sung, president of Unison, Inc., and long experienced with China, has cautioned:

It is important to recognize that there is a difference between what the Chinese can understand and what they can use. If you are selling technology to the Chinese, sell them technology which can be used, not technology that they can understand. They can understand anything, but are much more limited in what they can use.[9]

The geographical size of China's potential market exacerbates its infrastructure deficiencies. China is the largest developing country and the third largest geographically in the world (behind the USSR and the United States), stretching infrastructure needs far beyond what it is able to afford. It is, therefore, difficult to implement collaborative and synchronized actions across the Chinese economy. Thus the development of a national "China market," with attendant economies of scale in production and distribution, has been frustrated by its continued underdevelopment.

Security

Personal and family security remain the top priorities in economic motivations in China, stemming from the long tie to the land and reflected in the social security guarantees that have been made to the populace by the Communist government. When this works through the industrial enterprise, sapping its inclination for efficiency, the result is what the Chinese refer to as the "iron rice bowl." Guaranteed employment has affected income distribution and, consequently, consumer spending, both in amount and in composition. The family is the primary economic unit and remains the principal buyer, and despite the Communist effort to break up this unit, it remains so even under state ownership: "The dominant motive of workers in every Chinese state-owned enterprise is to maximize their family income and benefits."[10] The family unit historically provided economic security for its members, but families also lead to high inequalities in income and wealth and even in economic opportunities. To break up this unit in favor of "socialist equality," the government had to offer security through jobs for all and a guaranteed income for a basic "standard of living." In fact, one of the primary differences between Western and Chinese enterprises is the strong concept of the "employment provider" that is felt by the Chinese manager compared with the ideas of efficiency that are more typically associated with Western firms.[11]

Many consequences flow from such attitudes; among them is the reluctance of Chinese enterprises to engage in any innovative effort that might result in the loss of jobs either in that enterprise or in other enterprises that are associated with it and that often serve as a source of employment for other members of the (extended) family. The willingness of the government to break the "iron rice bowl" is highly unsettling to workers and bureaucrats alike, changing their orientations to security of income and thereby to consumption patterns.

Self-Reliance

The concept of communal self-reliance remains extremely important in understanding Chinese economic decision-making. The tradition of family and community self-reliance within the Chinese economy has been a source of frustration of recent efforts to eliminate or reduce economic redundancy, achieve economies of scale, and establish national markets. The concept of self-reliance does not extend down to the individual, who is to be protected and supported by the group to which he contributes and belongs. These attitudes have long cultural roots that made them extremely resistant to the efforts by the Communist regime to eliminate them and substitute larger collective associations.

In fact, the development of Communism reinforced this self-reliance. During the Civil War between the Chinese Communists and the Kuomintang, the Communists established enclaves (surrounded by Kuomintang forces) that served as their bases for revolutionary action. These border areas were self-contained, and took on all of the administrative and economic responsibilities of an economic system. In their isolation, the Communists were, of necessity, self-reliant. After the war, many of the enclaves' military commanders became public administrators. They carried with them an appreciation for the importance of doing everything within a closed group to achieve security.

A second recent reason for the acceptance of self-reliance was the Sino-Soviet split in 1959 and the widespread belief among Chinese leaders that the Soviet Union was willing to entertain a preemptive nuclear strike against them. As a means of reducing the vulnerability of China to such attack, Mao Zedong accepted the creation of significant redundancy within the economy—a "defense in depth" by "compartmentalizing" the economy to resist outside invasion. One of the legacies of this period are the "third-line" factories, which are still spread throughout the country, often in seemingly incongruous locations. This placement of productive resources for a defensive strategy has added to the fractionation of the economy and made it more difficult to establish nationwide linkages.

A third reason for self-reliance—and the one that carries the most weight today—is the recognition among many industrial managers that the Chinese industrial system simply cannot provide the degree of supplier dependability that a modern economy requires, particularly if the supplier is geographically distant. As a remedy for such inadequacies, the astute manager attempts to control as much of the system as possible, even to the extent of doing everything himself— being self-reliant—rather than entering into dependencies with other organizations outside of his control. Again, distribution links became seriously diverted from "efficiency" patterns.

Zero-sum Games

Another major departure from the assumptions underlying Western decision-making (i.e., from efficiency and, ironically, even from the Socialist goal of collective welfare) is the widespread view of the Chinese economy as a zero-sum game. Under this view, no one gains without some other entity suffering a commensurate loss. Such a world view is destructive of attempts at collaboration or partnership; but despite forty years of Socialist rhetoric, it remains a perspective held by almost any decision-maker within the Chinese economy. Patterns of enterprise purchasing and inventory retention are directly affected.

The reasons for the widespread acceptance of a zero-sum mentality within Chinese society are complex and varied. Traditionally, it arose out of an economy of scarcity and remained so even under the Communist regime. In addition, central planning typically provides only one primary source of resources for an enterprise, and the success of an enterprise depends on its gaining resources due it, despite scarcities.

There also is a traditional distrust within Chinese society for the types of economic cooperation that are associated with win-win strategies. This has been noted by a number of students of Chinese society,[12] including Max Weber.[13]

The zero-sum mentality is a compelling inducement for Chinese enterprises to become interested in a potential joint venture partner, to increase their options. Conversely, the same attitude leads to a resistance to "significant" success or profits for the partner, since this can be perceived as gained at the expense of the Chinese.

In one particular case that we are familiar with, the Chinese partner (which was assigned to the joint venture by the local government) perceived itself threatened by the joint venture; its acting on the basis of a zero-sum mentality left the venture a failure.

Absence of Opportunity and Opportunity Costs

Along with central planning and the vertical segmentation of the economy, through isolated ministries, came a reduction in the opportunities available to Chinese enterprises. Chinese enterprises were prevented both by the planners and by industrial administrators from expanding into new businesses or new geographical markets. They could not obtain the necessary resources, capital equipment, or labor skills to produce and sell new products; they could not access distribution systems that were geographically remote; they could not overcome local tendencies toward self-reliance and protectionism; nor could they spend their retained earnings in a manner that they chose. Thus they had little or no control over their own destiny, and as a result, the Chinese enterprise still resembles a single product line "cash cow," with little or no incentive or ability to diversify. Thus, for all intents and purposes, the enterprise has not faced opportunity costs; no recognizable next-best alternative existed. Therefore, alternative demand did not exist, and purchases followed the prescribed pattern from the prescribed suppliers at the prescribed prices. The emerging possibilities of market choices will undoubtedly be unsettling for enterprises, but they will open opportunities to sellers and opportunity costs to enterprises.

Hierarchical Decision Structures

The Chinese economic system can be thought of as a vertical system that stretches down from the industrial ministries, which are responsible to members of the State Council; through provincial and municipal bureaus, which are the local analogues and administrative representatives of the ministries; through provincial and municipal companies, which represent the division of specialized interests within the bureaus; to the enterprise. An example of such a vertical "slice" of the economic system might be light industry (see Figure 7.1).

Figure 7.1
Organization of Industrial Science and Technology Activities in the People's Republic

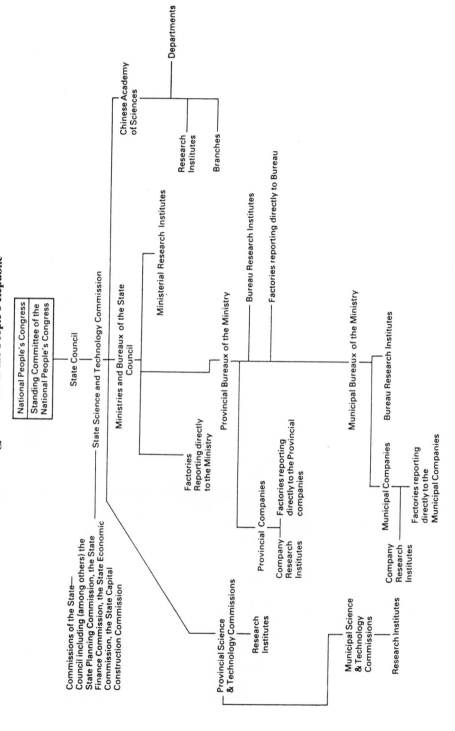

The Ministry of Light Industry reports to the State Council, which is the supreme planning agency. Directly below the ministry are the provincial units, for example the Liaoning Light Industry Bureau. The provincial bureau is guided by the ministry in technical matters and by the provincial government in administrative matters, ensuring that the ministry's requirements are met from appropriate factories and that the province's requirements are obtained from local factories. In major municipalities, there are local bureaus—for example, the Dalian Light Industry Bureau—functioning in the same manner as the provincial bureau. Sometimes conflicts between these authorities have seriously interfered with enterprise effectiveness. For example, reductions in direct requirements placed on the factories by the ministries as a result of decentralization may be offset by increased requirements from provincial and municipal governments. Thus greater discretion offered to the enterprise by the ministries is reduced by local authorities.

The responsibilities of a light industry bureau are too broad for effective management. Each bureau is thus subdivided into ''companies'' that represent and are responsible for major segments of activity, such as a product line. Thus underneath the Liaoning or Dalian Light Industry Bureau is a Liaoning (or Dalian) Bicycle Company, which is responsible for organizing and managing all of the bicycle production and distribution in the appropriate area. Below these companies are the enterprises that actually produce and sell bicycles. These enterprises tend to have a single product line focus, reflecting nearly four decades of strong constraints on what the enterprise could do.

Each of the layers in this slice of the economic system represents a possible decision-maker who must review, if not decide on, important issues, especially those relating to purchasing, production, and distribution. The number of the levels of the hierarchy that become involved with any particular decision is typically a function of the amount of resources (especially financial resources) that are involved. Depending on the amount of capital involved, plus the province in which the enterprise is located and the industry it is in, the locus of decision-making will be closer either to the enterprise or to the ministry in the economic hierarchy.

There also are cross-ministry disagreements on their ''turf'' or responsibilities. CATIC (China Aero Technology Import Corporation), a large import-export organization, wanted to develop a joint venture to produce the Xerox 2500 engineering-drawer copier. CATIC had been given the responsibility for engineering-drawing equipment by the aerospace ministry, but after a number of discussions between CATIC and Xerox, Xerox was informed by a section of the light industry ministry that they were to cease discussions with CATIC because copiers were the domain of the light industry group. Although never stated specifically, the indication was clear that continued discussions would impact the Xerox-Shanghai discussions for an office copier joint venture. CATIC told Xerox that they were fully authorized to conduct discussions on the engineering-drawing copiers, and they wanted to continue discussions, since the dispute was an internal Chinese matter. CATIC also was a good Xerox customer, and annually purchased a significant number of products for use in their 200 factories. In summary, there often are internal bureaucratic jurisdictional disputes between the ministries and bureaus that can slow decision-making and yet normally are never surfaced to the foreigner.

In addition, if the investment requires new capital construction, as well as technology, approval must come from the relevant planning commissions. And if new technological directions will result from this investment (i.e., state of the art innovation), approvals also must be obtained from the appropriate science and technology commissions. Then, to obtain an investment loan from the banking system, approvals from it will be required. The time and effort involved in getting even the most straightforward decision through the myriad bureaucratic levels can be considerable.

Horizontal Decision Structures

In many ways the Chinese decision system resembles a large matrix organization. The vertical columns cover decisions and resources for the technical endeavors of the system, whereas the horizontal rows carry instructions and resources for satisfying local needs. The organizations responsible for vertical relations also have horizontal claims on the system. The provincial or municipal bureau, for example, is not only a representative of the ministry in terms of allocation of quotas and resources, but also an organ of local government, responsible for satisfying local production and employment needs from the factories and work units under its jurisdiction (see Figure 7.1). The complexity and potential confusion of such a system have been described by the joint study group of the World Bank and the Chinese Academy of Social Science:

Until it was recentralized in late 1983, Shenyang Smelting Plant was under the Ministry of Metallurgy for raw materials and distribution of output, the province for electricity and other subsidiary materials, and the municipality for labor and finance. Financial targets came from the Municipal Metallurgy Bureau, and output targets came from both the Ministry and the municipal bureau. [14]

With such interwoven linkages, overlaid on the vertical columns, it is not difficult to see the potential for inconsistency, conflict, and delay. The Chinese system produces all of these.

Enterprises as Decision-Makers

At the heart of the economic system is the Chinese industrial enterprise. This organizational unit is an economic, social, and political entity, and as such differs considerably from its Western counterpart. The Chinese enterprise is seen by both workers and managers as an employment provider rather than as a profit center.

The Chinese factory also is the primary provider of social services to families of employees, providing subsidized housing, utilities, transportation, meals (usually breakfast and lunch) at work, medical care, day care and schooling for younger children, plus preferential access to sporting, cultural, and entertainment events. In Chinese society, the relationship between the worker and the work unit is both complex and intimate. From a Western perspective, it frequently appears that the work unit "owns" the worker and indeed, the power of the work unit over the worker is such that despite vigorous attempts on the part of the government to stimulate employment mobility among China's professionals, it remains difficult for skilled workers to change jobs.

The Chinese enterprise is responsible administratively to an industrial company (often composed of ten to twelve factories or enterprises and sometimes totaling 13,000 to 16,000 workers), which, in turn, is responsible to a local industrial bureau. The company (typically) assigns the local enterprise a production or sales quota (in gross units of measure); this serves as guidance for the enterprise in terms of both production and productivity. For an enterprise to pay its workers a bonus (which often represents as much as 40 percent of the worker's take-home income), the enterprise must have met its quota. Under the "managerial responsibility system," in which managers or enterprises promise performance against some benchmark statistic, the quota often serves as a plateau; once reached, the enterprise can charge higher prices for additional production (often sold on the open market), thereby having more autonomy in the production, marketing, or distribution of the product, or enjoy higher profit margins. These quotas are negotiated between the enterprise and the company, and tend to be set low enough to be achievable relatively easily.

Enterprises encompass the traditional managerial functions of manufacturing, research and development (R&D), finance, personnel, and marketing. An organizational diagram for a typical Chinese enterprise is shown in Figure 7.2. Major differences from Western companies in these areas include the influence of the party in personnel issues, the presence of workers' congresses as advisors to the management of the enterprise, and the relatively lower attention that the marketing function receives. All three of these issues are in an almost constant state of flux, however, Under the Zhou Ziyang reforms, the role of the party, although ambiguous, appeared to be declining; the role of the workers' congresses appeared to be mostly symbolic; and the role of marketing appeared to be increasingly important (see following section). In the aftermath of Tiananmen, some of this has changed. Marketing will probably continue to retain its newfound importance, but the role of the party within the enterprise is considerably more ambiguous today than it was before June 1989. Despite increased managerial autonomy being given to Chinese enterprises, the actual amount of managerial discretion that is vested in the enterprise manager is considerably less than that found in Western firms and is analogous to a division within a Western corporation. An interview with managers within the electronics industry revealed that as recently as 1986, despite the considerable autonomy granted, the following

Figure 7.2
Organization Chart for a Typical Chinese Enterprise

TECHNICAL SOURCES [70]   MEASURING OFFICE
QUALITY CONTROL DEPT [70]   QUALITY MANAGEMENT GRP
EDUCATION DEPT [7]+TECH SCHOOL   ALL CHECKING GROUPS
FINANCIAL DEPT [3]   SAMPLE TESTING LAB
                                          HEARING FACTORY PRODUCT
OFFICE OF THE CHIEF   REPAIRS GRP
ENGINEER [4]
                    PRODUCT DESIGN GRP
DESIGN DEPT[85]PRODUCT TEST RUN   CENTRAL LAB
             DESIGN STAGE   ALL PROCESSES GRPS
                                          DIVISION-SELECTION GROUP
PROCESS TECHNOLOGY   INSTRUMENTS OFFICE
DEPT [70]   TECHNICAL ADMINISTRATION

MOULDS WORKSHOP   MOULD AND TOOL MGT GRP

                                          STANDARDS
STANDARDS AND TECHNICAL   INFORMATION DEPT
RESOURCES OFFICE [10]   ARCHIVES
                                          TRACING AND DEVELOPING

POWER DEPT [80]
MACHINE REPAIRS WORKSHOP

OFFICE [10]   RECEIVING AND   RECEIVING GUESTS AND
                 SENDING REPS   SENDING VISITORS

                 PRODUCTION
                 DISPATCH GRP
                                          DOCUMENTS
                                          ARCHIVES, PRINTER
                 COOPERATIVES GRP   PHONE OFFICE
                 SELF-MADE PARTS
                                          OPERATOR CAR
                 WAREHOUSE
                                          SECRETARY TYPIST

(PLANNING AND ADMINISTRATION DEPT) [4]

                 TRANSPORTATION GRP
                 WAREHOUSE
                 ADMINISTRATIVE GRPS

WORKSHOPS
                                          TECHNICAL GRP
                                          ADMINISTRATIVE GRP
                                          PRODUCTION SHIFTS
CLINIC
CAFETERIA
KINDERGARTEN
SERVICE GROUP

Source: Hugh Thomas, Interview Notes, September 1980, as
depicted in William A. Fischer, "The Structure &
Organization of Chinese Industrial R & D Activities," R & D
Management, v. 13, no. 2, 1983, p. 70.

managerial functions remained the prerogative of the planners rather than the manager:

Policies and strategies

Approval of R&D projects

Quality

Training

Planning

R&D spending

Standards and specifications

Technology importation

Product pricing

Although the list varies across industries, the message is the same for all: despite increased managerial autonomy, different levels of government retain significant influence over many key business decisions.

Some enterprises sell their entire output to the market; others sell their output only after fulfilling their quota, which goes directly to the government. They are permitted to identify customers for additional output and to negotiate the specifics of the desired production. In many cases, this activity becomes outright marketing. After decades of selling directly to governmental organs, however, it is not immediately obvious who the customers are and who can best serve them. Unlike in the pre-reform era, in which product designs were uniform throughout an industry and sourcing and distribution were the responsibility of the state, the reformed Chinese enterprise is allowed to compete on the basis of design differentiation and is responsible for a substantial amount of its sourcing relations and almost all of its distribution. In mid-1990, as much as 50 percent of industrial products (35 percent of heavy industry) and more than 70 percent of agricultural products and consumer goods were allocated by market mechanisms rather than through the planning channels.

Major departures facing the Chinese enterprise manager under the reforms are the increased responsibilities that the enterprise faces for its own sourcing of material and components and its own sales. These, in turn, are affected by availability of financial resources and by management orientations to security or profit.

Before the current reforms, the enterprise remitted all of its profits to the state and, in return, received annual allocations of working capital plus grants of funds for investment. Today the enterprise must generate its own working capital out of its retained earnings and typically must secure its investment capital from the banking system in the form of loans.[15] This movement from a grant to a loan economy has been a major factor in introducing more discipline into the Chinese economy and sharpening decisions.

In human resources, the typical Chinese enterprise continues to rely on local government agencies for securing labor, and it is normal for a local government entity to be involved in the selection of management. But increasingly, with the acceptance of the "responsibility system," managers are being selected in a competitive manner, based on their proposals regarding contractual achievements. For example, the new director for the Anyang No. 1 Pharmaceutical Factory beat out thirty-two other applicants because he pledged to make the factory yield 2.85 million yuan in profits, 100,000 yuan more than the factory's planned target. The new director formalized this pledge with a contract signed with the local government, and in turn, he was allowed to select his deputies.[16] Under the contract responsibility system, who manages and what their objectives are set the parameters for market opportunities (in selling to the enterprise) and for competition in the marketplace.

ENTERPRISES AS BUYERS

For most foreign firms doing business in China, selling to the Chinese means selling to enterprises. Sales to the consumer are made only through a Chinese enterprise. The foreign firm must court the Chinese enterprise and seek to retain it as a customer. This is true for both industrial and retail sales.

Several key aspects distinguish the orientations of Chinese enterprises as customers: a lack of sophistication, an anxiousness to make profits instantly, and a lack of foreign exchange. Each of these hinders and retards the formation of a business relationship.

Sophistication of Buyers

Most Chinese enterprises, and the managers who direct them, are far less sophisticated in terms of technology, product characteristics, and quality and far less cosmopolitan in terms of world market experience than their counterparts in other developing countries. Although this situation is changing rapidly, Chinese managers simply have been isolated from the world market for too long to be completely knowledgeable or at ease with many aspects of international commerce.

Several consequences flow from this backwardness. One is that the Chinese are far less likely to recognize major shifts in market demand quickly enough, particularly when fashion is involved. For this reason, the Chinese found themselves purchasing large amounts of double-knit polyester technology and manufacturing capacity in ignorance of a pervasive rejection of double-knit apparel in major export markets. Fortunately China's domestic market was able to absorb much of this excess capacity, but this was simply a matter of luck.

A second consequence is the difficulty in discriminating among competing technologies. Although the Chinese are increasing their ability to forecast technologies (as a means of avoiding ill-timed technology acquisition), reports continue of Chinese firms paying top prices for already, or soon to become, obsolete technology. One consequence of this is an insistence on the part of many Chinese buyers that the technology they buy be the same as the selling firm uses in its own operations. Despite the fact that such technology may well be inappropriate for Chinese operating environments, the buyer is at least assured that the technology is not obsolete and that it works.

A third consequence is the frequent misunderstanding or misinterpretation of contracts by Chinese enterprises. Many of the Western "horror stories" and suspicions of unethical behavior stem not from malicious designs on the part of the Chinese, but from an unfamiliarity with international commercial behavior, affecting the terms of contracts that they see as acceptable (see Chapter 10).

Preference for Import Substitution

Since the establishment of the People's Republic, China has been an adamant supporter of import substitution as a guide to economic development. This view reflected China's approach of self-reliance as well as its lack of available foreign exchange, and it continues to be the dominant direction of Chinese import activity. The result has been a reduction in the vitality and pace of technical and commercial innovation within the Chinese domestic market and an absence of competition among Chinese enterprises. The approach continues despite the government's emphasis on expansion of export-oriented production; such encouragement flies in the face of an apparent attitude among some Chinese of having to suffer foreign economic contacts as an unfortunate but necessary cost of acquiring foreign technology and management skills.

Local Protectionism

Most Chinese managers are well aware of the threat posed by foreign competition and seek to protect their own enterprises from it. A significant amount of protectionist sentiment is found among the hierarchy of Chinese industry. Although the rallying cry for most of this sentiment is based on "infant industry" protection, in reality, much of it grows out of fears of long-term competitive deficiencies relative to foreign competition. These fears are so pervasive that protectionism is directed not only against foreigners, but also against other Chinese enterprises who seek to enter the market of another province. This separation of provincial markets is another obstacle to foreigners seeking to serve a national market in China.

Absence of a National Market

Local protectionism plus widespread deficiencies in infrastructure (e.g., transportation and national advertising media), self-reliance tendencies, and the importance of the local government agencies as leaders of industrial enterprises have prevented formation of a national market for most products within China. Any foreign firm hoping to align itself with a particular enterprise with the thought of accessing a large Chinese domestic market will probably be frustrated. Although Chinese enterprises or provinces may promise market exclusivity, it is not in their power or ability to grant it. They can neither provide access to other areas nor totally preclude competitors in theirs. More likely, the foreign firm will have to associate itself with and coordinate several Chinese partners, spread across the country, and overcome their automatic zero-sum expectations to access a substantial part of the Chinese domestic markets, both in volume and in geographical coverage.

An apparent plan of the state is to support several major foreign companies in specific industries and in separate regional markets for the benefit of having access of alternative technologies, to play one foreign investor off against another, and to keep import prices low and technology transfers flowing—for example Volkswagen in Shanghai, Beijing Jeep and Peugeot (Guangdong) in the automobile industry, plus Xerox (Shanghai), Toshiba (Wuhan), and Canon (Tianjin) in office copiers.

RELATIONS WITH CUSTOMERS AND SUPPLIERS

The new Chinese economic reforms seek to open markets to both domestic and foreign suppliers, the latter as it gains access to foreign markets. One of the problems for the foreigner will be to discover the best Chinese markets and the principal actors in them. This effort will require an ability to "read" China's development plans and changes in the economic system. Both efforts will be principally through the mechanism of a joint venture; though other channels are open, they are not preferred by the Chinese government, unless they bring new technology.

Understanding the buyer (or supplier or partner who will make a sale profitable) is a difficult task in China, given the differences in (a) ownership and control, (b) relations with customers, (c) distribution channels, and (d) supplier dependability.

Ownership and Control

Differences in ownership and control of customers and suppliers alter the marketing function in China compared with the West. Three types of ownership exist within the Chinese economy: "ownership by the whole people" (i.e., state-owned enterprises [SOEs]), collective ownership, and private ownership. SOEs constitute both the largest and the most important sector of Chinese industry. They form the backbone of the Chinese economy and have, until recently, been under the direct or indirect administration of one of the industrial ministries, bureaus, or commissions of the State Council. Since 1949, the Chinese government has viewed SOEs as the core of Chinese industrial capability and has given these enterprises both priority in obtaining resources and preference in most other aspects of commerce—the best equipment, the best-trained managers, and preferential access to foreign exchange, supplies, and any other desirable resources. Because of these advantages, these enterprises often also enjoy widespread brand recognition, at least in those regional markets where they are represented. In 1980, SOEs accounted for 22 percent of the total number of enterprises in China, but 79 percent of output by value,[17] down from 90 percent in the early 1960s, 90 percent of productive assets, and 69 percent of employment. The power and significance of the SOEs have diminished since the economic reforms, but only slightly. By January 1989, the SOEs' share of gross output by value had dropped to 58 percent, while the collective sector accounted for roughly 28 percent, the township-run industry sector accounted for 11 percent, and "other" accounted for 4 percent.

Although SOEs enjoy a large number of advantages over other enterprises, only during the period 1952–1965 did they demonstrate superior performance in industrial growth rates.[18] For the rest of the forty-year history of the People's Republic, collective enterprises (owned by communes, brigades, or teams), although lacking in advantages, witnessed far greater growth rates than did the SOEs. The reasons for this are ambiguous; but in general, SOEs suffered from excessive government interference brought on by their relatively greater visibility and from the fact that they were significantly more politicized. Collective enterprises grew at an annual rate of roughly 15 percent during each of the fourth, fifth, and sixth five-year plans (1966–1970, 1971–1975, and 1976–1980) versus 9 percent for the SOEs during each plan.

During the 1980s, the apparent discrepancy between industrial growth and productivity has been even more striking. Burdened by a variety of restrictive rules, the state sector fell well behind the collective sector in terms of productivity, motivation, and dynamism. (An example is a tax that escalates according to how large the compensation bill [bonuses] is relative to the basic wage bill; it has proved to be an impediment to managers who have been attempting to tie worker compensation directly to job performance, for the larger the bonus and greater the performance, the larger the taxes. Its impact is limited to SOEs, however, for it does not apply in collective or private enterprises.) For the foreign company considering a Chinese partner, the collective enterprise, despite its many disadvantages, appears to be more attractive in the smaller-scale, labor-intensive projects than SOEs. However, austerity measures introduced by the Chinese authorities in 1989, in particular the cutting back of loans to private and collective enterprises, and an additional 10 percent surcharge on aftertax profits may seriously harm productivity levels in collectively and individually run enterprises.[19] Similarly, new government assistance in the form of loans available for working capital, which were offered in mid-1990 to combat the damage of the economic austerity measures taken in mid-1989, were limited to SOEs.

China also has a small independently owned sector. Although it has received much attention in the Western press—"Capitalism Returns to China!"—it composes less than 2 percent of China's total employment and industrial output. Furthermore, its contribution to the overall economic picture is unlikely to change greatly in the next few decades. China is not ready for significant expansion of entrepreneurial activity. The venture capital system is only now emerging; there are still restrictions on the number of workers that an individually owned enterprise can employ, and in the absence of a national market, it becomes extremely difficult for any enterprise, especially a small, entrepreneurial one, to grow.

Still, the "value" of the private sector to the Chinese economy goes well beyond what these numbers suggest. The private sector has added an extra dimension to the life of the urban shopper: more goods are available, greater variety, better quality, than ever before; private retail offerings are available well after the normal closing hours of stores in both state-owned and collective sectors; and service has become part of the product mix. Life in China is richer because of the privately owned businesses that are springing up around the urban landscape, but the economy, as a whole, is not seriously affected.

Ownership has only been half the equation in describing Chinese enterprises. Leadership is the other, and often more important, half. No matter how owned, all Chinese enterprises have been included in the national, provincial, and/or local economic plans. For a long time, all goods and services and productive resources were allocated and assigned through these plans. But the influence and weight of the SOEs (which answer directly to the industrial ministry in Beijing and whose output was important to the national plan) would draw greater resources to the SOEs than could smaller, locally oriented enterprises. Before the economic reforms, SOEs were probably better joint venture partners because of their greater influence and resource endowments.

In the early 1980s, a significant redirection of Chinese industry took place, with most of the SOEs being reassigned to control by local authorities.[20] Economic power shifted to the provincial and municipal levels, leaving the ministries in Beijing with more of a coordinating role. Foreign firms were more attracted to deals with locally led enterprises rather than relying on Beijing ministries to arrange such ventures. Although similar attempts at decentralization had been attempted, the current policies were notable both in their duration and in the all-encompassing nature of the changes in authority relations. Enterprises were given increasingly greater managerial discretion as to products and operations responsibility and over the disposition of earned income to be used to reward workers and renew the organization for the future.

The first enterprises given managerial autonomy were collectives in industries not considered to be essential to national security or the level of well-being of the population. These enterprises, typically in light industries, were allowed significant discretion in determining product design, product mix, distribution, customers to be served, and reinvestment of earnings. A fair number of these enterprises moved aggressively into ventures and licenses with foreigners. These enterprises offered the opportunity to access the Chinese market or Chinese labor, and although they did not possess the advantages of the SOEs, they were eager and willing partners. The SOEs, although encouraged to engage in more foreign economic activity by the Minister of Foreign Economic Relations and Trade (MOFERT) and by the local foreign trade corporations under MOFERT's direction, were far securer (in having support of financing and resource allocations—the "iron rice bowl") than the collectives and, consequently, more cautious in embarking on risky activities. Also, SOEs found themselves more constrained by the economic demands of local governments, and so unable to respond to the opportunities offered by the new managerial autonomy.

Only in the late 1980s were the changes within the SOEs sufficient to make them a more attractive partner to foreign firms. This turnabout occurred when SOE managers saw the reforms as permanent, making them responsible for the fortunes of their enterprises. A particularly important change has been the promotion of younger, better-trained managers to assume positions of leadership within the SOEs. These new managers appear to be less tied to traditional ways of doing things in the face of the challenges and opportunities inherent in the new market influences.

The foreign firm seeking to enter China does not face a clear choice in the selection of a partner or of suppliers. Private Chinese enterprises are probably neither viable candidates nor reliable suppliers. These independently owned businesses are still too small, too constrained, and often too disadvantaged to be reliable performers. For the most part, collectively owned enterprises still have the most entrepreneurial vigor and the greatest freedom from bureaucracy, and for light industry–type of arrangements, they are probably the best choice. Collectively owned enterprises are best accessed directly through some sort of unofficial personal contact. Reliance on a ministry, or even a local bureau or company officials, will almost inevitably lead to contact with SOEs only.

SOEs are showing substantial signs of growth and aggressiveness, and should not be discounted as partners without careful consideration. In many industries, they alone have the necessary access to skills and resources to make them viable partners or suppliers. SOEs can be approached either directly through "official channels" or indirectly through informal, personal contacts. The risk of going through official channels is not only that it adds an additional level of bureaucracy to the partner search process, but also that the officials will attempt to steer the foreign firm toward a Chinese partner that they believe needs the assistance of a foreign partner.

Relations with Customers

For the joint venture aspiring to sell in the Chinese domestic market, or abroad, there are three channels to be considered: the foreign partner, the Chinese partner, and the joint venture itself.

Marketing by the Foreign Partner

Probably the most undesirable of the choices is that of relying on the foreign partner's abilities. Although the foreigner possesses considerably more marketing experience than the Chinese partner, and although the Chinese partner probably has little or no experience in dealing with a foreign product, the Chinese partner does possess one irreplaceable advantage: it knows the domestic market it has been serving. China has been far more isolated from markets abroad than most Westerners understand. As a result, although the Chinese consumer is gradually coming to recognize brand names such as Sony, IBM, and Coca-Cola, there is little value in other, less well known brand names in the domestic Chinese market; the consumer is simply unaware of these reputations.[21] Without brand recognition, there is little that the foreign partner can bring to the marketing function other than experience with making it more efficient and perhaps more effective. These are modifications rather than primary changes. Without some participation by Chinese organizations in the marketing function, the foreign partner faces a difficult task.

For selling the products of a joint venture in the international market, on the other hand, the assumption of sole responsibility by the foreign partner may in fact be the ideal arrangement. Presumably, the foreign partner is already familiar with international markets, and can operate in them in a reasonably informed manner. Furthermore, the ability to sell the joint venture's products in markets where foreign exchange can be earned should be a real incentive to the foreign firm seeking to repatriate joint venture profits.

Marketing through the Chinese Partner

Using the Chinese partner for domestic marketing is a means of taking advantage of its knowledge of the local market and access to channels of distribution, plus privileges and influence already exercised. Use of the partner must not, however, conflict with its existing business. The disadvantages of this approach involve the probable lack of sophistication on the part of the Chinese partner concerning distribution and marketing and the attendant loss to the foreigner of information regarding Chinese market conditions. If the product being sold carries an internationally recognized brand name, there also is the risk involved in tarnishing that reputation through careless attention to marketing details and brand protection on the part of the joint venture partner.

In almost all cases, there is little advantage, or even feasibility, in relying on the Chinese partner alone for marketing of the joint venture's products in the international market.

Marketing by the Joint Venture

A joint marketing effort through the venture itself is probably the most frequently used method of distribution and was the approach negotiated by Xerox with its partner. Joint ventures have gained both substantial autonomy and responsibility for achieving the success of their product. To the extent that the joint venture is able to meld the technical sophistication of the foreign partner with the knowledge of local conditions possessed by the Chinese partner, it should enhance the chances of gaining position in the Chinese domestic market. This requires the commitment and cooperation of both partners—something that cannot be taken for granted. The commitments of foreign partners often waver in the face of the expense of maintaining an expatriate presence in China, the mystery of Chinese culture and tastes, the difficulties involved in earning and repatriating a reasonable return on their investment, and the frustrations of dealing with China's stultifying bureaucracy. Similarly, the commitment of the Chinese partner often is less than full-fledged, as it struggles to produce a profit in the mainstream operations of the domestic company.

In pursuing international markets, the joint venture possesses no advantages by itself. The joint venture typically relies on the abilities of the foreign partner to enter international markets. A danger arises from this approach when the product of the joint venture is so different from the foreign partner's existing product mix that the transnational corporation possesses little comparative advantage in marketing or distribution. This latter problem arose for a Chinese brewer that had entered into a compensatory trade agreement with a European construction firm to build a new brewery. A certain proportion of the foreign exchange the brewer owed for the construction of the brewery would be generated through the export of beer, with the European building contractor responsible for the export of the beer, charging a royalty on each can or bottle sold. Beer was well outside of the contractor's product mix, however, and the contractor had no prior experience with consumer products. The Chinese brewer also had no experience in selling its product in foreign markets and yet was dependent on the success of its product in the European market to pay off the cost of the new brewery. The result was that little beer was sold in the foreign market and the brewery suffered a stain on its reputation for being unable to meet its loan obligations, even though it was not the party at fault.

Distribution Channels

Although China has clearly opened a significant role for market influences, some markets and/or products are still within the national or local plans, and their sale and distribution must conform to these plans.[22] For those products, the enterprise distribution plan is incorporated into the distribution plans of the governmental departments that, in turn, make sales to the designated customers. The products in question also can be ordered directly from the joint venture itself, and the joint venture has the right to sell, on its own, any output that exceeds what is demanded by the national or local plans.[23]

Marketers will find, however, a lack of organization and/or discipline throughout the distribution chain. For example, one of Europe's premier automotive companies sold trucks into China early in the "open policy" period, but it did not pay sufficient attention to the availability of maintenance or repair services. Shortly after the introduction of the trucks into China's northeastern Heilongjiang Province, there were scenes of breakdowns and abandonment of the newly imported trucks. The problem lay not in the automobile technology, which was arguably among the world's finest, but in the lack of training of Chinese truck drivers and the absence of a maintenance, service, and repair network. Today the reputation of that brand remains sullied by failures of a system that it did not understand and could not control. Marketing in China requires attention to the entire distribution and service chain that will support the product.

The alternative of establishing *new* channels for marketing and distribution remains difficult because of several persistent problems. The absence of a national market in the country means that the market served may be too small to support a service network or to establish a brand image in a cost-efficient manner. A firm that attempts to go nationwide with its products will probably face different local competitors in every province where local protectionism exists. The choice of a single joint venture partner becomes particularly difficult, as any specific partner is likely to be seen as an outsider in every other province. Furthermore, no single partner is likely to be able to provide adequate service outside of its home province.

Pricing of joint venture products remains somewhat outside the control of the manager. Most domestic prices are fixed by state or local agency and usually are allowed to float within a price band of plus or minus 20 percent. In 1988, in the face of serious inflation and the fear of political unrest, the government reduced price flexibility, reestablishing more government control. This is probably only a temporary setback, and China is likely to once again offer increased price discretion in the future.

Supplier Dependability

The abundance of relatively cheap, highly trainable labor within the Chinese market and the encouragement that the Chinese government provides to produce for exports make the issue of supplier selection important. As with any decision on source selection, a number of factors relating to manufacturing capabilities must be considered.

Securing Necessary Materials

Because of infrastructure inadequacies, foreign exchange scarcities, and government intervention, the ability of any particular potential supplier to acquire the necessary materials, equipment, or labor skills cannot be taken for granted. Supply and energy shortages continue to plague the economy and can lead to serious delays or interruptions. A survey of constraints on production among twenty sample enterprises, in the early 1980s, reported that for the most part, plan targets and the allocation of supplies do not constrain Chinese industry output. . . . The main constraints are demand and capacity. . . . The supply of electricity is a special case because it is almost entirely allocated, cannot be stored or traded, and is seldom self-generated. Electricity shortages are said to be responsible for the loss of as much as 20 percent of the gross value of China's industrial output.[24]

Meeting Quality Requirements

China has had persistent difficulty getting its industry to raise quality; its efforts in this direction are undependable. This can be a significant problem for the firm wishing to source intermediate products from China. The experience of Western firms appears to suggest that quality control does not have to be a problem if the foreign partner is willing to invest enough in establishing a quality-management program in the joint venture and to ensure that the program is consciously adhered to on a continuous basis. Such an effort takes more time and manpower than direct funding.

One limitation that appears to be difficult to overcome in China is the inability to require a supplier to adopt statistical process controls. Such direct "intervention" into the affairs of another organization is beyond normal Chinese relations.

Inventory Control

With inventory control, the primary problem is a lack of information. Most Chinese enterprises do not have the software, the hardware, or the raw data to establish the sort of integrated production control and inventory-management systems typically used in the West (MRP—materials requirements planning systems). Furthermore, until infrastructure deficiencies can be remedied, most Chinese managers will remain better off hoarding inventory, despite the new burden of a holding cost. The real cost of such inventory for the customer of such a supplier lies in the inefficient use of working capital, the confusion that accompanies such inventory buildups, probable machine interference, and a general lack of discipline. China's infrastructure deficiencies, its wide geographical expanse, the vertical segmentation of its industries, and the paucity of information within the society all conspire to make "just in time" an infeasible solution to China's inventory problems.

Labor Skills

In 1988, China began to free up its labor allocation system by allowing some university graduates to find their own employment. Despite such an unprecedented liberalization of the labor market, and despite continuing government proclamations regarding the desirability of greater labor mobility, most enterprises are essentially stuck with the labor skills they have and are unable to quickly obtain new or additional skills. One of the implications of such a situation is that a Chinese enterprise cannot easily adapt to significant market or technological changes on its own. Instead, it must either retrain its original labor pool or else join with another organization on a collaborative or contractual basis.

This means that unlike the West, where vendors are frequently relied on as sources of innovation,[25] such support is not to be expected from Chinese vendors.

For the various reasons mentioned in this chapter, China remains both compelling and frustrating as a place to do business. The attractiveness of the market is undeniable but is largely based on faith that someday it will become rich enough to support a profitable foreign presence. The frustrations of the market are omnipresent and often overwhelming. They arise in everything from a simple third world deficiency in infrastructure to the subtleties and sophistication of the world's most experienced bureaucracy. Although monumental change occurred during the 1980s, considerably more change will have to occur in the future if China is to become an attractive investment opportunity, much less to join the world economy.

NOTES

1. Negotiations for a Johnson & Johnson venture to produce Band-Aids in Shanghai took more than four years; Seagram spent more than two years establishing a drinks venture; RJR-Nabisco negotiations to establish a venture to produce Ritz crackers took six years. ("Beijing Opens the Door to Bubble Gum and Band-Aids," *Business Week*, August 8, 1988, p. 40.)

2. Jeffrey R. Taylor, "Consumer Forecasting," *China Business Review*, March–April, 1987, p. 22.

3. Wang Dashu, "A Sluggish Market: Causes and Counter-Measures," *Intertrade*, March 1990, pp. 51–53.

4. See *Statistical Yearbook of China, 1987*, p. 594.

5. A report by the *Christian Science Monitor* (April 5, 1990, p. 5) cites official Chinese statistics showing a widening gap between East and West provinces, with the West still held in the grip of state-owned enterprises. Delegations from the West have traveled to Beijing to seek redress.

6. Poverty in Xinjian Province in the far northwest and lack of funds for development and social services (including for construction of a mosque for the Muslim minority) led in mid-1990 to ethnic riots. The tensions also reflect longstanding repression of minorities by the Han.

7. See Jeffrey R. Taylor, "Consumer Forecasting," *China Business Review*, March–April 1987, p. 24, in which he collates the results of several Chinese studies of future income and consumption: Song Min and Liu Anping, "Income Elasticity Analysis of Consumer Goods and Forecast of Chinese Consumption Structure," *Quantitative and Technical Economics Research*, No. 1, 1984, pp. 27–35, 80; Yang Shengming, "Using a Statistical Data Approach to Forecast Consumption Structure for a Comfortable Standard of Living," in Li Xuezeng et al., eds., *The Structure of China's Domestic Consumption: Analysis and Preliminary Forecasts*, World Bank Staff Working Paper, No. 755, 1985; He Juhuang, "Demand System Analysis and Consumption Structure Forecasting," in Xuezeng et al.; Yuan Fengqi, Jin Xianglan, and Xie Fang, "Forecast of the Consumption Structure of China's People in the Year 2000," *Economic Research*, No. 10, 1986, pp. 5–6; Cheng Xiusheng and Tang Ruoni, "The Chinese People's Consumption in the Year 2000," *Economic Daily*, November 6, 1985, p. 3.

8. The *New York Times* recently quoted Xu Jiatun, director of the New China News Agency (a former member of the Central Committee of the Chinese Communist Party and de facto Chinese ambassador to and governor-elect for Hong Kong, as declaring that "capitalism is one of the greatest achievements of mankind." Barbara Basler, "China's Ear Is Its Voice in a Colony," *New York Times*, August 7, 1988, p. 3.

9. Comments made by C. B. Sung at the Graduate School of Business Administration, University of North Carolina at Chapel Hill, Spring 1984.

10. William Byrd and Gene Tidrick, "Factor Allocation and Enterprise Incentives," in Gene Tidrick and Chen Jiyuan, *China's Industrial Reform* (New York: Oxford University Press, 1987), p 62.

11. This can be seen in the relatively strong preference for "life-time employment" and the highest rating for "ideal situation" given to "welfare of the staff and workers" in factors influencing decision-making, among a sample of fifty industrial managers from the People's Republic, in Mun Kin-chok, "Characteristics of the Chinese Management: An Exploratory Study," in Stewart R. Clegg, Dexter C. Dunphy, and S. Gordon Redding, *The Enterprise and Management in East Asia* (Hong Kong: Centre of Asian Studies, University of Hong Kong, 1986), pp. 313–326.

12. Peter Fleming, *The Siege at Peking* (Hong Kong: Oxford University Press, 1983), p. 44; Robert H. Silin, *Leadership and Values* (Cambridge, Mass.: Harvard University Press, 1976), p. 53; and Barry M. Richman, *Industrial Society in Communist China* (New York: Vintage Books, 1969), pp. 264–265.

13. Silin, *Leadership and Values*, p. 46.

14. Gene Tidrick, "Planning and Supply," in Tidrick and Jiyuan, eds., *China's Industrial Reform*, p. 180.

15. There is some ambiguity about the source and conditions of funding for the most important state-initiated capital investment projects. It would appear that the funding still comes through the banking sector, but that the requirements for financial justification may be considerably less rigorous owing to the direct intervention by the state.

16. "Factory Directors Chosen Competitively," Xinhua English News Service, November 5, 1987, as reported in Foreign Broadcast Information Service, *Daily Report—China*, FBIS-CHI–217–87, November 10, 1987, p. 42.

17. Christine P. W. Wong, "Ownership and Control in Chinese Industry: The Maoist Legacy and Prospects for the 1980s," in Joint Economic Committee of the Congress of the United States, *China's Economy Looks Toward the Year 2000* (Washington, D.C.: U.S. Government Printing Office, 1986), pp. 599–610.

18. Ibid., p. 602.

19. *Journal of Commerce*, March 22, 1989.

20. Harry Harding, *China's Second Revolution* (Washington, D.C.: The Brookings Institution, 1987), pp. 124–128.

21. Like everything else regarding Chinese life and the economy, there are some dissenting opinions about China's ability to recognize and appreciate internationally known brand names: "Products that are household names in other parts of the world are increasingly finding their way into Chinese lives. In November [1987], Kentucky Fried Chicken Corp. opened the first Western fast-food restaurant in China, opposite the austere mausoleum of Chairman Mao in Beijing's Tiananmen Square. The 500-seat unit, which can fry 2,300 pieces of chicken an hour, is expected to ring up daily sales of $7,000. . . . In a Chinese version of the cola wars, Coca-Cola Co. and PepsiCo Inc. are aggressively expanding distribution, Kodak, Fuji, and other foreign film suppliers have attained a 70

percent share of the color film market. Nescafé and Maxwell House are waging coffee combat in a land of tea. Says Raymond So, manager of J. Walter Thompson China: "People in China are the most brand conscious in the world. If you can afford imports, you're fashionable." *Business Week*, January 25, 1988, pp. 68–69.

22. The number of products still under the planning system has declined rapidly: "The number of industrial products allocated under mandatory planning, which had been more than 500 at the height of central planning in the 1950s, was reduced first to 120, and then to 60. The comparable number of agricultural commodities was reduced from 29 to 10 in 1984 and then to zero in 1985, with the adoption of the procurement contract system." Harding, *China's Second Revolution*, p. 109.

23. Zhang Xinda, "On the Question of Markets for the Products of Joint Ventures in China" (Paper prepared for a Conference on the Role of Foreign Investment in National Development with Special Reference to China, sponsored by the Institute of World Economics and Politics of the Chinese Academy of Social Sciences and the Sloan School of Management, Massachusetts Institute of Technology, Hangzhou, China, March 25–30, 1985), p. 27.

24. Gene Tidrick, "Planning and Supply," in Tidrick and Jiyuan, eds., *China's Industrial Reform*, p. 189.

25. Eric von Hippel, *The Sources of Innovation* (New York: Oxford University Press, 1988).

8

China as a Production Base

China is blessed with numerous resources, sufficient for almost any industrial complex it wants to establish. It contains varied mineral and agricultural resources, several sources of energy, ample water,[1] and the world's largest supply of labor. What it lacks is access to these resources, which can be gained only through appropriate infrastructure. This, in turn, can be built only with capital, skilled labor, and management. These gaps in access, rather than the abundance of (untapped) resources, are the focus of this chapter.[2]

LOCAL SOURCING PROBLEMS[3]

One of the attractions to foreign business of producing in China is the abundant low-wage labor available and the current investment incentives offered by various governmental levels to reduce total costs. However, mere access to this labor and its skills and to natural resources often is insufficient, for they are barely adequate to meet the basic needs of China's population in its domestic manufacturing. Most civilian goods are of low quality and cannot meet competition in a sophisticated international market. The foreigner in China is urged by the government to export to earn foreign exchange to finance its business there. The foreign direct investment venture must, therefore, be concerned with the adequacy of the production base not only for itself, but also for its local suppliers, who must become both more sophisticated and more efficient so as to meet worldwide competition.

Chinese Manufacturing Equipment

In general, the equipment used in manufacturing processes in most Chinese factories is out of date. Although age varies from factory to factory, industry to industry, and locale to locale, the average vintage in most industries is 1950s or earlier. Such old equipment might not be a particularly damaging liability in a closed and protected domestic market of the sort that existed in the pre-1978 period, but the real cost of relying on it is felt when the economy opens up to foreign competition and modern technologies. At that point, the reliability, efficiency, flexibility, and quality that are typically associated with modern equipment can place a Chinese enterprise at a significant competitive disadvantage. (The military and space enterprises are exceptions; many have the skills and equipment but lack efficiency.) Ironically, the one sector of the Chinese economy that has shown the most promise as a result of the economic reforms—the non-state enterprises—has been the least able in the past to gain access to modern equipment of foreign origin. As a result, this sector, although more productive than the state-owned sector, is even further behind in terms of equipment sophistication.

Without modern equipment, which provides a degree of manufacturing flexibility but also the standardization of products and processes inherent in automated production, it is much more difficult for the Chinese to compete with foreign firms on the basis of reliability of delivery or quality. China's attractiveness as a source of cheap labor does not offset the equipment disadvantage, and in a sense, the lack of labor skills (evidenced in low wages) prevents adoption of more sophisticated equipment—as does the "iron rice bowl," which requires employment of labor when capital equipment may be needed for high volume and quality control.

Productivity

Chinese productivity growth attributable to increased efficiency from existing production resources has actually been quite low. Almost all of the productivity improvement that has occurred under the People's Republic has been the result of adding more labor to the existing plant and resources rather than getting more out of the existing labor force.[4]

Growth in productive efficiency occurs most readily through the exploitation of economies of scale. Yet China has had considerable difficulties achieving them, despite having a centrally planned economy. The reasons for this relate to earlier discussions of the adherence to a tradition of self-reliance within the economy and within each province, plus a limited capacity for truly centralized orchestration and control owing to infrastructure deficiencies and the persistence of local protectionism within the domestic economy.

The failure to exploit economies of scale can be seen in many industries. China is reputed to have more automobile factories than any other country, but it ranks no higher than twentieth in the number of automobiles produced.[5] In 1984, there were 140 bicycle factories in China, 83 more than should have existed to serve China's population efficiently; half of all television and watch factories and 80 percent of all makers of refrigerators and washing machines were "woeful squanderers of raw materials and fuels."[6] In 1982, China produced 190,000 refrigerators in 103 factories, compared with foreign manufacturers who often produced more than one million units in a single factory.[7]

Consequently one of China's principal comparative advantages as seen by advanced countries—cheap labor—is diminished, sometimes strikingly, by poor productivity. Despite its "giant" scale in population, China is a "pygmy" in production units and productivity.[8]

Product Design

Along with laggard productivity, Chinese enterprises typically are backward in product design. While Japan is being recognized not only as an astute manufacturer, but also as a leading industrial designer, China struggles with product designs that are decades behind international standards. China's estrangement from the world economic and design communities was a major factor, but its "big-market mentality" and the monopolistic position of Chinese factories also have been contributors. Because the Chinese hope to sell in international markets, they must master the intricacies and subtleties of avant-garde design and fashion—an approach that sometimes is as hard for them to take seriously as it is to master. Design often is regarded as an arcane and impenetrable science (or art) by Chinese managers who have never had to pay attention to aesthetic requirements. Yet it is essential to do so if Chinese enterprises are to make their mark in most international product markets.

Consequently China is beginning to take strides in incorporating modern design into some products, such as men's suits and ties and packaging for beverages (aluminum cans with flip tops for beer, plastic two-liter bottles for soft drinks) and by mimicking some trademarked logos and designs, such as the omnipresent Mickey Mouse. In one isolated sign of progress, in 1985, a Chinese dress won first prize at the 50th Paris International Fashion Fair.[9] Yet notable differences remain between products produced for the domestic market and those produced for international customers, as well as between the ability to faithfully copy a pattern or design obtained from abroad, which can be relatively easily done, and the ability to create attractive and fashionable designs, which is more difficult to do.

Quality

Discussions of Chinese manufacturing among Western businessmen inevitably turn to "horror stories" regarding lack of attention to quality control. This also is true among Chinese, who understood the results of not paying attention to quality. Poor quality has persistently plagued both consumers and industrial buyers, neither of whom have developed any confidence in the ability or willingness of Chinese manufacturers to meet product performance consistently or appearance standards on a level commensurate with world-class expectations.

Interviews with Western businessmen trading and/or producing in China in the late 1980s suggest that improvements are being made in the level and dependability of quality in Chinese manufacturing. One hosiery manufacturer, for example, observed that the Chinese offer for export both quality and variety in colors that surpass those available anywhere else! Yet, as with design, significant differences exist between the quality of products made for the domestic market and the quality of products produced for international buyers.

Quality control in Chinese industry remains a dilemma. The ability to produce high-quality products is certainly evident in many of the most advanced factories in the country. However, problems in sourcing, material availability, worker motivation, equipment vintage, and distribution conspire against dependability in quality. Furthermore, the continuing seller's market saps enthusiasm of enterprises for maintaining a strong and durable commitment to quality programs. The rise of domestic competition and the threat of imports are providing an appropriate stimulus for correction, however.

Shop Floor Control and Manufacturing Information Systems

Aside from the ubiquitous, but often inconsistently used "total quality control" paperwork on the shop floor, there usually is little to be seen in the way of shop floor control in Chinese factories. This suggests that there is an apparent disparity in documentation and decision-making between Chinese and Western factories regarding job routing, batch-size determination, delivery dates, and customer identification. Presumably, such information does exist in Chinese factories; but by its absence from visibility on the shop floor, it is apparently not accorded the same degree of importance as in the West.

The lack of attention given to manufacturing information has again occurred because of a lack of discipline in a seller's market and the absence of opportunity costs associated with manufacturing decisions. These relax the pressures for product design changes, quality assurance, schedule performance, inventory, and labor productivity. Consequently little attention has been paid to prioritization, inventory, batch-sizing, capacity deployment, or even make-buy decisions that are usual in a competitive Western manufacturing firm.

China's lack of manufacturing information systems also is due to its relative lack of information infrastructure, including computer technology and data integrity, plus a low level of telephone technology for the gathering, processing, and transmission of manufacturing-related information. Deficiency in data integrity is the result of little knowledge about the markets to be served, the true cost of the resources involved, and past penalties (with no potential rewards) associated with the transmission of "honest" information about problem areas.[10]

Only in the mid-1980s did Chinese factories begin installing Western-type cost accounting. A study commissioned by Xerox found that its potential partner categorized all costs into labor, materials, and overhead. The latter included all expenses from staff salaries to new-product development. Unit manufacturing cost was unknown and unneeded in their system.

Inventory

Chinese enterprises continuously hold excess inventory. Some significant amounts of this is finished-goods inventory, produced in the "spirit" of growth to serve the seller's market but no longer suitable for a market in which the buyer has considerably more discretionary control over purchasing decisions. During the 26 years between 1953 and 1981 (except 1958–1960, for which accurate data are not available) the stockpiles of steel products held by Chinese industry annually were more than half the production in each year and more than the total production in ten of these years.[11]

More alarming, however, are the amounts of work-in-process inventories that are probably the result of poor supply dependability, poor quality, and poor batch determination. Although such inventories often are excessive, they can be justified in an environment of shortage and schedule delay, in which the carrying costs were historically negligible. Today, however, such high inventories become a problem of considerable magnitude, raising competitive costs, since work-in-process inventories represent an investment of working capital that yields no return, requiring holding space on the factory floor, adding to the complexity of management and shop floor control, raising the probability of inventory shrinkage and obsolescence, clogging up a factory's "arteries," increasing the likelihood of machine interference, and stretching out deliveries.

Labor Morale

Before the economic reforms, the morale of the Chinese work force was quite poor. Salary increases and promotions had been suspended for most of the Cultural Revolution, and workers had limited or no visible careers. Consequently work was frequently looked at as necessary but unsatisfying and uninspiring. Furthermore, Chinese workers had little or no mobility, leaving them to regard their future as little more than continued repetition of their depressing current situations. The condition was such that one well-known observer of Chinese work life suggested that the ironic legacy of Mao Zedong's repeated attempts to mobilize Chinese workers by appealing to their "spiritual" (i.e., "service") motivations was a heightened rather than a diminished receptivity to material rewards.[12]

Today, as a direct result of the economic reforms, Chinese workers are increasingly being rewarded for their efforts and accomplishments, linking performance to pay. By 1985, the use of time wages in state-owned enterprises had declined to 60 percent from 85 percent in 1978, while the use of piece rates had risen from 1 percent to 10 percent over the same time period.[13] Evidence of the dramatic improvement in the cash income of urban households because of economic reforms can be found in the increase in total nominal monthly income for these households during the period between January 1986, when it was 89 yuan (of which 68 yuan were wages and 11 yuan were bonuses, plus 10 yuan for subsidies) and February 1988, when it was 111 yuan (of which 83 were wages and 28 were bonuses and subsidies).[14]

China also has the good fortune to have a work force that is receptive to training. Despite the low productivity that has been witnessed in the Chinese economy, and despite the infrastructure problems that make doing business there difficult for foreign firms, China's pool of low-wage labor is one of its great assets because of the wealth of eager and willing human talent that these workers represent. They will undoubtedly facilitate China's entry into the world economy because of their potential for learning.

TRANSPORTATION

Access to materials and markets in China is seriously hampered by inadequate transport. Efforts to correct it are continuing, but the gap is large and seems to increase, as demand rises faster than supply.

Traffic Growth

China's transportation infrastructure is severely congested through extremely heavy use. The freight carried by China's transportation network increased more than thirty times between 1952 and 1988, from 315 million tons to more than 10 billion tons, with by far the largest tonnage going by road (five times that by rail and seven to eight times that by water); the distribution remained relatively stable for a decade or more, with rail at 20 percent, road at 70 percent, water at 8 percent, and pipeline and other at 2 percent. Only after 1983 did rail decline to under 15 percent (in 1988) and road transport rise to 75 percent.[15] Freight demands will become heavier, doubling or tripling in the next fifteen years, as China pushes ahead with its modernization programs and opens more to foreigners.

A closer analysis of freight traffic in China reveals that although freight volume is greatest by road, road haulage is predominantly over short distances. Long-distance transport is dominated by rail and water networks (see Table 8.1).

In comparison to other countries, freight traffic imposes a heavy burden on China's transport system. Using the standard ton-kilometer (tkm) measurement (one ton of freight moved one kilometer), China's economy generates more than 3 tkm for every dollar of gross national product (GNP). This compares poorly with India, Brazil, and the United States (less than 2 tkm per dollar GNP), although it is better than the USSR (4 tkm per dollar GNP).[16]

Table 8.1
Freight Traffic, 1979–1988 (billion ton/km)

Year	Rail	Road	Water	Air	Pipeline	Total
1979	560	74	456	-	48	1138
1980	572	76	505	-	49	1203
1981	571	78	515	-	50	1214
1982	612	95	548	-	52	1404
1984	725	154	634	-	57	1569
1985	813	169	770	-	60	1813
1986	876	212	865	-	61	2015
1987	947	262	950	1	62	2223
1988	988	298	998	1	65	2350

Source: China Statistical Abstract, 1989, N.Y.: Praeger, p. 51.

The principal reason for this volume of freight is the long distances between the geographical location of resources and that of major industries and markets in the cities. Most resources are in the western half of the country, whereas the industries and markets are in the eastern half. This separation generates much transportation of resources; coal shipments alone make up a substantial proportion of railway freight shipped to eastern cities and to ports for export.

The Chinese policy of self-reliance and strategic location of key industries throughout China (regardless of economic effectiveness) have placed additional demands on the transportation network. Every province (except Tibet) has a steel mill, although iron ore is found in only a few provinces. Because the steel-making process uses about five tons of input for every one ton of output, it would be more economic to transport finished steel than to ship iron ore and coking coal to the dispersed steel mills.

The rapid economic growth experienced by all sectors of the Chinese economy has further burdened the transportation network. Shanghai, for example, has become a major transport bottleneck because of the need to transport raw materials and foodstuffs from the Chinese interior into Shanghai, to export and import goods and materials through its ports, and to distribute manufactured goods to the domestic market.

Passenger traffic also has increased nearly forty times since 1950. Even since 1978, it has risen three and a half times, as shown in Table 8.2. The three major contributors to this increase have been the rise of domestic tourism, the opening of urban and rural markets, and the increase in intracity traffic. Domestic tourism still involves relatively short traveling distances, but the number of Chinese who are visiting tourist areas is large and growing. Foreign tourism, as indicated in Chapter 4, increased sharply after 1978 but declined after Tiananmen into 1990.

The reopening of urban and rural markets has encouraged those producers

Table 8.2
Passenger Traffic, 1978–1988 (billion person-km)

Year	Rail	Road	Water	Air	Total
1978	109	52	10	3	174
1979	122	60	11	4	197
1980	138	73	13	4	228
1981	147	84	13	5	250
1982	158	96	14	6	274
1983	178	111	15	6	309
1984	205	134	15	8	362
1985	242	157	17	12	428
1986	259	198	18	15	490
1987	284	219	20	19	542
1988	326	253	21	21	621

Sources: Statistical Yearbook of China, 1986, p.322; and China Statistical Abstract, 1989, N.Y.: Praeger, p. 52.

that are able to make the intrarural and rural-urban journeys to local markets to do so, increasing their incomes substantially. Finally, passenger traffic within the cities also is growing as economic activity and urban populations rise.

Network Expansion and Improvement

Since Liberation in 1949, China has made significant progress in the building of its transport infrastructure. It raised rail lines from 22,000 kilometers to more than 44,000 kilometers in 1978, of which 1,000 kilometers was electrified by that date; roads were increased eleven-fold from 80,000 kilometers to 890,000 kilometers in 1978; inland waterways, from 74,000 kilometers to 136,000 kilometers by 1978; beginning with no commercial air transport in 1949, nearly 150,000 kilometers were available in 1978; pipelines rose from zero to more than 8,000 kilometers in 1978. Since that year, waterway capacity has dropped and airways risen sharply, with rail and road increasing, and pipelines lengthening by nearly 80 percent, as shown in Table 8.3.

Despite the doubling of the railways, an elevenfold increase in roads, and a twentyfold increase in air routes, demand continues to outrun supply. Indeed, it was not until the seventh five-year plan (1985–1989) that the transportation sector was designated as a top priority for state investment. In that plan, about 13.5 percent, or 51.4 billion yuan, of the state capital construction budget was allocated to transport, of which railways received the lion's share, or roughly 32 billion yuan; air, 2 billion yuan; and roads and waterways sharing 18 billion yuan. High priority still needs to be assigned to improving the transportation of

Table 8.3
Transportation Lines, 1978–1985 (1000 km)

Year	Rail	(Electric)	Road	Inland Waterways	Air	Pipe-line
1978	49	1	890	136	149	8
1979	50	1	875	107	160	9
1980	50	2	888	108	192	9
1981	50	2	898	109	218	10
1982	50	2	907	109	233	10
1983	52	2	915	109	229	11
1984	52	3	927	109	260	11
1985	52	4	942	109	277	12
1986	52	4	962	109	324	13
1987	53	n/a	982	110	389	14
1988	53	n/a	996	109	374	14

Source: Statistical Yearbook of China, 1986, p.302 (adapted)

energy resources (coal and oil), developing transportation links between the ports and China's hinterland, and upgrading the ports themselves.

Rail

Railways carry nearly 15 percent of the total freight and more than two-thirds of the tonnage per kilometer, plus more than half of the passenger-kilometers in China. Under such strains, it is notable that passenger trains keep reasonably on schedule and seldom are late.

The emphasis is on making improvements to the existing network, rather than on a massive expansion of new lines. Such improvements include further electrification of the system, double-tracking, and replacing steam trains with diesel (or electric, where appropriate) locomotives. Much of the new investment in the railway system is in so-called local railway systems, which are built and operated by local governments and enterprises with some state assistance. The local railway networks now total almost 6,800 kilometers and are not counted in national statistics.[17] New rolling stock is being purchased from East Germany, Poland, Sweden, France, and the United States; in addition, a technical assistance agreement with British Rail Engineering, Ltd., will lead to design of three prototype coaches and help in coach design, manufacture, and production.

Besides capital improvements in the railways, some pressure on the system has been relieved by discouraging short-distance haulage by rail through the imposition of surcharges on passenger travel under 100 kilometers and freight movements under 200 kilometers. Nevertheless, without adequate highways and trucking, it is clear that the rail system will remain a major weakness because it is a vital cog in China's transport infrastructure, and future demands on the system will increase.

Road

China's road system is another weak link in the transport infrastructure. Although Table 8.3 shows a sizable growth in roads since Liberation, it masks the facts that China's road network is still sparse compared with the size of the country and that the quality of these roads is exceedingly poor. Of China's 995,000 kilometer of roads, it is reported that 83 percent are all-weather (surfaced mainly with mixed bitumen, sand, and gravel), with 24 percent paved with high-standard concrete.[18] This may be an optimistic estimate. Many of the "all-weather" roads are unsuitable for heavy trucks. As much as one-quarter are little more than mud tracks that are seasonally impassable and unsuitable for anything but tractor transport.

The system itself tends to consist of roads radiating from cities, without a coordinated interurban or interregional network of highways, forcing the shipping of goods by rail. Where interurban or interregional carriage of goods and passengers is feasible, it is still slow, and subject to constant delays caused by traffic congestion, flooding, or road repair.

Efforts are under way to improve road conditions so as to shift some of the burden for freight haulage away from the railways. A "national network" consisting of 110,000 kilometers of roads has been designated, with the aim of linking provincial capitals with one another, with the central authorities in Beijing, and with the important coastal cities. Major highways are being constructed around key cities. But these projects will take years to complete.

Beyond road conditions is the lack of trucks for transport. China has acknowledged the need to use more fuel-efficient trucks that are capable of carrying larger loads. In the countryside, it concedes that tractors for haulage—especially the small, two-wheeled "walking tractors" that are commonly adapted for use as vehicles—must be replaced by smaller, affordable trucks. The production of more efficient trucks, large and small, will impose further demands not only on the road system, but also for the production of higher-quality fuel supplies— including diesel—and the establishment of a fuel distribution network.

Waterways and Ports

Waterways were the common means of long-distance transport in traditional China. After being more than doubled in the 1950s, inland waterways were largely forgotten by Chinese planners. Because of the proliferation of irrigation and drainage projects and a general neglect of the waterways (with decollectivization in the Chinese countryside), the network of navigable waterways has shrunk by 30 percent from its peak of 162,000 kilometers in 1962 (see Table 8.3). Chinese planners are considering more extensive use of these waterways for two reasons: first, waterways are immediately available to reduce some of the traffic burden, and second, the utilization of existing waterways will reduce the often profligate diversion of agricultural land to needed road and rail construction.

Coastal shipping also would alleviate some of the burden of north-south rail routes, and China has made important progress in enlarging its merchant shipping fleet, in particular its container capacity. But increases in coastal shipping capacity only add to the congestion already found in China's major ports. On any given day 400 to 500 ships can be found waiting to dock at most major ports, with waiting times of thirty or more days. At major ports, like Shanghai, sixty-day waits are not uncommon. For some foreign ventures, these delays can be unbearably costly. One report noted that "even a small vessel of 2,000 to 3,000 tons can clock up demurrage charges of U.S. $10 million."[19] Consequently port construction in China's fifteen major coastal cities has been a priority investment target of Chinese planners. By 1990, China hopes to add 120 new berths in these cities, increasing its total cargo handling capacity from 300 million tons annually to 500 million tons.

Foreign investment and soft loans (especially from Japan and the World Bank) have played an important role in China's port development—a recognition of the potential damage that limited port facilities would have on China's desire to increase export earnings. Foreign investors have been attracted by additional incentives offered by China to develop port facilities. These incentives (for contracts of fifteen years or longer) include reduced income tax rates and the guarantee of adequate docking fees. The port of Mawan in the Shenzhen Special Economic Zone, for example, is the result of a $60 million investment by the Sum Cheong Piling Co., Ltd., of Singapore.

Air

Air travel in China is still in the early stages of development. Although its growth since 1978 has been dramatic, only 7.5 million passengers are carried annually, a level reached by the United States some forty years ago with one-fifth the population. Improvements in air transport will be slow on two counts. First, China still relies on foreign companies for its civil air fleet, a reliance that places a serious drain on foreign exchange. China has signed an agreement with McDonnell-Douglas for both the supply of aircraft and the training of Chinese personnel for the development of domestic manufacture (see Chapter 11 for details). However, China will remain dependent on foreign suppliers for some time to come.

Second, China's airports are in poor condition. Virtually all date back to World War II and need heavy investment to meet modern standards. Further, support infrastructure, ranging from a coordinated traffic control system to warehouse facilities, is inadequate. Again, the seventh five-year plan has sought to address some of these problems, but progress will be slow.

China's transportation system has grown quite rapidly since 1949, but it remains inadequate to serve the demands; growth in quantity has not been matched by a commensurate growth in quality. Beyond inadequate infrastructure, the means of transport and the backup facilities (e.g., warehousing, distribution networks) are lacking. This was perhaps most dramatically illustrated in 1985 when China had its largest grain crop to date. Despite the record harvest, much of the surplus went to waste, rotting either at source because storage facilities were too small or in transport containers because of unloading delays.

The emphasis placed on upgrading transportation facilities in the seventh five-year plan is a recognition of the vital role this sector must play if China is to realize its modernization plans. It goes only a small way, however, toward resolving the many difficulties that confront this sector.

SKILLED LABOR

China's skilled labor presents a paradox. China has the world's largest pool of cheap labor, and it is attractive in its level of education and its willingness to comply with the demands of an industrial society. As a direct result of the incentives associated with the economic reforms, Chinese labor occasionally has made sizable improvements in productivity, especially in the collective sector. Furthermore, they have even shown initiative when given positions of responsibility and involvement in decision-making. Yet skilled Chinese labor is in short supply, and Chinese workers, in many ways, are captives of their "dan wei" ("work units," or factory), so there is no pull of alternative opportunities to induce learning new skills.[20] The factory is the primary economic unit, after the family, and plays a central role in the distribution and redistribution of the wealth in the country. As mentioned previously, the "dan wei" provides wages, food allocation stamps, housing, and retirement income, and is the vehicle of administration and control of a variety of social programs including recreation; even a social event such as a dance will be held in one of the rooms of the "dan wei." Thus the worker has many bonds to his "dan wei," and change associated with greater professional mobility can be traumatic. There is no national labor market to facilitate career mobility. Consequently China provides the attraction of a promising labor market but one that often is particularly difficult to access.

Skill Shortages

It is not unusual to hear foreign managers in China complaining about the quality of Chinese labor. As a direct result of the Cultural Revolution and economic isolation, a whole generation of the Chinese work force was not exposed to modern technology or work methods that are taken for granted in the West. Consequently many workers are lacking in training that is quite basic. Furthermore, much of China's work force is perceived as lacking discipline, a characteristic that reflects the system of job protection. The large, state-owned enterprises were regarded as being particularly safe places to work because they could afford to make mistakes—"drop their rice bowls"—without suffering.

This is the origin of the characterization of permanent employment as "iron rice bowls." Because of their state support, they could maintain employment despite losses.

Less favored organizations had to be more vigilant, for their "rice bowls" were ordinary porcelain and would break if dropped. The "iron rice bowl" mentality remains a major problem affecting Chinese labor productivity, despite a decision to eliminate it by phasing in labor contracts, plus a vigorous campaign by the Chinese government to overcome it through greater competition, an increased emphasis on market performance and profit, greater accountability, and increased labor mobility. Even when these pressures are really applied and enforced, upgrading of skills is totally the initiative of the workers themselves and foreign investors, since the work force that was in place in 1986 has "grandfather rights" in terms of guaranteed employment.

Sources of Labor and Labor Mobility

The sources of Chinese labor and the mobility of that labor differ significantly, depending on the level of skill involved. Labor possessing low skills typically is obtained from local municipal labor bureaus. Many such workers are youths who have completed high school but who were not chosen for higher education. Foreign joint ventures are permitted to administer tests of both intellectual and physical capacities to workers and to refuse any offered by the labor bureau who do not pass. They also are allowed to impose a probationary period to gauge the worker's performance. Urban unemployment among youths is sufficiently high to permit providers of attractive jobs to be discriminating without serious penalty. Newly promulgated regulations do allow greater reliance on newspaper advertising and other forms of direct recruiting; however, some restrictions will probably remain to encourage the use of local people in the work force, which is a primary obligation of local governments.[21]

The hiring of skilled workers, particularly those with higher educations, is different from the employment of the relatively unskilled. Until recently, college students filled out "wish lists" in their senior year describing the position and location that they preferred, with location usually considered more important than position. These desires were matched by school officials against job opportunities that were being offered by state enterprises. Apparently, serious attempts were made to match students and jobs satisfactorily, but such a system is quite complex, and many students expressed dissatisfaction with their assignments, especially since they are "lifetime." The university students who struck for greater openness in 1989 were just such a select group of potential future cadres and bureaucrats.

The Chinese government has recently announced that college graduates can interview and find their own jobs. Although this system is too new to draw conclusions as to results, it does represent a step toward the creation of labor mobility and a national job market within China.

Career mobility among China's skilled workers has been a particularly vexing dilemma for the Chinese government. Despite more than eight years of calling for greater freedom in job choices, professional mobility remains more a dream than a fact and a continual reminder of the lack of individual freedom. The basic impediment to professional mobility in China is that the individual who wants to leave an organization for a job elsewhere must first secure the permission of the enterprise where he or she currently works. In a society where higher education has traditionally been relatively rare, and where the organization is not free to go into a job market to hire people whenever it needs them, an organization that already possesses someone with scarce skills is not going to be easily persuaded to part with that person. Therefore, even if the skills that the person possesses are not currently useful to the enterprise, the costs of holding that person and the probability of replacing them are both so small that it makes sense to deny permission to move than to respond to the interests of the state or the wishes of the individual.

Wages and Compensation

The average Chinese worker employed at a Sino-foreign joint venture in 1988 cost US $95.50 per month;[22] of this, take-home pay amounted to $45 and subsidies, $50.50.[23] Take-home pay usually consists of $35 in basic wages and $10 in bonuses, and the subsidies consist of 50 cents for education, $9 for housing, $4 for medical insurance, $7 for retirement insurance, $7 for labor welfare, $9 as a service fee, and $14 for general welfare. Most of these subsidies do not go directly to the worker, but are paid to various agencies, both within and outside the joint venture, that administer the specific benefits. This compensation package varies widely by locale ($151 per month was the average in Shanghai in 1989), but the general form is representative of most joint venture situations. In 1986, the basic wage paid by foreign joint ventures in China was 41 percent higher than that paid at Chinese state-owned enterprises, with that amount over normal levels going to the state "in lieu" of taxes.

A particularly irritating dimension to the compensation issue in foreign joint ventures is the often wildly inflated salary demands that are associated with the Chinese managerial staff, especially when compared with the wages that are actually received by Chinese managers. In one particularly blatant example, the Chinese general manager of a Japanese joint venture was "paid" in excess of 9,000 yuan (US $2368 at the then current exchange rate) per month by the joint venture, of which he received less than 300 ($79). Despite the appearance of deceit and unethical behavior, there may in fact be a reasonable rationale for such practices. Most Chinese have been taught from childhood about Western exploitation, and the government is determined to resist its reappearance. It is insulting to the Chinese and a loss of face to see Western counterparts in management earning far more than the Chinese, who often perform the same jobs. Indeed, the Chinese authorities complain that although most expatriate workers are competent, they are typically no more (and some *less*) so than their Chinese counterparts. Therefore, some equity in salaries is justifiable.[24]

Unemployment and Underemployment

A most difficult situation began to emerge during late 1989 that tended to upset the people and undermine party power—the rise of significant unemployment.[25] Underemployment—too many workers for the tasks required—has been a historical fact in China for some years, with factories forced to take workers on their payrolls. As a consequence, "five people ate the rise of three" and productivity declined and production sagged. An estimated 30 million urban workers were "unemployed on the job," with roughly half the rural work force in a similar situation.

Despite the underemployment in the cities, rural workers have surged into them, seeking a better life. The increasing productivity of private plots has released farm workers, and the baby boomers of the 1960s are increasing the labor force coming into the cities by an average of 20 million each year, with former retirees also reentering the labor pool. Consequently some 150 million rural workers are flooding the cities, with the figure expected to exceed 250 million by the year 2000. Despite efforts by authorities to force (expel) the immigrants back to the rural areas, the effort to migrate is virtually impossible to stop, given the disparity in living standards, as shown in Chapter 7. It is expected that unemployment of new entrants into the cities will remain around 50 percent far into the late 1990s. This condition can only exacerbate the problems of welfare and social services in the cities, increasing tensions.

MANAGEMENT

In OECD (Organization for Economic Cooperation and Development) economies, management would be held responsible for the deficiencies in enterprises resulting in high costs, low productivity, and poor quality. But in China, management at the enterprise level has had few of the levers of decision-making that characterize Western market systems. To move from the historical patterns of management in China to those required for international competition will require education and experience in several dimensions.

"Traditional" Chinese Management

Chinese management is in flux because of the dramatic changes that economic reforms have created in the environment of the more than 400,000 urban economic enterprises in which managers work. According to Deng Xiaoping and other Chinese leaders, a new form of "Chinese management" ultimately will evolve from this turbulent situation. While the current regime is seeking to modernize management, it is difficult to define what constitutes Chinese management. For the most part, Chinese managers remain in the traditional mold—typical of that found in centrally planned economies rather than in Western countries.[26]

The Development of Management Cadres

Management in China is very much an individual art. In modern societies, managerial techniques are professionalized and standardized, by virtue of participation in and instruction from a variety of recognized educational fora (e.g., university M.B.A. programs, professional journals, American Management Association, and management development programs). In contrast, the Chinese manager must learn the necessary skills almost on his own, without access to consultants to supplement his knowledge or that of his staff. The result is a managerial cadre that is undereducated, unprofessional, and often unsophisticated, punctuated by individuals who are truly "characters," and who are developing their own managerial style unfettered by any presumptions of professional behavior.[27] There has been a high failure rate in management; in one situation in a Beijing enterprise, a manager was removed in favor of a younger one, only to be returned when the successor proved to be even more inept; all the while, discussions continued on and off with the foreign investor without his knowing of the shifts. This experience is repeated in other enterprises, emphasizing the existence of considerable experimentation.

Social Responsibility

Because the Chinese work unit is the basic provider of housing—and frequently of education, health care, and even a wife (or husband)—it often is remarked that the Chinese enterprise director is more of a "mayor" than a manager. He or she (China is not a totally male-dominated society, as is Japan; one often meets women among top officials, but there is more pretense than substance to sexual equality) is continually involved in the domestic and personal affairs of the workers to a degree unprecedented in the West. Furthermore, because of the political and even "spiritual" (read "service") role of the work unit and the Communist Party within Chinese society, the enterprise director plays an influential role in even intimate aspects of Chinese life as well. The integration of life with the enterprise is buttressed by the fact that because the work unit is the traditional source of housing for its employees, most Chinese managers live "cheek by jowl" with their employees, and thus can never escape their roles.

The social responsibility that a Chinese manager feels was well demonstrated in a survey of ninety-four enterprises made when a provincial enterprise law was to give them the authority to reduce surplus labor in their factories. Before the law was in place, 69.5 percent of the managers expressed a desire to cut their labor force. After the law went into effect, only 6.6 percent of the managers made any major staffing changes, 69.1 percent reported minor changes, and the remaining 24.3 percent made no changes. Clearly, factory managers continue to feel social pressures in making management decisions.[28] And reductions in the labor force are just as unattractive to Chinese as they are to Americans.

Family Roles

The strains that arise from the "intimate" contact found between Chinese managers and their work force are made greater by the heavy reliance the Chinese management cadre has placed in the past on various forms of nepotistic rewards and favors; advancement is based on personal loyalty rather than on merit.

The Chinese traditional use of *guanxi* has, in many cases, not only resulted in bad decisions,[29] but also in the appointment of bad managers. Although such practices are attacked by the government, which recognizes the importance of merit in the selection of managerial personnel, the traditional reliance on *guanxi* by the Chinese has made it a quite durable practice. In a society impoverished in education, communication, information, and freedom of decisions in markets, and in which interpersonal trust has repeatedly been abused in the past, reliance on *guanxi* is probably rational behavior. It was, however, brought under severe criticism, being a major source of the discontent in the student hunger strikes in 1989.

Bureaucratic Ties

The matrix relationship that exists between the enterprise and the myriad of ministries, bureaus, companies, and agencies makes the role of the Chinese manager even more complex. Now that career advancement is a possibility for the manager who performs, and now that managerial autonomy is considerably greater than it has been—and linked directly to the quality of the workers' lives—there is considerably greater pressure on the Chinese enterprise managers to perform. Yet, for the most part, they are inadequately prepared to do so within a modern, competitive marketplace that demands sophisticated managerial skills.

The managers' task is made harder by the fact, noted earlier, that the ministries and bureaus have not given up as much of their decision-making prerogatives as the reform movement has suggested, or as the enterprise managers would like. For this reason, it should not be surprising that in a 1986 survey of 300 managers of Chinese electronics factories, more than half expressed a desire to be relieved from their positions.[30]

Specialization in Management

The complexity of participation within such a matrix works against attempts to systematize the managerial role and is exacerbated by the reliance on negotiation rather than on direct authority that is characteristic of Western management. Consequently the Chinese management role is better explained in terms of "holistic" or "fluid" managerial styles than "specialist" and "systematic"—a style the fits with Confucian culture and is encouraged by the traditional social role imposed on the Chinese manager.

Furthermore, there is less distinction between functional responsibilities within

a Chinese enterprise, owing to the nascent stage in which many of these previously unnecessary functions are found. In such cases, in which specialists are
scarce, good managers are drawn from many backgrounds to develop the new
role that is required. For example, many Chinese enterprises have aggressively
developed a marketing function without relying on marketing specialists or doing
market research.

Managers as Information Conduits

Unlike Western managers who pride themselves in their role as decision-
makers and resource allocators, the managers of Chinese enterprises more typically see themselves as "information conduits"—channels to bring information
from higher authorities to the workers and information from the workers to
higher authorities.[31] This attitude stems from a long tradition of oriental despotism, under which the central figure made all important decisions (with or
without advice) based on information supplied.[32]

Accordingly, it frequently is difficult for Chinese managers to act as decisively
and with as much dispatch as foreign counterparts might expect or desire. It is
not surprising that being an information conduit is preferred to being a decision-
maker when electronics factory managers perceive that

if they do more, they make more mistakes; if they do less, they make fewer mistakes;
and if they do not do anything, they still make mistakes. If the manager makes a few
mistakes he takes criticism from above and below and blame for all those around him.
Managers who commit minor mistakes are accused of having an improper working style.
They are interrogated by the party rectification committee. Managers who make serious
mistakes are forced to resign and fear imprisonment.[33]

This problem is compounded by the fact that China is an information-poor
society, so that even the decision of what information to present and how is
difficult—unless mandated by government. Although modern management is
typically associated with open, explicit, and dissemination-oriented communications systems, China remains a society of secretive, implicit communications
characterized by information-hoarding. In recent memory, there has not been
any positive inducement for a Chinese manager to share information or for that
information to be accurate when it is shared.

One of the characteristics of an information-poor society is that communication
becomes a luxury rather than a necessity. In addition, there is a great reliance
on the propagandistic character of *all* information exchanges. As a result, the
concept of an information society espoused by Western futurists and operation-
alized to some extent by modern management information systems runs into
social contradictions as well as hardware deficiencies in the Chinese context.

Management as a Frustrator of Economic Development

For the reasons described in the previous sections, the current state of managerial professionalism and technical sophistication among Chinese managers is so inadequate that the radical economic reforms sought often are frustrated by an inability to implement them. Similarly, the typical Chinese enterprise is unable to respond to what in the West would be considered normal changes in market demand, product design, and technological innovation. Despite improvements, most Chinese enterprises are still led by people who have little or no higher education. Consequently, without the breadth associated with higher educational experiences, these managers interpret national market changes as similar to those of local markets, with the result that they cannot adjust appropriately.[34]

Specific inadequacies in Chinese managerial techniques cover a wide range of activities. The most significant inadequacies are seen in the knowledge and use of modern management techniques. Figure 8.1 offers some insights into areas of management expertise that appear to be deficient in China. Among these are (a) marketing, especially understanding who the customers are and what they want in a product or service; (b) the ability to manage a multiparticipant (i.e., vendors, customers, distributors) manufacturing operation efficiently and effectively, in response to the demands faced by a product mix characterized by both high volume and high variety; (c) investment analysis and a familiarity with alternative methods of financing an industrial enterprise; (d) the establishment of internal corporate information and control systems; and (e) a variety of human resource management techniques, particularly those relating to performance evaluation and reward, and the concepts of directorship and corporate governance.

Reforms in Management

Management development and reform of the managerial environment are both directly and indirectly at the heart of much of the economic experimentation that is taking place in China as a result of the economic policies of the Deng Xiaoping administration. Essentially, there are four major means by which the position and environment of the Chinese manager are changing dramatically as a result of these reforms.[35]

Decentralization of Managerial Authority

Throughout the period of its governance over the People's Republic of China, the Communist government has repeatedly vacillated in its support of centralization of the economic system. Major oscillations between centralization and decentralization have occurred. The current economic reform program went further than any previous attempt at decentralizing the economic system before the retrenchment in late 1989; it did so not only by having the central ministries divest themselves of a considerable amount of involvement in the day-to-day affairs of specific industrial enterprises (the leadership of which has been passed

Figure 8.1
A Non-comprehensive Sample of Functional Management Knowledge That
Appears to Be Lacking in the Chinese Management Community

MARKETING   HUMAN RESOURCES

Market Research   Motivation & Incentives
Advertising   The Concept of Directorship
Product Design   The Role of the Manager
Industrial Marketing   Executive Compensation
Consumer Marketing   Organization Design
                                   Leadership Styles

MANUFACTURING   FINANCE

Total Quality Control   Investment Analysis
Managing High Volume/   Credit Analysis
  High Variety Operations   Methods of Financing
Value Analysis   International Finance
Inventory Management
Manufacturing Information
        Systems   ACCOUNTING
Distribution Systems
Establishment of Control   Auditing
        Systems   Public Accounting

ETHICS AND COMPARATIVE
    MANAGEMENT

CONTRACT LAW   MANAGEMENT OF SCIENCE AND
                                             TECHNOLOGY

                                   Anticipating Technological
                                         Change
                                   Managing Innovation and
                                         Creative Groups

Source: William A. Fischer, "The State of Chinese
Industrial Management," in Nigel Campbell & John Herley
(eds.), Advances in Chinese Industrial Shades: Joint
Ventures & Industrial Change in China, Greenwich, CT, JAI
Press, 1989.

to regional authorities), but also by providing the enterprise managers with
significantly greater discretion in managerial decision-making. This greater managerial autonomy has been part of and necessary for the introduction of a greater
play of market forces than has previously existed in China.

Although it differs from province to province and industry to industry,[36]
today's Chinese manager has considerably more autonomy over certain major
areas of business than has heretofore been the case. In particular, the Chinese
manager is now transitioning to a role in which he is responsible for developing,
producing, and distributing the products that his enterprise produces for customers in a competitive market. Progress is being made slowly. To date, most

Chinese managers do not have the authority or knowledge required to fulfill their responsibilities. Although still lacking control over the pricing decision, the enterprise manager can make capital investment decisions and advertise, and has new powers that affect the hiring and firing of the work force. Unlike in the past, when most decisions were made at the company level or higher, today's enterprise is responsible for its own working capital and investment capital and for earning enough profit to supplement worker salaries with bonuses and incentives that provide a higher standard of living.

Despite the rather surprising changes that have taken place in managerial autonomy, the Chinese manager is still not totally empowered to perform his job. The all-important product-pricing decision is still the prerogative of higher authorities, and employee hiring and firing decisions are complicated by a variety of exogenous factors. Particularly troublesome are those situations in which different portions of the economic system have experienced different degrees of autonomy, leaving the relatively more autonomous enterprises constrained by their less autonomous counterparts.

Greater Accountability

One of the most profound changes that has occurred as a result of economic reform is the considerably greater degree of economic discipline that has been introduced into industry.[37] This is primarily the result of the movement from a "grants economy" to a "loan economy." Under the new regime of relying primarily on bank loans for investment capital, real changes are being seen in the behavior of Chinese enterprises. No longer are Chinese managers cavalier about undertaking new projects, secure in the knowledge that if the project failed, they would still be protected by support from government agencies. Instead, the Chinese enterprise must borrow its investment capital from banks, which, in turn, expect repayment with interest on their loans. As a result, Chinese enterprises appear to be much more cautious in their investments, placing considerable emphasis on the suitability of prospective new technologies for their specific operating environment (even to the extent of involving their customers and suppliers in the investment process), and worrying about reliability and the time it will take to get the technology up and running, and generating cash flow to pay off the loan.

Although there is still some uncertainty among "China watchers" about just how much clout the banks actually have when "nationally important" projects are being considered, it seems clear that the Chinese managers themselves perceive the banks as being an important constituent that they do not want to antagonize, and so they appear to be altering their behavior in important ways. One consequence of this new discipline is that China's traditional insistence on state-of-the-art foreign technology, with "all the bells and whistles," has diminished; more appropriate technology is now sought. Increasingly, Chinese firms appear willing to consider older and "intermediate" technologies in an effort to ensure reliability and "fit" in their production systems.

Profit has, in principle, become the primary measure of performance and the principal measure of accountability in Chinese industry. Although there are, theoretically, a number of indices by which Chinese managers are measured, profit has taken priority among them. One particularly important reason for this is that the workers' bonuses, which represent an appreciable proportion of their take-home pay, depend on profits being earned. Without profits there are no bonuses, and without bonuses (which have become part of the workers' assumptions of "permanent income"), the labor force will be come restive.

Managerial contracts increasingly bind the manager to promises made to the local company or bureau; they, in turn, are the basis on which the manager's bonus or penalties are assessed. Also, a variety of other, often customized indices are considered in appraising managerial performance (loss reduction as a goal is being used in a number of instances in which the enterprise in question has historically not been a profitable venture and the manager is being asked to undertake a "heroic" task).

The main conclusion is that despite the complexity of the while situation, accountability is now very much the desired norm in Chinese industry, unlike the situation of only a few years ago, when there was little or no managerial accountability.

Incentives

As a result of the recent reforms, the use and types of incentives used in industry have been transformed. Since the 1950s, the Chinese have experimented with a wide range of incentives. They have moved from moral suasion and mass mobilization efforts, which relied on the patriotism and ideological allegiance of the people, to an emphasis on material incentives. Today a wide variety of material incentives, including piece-rate schemes, are used to motivate both workers and managers. Although there is still considerable debate as to the optimal scheme to be used, China is committed to tying pay to performance, supported by the new "socialist principle" of "to each according to his work" and the law of value.[38]

One recent change is a growing acceptance of managerial staff also sharing in managerial incentive schemes, sometimes at reward levels far above those of the average worker. This represents a rejection of the long-held and widely practiced reluctance of managers to reward themselves for superior performance for fear that they would be criticized for exploiting the workers. Today it is widely publicized that managerial "brainwork" is potentially more important than labor in the success of the enterprise, but many managers still reject large bonuses for fear of criticism.

A second, less direct material incentive that seems effective is the newly accepted idea of a career. Until recently, advancement in one's profession was the result of many factors, most of which were political. Managers were reluctant to discuss, and appeared not to think about, personal advancement or the concept of a career *in* business. Today, however, with performance being the most important criterion for advancement, most managers are being selected and promoted on the basis of their professional and technical expertise, and the concept of a career has emerged, with opportunities for career advancement catalyzing managerial behavior.

Organizational Flexibility

Given the previous vertical segmentation of the Chinese economy, there was little reason for experimentation with organizational design. The result was near uniformity of organizational structures even across widely different industries. Today, with increasing managerial autonomy and the need to perform, greater variety is emerging. Typically, this is occurring more through the creation of relationships *between* organizations than *within* them. Nevertheless, as a result of a wide range of domestic joint ventures, Chinese organizations are being restructured, and becoming more responsive to markets in the process.

Transfers of Foreign Managerial Skills

The lack of managerial sophistication in Chinese enterprises significantly hampers attempts to forge a new domestic, market-influenced economy to increase China's international competitiveness. This gap is a primary concern of the Chinese government, which has repeatedly stressed the need for improving China's managerial skills, particularly through learning foreign management techniques. Given China's heritage of central planning and the number of managers necessary to guide some 400,000 economic units within the country, there is a general lack of competent managers and managerial talents. This is not due to lack of abilities, but to poor educational and training programs. In addition, even well-prepared Chinese managers are relatively unprepared for decision-making in respect to market influences. Consequently their performance in many world markets has not lived up to their expectations.

Differences between Chinese and Western management styles and practices are not as immediately apparent as one might initially believe. In fact, many Western management experts have been struck more by the similarities that exist than by the differences. Nonetheless, as suggested by China's cultural orientations (Chapter 5), there are significant differences in reasoning between China and the West, including perception and cognition, reflected in managerial decision-making. Relations are bilateral and hierarchical, with a strong feeling of social responsibility regarding these relations, especially in the work place.[39]

For the firm doing business in China, either as a seller to the Chinese market or as a producer within China for export abroad, the introduction of modern management practice becomes almost a necessity. The choice of the most efficient means of doing this is not clear-cut. One way of transferring managerial training is to introduce expatriate managers to provide continuous, on-the-scene instruction as part of performing the daily job. A number of service operations, such as the Jing Guo Hotel in Beijing, operated by the Peninsula Group of Hong

Kong, have relied on just such a mechanism to introduce the subtle and complex tradition of service that maintains their international reputation.

An alternative method is to create formal training programs for the Chinese staff. This can be done at the Chinese location and is an efficient means of training a large number of people. But several problems can arise with such approaches, including the selection of attendees for such training; an inability to attract the sort of worker or manager for whom training would appear to be a desirable investment; and the sudden and unannounced transfer of newly trained personnel by government officials to disperse technology to other factories, shortly after they have finished the training program provided by the foreign firm.

Problems Remaining

Without denying the significant improvement that has been made in the Chinese manager's position, there still remain broad areas of dissatisfaction with prerogatives not granted and ambiguities not resolved.

A 1986 survey of 300 factory managers in the domestic electronics industry noted five key problems faced by contemporary Chinese managers.[40] First, many rapid and wide-ranging changes in macroeconomic policies have been imposed on the enterprises seemingly capriciously, especially the movement to a loan economy and the growing importance of foreign exchange.

Second, the administrative function is still too complex. Despite the "decentralization" of the Chinese system, there has been a renewed proliferation of government offices to which the enterprise must answer. Direct-line reporting to the ministries has been eliminated, but the bureaucrats continue to impose controls. This has increased the level of administrative complexity the enterprise manager faces because the local government with line control often is at odds with the ministries.

Third, full autonomy has not yet devolved to the enterprises, particularly in matters of personnel pricing and finance. The relative inability to hire in a national market or to fire incompetent workers, to have a free hand in establishing wage differentials, and to freely employ "equity" capital remain major problems.

Fourth, the continuing ambiguity and competition between the factory manager and the enterprise's Communist Party secretary make it difficult for the factory manager to make adjustments, handle employers, set policies, and lead when the party officer and the factory manager disagree. Although, officially, the enterprise director has undisputed control over the enterprise, considerable uncertainty remains at the factory level over just what that means. This uncertainty is the result of more than three decades of the party secretary being a most important actor in enterprise decision-making and in the personal fortunes of individuals. Today, although the government is emphatic that leadership lies with the manager, many workers believe that "managers may come and go but the party secretary will linger on." This ambiguity is exacerbated by party secretaries who are openly reluctant to give up their positions of authority and power and become relegated to what often is described as a "cheerleading" function. The fact that the Chinese press is replete with descriptions of factories in which the party secretaries and committees are unwilling to give up power and in which they actually impede economic performance emphasizes the significance of this problem. Finally, the adjustments that have had to be made in changing from a command economy to one that contains market influences and the pressure of public opinion make the factory manager's job considerably more difficult. One manager commented that he feared that once the factory manager responsibility system was implemented, the factory manager would become the center of criticism. As a result, the Chinese manager faces responsibilities that are changing and for which he is ill-prepared.

RESEARCH AND DEVELOPMENT

Unlike many developing countries, in which science and technology have been regarded as largely unaffordable luxuries, the People's Republic of China has consistently supported a wide variety of scientific and technical activities, including industrial research and development (R&D).[41] As a result of this support, China enjoys several advantages that are not found in most developing countries. China has a relatively large population of technical workers, many of whom have had some formal training in their specialties. In addition, China has several research institutes that are world leaders in their field of research, though they typically are involved in either military technology or pure science.[42] The Chinese were the first to synthesize insulin; they succeeded in launching space satellites, and reported successes in superconductivity in 1987, almost immediately after the first findings from Houston. These are testimony to its scientific and technical capabilities in a few highly visible areas. Other examples exist of advanced, although not world-leading, capabilities in research institutes in other fields. In addition, a number of academic institutions with scientific and technical specialties have close ties with industry. In short, China has a remarkably well-developed and well-endowed scientific and technical base for a developing nation.

As with any developing country, China's scientific and technical systems have several major deficiencies, resulting principally from inadequacies in the social, economic, and technical infrastructure. They involve poor equipment because of scarcities in foreign exchange, poor or unavailable technical capabilities (both hardware and software), inadequate educational facilities and offerings, the absence of particular skills and knowledge, unavailable information, and poor research materials and information.

These problems constrain China's ability to achieve world-class levels in a wide range of science and technology, limiting real achievements to a few well-endowed institutes. Furthermore, such deficiencies are exacerbated by problems that have been caused by four decades of central planning. Though the bureaucracy supported the pursuit of science and technology, it has also been a major source of frustration.

Structure and Organization of R&D

The Soviet influence on China's industrial economy also is reflected in the structure of industrial R&D activities.[43] China's scientific and technical activities are organized vertically in each sector, stretching from the State Science and Technology Commission (under the State Council) down to the Provincial and Municipal Science and Technology Commissions and into the institutes and enterprises. The R&D activities in each industrial sector occasionally are linked through a science and technology division of the ministries at the top, stretching down through similar divisions at the local bureau and companies to the enterprise or independent research institutes. Applied and industrial R&D also are increasingly being conducted in the research institutes of the Chinese Academy of Sciences, which itself vertically controls a set of institutes occasionally linked to the other two sets.

The strength of all such systems, according to socialist logic, is the ability to fully utilize scarce resources by means of the centralization of control and coordination of all activities, which allows for the supposed optimization of resource allocation. In those few cases where such control and coordination have actually been operative—as in setting a high priority on synthesizing human insulin,[44] and, presumably, the cases of the development of the atomic bomb and the pre–Cultural Revolution computer industry—central control *has* helped China to mobilize its scarce resources to become a world leader. For the most part, however, the system simply has not worked, with the consequence that Chinese science and technology, like the rest of China's industrial system, is severely fragmented along vertical sector lines, with little horizontal transfer of technology.

The recent economic reforms have shifted the role and funding of R&D throughout and across all sectors. The research institutes, including those of the Academy of Sciences, eventually will be required to earn their own support. One reason for this edict has been the frustration of Chinese science and technology planners with the gulf existing between the producers and consumers of R&D and the need to bridge this gap by forcing institutes to seek ways to serve their intended markets.[45] Faced with uncertain futures and the expected loss of government subsidies, some research institutes, including some that are academically oriented, have become quite aggressive in the pursuit of clients for their R&D services. Still, most research institutes continue to receive a substantial amount of their budgets from governmental grants, but research institutes in industrial enterprises are dependent on an allocation of the enterprise's retained earnings for their support.

R&D at the Enterprise Level

The great bulk of Chinese industrial R&D is performed at the enterprise level, and is similar in approach to that in the United States. Industrial R&D managers the world over face the same general problems: resource constraints and the difficulties of managing intellectuals in situations characterized by longtime horizons and considerable uncertainty.[46] In the Chinese enterprise, R&D activities usually are led by the chief engineer,[47] who typically is a vice-director of the enterprise, having considerable managerial influence because of the technical resources under his authority:

> The Chief Engineer in today's Chinese industrial enterprise is a fairly formidable figure. He is clearly at least the equivalent of a vice-president of R&D in a Western firm. The chief engineer is usually personally involved in making the final decisions on technical project selection both within the technical groups of the enterprise and often within the workshops as well. Because of his influence over the enterprise's funding for technical activities, the chief engineer tends to have his finger on the total technical pulse of the enterprise.[48]

The term "chief engineer" is an honorific title as well as a job description in most Chinese enterprises; he may have no more than a college degree with a technical major. Increasingly, however, as part of the reforms, younger and better trained members of the enterprise are being selected for this position out of R&D and production operations.

The chief engineer typically is responsible for three technical groups: the design group (or research institute), the process technology group, and the workshop technical teams. The design group is chiefly responsible for new product development, whereas the process technology group is responsible for process selection and development decisions, and the workshop technical teams are devoted to process improvement. In many factories, the chief engineer also might be responsible for quality control, trial production, and the technical information office.

Most technical workers in Chinese enterprises have far less formal education and considerably less scientific sophistication than their Western counterparts. As a result, they frequently are not well informed about the state of the art in related scientific and technical fields outside of China. This situation will change as China increases its exposure to the outside world. Most Chinese technical workers do, however, have a significantly greater amount of experience on the shop floor, which frequently leads to the development of imaginative, if somewhat primitive, solutions to process problems. Because of the relative lack of formal training and sophistication, Chinese technical groups frequently rely on reverse engineering as a primary means of introducing new product designs in the domestic market, relying on the Chinese strengths in pragmatism and experience-based know-how. This practice has resulted in the copying of some product weaknesses in precise detail—ones that were later corrected in the West and remained undiscovered in China.

R&D in Joint Ventures

Given the traditional reluctance of multinational corporations to share or relocate R&D abroad,[49] the amount of R&D that is being supported by foreign interests in China is extremely small. China would like to see more foreign-sponsored R&D take place there, using Chinese engineers and scientists. The primary obstacles to such activities, beyond the reluctance on the part of transnational corporations, include suspicions about Chinese willingness and/or ability to protect shared intellectual property, a perceived lack of skills in relevant scientific and technical communities in China, and deficiencies in infrastructure. The first two are clearly diminishing, but slowly.

As a result of enhanced competition domestically, Chinese enterprises are increasingly seeking to protect intellectual property. Deliberate sharing of intellectual property with erstwhile competitors is no longer the significant danger that it was only a few years ago. With further improvement of intellectual property laws in the Chinese domestic economy, such dissemination should become less of a problem. Nonetheless, China continues to be burdened by the reputation of a "copyright pirate." In 1989, China was identified by the International Intellectual Property Alliance as being the world's leading violator of intellectual property rights. Estimates of losses in China for 1988 were placed at US $418 million. In one case alone, Collier Macmillan reported print runs of more than one million copies of its *English 900* textbook in China without compensation, a loss conservatively estimated at US $100 million a year.[50] China has been working on improving its position in this regard, and in late 1990 issued a copyright law that was close to Western practice.[51]

The scarcity of adequately trained Chinese scientists and engineers also should be reduced as educational institutions improve and as Chinese faculty and graduate students return from studying abroad. Despite the huge numbers of Chinese studying abroad, it will take a relatively long time to bring them back to China and reintroduce them into the various Chinese scientific, industrial, and academic communities. The treatment of the student reformers in 1989 will probably delay this process even more. This delay will frustrate transnational corporations in tapping Chinese domestic science and technology talent.

NOTES

1. The supply of water is sufficient in the main, but shortages of rainfall, incorrect estimates of groundwater supplies, and wasteful uses of water have created scarcities in the northern provinces. (See the report by Ann Scott Tyson, "Water Is Running Out in China," *Christian Science Monitor*, June 5, 1990, p. 12.)

2. A caution is in order, however, for China's timber and forest resources are fast

diminishing. A report in the *People's Daily* (Beijing) warned of a serious drop in forests from nearly 13 percent of the land to less than 9 percent by the year 2000 unless strong measures were taken. This percentage compares with 66 in Japan, 35 and 33 in the USSR and the United States, and between 20 and 30 in each of West Germany, France, and India. At the current rate of consumption, it was anticipated that state timber enterprises would be out of business by the end of the century, especially since only 10 percent of the trees planted survive. The results are more widespread, in that soil erosion occurs with silting into the rivers, more readily causing flooding. (See *World Press Review*, September 1990, p. 42).

3. This section borrows extensively from a paper by William A. Fischer, "China's Manufacturing Capabilities," Working paper, Center for Manufacturing Excellence, University of North Carolina Graduate School of Business, April 1989.

4. Dwight H. Perkins, *China—Asia's New Economic Giant* (Seattle: University of Washington Press, 1986).

5. In 1978, China produced 150,000 motor vehicles in 130 separate production enterprises in twenty-six provinces under the jurisdiction of several ministries. Gene Tidrick, *Productivity Growth and Technological Change in Chinese Industry*, World Bank Staff Working Papers, No. 761 (Washington, D.C.: The World Bank, 1986), p. 13.

6. Willy Wo-Lap Lam, *Toward a Chinese-style Socialism* (Hong Kong: Oceanic Cultural Service Co., 1987), p. 109.

7. Tidrick, *Productivity Growth and Technological Change*, p. 13.

8. Charles N. Stabler, "Looking Toward China for Growth in Trade," *Wall Street Journal*, November 16, 1987, p. 1.

9. Lynn Pan, *The New Chinese Revolution* (London: Hamish Hamilton, 1987), p. 119.

10. Here we are referring to the disastrous effects of admitting actual situations in the years of the "Learn from Dazhai" mobilization, in the late 1960s.

11. Tang Zhongkun, "Supply and Marketing," in Gene Tidrick and Chen Jiyuan, *China's Industrial Reform* (New York: Oxford University Press, 1987), p. 221.

12. Andrew G. Walder, "Some Ironies of the Maoist Legacy in Industry," in Mark Selden and Victor Lippit, eds., *The Transition to Socialism in China* (Armonk, N.Y.: M. E. Sharpe, 1982).

13. Oiva Laaksonen, *Management in China During and After Mao in Enterprises, Government, and Party* (Berlin: Walter de Gruyter, 1988), p. 256.

14. The University of Illinois at Chicago and the China Statistical Information and Consultancy Service Center, *China Statistics Monthly*, April 1988, p. 112.

15. *Statistical Yearbook of China, 1989* (New York: Praeger, 1990), pp. 50–51.

16. Jacques Yenny, "Modernizing China's Transport System," *China Business Review*, July-August 1986, pp. 20–23.

17. Thawat Watanatada, Clell Harral, and Pam Baldinger, "Railways," *China Business Review*, March-April 1989, pp. 14–19.

18. Chen Yuanhua, "Highways," *China Business Review*, March-April 1989, pp. 28–30.

19. *Journal of Commerce*, March 22, 1989.

20. Gail Henderson and Myron Cohen, *The Chinese Hospital* (New Haven, Conn.: Yale University Press, 1984).

21. J. P. Horsley, "The Chinese Workforce," *China Business Review*, May-June 1988, pp. 50–55.

22. Much of this section relies on the article by Jamie P. Horsley cited in note 21.

23. *U.S. Joint Ventures in China: A Progress Report*, National Council for U.S.-China Trade, 1987, Washington, D.C., as quoted in Horsley, "Chinese Workforce," p. 51.

24. "Who's the Boss?" *Intertrade*, August 1987, pp. 10–11.

25. See *Christian Science Monitor*, October 4, 1989, p. 1, and October 6, 1989, p. 4.

26. Wenlee Ting, *Business and Technological Dynamics in Newly Industrializing Asia* (Westport, Conn.: Quorum Books, 1985), pp. 110–111.

27. Ting has referred to "traditional" management as being more "entrepreneurial" than modern management. This is in fact the case, if you ignore the popular image of the entrepreneur as a savvy struggler against bureaucracy and recognize instead that entrepreneurship also is experimentation.

28. "More Cracks in the Iron Rice Bowl," *Far Eastern Economic Review*, March 24, 1988, p. 89.

29. William A. Fischer and Denis F. Simon, "The Managerial and Technical Issues in Technology Assimilation," paper presented at a conference on Technological Change and Economic Performance in the People's Republic of China, Woodrow Wilson Center, Smithsonian Institution, Washington, D.C., April 1987.

30. Zhang Zhongfang, "Managing a Factory Is Difficult: More than Half of All Managers Want to Be Relieved, Reports a Sampling Survey of 300 Chinese Factories; the Head of the Factory Managers Research Association of the China Electronics Industries Association Analyzes the Causes for Our Correspondent," *Jiefang Ribao*, August 23, 1986, pp. 1, 3; trans. Foreign Broadcast Information Service/China Report/Economic Affairs, JPRS-CEA–87–00 6, January 28, 1987, pp. 52–55.

31. This has been demonstrated in some unpublished work by Joseph Alutto, at the National Center in Dalien in 1984.

32. Karl A. Wittfogel, *Oriental Despotism* (New York: Vintage Books, 1981).

33. Zhongfang, "Managing a Factory Is Difficult," pp. 54–55.

34. William A. Fischer, "Market Influences, Technological Innovation, and Managerial Education in Chinese Industry," University of North Carolina Graduate School of Business Administration, Working Paper, Summer 1989.

35. William A. Fischer, "Chinese Industrial Management, Outlook for the Eighties," Joint Committee of the Congress, *China's Economy Looks Toward the Year 2000* (Washington, D.C.: U.S. Government Printing Office, 1986).

36. The problem here is that China is literally in the throes of great experimentation, and what happens in one place or in one industry may very well be at the initiative of a single official who is experimenting on his or her own. As a result, it is difficult to speak of these reforms as if they are standardized.

37. Denis F. Simon and William A. Fischer, *Technology Transfer to China* (Cambridge, Mass.: Ballinger, forthcoming 1991).

38. Xue Muqiao, *China's Socialist Economy* (Beijing: Foreign Language Press, 1981).

39. W. A. Fischer, "The Transfer of Western Managerial Knowledge to the Chinese," Paper presented at the National Meeting of the Decision Sciences Institute, Honolulu, November 1986; see also Wenlee Ting, *Business and Technological Dynamics in Newly Industrializing Asia* (Westport, Conn.: Greenwood Press, Quorum Books, 1985).

40. Zhongfang, "Managing a Factory Is Difficult," p. 54.

41. Two books by Richard P. Suttmeier chronicle the development and support of science and technology in the People's Republic of China: *Science, Technology and*

China's Drive for Modernization (Stanford, CA: Hoover Press, 1980), and *Research and Revolution* (Lexington, Mass.: D. C. Heath, 1974).

42. For an assessment of China's capabilities in science and technology that concludes that these may not be adequate for industrial competitiveness in the world economy, see Denis F. Simon, ''China's Economy Confronts the Challenge of the Global Technological Revolution,'' *Business in the Contemporary World*, Spring 1989, pp. 98–114.

43. Much of this section is drawn from William A. Fischer, ''The Structure and Organization of Chinese Industrial R&D Activities,'' *R&D Management*, 13, no. 2 (1983): 63–81. This source contains considerably more detail about the actual workings of this system and remains reasonably accurate five years later.

44. Hu Youngchang, Jiang Chengcheng, Chen Changqing, Luo Deng, and Huang Aizhu, ''The Policy Adopted for the Total Synthesis of Insulin and Yeast Alanine TRNA and the Manner in Which the Work Was Organized,'' paper presented at the National Academy of Sciences U.S.-China Science Policy Conference, Washington, D.C., January 1983.

45. The model of Korea is appropriate. See J. N. Behrman, *Industry Ties with Science and Technology Policies in Developing Countries* (Cambridge, Mass.: Oelgeschlager, Gunn & Hain, 1980).

46. William A. Fischer, ''Do We Stand on Our Heads While We Work?'' *Research Management*, 26, no. 2 (1983): 28–33.

47. William A. Fischer, ''The Chief Engineer,'' *China Business Review*, November-December 1983, pp. 30–34.

48. Fischer, ''Structure and Organization,'' p. 69.

49. Jack N. Behrman and William A. Fischer, *Overseas R&D Activities of Transnational Corporations* (Cambridge, Mass.: Oelgeschlager, Gunn & Hain, 1980).

50. Clyde H. Farnsworth, ''China Called Top Copyright Pirate,'' *New York Times*, April 20, 1989, p. 31.

51. See Pitman Potter, ''Bettering Protection for Intellectual Property,'' *China Business Review*, July-August 1989, and Peter A. Schloss, ''China's Long-awaited Copyright Law,'' *China Business Review*, September-October 1990.

9

Contributions of Foreign Direct Investment

One of the main problems in foreign direct investment (FDI) is that of achieving an arrangement between the foreign investor and the host country that is seen as in the mutual interest of both. The contributions that the foreign investor considers that he is bringing are not always the ones sought by the host country, and sometimes the contributions sought by the host country are not willingly provided by the foreign investor. Furthermore, the contributions sought and those available change over time and sometimes are altered by unforeseen circumstances. Therefore, negotiations are always imminent. The foreign investor should prepare for negotiations by delineating the potential contributions of each party; to do so requires an understanding of the differing contributions available from different types of companies and projects. On their part, Chinese officials need to become more aware of the limitations faced by private companies on their ability and desire to contribute to developmental objectives other than direct response to markets.

CONTRIBUTIONS SOUGHT BY CHINA

The contributions sought by China are directly related to the developmental strategy adopted by the government. The World Bank has delineated five models of development: (1) highly open economies, readily permitting inflows and outflows of foreign investment, with few barriers to trade; (2) relatively open economies, which remain open on investment flows but promote exports and protect several sectors; (3) economies formed into an open regional market, with free trade and investment inside, but with selective protection of industries against imports and inward investment; (4) highly protected economies, with quite selective entry of foreign capital and targeting of specific industries for support and protection; and (5) economies that are closed to imports and FDI.[1] There are virtually none in the last category, and even the highly protected economies are dwindling in number. China is not a member of any regional association and is not expected to be in the twentieth century; it is not ready to open its economy to the extent of the highly advanced countries. Its own assessment of development experience is that those following a strategy of relatively open economies with selective protection and support (category 2) have achieved the highest rates of growth. Such countries follow an export-oriented development, promoting technology and competitive processes in support of greater exports. These governments provide protection to infant industries and support new enterprise formation by a variety of techniques. Neighboring countries of Asia have provided such models of success. It is this strategy that China has chosen to follow ultimately, though it has not yet achieved a complete application.

Today China remains effectively closer to category 4, highly protected economics with quite selective entry of foreign capital and targeting of specific sectors for support. The domestic market is in essence protected from foreign competition by the dual-currency system, since sales in the domestic economy must be accompanied by exports for the hard currency needed for profit repatriation of the joint venture. And for the reasons discussed earlier, exports from China in areas other than labor-intensive and basic-resource industries are still difficult to achieve on a profitable basis. Although it has not been publicized, China may have the intention of protecting some industries for development of export capabilities. Immediately after Beijing-Jeep and Volkswagen began production, China restricted the import of autos through high taxes (equal to the purchase price) and limited import licenses for autos.

In applying a guided but open policy, four distinct contributions are sought from new investment, whether domestic or foreign, though some are more effectively made by foreigners because of their greater experience in international competition: (1) investment to substitute for existing imports, to increase the domestic base of production and relieve the balance-of-payments pressure; (2) investment to promote exports, initially relying on labor-intensive processes— as in the textiles and apparel industries—again increasing the domestic base and adding to foreign exchange earnings; (3) investment to substitute for imports but to utilize technology and capital-intensive processes, upgrading the production capabilities and preparing for eventual export of the products; (4) investment to exploit natural resources, thereby stimulating production and export of agricultural and mineral products and expanding the value-added through processing. Of these four, two are oriented toward the expansion of the domestic market (and reduction of imports) and two are oriented to entry into foreign markets. China has not yet found an appropriate balance among these contributions and may not for some time, given the fact that it has a number of deficiencies within the economy that are likely to remain. To help most effectively, an accommodation is required among the contributions of FDI, the conditions of the internal economy, and developmental goals.

Goals

China has set a goal of quadrupling the total value of agricultural and industrial production between 1982 and the year 2000, which would mean a $1 trillion gross national product (GNP) at that time. At a minimum, China would require $100 billion of foreign capital (direct and portfolio) over the remainder of this century to achieve this goal. Given the delay in utilization of funds committed, this will mean roughly $10 billion per year in commitments during the last decade of the century. Although this seems a large figure, it would still be only about 1.3 percent of the total GNP in that last decade, which would amount to about $7.5 trillion in aggregate over the ten years if the goal is to be reached. Compared with the nearly 5 percent of total European GNP that was contributed by foreign aid and investment under the Marshall Plan for European recovery, there is substantial room for greater contribution of foreign funds. Not all such funds will have to come from direct investment, however, since China also is borrowing abroad for various infrastructure projects. Still, there is room for significant additional contributions from abroad through direct investment.

Sectors Targeted

China's plans for economic development have categorized the sectors that are appropriate for the introduction of advanced technology as follows:

A. Certain important machine tools, electrical products and instruments and meters that China cannot manufacture now;

B. Scarce goods which China can produce in small quantities and inferior quality;

C. The products which are used in tourist, catering, and other services and can earn foreign currency;

D. Needed products that heavily depend on raw materials, parts and auxiliaries produced by China;

E. Products of advanced enterprises that are newly operational. It takes time to market these products abroad, because the workers have to familiarize themselves with the work;

F. Parts and auxiliaries that may strengthen the competitiveness of our exports and increase foreign trade earnings;

G. Products that are helpful to the development of our newly emerging industries;

H. Products whose manufacture will not require funds, construction materials and means of production from the state, have ready markets, cause no problem of foreign currency balance and meet the market demand.[2]

In these areas, the domestic market will be opened on a selective basis to joint ventures. The determination as to whether or not the joint venture can serve the domestic market will depend on the degree of advanced technology, on the use of the products (including home demand), and on competitiveness in the international market. The division of domestic and foreign sales also should be made on the basis of the plans of the various ministries for development and technological transformation as well as the potential social and economic benefits from their serving domestic demand. These determinations will be made not by the foreign enterprises or even the joint ventures, but by the government officials approving the contracts.

The contributions expected from joint ventures may in fact shift over time. Thus, although some joint ventures may be approved to open up international markets, they may initially serve domestic markets. The China Schindler Elevator Company, Ltd., mainly serves the domestic market, but it is expected to produce predominantly for export in the future. On the other hand, more than 90 percent of the products of both the Dynasty Wine and the Hangzhou West Lake Retin Works Company, Ltd., are sold in the advanced countries of Asia, Europe, and North America. The work shoes made by Nantong Liwang Company, Ltd., are exported 100 percent to Japan, since they are used only by Japanese rice farmers. Still another category is the added processing of indigenous materials to enhance value-added, such as the woolen sweaters of Xingjiang Tianshan Woolen Products Company, Ltd., and the products of Shanghai Gaoshi Essence Company, Ltd.

Finally, there are those joint ventures that will be principally oriented to the domestic market, substituting substantially for imports—such as the automobile industry. Eighty percent of the vehicles produced by Beijing Jeep Company, Ltd., are for the home market; all Santana cars produced by Shanghai Volkswagen and the colored plate glass produced by Shanghai Yaohua Pilkington Glass, Ltd., are sold almost wholly in the home market; however, Shanghai Yaohua Pilkington must export 15 percent of its production to earn foreign exchange for profit remission and import needs. The automotive industrial instruments and meters of Shanghai Foxboro are principally for the domestic market, and two-thirds of Camel cigarettes, made by Shanghai China–U.S. Tobacco Company, are distributed domestically. Finally, much of the petroleum produced by joint ventures has been sold in China because of a general scarcity.

Involvement of foreign capital is seen in China as a phase in overall development, maintaining the country's high degree of self-reliance, but with greater openness to the international economy. This will be done through careful guidance of the FDI into large-scale projects with long-term payout plus much smaller-scale projects in light industries with more immediate returns. In both cases, the concept of "equality and mutual interest" does not necessarily include ready access to the domestic market by the foreign joint ventures.

The role of joint ventures is more valuable for technology transfer, management know-how, and access to international markets than for initial capital contribution. The major part of China's requirement of $10 billion per year of capital can only be obtained through international borrowing. The capital contribution that will be made through normal joint venture activities will simply not be sufficient to do more than capitalize these ventures. China's capital requirements extend far beyond these to build appropriate infrastructure.

TRANSNATIONAL CORPORATION CONTRIBUTIONS

It is largely in market orientation that a divergence arises between China and foreign transnational corporations (TNCs). Save for the resource-oriented companies, pursuing oil and mineral resources, the major interest that foreigners have in China is to develop the domestic market. There are few opportunities for sourcing of components or assemblies in China for use in more advanced countries that are not also more readily available in other developing countries. The low wages of workers provides a potential export advantage for domestic enterprises, but these low-wage patterns are not always permitted for the foreign joint ventures, reducing somewhat the contribution they can make to export capabilities. In addition, the labor content in many products in the world market is dropping because of automation. Although incentives are provided through tax waivers, it is the *total* cost of operation that a TNC examines. "Normal conditions of production" in China make it difficult to export, reducing the effectiveness of tax incentives.

Further, given the orientation of China to self-reliance (read as "limited autarchy"), many TNCs see the contribution of advanced technology as the development of potential competitors for the future. Although some are willing to accept the risk, others are willing to contribute only less than the latest technology.

TNC Perceptions

TNCs see their major contributions not just in terms of technology, capital, managerial skills, and market penetration, but in the entire capabilities of private enterprise leading to invention, innovation, market expansion, and competitiveness. These require a high degree of flexibility in management and technical processes, in turn necessitating a policy of nonintervention by governments. On the other hand, the TNCs seek from government a high degree of stability and certainty in policies toward the private sector. They do not mind the existence of government plans; in fact, plans that provide some certainty and support for development are welcomed. Obstacles to TNC contributions are uncertainty and continued change in the terms of reference or guidelines for the private sector or foreign investor.

Given the developmental stage in which China finds itself, it is not feasible to open the economy in the same way that Singapore or Hong Kong did. Existing industries and enterprises require nurturing and improvement before they can stand on their own. Without such careful guidance, fledgling Chinese enterprises could be seriously set back by foreign joint ventures or even substantial imports, as occurred with the Shanghai domestic computer industry when imports rose substantially in 1985.

Prerequisites for Technology Transfer

Because the Chinese government places so much emphasis on acquisition of advanced technology and processes would enhance the capabilities of existing enterprises, it is necessary to look at the conditions that would make the contributions of foreign technology most effective.[3] The mere transfer of technology from overseas is by no means enough to make the contribution effective. There must be an entire system for receiving the technology and utilizing it effectively, as well as a process of careful selection so that it is not wasted through inefficiency or nonuse. TNCs themselves are not always overtly aware of what is necessary for recipients to utilize the technology effectively. Some have simply passed technology to a recipient in written or oral communication, leaving the host company to use it in the best way they could see fit. In many cases, there is insufficient ability to receive and utilize current technology.

Effective technology transfers have four prerequisites: the *ability* and *willingness* of the owner of the technology to transfer it and the *willingness* and *ability* of the recipient to use it. If any of these is absent, the expected contributions are not fully achieved. Most of the attention paid to technology transfers is focused on the *willingness* of the licensor and the *willingness* of the licensee or his government to participate in the transfer. Much less attention has been paid to the relative *abilities* of each partner, but these often are much more important in consummating the actual transfer and making it effective.

Technology Export

In the foregoing comments on China's orientation, we have noted a strong willingness on the part of the government and of enterprises to accept foreign technology, but the willingness of the foreigner to release it and to actually transfer it is much less strong. This is partly a concern that a future competitor will be generated, particularly if the licensor is precluded from long-term participation in any joint venture. But the willingness also is reduced by the historical lack of appreciation in China (as in Taiwan) of the need to extend protection of trade names, copyrights, and patents. The traditional attitude remains in China that "machines can be owned, but knowledge belongs to everyone." This stance is taken at the same time that objections are made that royalties are "too high," draining foreign exchange and raising costs of the ventures. The West considers that knowledge belongs to whoever creates or acquires it, and that this proprietary interest is important in the stimulation of invention and the movement of invention into commercialization through innovation. Know-how, which may be different from technology, often is the Western company's sustainable competitive advantage, and is so valued.

Historical science in China (as discussed in Chapter 5) did not lead to extensive commercial activity; this may be partly explained by lack of ability to appropriate the rewards for these discoveries. Much of the technology in China that was used in economic development arose out of the need to resolve certain problems, such as bridge construction, buildings, and recording of events chronologically. The development of enterprise that arises through invention and innovation, and that leads to profit for the principal actors, does not frequently appear in China's economic history.

The *willingness* of the owner of proprietary technology also is related to the terms of the agreement, including the price or returns received. There normally are some thirty topics considered for inclusion in licensing agreements—whether to independent or related licensees—that delineate the responsibilities of the licensor and those of the licensee; each one of these provisions is tradable against others and particularly against the financial returns. Thus the right to receive back improvements made by the licensee would tend to reduce the royalties agreed to under the license. Similarly, a request by the licensee to have an exclusive right to use the technology would increase the royalty rate. As with most developing countries, China has continued to undervalue technology (seeking to negotiate low royalties) as compared with world practices or what a potential licensor considers appropriate; this is part of the zero-sum mentality discussed earlier. Royalties and expatriate salaries—two negative subjects in China—are both viewed as a form of Western exploitation: The Chinese consider that these rich companies should absorb such expenses themselves for the privilege of doing business in China.

Perhaps of even greater importance to the effectiveness of a technology transfer than the supplier's *willingness* to transfer a technology is the *ability* of the licensor to transfer the technology so that it can be readily understood and put into practice by the licensee. Not all potential licensors are so capable. Companies with extensive practice in such transfers are more likely to know how to do so effectively; on the other hand, they may be so standardized in their approach that they cannot make appropriate adaptations for different cultural, economic, or social settings. Some companies essentially transfer a standardized package and let the licensee sort out how it is used. Others, who are new to the game, will be learning by doing, and therefore will not be as capable in making the technology understood by a licensee or know how to adapt it to different conditions and different materials. Most Chinese companies will insist that the technology transfer agreement is not satisfied, and no payment will be made until they have successfully produced some number of items using it. This leads to negotiation on the conditions under which the items are to be successfully produced, with or without a foreign company's assistance. Issues in such negotiations include whether the licensee has to train Chinese personnel, the cost of such training, and over what period of time this effort will endure; the number of items that must be produced before licensee is considered ''capable''; and the criteria of ''adequacy and capability.''

Not the least of the problems of licensors is their unfamiliarity with different cultures and operating environments and the way in which these are related to technology. They, therefore, cannot anticipate the problems and sometimes will underprice the cost of transfer, only to become frustrated later as costs rise in meeting unanticipated situations. The desire on the part of many developing countries, including China, for technology from medium-sized or even small companies may produce licensing agreements but not effective transfers because of a lack of experience in transferring technology.

Given time and a willingness on the part of both parties each to go through the process of learning, most licensors eventually will find a way to effectively transfer technology; a few simply give up the game, being unwilling to take the time or make the effort to do so.

Technology Absorption

The most important aspect of all is the *ability* of the host country and licensee to effectively absorb the technology. This ability is taken for granted on the part of most developing countries. As a consequence, frequently not enough is done to make certain that the receptiveness actually exists.

A substantial effort is required in building a scientific and technological infrastructure not only within the recipient, but also surrounding and supporting him. A sufficient scientific base is needed so that appropriate agencies or entities can screen the technology coming in to make certain it is the right technology for the situation or the enterprise receiving it and is what the country wants. The recipient should be adequately prepared technically, as well as managerially and psychologically, to accept, adapt, and use the technology. Xerox, with the support of its joint venture partner, is having six Chinese engineers from the joint venture spend a year in the United States with Xerox, so they become more familiar with basics and the technical process in a copier. This is in preparation for the joint venture–Xerox development of a follow-on copier product.

Secondary and tertiary parties (suppliers and vendors) should learn how to match the technology with their own technological advance so as not to undercut the value of the technology received from abroad. For example, suppliers producing parts of a lower quality than that required by the technology recipient will undercut the value of the technological advance by rendering it ineffective. Vendors who do not know how to maintain and repairment equipment that is produced with or that embodies high technology will leave the equipment in disuse longer than is appropriate, leading to an uneconomic situation of high cost and low returns for the technology transfer. Upgrading these vendors is one of the main goals of the national integration of the first Xerox copier to be manufactured by the joint venture. The other goal is to reduce the import content of the first copier to make it less expensive in the domestic market in terms of foreign exchange.

The licensee itself must be technically, psychologically, and organizationally prepared to use the technology, or else it simply sits on the shelf or is applied ineffectively. Despite a willingness to receive it, there frequently is an unwillingness to make the necessary adaptations or changes in the enterprise's organization, power structure, work force employment, employee skills, and level of employment—all of which upset the existing system. Relatively few developing countries have created the scientific and technological infrastructure necessary to receive, adapt, and use technology transferred from abroad.[4] To conserve the resources of the host country and make certain that the development occurs in the most effective manner, it is necessary to have a scientific community that can assess "appropriate" technology and also distinguish between what is necessary for the national interest and what is desirable from the interests of the receiving enterprise.

These distinctions are necessary if an approval process is to be useful. For example, the Chinese government seeks import substitution as a means of generating economic growth, but the protection of the domestic market with a considerable amount of unsatisfied demand provides little incentive to an enterprise to actually apply technological changes either to expand the market or to reduce costs. Thus there is a link between the development strategy of the government and the willingness of enterprises to act in concert. Only if there is competitive pressure, which is generated either by additional enterprises in the local market or by an opening to the international market through imports or exports, does the pressure to compete increase the pressure to make effective adaptations and use of imported technology. This is evident in China's case, where even the limited domestic competition that has emerged under the new reforms is sufficient to encourage enterprises to acquire foreign technology.[5]

Diffusion of Science and Technology

To make the imported technology most effective, there has to be a diffusion throughout the economy, not only of the specific technology, but also of new technological orientations. Lead sectors have to be stimulated to use advanced technologies, which then can press on both suppliers and vendors the necessity to raise their technical abilities. In turn, these secondary and tertiary parties will require scientific and technological support from a national industrial research network. If there is no such network, the imported technology is likely to be ill-suited for the nation's needs, though it may be seen as desirable by an individual enterprise.

For technology transfers to make their maximum contribution to the host country's development, a sufficient scientific and technological infrastructure is necessary, and it requires at least concomitant support for continued improvement. To stimulate the educational system to include a scientific and technological orientation, appropriate careers must be available in research institutes, and these opportunities must be seen as desirable. To do this will require the establishment of a viable research and development (R&D) network both within enterprises and outside in independent institutes. These institutes need to have central support either through the government or through an independent agency of the government that can speak for their interest at times of budget consideration. For the most part, China possesses all three prerequisites.

Only if there is sufficient scientific manpower and technological expertise to assess imported technology will a country be able to determine the most appropriate technology for its needs and to bargain for that technology effectively. It must have sufficient ability to determine some of the needs beforehand, not relying wholly on the foreigner to come forward. China's orientation is to wait for the foreigner to take initiatives, which is basically a function of the fact that it does not have sufficient information about what is going on in the outside world to make prior selections. But this limits its bargaining position and makes it wary in the bargaining process, simply because it does not have an appreciation of the universe with which it could be dealing. It considers itself weak compared with the strengths of the foreigner and the information that the foreigner might have; China, therefore, bargains from a weak and suspicious position, which makes coming to an appropriate agreement difficult. As a partial remedy, the China International Trade and Investment Corporation has invested several million dollars in its U.S.-based venture capital fund as one way of learning about external technology. A result has been Chinese ownership of several firms in the United States and the opportunity to place Chinese executives in them to gain experience.

Without a suitable scientific and technological network, it is virtually impossible to plan for international technical cooperation or to make certain that the resources of the country are used effectively. Therefore, the foreigner faces "on-again, off-again" policies or orientations by the host country, and this reduces the contribution they are willing to make.

The same R&D infrastructure is necessary to help each enterprise in assessing the usefulness of particular technologies, and also for guiding them to appropriate sources. This is a matter not only of information, but also of contacts with appropriate decision-makers in enterprises and governments.

Finally, if there is too great an estrangement between the officials in enterprises and those in government dealing with scientific and technological matters, the former will be uninformed and the latter will be largely irrelevant to industrial needs. There has to be a continuing link between the activities of the government institutes and policymakers and those who are the actual recipients of technology. This structure does not exist in China, save in a few instances, and it must be built. During the process of its construction, a good many false starts and detours can be expected. But without it, there will be selection of unsound or irrelevant technologies, fruitless attempts at adaptation, or failure to adapt when necessary—all resulting in an ineffective assimilation or use of the technology. The contribution of investment, therefore, will be minimized rather than maximized. Without such a network, the government cannot ascertain needs, assist enterprises, or assess enterprises' latent capabilities so as to make effective use of foreign technology. Such a network would help to examine the impacts of the technology and the opportunities it opens up. Technology is not merely an addition to existing resources; it can and does change labor-capital ratios, the amount of labor required, the skills required, and the material inputs. It also changes the necessity for repair and maintenance and even the patterns of use of the final product.

Consequently it is necessary to have a network that can help in the selection of particular technologies to be transferred; the particular enterprises that can make effective use of it and will do so; the means of and assistance in making appropriate adaptations to the technology, given domestic demands and material supply; and the technologies necessary to stimulate export abilities and, therefore, to be an engine for economic growth.

Embodied Technology

Because China does not have the requisite R&D or scientific and technology networks for effective transfers, it must rely, to some extent, on the import of technology embodied in components or assemblies, which the country is not yet ready to produce. This involves combining the technologies of the advanced countries in imported components with those that China can effectively produce through its own suppliers. This combination, which leads to joint manufacturing and assembly through imports of completely knocked down products, has been a substantial portion of investment in most developing countries, especially in the early stages of development. It has not, however, been large in China, partly because of the requirements (mostly for foreign exchange) laid down by the government.

TYPES OF FDI AND THEIR CONTRIBUTIONS

At different stages of development, a country relying significantly on FDI will find that its reliance on various categories of such investment also will differ. The categories vary from country to country according to the resource base within each, its demand structure, and its relation to the world economy. Five basic categories of foreign investment need to be distinguished: development of raw materials, labor-intensive manufacturing, process manufacturing, assembly manufacturing, and service activities. Each makes different contributions and faces different problems in making those contributions. A host government has to take these differences into account if it is to receive the most effective and desirable contributions from these types of investment.

Differential Contributions

The differential contributions of these five types of FDI can be set forth in a matrix form in which the *relative* contribution to China's development objectives can be noted as high, moderate, or low, as in Figure 9.1.

Once again, the contributions of each of these categories of FDI, as seen by the Chinese government, are different from the TNC's views. In fact, the desired

Figure 9.1
Potential Contributions of Different FDI Projects

Contributions	Raw Mat'ls Dev.	Labor Intense Mfg.	Process Mfg.	Assembly Mfg.	Services
Employment					
- levels	Moderate	High	Mod.	Mod.	High
- skills	High	Low	High	Mod.	Low
Domestic production	High	High	High	High	High
Supplier production	Low	High	Mod.	Mod.	High
Vendor services	Low	Mod.	Mod.	High	High
Import substitution	High	High	High	High	Low
Exports	High	Mod.	Mod.	Low	Low
Advanced technology	Mod./High	Low	High	High	Low
Capital inflows	High	Mod.	High	Mod.	Low
Imports					
- equipment	High	Mod.	High	High	Low
- components	Low	Low	Mod.	High	Low
Cost reduction	Mod.	Mod.	High	High	High
New Product Development	Low	Low	Mod.	High	Mod.
Domestic competition (catalyst to)	Mod.	High	High	High	High

contributions on the part of each frequently are in dispute, as is particularly the case with reference to penetration of export markets, the balancing of foreign exchange, and repatriation of profits.

The different categories of FDI indicated above are exemplified by the 840 Sino–foreign equity joint ventures established between 1979 and 1984. When grouped according to these five categories, the various products are distributed as shown in Figure 9.2.

If one looks only at the potential among these various categories for balancing foreign exchange, for example, the service activities will clearly lead to an increase in foreign exchange reserves through services to tourists or foreign

Figure 9.2
Categorization of 840 Sino-Foreign Joint Ventures, 1979–1984

Raw Materials	Service
Oil	Hotel
Coal	Taxi and Rental Cars
Mining-Granite	Printing and Photography
	Restaurant
Labor Intensive	Repair Services
	Tourist
Clothing	Consulting
Shoes	Building
Furniture	Transportation
Construction	Advertising
	Amusement Centers
Process Manufacturing	
	Assembly Manufacturing
Food	
Fishing	Computers
Winemaking	Calculators, Watches
Textiles	Magnetic Disks
Steel and Aluminum Windows	Telephone Switching
Equip.	
Plastic Zippers	Control Systems
Videotapes	Elevators
Perfume	Tvs
Concrete	Autos
Bricks	Bicycles
Chemicals	Toys
	Printing Equipment

Source: Shapiro, James E., "China Joint Ventures: Benefits, Problems and Solutions," Discussion Paper for Pacific Forum Conference on Enterprise, Economics and China's Development, Beijing, PRC, October 17-19, 1986.

investors in China. Even advertising and repair services, which would be least oriented to the foreigner, will at times produce foreign exchange. A second measure is that of national integration, or the involvement of local supplies of parts or services. Here again, the service sector makes a substantial contribution to this objective, relying principally on domestic resources, save for the import of some aspects, such as building materials or taxis. The development of services in the hotel, transportation, and financial sectors builds national integration in ways not previously existent.[6] The raw materials sector, being export-oriented, also will add to foreign exchange. It is essentially oriented toward transportation, processing, and utilization of domestic supplies and is, therefore, high on the list in national integration. The clothing industry also is export-oriented and utilizes large volumes of domestic raw materials and labor, but it is considerably more fragmented in terms of production location, integration, and distribution. Even the process-manufacturing industries frequently will be export-oriented and are clearly reliant on domestic components. Thus all of the joint ventures, except

Figure 9.3

Contrasting Goals of Technology Transfers and Joint Ventures

<u>CHINA</u>   <u>FOREIGN FIRN</u>

<u>Technology Transfers</u>   <u>Technology Transfers</u>

Secure (less-than latest   Earn Profits on Sale of
    Technology   Technology and Parts until
                                                    National Integration
For Internal Use   Complete
- improve living standards
- develop infrastructure   and/or
- national security
                                                    Secure Source of Low-cost
To Export Parts/Products   Production
    and Earn Foreign
    Exchange in the Long
    Term

To Reduce Foreign Exchange
    Expenditures

<u>Joint Ventures</u>   <u>Joint Ventures</u>

JV Only Way to Secure   Earn Profits on an On-going
    Technology   Basis from PRC Domestic
                                                    Market
Insure Continuing Source of
    Latest Technology   and/or

To Export Parts/Products   Secure Source of Low-cost
    and Earn Foreign   Production
    Exchange

Better Opportunity to
    Export

Management Efficiency

the assembly manufacturing category, are inherently oriented to national integration and frequently to the earning of foreign exchange through direct exports.

Just as the contributions of the five categories of FDI to national goals differ, so do the perspectives as to the value of those contributions by the TNC and Chinese officials. For example, the contributions of joint ventures can be compared against technology transfers from the perspective of China and the TNC, as seen in Figure 9.3.

Importance of Assembly Manufacturing

The investment in assembly manufacturing raises quite different problems because it operates under a more complex setting; it must import components and it cannot quickly balance foreign exchange. Of the 840 joint ventures noted above, only about 50 could be classified as assembly manufacturing. Of these, about two-thirds were electronics (watches, calculators, computers, and televisions). Calculators and watches are, however, basically micro-processor chip technology, which is process manufacturing and done elsewhere. The assembly manufacturing aspect is packaging the chip in a case and calling it a watch or calculator. Televisions and computers are not yet exported from China in any meaningful quantity and are essentially "import substitution" investments, reducing the expenditure of foreign exchange directly. The remaining third (less than twenty joint ventures) are those such as Beijing Jeep, Shanghai Volkswagen, and Shanghai Foxboro. None of these yet balance foreign exchange through exporting the production of the joint venture essentially because they import substantial portions of the final product and will do so for some time, awaiting the ability of domestic manufactures to supply critical components.

The Chinese aphorism "what is practical will happen" also implies that the impractical or unreasonable will *not* happen; this is borne out by the small number of such assembly manufacturing ventures. Despite the importance of this type for transfers of embodied technology, foreign investors are not significantly entering into this category because the balancing of foreign exchange in the near term is not possible, if the joint venture begins manufacturing with imported parts sets. The balancing of foreign exchange on an annual basis may take eight to ten years, and on a cumulative basis up to fifteen years. The delay lies in the need to combine sufficient quality cost reduction and up-to-date technology in the final product for competition in international markets, and at the same time develop a reliable supply of domestic parts.

Thus the major obstacles to a more substantial contribution from this category are the high cost of production in China of critical components, the time required to achieve national integration, and the continued advances in related manufacturing technologies by foreign competitors, which keep Chinese suppliers "running behind."

One reason Chinese production costs are high is overemployment in most of the factories. This is the result of a high degree of inefficiency in the productive processes; a high degree of indirect labor, as the factory serves an important role in the provision of social welfare services; use of the Chinese enterprise by society as an employer of last resort, rather than as a means of productive efficiency; the consequent difficulty of laying off Chinese workers; and, in the absence of other economic objectives, the employment of family members as a perk of one's being employed in a state-owned enterprise. Scrap and rework also are high, further increasing costs. The cost of production in China will not reach equality with other countries for another five to ten years at least, even in sectors given a high priority.

The national integration of components from local suppliers is slower than frequently is anticipated by government officials for several reasons. For the foreign licensor or joint venture partner to maintain control of the manufacturing process in terms of scheduling and quality, only a single component or subassembly from domestic sources can be introduced into production at a given time. This means that the integration of national suppliers tends to be sequential—from part to part—rather than many within a given year. The process of sourcing parts starts with procuring and testing samples. When the sample parts meet specification, quality, and cost requirements, production parts must be procured and tested. Sometimes the differences in the fabrication methods for sample parts and production parts will cause performance problems that must then be corrected. The typical period of time to nationally integrate a single subassembly is, therefore, six to eighteen months, but only if the sample and production parts promptly meet specification, quality, and cost requirements, without repeated rework. This is true for China as it is for other developing countries, raising the prospect of a long wait before achieving profitability and foreign exchange balance. The problem is exacerbated in China because the government has lost control over the sequencing and pacing of foreign technology acquisition. Instead of a lengthy but predictable process unfolding, the Chinese experience is more likely to be both lengthy and unpredictable. A case in point is the importation of color television assembly lines, requiring substantial foreign exchange with little or no prospect of integration or complementarity among the lines. This is a problem that the Chinese government is particularly sensitive to, since by mid-1990, 166 such lines had been imported into China by enterprises exercising their newfound autonomy.

The empirical evidence indicates that a national integration plan of 15 percent per year (by value of the imported parts set) is achievable. The *Asian Wall Street Journal* reported in April 1986 that Shanghai Volkswagen would be 90 percent nationally integrated by 1992, a seven-year period from its inception. Sanyo could achieve only 28 percent in two years. The city of Wuhan, working with Toshiba, faces a struggle in achieving 70 percent in three years. Most of the time, however, the publicized targets are not achieved with the quality, cost, and delivery performance associated with world-class competitors. The time required to achieve national integration may be shortened by using only the best factories and not paying much attention to their costs, but this would reduce the profitability of the joint venture. Not seeking the most cost-effective means of production also will lengthen the time to reach parity with the cost of production in foreign countries, leaving the joint venture noncompetitive and, therefore, unable to achieve exports and balance foreign exchange.

Products that were designed in another country for that market will have been designed with a bias to the manufacturing strengths and operating environment of the original target country. Motors and other components will be selected from those readily available or easily fabricated in that country. Therefore, duplicating these parts in China will always be lengthy and usually too long for successful exporting in sectors that are high tech and rapidly changing. The obvious way of reducing the problem of national integration to the minimum is to design the product initially for manufacture in China. To do this, access to the domestic market is required; a technology base and new product development capability in such ventures also would be critical for their long-term success.

A final obstacle to successful national integration in this category of investment is the continuation of advances in technologies in foreign countries manufacturing competing products. Continued progress is being made in the design (computer-based design) and manufacture (computer-aided manufacture) of products as well as in the products themselves. Simple products are becoming high tech in terms of their processes and even some of their components. For example, a copier is a small chemical plant running inside a box, with a combination of photography and xerography. Both photography and xerography have been digitized today, facilitated by the increased use of electronics and microcircuitry. Microprocessors also are replacing cams and timing chains in the most basic products.

These three obstacles to success in assembly manufacturing can be resolved, but only at considerable cost and effort. This would involve at least three developments: (1) large investments must be made by the joint ventures in the technologies needed to reduce the cost of new-product design and production; (2) factories must be organized efficiently and function only as business enterprises; (3) new-generation products must be designed in China in conjunction with Chinese suppliers. These developments will permit state-of-the-art products to be introduced into the international market at a competitive price, along with a 70 to 90 percent level of national integration. Such investments in new-product technology will be large and costly for the joint venture enterprises, requiring the joint ventures to be profitable in both renminbi and foreign exchange.

The implementation of the solutions above—for increasing the contributions of assembly manufacturing joint ventures—will require a strong central planning system to coordinate the efficiencies of centralization with the strengths of the municipalities and provinces to achieve a synergistic result for China. Ironically, this is the very opposite of the decentralization that the current reforms were seeking before mid-1989, after which strong centralized control reemerged.

Policies to Increase Contributions

Other countries have adopted policies to enhance contributions of the assembly manufacturing investor. This includes joint ventures for marketing and for import substitution for selected products with large domestic requirements and with technologies of long-term importance.

Joint Venture Marketing Companies

Permission has been given for the establishment of joint venture marketing companies selling the selected products imported from foreign companies that also are willing to transfer technology. After the joint venture companies doing this become financially strong through profits from domestic sales, they can begin to develop their own products, with the assistance of the foreign companies.

The advantages for China would be participation in the marketing profits and the concentration of these profits for future product development in China. In the interim, China also would gain industry knowledge through marketing, repair, and maintenance of the products.

Import Substitution Joint Ventures

Manufacturing joint ventures have been formed that nationally integrate the selected products but do not export the final product, therefore avoiding the problems of international quality standards and export competitiveness. The foreign investor strives to aid the balance of foreign exchange through other purchases in the host country, and the foreign investor is assured of a reasonable rate of return by guaranteeing foreign exchange conversion of sufficient profits. Depending on their domestic market share and profits, these joint ventures are expected to be profitable enough after several years to finance new products designed in the host country.

In China's case, foreign exchange requirements for importation of parts would cease when the cost of production in foreign exchange fell to that of the import price. The pressure of foreign exchange requirements should stimulate Chinese factories to speed up cost reductions. The foreign investor's rate of return also could include an incentive for faster national integration. When the cost of production in China decreases below foreign costs, there could even be a limited export market, depending on the technology finally adopted and the final cost of production compared with that in other countries.

Manufacturing and Development Joint Venture

Another form that would add substantially to China's development is a manufacturing joint venture (which also could include a domestic marketing company for the foreign investor's other imported products as appropriate) that assembles and nationally integrates the approved product for sale in the China market. The joint venture also should promptly begin to develop a new product designed for the local market with imported technologies but *not* with imported parts. This venture would fill in and enhance the design capabilities existing in China, with some support from the foreign partner.

For selected products and technology in China, this option represents a potential improvement in the ability of its joint ventures to earn foreign exchange in the international market through taking advantage of the Chinese domestic market. For some products or technologies that are critical in developing the urban and economic infrastructure, in meeting the targets for raising the standard of living in China, and for national security, it would be useful to establish this third kind of joint venture.

This would require a domestic market large enough to offer economies of scale in production and distribution. Because of the critical nature of the products, the best Chinese factories would be the only ones considered for partnership in such ventures. (From the Chinese perspective, there are advantages in linking weak Chinese factories with competent foreign partners, to upgrade the Chinese facilities, but this reduces the effective transfer of technology and slows national integration.) The issue is not between large and small factories, but between those that are efficient and inefficient, competent and incompetent, technologically prepared and technologically backward. The more efficient, capable, technically prepared, and competent companies will know how to accelerate national integration and how to utilize foreign technology at the same time. They also would be able to accelerate technology transfer even to less capable suppliers, but even here, the best supplier should be sought to reduce costs and spread the benefits throughout the country as quickly as possible.

Paired with these best Chinese factories should be the best foreign partners possible. This means technological leaders, those with international experience, those with broad access to foreign markets and, therefore, experienced in international competition, and those sincerely willing and able to transfer technologies. Matching these willing and able partners is probably the most important and difficult task in the formation of this new type of joint venture.

To make certain that there are sufficient profits in renminbi as well as in future foreign exchange earnings for new-product development, the market available to the joint venture must be of significant size. It might be argued that even if as much as two-thirds or three-quarters of domestic demand would be met by the single joint venture, operating so as to achieve economics of scale, this oligopolistic structure would not be too high a price to pay for development. No single monopoly should be permitted, for some protection is needed against a natural disaster in the dominant plant, and some competition is needed for comparison in terms of efficiency and quality. Some competitive comparisons could still be achieved through selective imports of similar products.

These selected joint ventures, given their strong market position, would need a government agency to work with and oversee them, helping to speed up national integration by identifying potential suppliers. In addition, export prices would need to be carefully determined, since China's cost accounting systems leave it at a competitive disadvantage. Until China has moved to a more export-oriented economy and established accounting standards consistent with those in other countries, its cost of production will continue to be distorted by the pricing of raw materials and the costs absorbed by the Chinese factory as provider of social services to families of employees. A government agency to monitor international prices and advise joint ventures (and local factories) on pricing would be helpful in this regard. Industry price trends are critical, in that any new product coming from the joint ventures must be price-competitive on the world market at the time of its introduction.

To be competitive internationally, an effective cost-price structure and high-quality products are required. Because many of the enterprises do not know the needed quality characteristics, government assistance in achieving quality levels will be needed—tied to the technological institutes that are serving the various ministries, as proposed earlier. Even with relatively comparable quality, China initially will need to offer a 25 to 35 percent discount to customers for industrial products to get them to switch sources of supply. Any customer shifting supply sources will perceive that it is assuming significant risks and must justify these with significant cost savings. These risks, beyond just meeting production specifications, are quality over the long-term, timeliness of delivery, the ability and willingness of the Chinese to assist when technical and other problems occur, the future availability of replacement parts, plus the loss of an established supplier who has previously provided this type of product support.

The government organization whose responsibility it would be to monitor quality and price would need to understand these issues and gradually bring China's export prices closer to the international price over a five- to ten-year period. Quality is so important that if foreign purchasers become concerned over the quality of Chinese products, it would be impossible to gradually raise China's export prices or to export significantly to developed countries. Thus the highest priority must be given to technological assistance in cost reduction, to be able to sustain international discounting and to improve and maintain quality at levels required by customers.

The quasi-monopolistic position of such selected joint ventures should not be permitted to provide excessive profits to the foreign partner. This could be avoided through negotiation of a guaranteed reasonable rate of return in the original agreement. Such a guarantee would be acceptable because of its reduction of risk for the foreign investor. The joint venture profits, which would tend to be large, would then be retained in the joint venture to be invested in the latest production technologies and new-product development and engineering. This third type of selected joint ventures has not been fully tested in other developing countries, but they have not had the same attractiveness that China does with the large size of its potential domestic market.

Finally, the fact of a government-owned enterprise being the joint venture partner puts the government completely into the decision-making process, and these selected joint ventures should not become private until they are firmly established and can sustain competition in the marketplace, which would be opened at that time to other companies. These suggestions are not proposed as a panacea, but to stimulate discussion of imaginative solutions for the unique conditions of China.

NOTES

1. *World Bank Report*, No. 5206, CHA., p. 135.

2. "On the Question of Markets for the Products of Joint Ventures in China," paper presented before the MIT-CASS Conference in Hangzhou, China, March 25–30, 1985, p. 23.

3. Further illustration of these arguments is found in J. N. Behrman, W. A. Fischer, and D. F. Simon, "Transferring Technology to China," *International Trade Journal*, Fall 1989, pp. 49–67.

4. See J. N. Behrman and H. W. Wallender, *Transfers of Manufacturing Technology within Multinational Enterprises* (Boston: Ballinger, 1976), and J. N. Behrman and W. A. Fischer, *Overseas R&D Activities of Transnational Companies* (Cambridge, Mass.: Oelgeschlager, Gunn & Hain, 1980).

5. See William A. Fischer and Denis F. Simon, ''The Managerial and Technical Issues in Technology Assimilation,'' paper presented at the Conference on Technological Change and Economic Performance in the People's Republic of China, Woodrow Wilson Center, Smithsonian Institution, Washington, D.C., April 1987.

6. See W. A. Fischer, ''The Political Economy of Service Operations in the Developing World: The Case of China,'' paper presented at the National Meeting of the Decision Sciences Institute, Las Vegas, November 1988.

10

Negotiating a Joint Venture

Joint ventures, whether separated 400 or 4,000 miles from the parents, are a continuous negotiation. A successful negotiation of a joint venture is an agreement to continue negotiation on a long-term basis to achieve, ideally, common, or at least complementary, goals. The foreign partner will continue to negotiate with the Chinese management in the venture, with government departments, and often with labor over expatriate requirements, welfare fund contributions, import licenses, and so forth. In turn, the Chinese partners are negotiating in the same ways about foreign exchange and exports. In addition, negotiation occurs with suppliers, with vendors, with bankers, and so on. Much needs to be learned in the initial negotiation process about each other's commitment, values, and goals so as to be prepared for subsequent negotiations and the conditions under which they will take place. It is the purpose of the initial agreement to set the terms of reference for subsequent negotiations. Therefore, there are several stages that set the parameters for subsequent stages, usually narrower in scope; the larger scope can always be returned to, since there was an initial agreement on general principles and the choice of each other as long-term partners.

This continuous-phase nature of negotiations in China is not acceptable or understood by most Western businessmen, who see each stage as being completed before going to the next one. In their view, issues that have been settled are not to be reopened; yet they often are between partners even in the United States and with Japan. But the Chinese view that every part is simply a segment of the whole means that any change calls for a reexamination of how it affects the entire relationship. This reassessment calls for repeated adjustments on the part of inexperienced Western negotiators.

The Western negotiator starts at a disadvantage when he takes the initiative in going to China to seek out opportunities, for he is seen as the supplicant, competing for the China opportunity against other foreign investors. China has already indicated that it wants to have foreign direct investment, but it has not said so specifically for each sector, though some priorities have been set, or to each foreign enterprise. The Western company is the suitor and is expected to make the first offers and the later concessions. Further, the setting is within China, whose culture thereby dominates, and whose government retains ultimate control over the agreement.

The Western company is an outsider attempting to get in, and the game and playing field are complex, hierarchical, unfamiliar, and seductive. Pursuing the game analogy, the foreigner needs to answer the following questions:

Who defines what the game is, and what is it?

Who sets the rules and can change them?

What are the rules?

Who supplies the equipment used?

Who are all the players?

How many teams are playing?

Who is on which side?

Who keeps score and how?

Who determines the winner—if any?

Who decides when the game is over and by what criteria?

Who gets to keep what after the game?

The Westerner is at a disadvantage in answering these questions, in comparison to competitors from Eastern countries, particularly those from societies with cultures close to the Chinese.

Japanese as Negotiators with China

The Japanese have several advantages in negotiating with the Chinese, but they arise more from familiarity and hard work than from the closeness of cultures.

The Japanese will pursue the opportunities in China both aggressively and extensively. They are located in multiple areas and cities, ferreting out business, staying there for the long term. Many have the ability to work in Chinese, despite its complete distinctiveness in oral communication.

They also are exceedingly flexible in meeting the demands of the situation, though they clearly are unwilling to "give away the store." They are adaptable to the more spartan living conditions throughout China, especially outside the major cities. This results partly from many of them having been in China or at least being familiar with it through the Japanese occupations in Manchuria and Northern China for long periods.

The Japanese are willing to spend the time and effort to learn the customs and business practices before entering into negotiations. They do their homework, sometimes knowing more about the limits of regulations and authorities (and sometimes even the Chinese negotiators' bottom line) than do the Chinese counterparts.

Unless the foreigner understands the Chinese approach, he frequently finds himself making early and sometimes sweeping commitments, so vaguely defined that the Chinese can later call for specific agreements as fitting within the broader commitments made earlier. The play and counterplay between specifics and generalities in the Chinese pattern of negotiation often are confusing to the Westerner, resulting in frustration and defensiveness. It is, therefore, necessary to understand the orientations that the Chinese bring to the negotiating table, including cultural orientations, to reach a successful agreement. The Westerner needs to prepare, to learn the processes and the issues in negotiation, to understand the scope of an agreement and its implications, and to become familiar with the various levels of approval that are required.[1] Once a joint venture agreement is signed, negotiations on implementation begin.

PREPARATION

As emphasized in the preceding chapters, the preparation for negotiations consists in becoming as familiar as possible with key aspects of China's orientations, goals, and behavior—its culture and value system, the working of its economy, its political system, social behavior, the legal system, and the role of management. The effects of these "institutions" on negotiations can be summarized as follows.[2]

Institution and Characteristics	Impacts to Be Expected
Value System	
Sino-superiority	Resistance by labor to assimilating foreign techniques and skills
	Lack of empathy for risks and problems of foreigner
Primacy of authority	Necessity for control to achieve cohesion
Loyalty	Adhesion to interests of one's own group, even without direct personal "benefit"
Ideology of socialism	Baggage carried over, elevating politics over economics
	"Big-market" mentality
Motivation	Distrust of private transactions
	Inhibition of entrepreneurial and competitive behavior
	Suspicion of profit motive and any benefits accruing to foreigner
	Zero-sum mentality

Economic System

Population pressures   Labor surplus

                               Employment security sought

                               Low mobility—rigidity

Egalitarianism   Fear of scarcities

                               Support of "grants economy"

Fiscal weakness   Tendency to and fear of inflation

                               Lack of control of budget and of money supply

                               Conflicts over public investments

Regionalism   Unbalanced development

                               Regional jealousies

                               Lack of "national market"

                               Protectionism

Political System

Strong central control   Continued economic planning

                               Central decision-making

                               Price controls

                               Limited market decision

                               Interventions in enterprises

                               Conflict among levels and units of government

                               Instability with efforts to reduce government control

Social Behavior

Familialism, Individual-   Suboptimization—priority to self and family over organi-
  ism, Particularism   zation or country

Corruption   Pervasive inefficiency

                               Low philanthropy; high greed

Friendliness   Openness to foreigner

                               Cordiality

                               Lasting relationships

Superiority   Discrimination by race or color

                               Mistrust when "lower" gain

Legal System

Rule by law, not rule of   Ambiguity in contracts
  law   Avoidance of details in interest of others

                               Focus on personal commitment by others

                               Careful negotiation, with renegotiation

Management Style

Traditional roles and lack of modern concepts and techniques	Lack of strategic focus
	Loose central coordination
	Poor linkages among projects
	Bureaucratic inefficiency and infighting
Risk avoidance	Noncompetitive ethic
	Lack of personal or managerial incentives to raise productivity
	Lack of competition among managers for better career paths
	Inadequate use of specialists

Once the background is perused, the next step is to study government priorities to determine which of the company's products or activities has the best chance of success in China. To know that the government has already set a high priority on production of the company's product provides a foreigner with a stronger bargaining position. The government also may have some specific enterprises that it considers the most desirable partners. This phase of preparation, therefore, involves a prefeasibility study, looking at the various opportunities in China and potential partners.

Lack of Information

A major obstacle at this stage, and at virtually all subsequent stages, is the paucity of information available to the foreigner. It is difficult to uncover potential partners, what their capabilities and interests are, what commitments they can make, the kind of support that a local government might give—all before formal negotiations are begun. The fact that the Chinese have equally little information on the nature of Western companies, their reputations or abilities, their objectives and operating styles, merely balances the mutual ignorance. But this condition does not necessarily make for successful negotiations. Rather, it significantly alters the content and duration of the negotiations, since both sides are attempting to protect themselves against the unknown.

The Chinese will attempt to obtain a sweeping commitment from the foreigner in the form of a general statement of intent or memorandum of understanding (MOU), within which they later nail down the details. Conversely, the foreigner will seek to take small, specific steps, gradually building to a securer arrangement. Thus interim technology transfer agreements, interim sales of components or final products for introduction into the Chinese market, and interim training of Chinese managers or officials either in China or abroad have been ways of gathering information about the market and the potential partner that could not be gained through research.

So as not to signal too great an initial interest, the Western company is well advised to send a small team—no more than two or three—for the preliminary stages. The members should be chosen for their ability to understand and observe practices in a different country as well as for their understanding of corporate objectives and authority to make decisions. The more experienced the team, the greater the likelihood of success, since they possess information from practice. The MOU is a worthwhile step in negotiations for the Western parties as well. It documents understandings and decisions, and creates a valuable record for discussions at the home office as well as for new personnel joining the joint venture at a later time.

Translation in Negotiations

With translators sometimes not understanding the essence of an issue in negotiation or not knowing the nuances of the languages, miscommunication is a constant risk. During one of the early Xerox-Shanghai Movie and Photo Industry Company (SMPIC) discussions, Xerox offered to provide some equipment at its cost—meaning without any markup or profit. Xerox's negotiator said: "We will do that at our cost." But the word "cost" was heard as "expense" by SMPIC, since the same word in Chinese is used for both English words. SMPIC understood that the action was to be at Xerox's "expense," which would have included all transport and set-up costs. The error was caught during the drafting of the MOU, before it was communicated to all of the Shanghai bureaus and departments concerned. At least two knowledgeable translators, good notes, and avoidance of business slang are prudent.

In another set of discussions regarding modifications in some of the financial assumptions in the feasibility study, the Xerox financial officer turned to coauthor Shapiro and said, "I'll raise the red flag if they create a problem." The English-speaking Chinese who were present looked surprised, for the red flag in China is not a danger signal, but a positive sign.

Of great importance in preparation is achieving an appreciation within the company headquarters of the complexities of negotiating in China, the lack of information, and the likelihood of a long duration with seeming advances and retreats, so that executives do not become frustrated and make the situation more difficult for their own negotiators by holding unreasonable expectations or sending impossible instructions. Headquarters also should understand that an agreement eventually sent for approval is not likely to be similar to agreements negotiated with European companies, and even if it has the same format and general content, it will not be read the same way by the Chinese. The Chinese are much more concerned with the spirit and intent of the agreement than with the letter of the contract or its specific provisions. It is seen as even more like a marriage contract than the agreements among Western countries; commitments are seen as enduring. It is seen more like the sixteenth-century contract in China for forming a business partnership, which stated that it was formed by each of the parties having taken "an oath by drinking blood-wine to work together in harmony and share both profits and losses. They will not disagree, feud, or seek separate profits. The party that breaks this contract will be persecuted by gods and men alike."[3]

Perceptions of U.S. Business

At the end of the Xerox negotiations, at a time when friendships had been strengthened through mutual understanding, a senior Shanghai official who had dealt with foreign corporations for some years both inside and outside of China, was asked what was his greatest concern about joint ventures. Despite the many issues involved in developing a joint venture, he said simply, "Earning foreign exchange and the changing priorities of the foreign partners."

Most readers of the U.S. financial and business press would readily agree. Corporations are shown as having moved through periods of diversification, centralization, and, more recently, a "stick to your basic business" approach. This is one example of changing corporate directions. Domestically and internationally, U.S. corporations are entering joint ventures and similar arrangements even with competitors at an impressive rate, but there is no guarantee that these alliances will meet expectations and survive long term. This also is apparent to Chinese economists, who watch the United States closely. Thus they may think that their relations with U.S. companies will be considered as merely tactical by the United States because of changes in the policies of both transnational corporations (TNCs) and the government.

Obtaining adequate information early is made more important by the fact that it is difficult to change partners in midnegotiation. To cut off negotiation with one company and then seek another is seen as improper behavior and may be strongly or completely opposed by the central government, in support of the local or provincial government's interest in the original enterprise. It would be a loss of face for the Chinese negotiators.

Chinese Orientations

Chinese orientations to negotiation stem from their own cultural background and from their objectives. The procedure has a logic that is distinct from that in the West and is a source of continuing misunderstanding and confusion for Western negotiators. The MOU promptly sought by the Chinese side is not unusual in Western diplomacy, but it is not usual in business dealings. And the Chinese use this as the umbrella that covers and guides all subsequent agreements. Later, when the Chinese negotiators are not achieving what they want, they will refer back to the general understanding to show that it is not being fulfilled. Western negotiators may be surprised (and suspicious) to find the Chinese drafting a MOU even when no agreements have been reached. It is their way of showing their efforts in negotiations to higher levels of authority.

Despite an aversion in the early stages to specifics, when detailed provisions are written into the contracts, Chinese negotiators adhere closely to these terms. Details are carefully defined, since the Chinese expect literal adherence to them— at least when it is in their favor. The written word is revered, but the fact that there are two sets of written words—the details and the general understanding—

permits the Chinese, in the event of a dispute, to select whichever set they want to rely on. In either case, the foreign partner is supposed to accommodate, *since he is rich and more able to do so.*

Negotiation Advice

Western negotiators will be introduced early to the phrase "Through friendly negotiations and mutual agreement. . . . " It is the Chinese solution to the many "what if" questions that arise during contract negotiations. An experienced manager for AMF Asia offered the following explanation: The Chinese approach is to fully negotiate until there is a mutual agreement, and the process works because it is impossible to specify in contract language, especially in advance, all of the situations that may give rise to disagreements in the future. Therefore, establishing a relationship under which resolution of differences will be achieved through mutual agreement removes the trauma and delays of protracted contract discussions regarding "what ifs." His recommendations: Accept and utilize the "mutual agreement" solution to "what ifs" because ultimately, it is the only viable position to take so that the joint venture has an opportunity to survive long term.

If there is a need to go to arbitration or the courts, the joint venture has a questionable future. The real issue, from the Chinese perspective, is whether both parties have acted in a virtuous (honorable) manner in regard to the disputed incident.

Writing such contracts in legalese, when the Chinese do not have a tradition of such specificity of legal terms, will require other lawyers to interpret what the initial lawyers wrote; but to the Chinese, it is the managers who should interpret what is right and proper in the current situation and for the future. These could not be fully foreseen at the time of negotiation and should not be subjected to legal interpretations.

Western businessmen see such general memoranda as merely preambles to the specific, operative provisions to be negotiated later. Professor Lucian Pye, who has long been a student of business negotiations, emphasizes the psychological dimension of Chinese orientations. The Chinese seek to get the Western negotiator to make general commitments that exaggerate his capabilities or contributions; in the process, he is induced to feel indebted to his Chinese hosts. Then the hosts play on the guilt or obligation of the foreigner to extract additional concessions. Because the foreigner is richer, and thereby more obligated to adjust, the Chinese prefer to settle disputes directly with their partner rather than turn to arbitration by an international entity. This would be seen as external interference in internal Chinese affairs and absolutely unacceptable, given China's history of foreign intrusions.

These "psywar" tactics include controlling the setting and pace of negotiations. The foreigner is requested to start the discussions by indicating what his objectives are, forcing him to show his hand. He is then asked to make concessions, beginning a process of concession and counterconcessions, in which the Chinese are always one step ahead. Guilt is imposed by suggesting that nonagreement will lead to a "failure," which is contrary to the prior memorandum of understanding.[4] The Chinese also use time and delay tactics quite effectively. At times the delay may not be tactical, but simply a necessity because of the inability to obtain agreement among the various parties involved on the Chinese side. The usual eagerness on the part of Americans to negotiate quickly plays into the hands of the Chinese.

One American manager seemed surprised to discover that the "Chinese lack the knowledge that 'time is money.' "[5] As noted earlier, this concept of money is traditionally foreign to the Chinese, though recently such statements have been displayed in factories. Further, the enterprise negotiator is not going to rush to an ill-considered agreement just to "save time" when he knows that the contract has to be concurred in by a bureaucratic official who has the power to criticize the decision-maker to his superior government officials. Other concepts of money would more readily come to mind on the part of a Chinese manager in a centralized bureaucracy: "Money not used [committed] now can be used later"; "Money used unproductively is wasted"; "Money used [committed] now cannot be used later." The idea that money is wasted because time is spent deciding how best to use it would not come to mind. Time is spent, therefore, protecting the use of money and the individual decision-maker. Because there are many such individual decision-makers in the hierarchy of negotiations, it *takes* time. They are, therefore, less concerned to set a fixed agenda and to complete it on any given schedule, particularly one that is not of their own making. Once set, they are next to impossible to change.

Agenda Setting

In one negotiating session between Xerox and a Chinese enterprise, there were six issues on the agenda, divided among full-day and half-day periods over a five-day week. The last half day was for the MOU, but from past experience, Xerox learned that the MOU always took most of a full day, since the written words required redefinition and often renegotiation. Xerox attempted to advance the schedule a half day by agreeing quickly to the Chinese position on one of the issues and moving on to the next topic. This gained no time; rather, a lot of frustrating discussion followed as to what, precisely, Xerox had agreed to, with the Chinese pushing for deeper concessions.

Perhaps Xerox's action aroused suspicions with the Chinese. The wisest course is to set the agenda mutually and then be prepared to stick to it, never letting time become a factor in your considerations. Western negotiators must have as much time and patience as their Chinese counterparts. Because of the many Chinese levels involved, it may be impossible for the Chinese, without warning, to advance the agenda. They simply may not have prepared their positions for such an event.

For the foreigner, who considers that he is on a time budget, this can be quite frustrating—as it is back at company headquarters, where there is even less information and understanding of Chinese orientations. The corporate staffs of head-quarters companies, which usually emphasize reports "on time" and long-range plans, are bothered by long drawn out negotiations, and are psychologically un-prepared to cope with the inability to project future relations. Further, the unpre-dictability of which issues will be the sticky ones leaves the headquarters officials frequently unable to quickly "staff out" requests from the negotiating team.

The process of negotiation for the Chinese is one of "getting to know you" and finding out the areas of mutual accommodation. They are much less con-cerned with nailing down specifics to "maximize their position" than with getting an agreement that binds the parties to future specific commitments. They talk of lifelong friendship because they normally make heavy demands on friends to assist in their material progress, rather than rely on profit-oriented, arm's-length dealing through a free market. Friends are seen as continuous one-way givers, with the wealthier or stronger able to offer more to poorer or weaker friends, and therefore expected to be even more forthcoming. The stronger and richer are recompensed simply by being recognized by others as having the higher position and greater prestige. They need no material benefits but are elevated in stature. The Western countries are in this position compared with China and are expected to give repeatedly, particularly in the area of technology.

The Chinese attitudes toward advanced technology also reflect a psychological orientation to relations, in that the United States is *expected* to transfer only the latest technology; otherwise, it is not fulfilling its responsibility to the poorer or weaker supplicant. Again, for lack of an advanced technology base, the Chinese are wary that they will be given less than the latest technology. This concern is increased by the fear of Chinese negotiators that their superiors will accuse them of agreeing to unsatisfactory terms. Fear of not obtaining enough from American companies is fed by the frequently exaggerated claims of companies in their advertisements and by their demands for quick profits out of the venture that the Chinese consider excessive. (A demand for quick returns by the U.S. partner may be interpreted by the Chinese as a signal that the technology is hearing obsolescence and, therefore, will not be worth much in the future.) Both of these foreign positions indicate to the Chinese that there is considerable room for maneuver on the part of foreign companies, who *should* give more to the Chinese partners.

Finally, there is a preference among the Chinese to deal first with "soft" issues that do not have market criteria for decision-making and are much more a matter of relations, such as employment policies, training, organization, se-lection of managers, and role of the board. The "hard" issues stemming from market considerations of price and profits are left to the last, partly because they are seen as outside the control of the joint venture itself, partly because agreement on "soft" issues shows the extent to which the partners do have mutual interests and values and can work out the more nebulous relations. Once this is done, even the hard issues can sometimes be concluded fairly rapidly. Conversely, it is the American approach to focus on the hard issues first, since they are quite specific, and then move to the more nebulous ones. To them, if agreement cannot be reached on the bottom-line, there is not much sense in negotiating other provisions.

The Chinese orientation is displayed in three steps: The opening game lays out broad intentions, objectives, and relations in a "memorandum of understanding," which establishes the framework for future negotiations and provides the Chinese with terms of reference against which to measure specific provisions. The mid-game is played at a more leisurely pace, through fits and starts, progress and reversals, and focuses on the soft issues, though a lot of detail may be covered, such as the specifics on the technologies transferred, the documentation available, training, product liabilities and guarantees, delivery schedules of components, material supplies, and organizational structure. The end-game can be drawn out or short, depending on circumstances outside of the firm—the availability of foreign exchange, the existence of competitors, the ability of government departments to make decisions, and so on.

This sequence, like that of negotiations with the Japanese, involves virtually all of the parties who will ultimately implement the agreement, and therefore has the *potential* of permitting a relatively fast approval of the joint venture documents. Here, again, the Chinese are at an advantage simply because their people have been close to the negotiations and more directly involved, whereas only a few officials from the foreign company have had that opportunity. Even after signing, Western negotiators usually have to obtain agreement and commitment from those who will be directly involved in implementing the project; this process usually requires substantial additional time, causing a delay that can raise doubts in the minds of the Chinese as to the full commitment of the Westerner.

One final caution emerges out of the discussions in Chapter 5 on Chinese culture. Given the several levels of government and the officials of the enterprise itself, there is considerable concern for the saving of face. Considerable effort is required to discern the situations in which face is being protected and those in which the issue is itself significant.

Fax and Face

The Chinese concern with face is not just a matter of culture or courtesy. A joint venture on telecopiers (fax machines) was projected between an American and a Chinese enterprise, assembling semi–knocked-down kits imported from the United States. A formal contract was signed, with Chinese television coverage, for the delivery of $5 million of copiers, some semi–knocked-down kits, some completely knocked-down kits, and some machines to assemble the kits. The Chinese enterprise had tested the machines before the contract signing because there were problems of static on the telephone lines in China. The first 200 units installed in Chinese departments and bureaus did not work as the test models had, and after some troubleshooting by the American firm, it was found that the proper set-up adjustments had not been made by the Chinese engineers to handle variations in the incoming signals. The Chinese then sought to cancel the contract.

The desire to cancel the contract stemmed from the unwillingness of the Chinese manager to tell the ministry that the machines had been installed incorrectly. The American manager responsible for the negotiations considered that such an error was understandable, given the unfamiliarity with a new machine. The Chinese manager asserted that such an admission would be a loss of face.

As a consequence, the $5 million contract was quietly terminated and the Chinese enterprise lost an opportunity for a new marketing opportunity and new profits.

PROCEDURES AND ISSUES

The fact that the Chinese factory or enterprise is owned by the people and, therefore, responsible in most situations to a local or provincial government (and indirectly to the central government ministries) means that procedures of negotiation are hierarchical and involved. A number of steps are required, and the officials at the different levels of government are not always in communication with one another. Further, different governmental agencies are concerned with different aspects of the agreement, and their representations on those in which they have an interest may upset the balancing of trade-offs being negotiated between the two primary partners.

Procedures

Although there are no set procedures, and the negotiations can start on virtually any aspects, a number of steps must be taken before final agreement is reached.

(a) Selection of a potential partner with whom to begin negotiations is a complex and tenuous first step. It is not acceptable for the foreigner to negotiate simultaneously with two or more Chinese enterprises. The Chinese government may be negotiating on the same type of project with a number of foreign companies, even beyond the exploratory stage; however, at some point, preclusive pairings are made between a Chinese enterprise and the foreign TNC. The actual selection of a *potential* partner should be discussed with different levels of government to ascertain the interest of each in the particular project and its willingness to provide incentives or support, *and* to be certain that the Chinese enterprises being considered as partners are within the purview of the ministry with responsibility for the class of products to be manufactured. It is not easy for the foreign company to know the enterprises that would make the best partners, and some that would appear unattractive might become more attractive through governmental support or encouragement. But government officials may have favorites they are eager to push forward, despite, or rather because of, their inabilities.

(b) Determination of the composition of the negotiating team is a critical step. The Chinese team frequently is introduced to the foreign team only by their business cards, with their individual roles and positions never being explained. The composition of the Chinese team will change according to the issues being discussed, though the leader will remain throughout. Being rank-conscious, the Chinese will respond with a person of similar rank to that of the person representing the foreign company. Therefore, the higher the company official, the higher the Chinese official, leading to less need for consultation with higher units on the part of both negotiators. It is not always easy to determine who the final decision-makers are on the Chinese side. At times, the entire team consults, but the process of doing so frequently is hidden, in that the team retires to an adjoining room to work out its position. Even the process of referral back to other involved agencies or departments clouds the decision-making process from the view of the foreign negotiators. It is, therefore, difficult to know whose interests to emphasize to achieve agreement. But, ultimately, as the representative of the people at the factory, the manager (with concurrence from the factory's party office, in some cases) must agree. Neither the central government ministries nor the local government departments or leaders are likely to force any decisions on the factory or enterprise manager. They will only urge progress and offer support.

(c) Selection of time and place for the negotiations usually will be determined by the Chinese side, with the foreign negotiator able only to determine the length of his stay for any given phase. For a joint venture, the time required from initial contacts to contract signing frequently ranges from three to ten years. The actual process of negotiation usually will be shorter, but eighteen months to three years is not unusual in that phase. Less than two years is probably too short for the potential partners to learn each other's values and commitment.

(d) An interim agreement may be appropriate to begin test marketing the product or to provide technology for the improvement of the Chinese product to show what can be done in process manufacturing and in marketing of improved products. This step could be phased into the longer-run agreement; or it may be terminated as a completely separate activity and not to be continued once the major project is under way.

(e) Referrals by both sides to higher levels of decision-making typically will be required during the negotiations; at critical times and for important issues, it may be advantageous to be proactive among the different levels of the Chinese government, since they often are not in regular contact with a given negotiation and, in any case, are dealing with a number of foreign investments at any given time.

(f) The signing ceremony will be programmed jointly or by the Chinese, with appropriate officials in attendance for ceremonial purposes or for participation in signing of the document. It often is an appropriate time for the foreign investor's chief executive officer or chairman to visit China and visually affirm the commitment to the venture by both China and the foreign company.

Issues

Every aspect or provision of an agreement is an issue for negotiation. Some negotiation issues are of critical importance, whereas others, though less important in some negotiations, become matters of lengthy bargaining. The major matters must be settled satisfactorily, and once done, the minor matters are settled fairly readily.

Major	Minor
Pricing	Role of board
Technology transfers	Management
National integration	Dispute settlement
Foreign exchange	Technical specifications
Costs and profits	Training of Chinese
Exclusivity	Proprietary rights
Valuation	Termination
Feasibility study	Taxes
Loan guarantees	Labor
Access to materials	Force majeure

Price is a prime concern of Chinese and Western negotiators, but for different reasons. The Chinese are concerned with the price of the imported parts and the license fee, since government officials can understand them more readily in determining whether China received a "good bargain."[6] This aspect permeates much of the negotiation and is on the minds of the Chinese, despite the fact that it may be one of the last issues concluded. Selling price in the domestic market is of major concern to the foreign investor because it determines the profitability of the joint venture and is government-controlled. Both partners are concerned with the export price because it drives foreign exchange requirements and earnings.

The Chinese are particularly questioning on the price issue because they do not understand the cost structures and pricing practices of Western companies and usually do not use Western cost accounting practices. Here, again, the lack of information extends the negotiations and raises some frustration for both parties.

The issue of competitive pricing enters into the success of the joint venture, which must face other companies in China and eventually seek to penetrate foreign markets, if that is feasible. The negotiation is constrained somewhat by the fact that the foreign partner, if asked to include the final product in his own distribution network, must achieve prices that are competitive with other sources of supply. The lack of understanding of how these foreign operations determine their prices and what a "competitive price" is internationally make for considerable anxiety on the part of the Chinese, whose political or managerial careers could be seriously affected by giving away too much to the foreigner.

Technology transfer is "most wanted" by the Chinese, so they are concerned with the level of technology, the scope of the transfers, how current the technology is, and the royalties or fees to be paid. As with most developing countries, the desire is for the latest technology, even though they cannot effectively use it; that is, they are not prepared or able to absorb it (as discussed in Chapter 9).

The Chinese are so concerned to have adequate knowledge of the technology that they demand a significant amount of technical information in the bargaining process itself. Unfortunately, because of their noncompetitive economy, they have not always been found to be careful about its dissemination, sometimes commenting to one negotiating partner about the technical information or offer of a competing Western company. Although sometimes they lack information about technical processes, they are becoming educated through the bargaining process.

Although recent evidence has arisen that the Chinese are willing to take "appropriate" technology (i.e., what they can use effectively), it often is difficult for the foreign negotiator to persuade them to do so. This issue is an acute one, since they are seeking to raise quality to international levels to be able to export. The more advanced the technology, the more complex the negotiation over this issue, if for no other reason than it may come under the Coordinating Committee regulations or the export controls of the United States. These controls constrain the export markets for the products coming out of China under the technology license.

National integration also is a joint priority. It is sought by the Chinese to raise local content, to diffuse the technology, and to be able to produce the item themselves in the future, if necessary or desirable. It is an important priority to any foreign investor seeking to export from China, for without a significant level of national integration, production costs are raised compared with competitive locations elsewhere. The negotiation raises the question of the pace of integration (always longer than the Chinese desire), the prices to be paid to domestic suppliers, delivery schedules, and the transfer of technology to the suppliers to make the part and maintain quality.

Foreign exchange earnings and access to foreign exchange are the most critical of issues for both partners. Because the foreign partner is most interested in the domestic market, in almost all types of joint ventures the Chinese insistence on earning foreign exchange through exports (as discussed in Chapter 9) raises a difficult problem—one that normally is left (unfortunately) until the last stages of the negotiation. One of the problems related to exports is that Chinese enterprises (or factories) typically use a separate import-export organization to conduct foreign commercial transactions; these organizations receive a small percentage of the value as compensation. Consequently the enterprises themselves know little of the problems of exporting or the export markets. They are relying on the foreign partner to conduct their business without understanding its problem, and insist on specific performance.

The Chinese want to earn foreign exchange as soon as possible through exports, in addition to reducing the cost (and sometimes quantities) of imported parts.

The foreign partner wants to be assured that sufficient foreign exchange loans will be made available to the joint venture. Any of the three levels of government (central, provincial, or municipal) can provide access to foreign exchange, if the project is of critical importance. Discussions with these entities extend the bargaining process with the enterprise manager still further.

Costs and profits are linked in the minds of both sets of negotiators, but their approaches are quite different. On no other issue is the Chinese saying "Same bed, different dreams" more appropriate. The domestic costs of the joint venture are seen by the Chinese as part of their benefits or returns. Consequently they will seek to raise the salaries of managers, wages of labor, and costs of raw materials, if they can do so without damage to the prospects of the joint venture (as they see it). They also regard profits as a cost, since they see half of them going outside of the country (the zero-sum mentality). They may seek to reduce profits, therefore, since they have little experience in using profit for long-term investment. Although they currently are talking in a profit-oriented way, mind-sets are difficult to change, particularly among bureaucrats with no commercial experience.

To the foreigner, costs of imported components and kits are returns to his company, as are profits. Thus both sides are willing to raise some costs, even at the expense of profits, since the returns to them are commensurate with the costs selected.

There are ample items in the project that have no hard cost structures—training, engineering consultation, expenses of traveling personnel, royalties, and so on—leaving them open for negotiation. The apparent high costs of these activities supplied by the foreign investor leads the Chinese to consider that there is always some "fat" in the deal that can be reduced through higher wages, taxes, or reduced prices of the final product. Any service fees to the foreign partner are seen by the Chinese as "nonproductive" or already amortized on the books of the foreign company, so that all that needs to be paid is out-of-pocket expenses. An agreement to reduce costs to that level later is a test of the rich foreign company's sincerity and graciousness toward the weaker and poorer Chinese.

A serious issue arises from the lack of cost accounting on the part of the Chinese, so that the foreign partner is left without hard data on the past experience of the enterprise with which it is negotiating. It will be some time before trans-actions of Chinese procedures are satisfactory and still longer until Western accounting systems are introduced. Consequently the laws on foreign investment specify what net profit is: a series of deductions from gross income, including operating expenses, income tax, and set-aside for three funds—a reserve fund, a fund for bonuses and welfare for workers and staff, and a fund for expansion of the enterprise (usually totalling between 15 and 20 percent of net income after taxes). Sometimes the reserves are left to the determination of the board of directors. Net profits can be paid to the partners as dividends on the decision of the board of directors, unless specified otherwise in the joint venture contract.

The *valuation of contributions* is difficult for reasons indicated above having to do with cost information and accounting procedures. The valuation procedures in the West are simply not used in China, and the different contributions that each makes leaves a balancing of contributions rather arbitrary. In addition to capital (in renminbi), the Chinese will be contributing an existing plant in some cases, or only land, labor, and access to raw materials and a potentially large domestic market. The foreigner will be contributing capital, management, and technology, plus potential access to a foreign market. Only the capital contribution has a hard value, for even the land is owned by the state and has no market price.

Despite the difficulties of making adequate valuations, says one American observer, it is interesting how often the value of the contributions of the Chinese equal precisely 50 percent of the capitalization of the joint venture, with no Chinese capital contribution. Optimistically, this could result from a careful pruning of the total value of the project, so that what the Chinese are willing to contribute is in fact 50 percent of the total. The Chinese also view foreign exchange funding through joint venture loans from Chinese financial institutions as part of their contribution—perhaps the most important in their view.

The *board of directors* usually has the responsibility for making decisions on changes in products or processes, and on serving domestic or foreign markets. Only the board will have the ability to initiate discussions with Ministry of Foreign Economic Relations and Trade (MOFERT) and other departments in charge to remove bureaucratic intervention. Agreement should be reached early that the board will take such initiatives, and that the foreign partner's board members are particularly expected to do so. Further, the issues on which voting is required should be delineated, with the voting patterns necessary for decision also decided—that is, which issues will require unanimity (such as revision of the articles of agreement, termination, expansion, or merger), which taken by a two-thirds vote or by a simple majority. In addition, a requirement may be added that on every issue, a minimum of one director from each side should be found voting with the deciding group. Voting is not the normal procedure for the Chinese, who prefer to take decisions by consensus after adequate discussion—which may require days. But any foreign investor who believes that he can, in any foreign country, insist on performance by voting or resorting to the joint venture contract will have a short-term venture.

Management is the joint responsibility of the two partners, with the managing director frequently appointed for an initial period by the foreign partner and the deputy appointed by the Chinese, from which also comes most of middle management. It is difficult, if not impossible, to recruit Westerners for middle management who know the Chinese language, who will live in that cultural environment for some years, and who see this as a career opportunity. In addition, the costs of expatriates are greater than the joint venture usually wants to sustain; and if salaries are sufficiently differentiated to attract a foreigner, there is a potential for dissatisfaction on the part of the Chinese managers. Provision should be made for senior foreign managers to visit the operations as appropriate to assess progress and determine how to meld the joint venture into their parent company's long-term strategic plans.

Compensation for foreign managers, including the managing director, typically is a difficult issue because it sets a pattern for Chinese management that is far out of line with competing domestic companies. The principle of "equal pay for equal work" is insisted on by the Chinese, but the salaries of foreign managers are several multiples of that received by Chinese managers. The government usually insists that the salary of Chinese managers be equal to that of Westerners and be paid by the joint venture to the government (or the factory's welfare fund), with the government keeping all but the locally competitive take-home remuneration it pays the Chinese manager. This practice raises the costs of the venture and reduces the profits to both parties, but it increases the revenue to the government, which is part of the benefits sought by the Chinese. If the foreign partner pays an expatriate manager at the Chinese level and deposits the remainder of a normal salary in the home country, the foreign partner is subsidizing the joint venture substantially.

The Chinese also are concerned about high fringe benefits and other perks for foreign managers. Due attention should be paid to spelling out all of the remuneration and benefits to expatriates. When the general manager of one of the early Shanghai joint ventures with a high-tech U.S. firm was asked what was the most difficult issue he was dealing with (after the first year's operation), he replied, "Expatriate salaries and annual increases." Taxes that have to be paid by expatriates also are complicated, for even an aggregate of thirty days in China or a residence permit allowing visits up to ninety days (regardless of days spent) can lead to a determination that the foreigner is a "Chinese taxpayer." He then is expected to pay individual income tax on his entire annual income, regardless of where earned. Such taxes are difficult for the Chinese to administer and are a subject of negotiation.

Domestic materials are under the allocation of the Chinese government, and any joint venture can be stymied by the lack or irregular supply of materials necessary for production, as well as their inflated prices. The negotiators should ascertain that the joint venture is of sufficient priority to warrant a continuous and appropriate supply of materials and energy, although even this is difficult. Again, this part of the negotiation requires government departments beyond those immediately responsible for the joint venture.

Labor supply would not appear to be a critical issue when there is an enterprise in existence because a labor force is already employed. But skilled labor and good managers are in high demand and difficult to find even with government support and assistance. Most Chinese companies are faced with overemployment; labor is simply assigned to them, and they must pay the going wages. The joint venture negotiations should stipulate that the board has the ability to determine the level of employment, to hire workers as needed, to fire those that are redundant or incompetent, and to determine appropriate wages. Here, again, the government frequently insists on wages higher than usual to compensate it for benefits such as low-cost housing and medical care. The workers will get only standard wages. In one instance, the joint venture determined that the workers should be given incentives out of the profits of the venture; it made such a provision, only to be stopped by the department in charge for excessive wages.

Exclusivity often is desired by both parties to the venture, pending approval by the relevant government departments. Exclusivity is not only a matter of whether other companies might have similar technology or be licensed with the same technology from the foreign company, but also a matter of market concentration—that is, the number of competitors that the government will permit in a given sector. In some instances, the total market may be so small that economies of scale cannot be reached, as would be required to reduce costs and raise quality to international standards. If this is the case, an agreement by the government to concentrate production in a few locations becomes part of the negotiations. Here, again, the local partner has the same interests as the foreign company and will strengthen the presentation to the appropriate government agencies. One qualification is that, given the market fragmentation, absence of a Chinese national market, and the relative power of local officials, even assurances by national officials of broad market exclusivity may not be feasible or, if given, may not be enforceable in practice.

Proprietary rights in patents, trademarks, copyrights, and know-how have not been historically protected in China. The lack of a competitive economy has been a primary reason for the lack of innovation (application) of invention in China, except through government projects—armaments, bridges, and even astronomy (which was supported by the emperor). The Chinese partner has contrary interests both in disseminating or diffusing the technology, usually at the request of the department in charge or another government entity, and in keeping it within the enterprise for competitive purposes. Both pressures exist, and the essential ingredient is good faith on the part of the Chinese partner. China has promulgated a law protecting patents, but there is as yet little experience in its implementation.

Disputes that cannot be resolved through the board of directors or in consultation with MOFERT are expected to be resolved through arbitration or conciliation. As indicated in previous chapters, there is little desire for litigation on the part of the Chinese enterprise, and it behooves the foreign partner not to press that route unless absolutely necessary. Arbitration is sought by the Chinese only reluctantly and even then through their own Foreign Economic and Trade Arbitration Commission of the China Council for the Promotion of International Trade, rather than going to international arbitration. Sometimes the Arbitration Institute of the Stockholm Chamber of Commerce is accepted as a neutral body or the U.N. Commission on International Trade Law. Use of the laws of the foreign country is not acceptable to the Chinese government, but reliance on the law of China is a problem for the foreign enterprise. The choice of applicable law frequently is left to the arbitration tribunal to which the dispute is referred. Sometimes acceptance of a tribunal is explicitly stated in the agreement, so as to waive any sovereign immunity that might attach to a state enterprise.

A dispute arising over expropriation or confiscation by the Chinese government would probably lead to arbitration, unless there is a bilateral investment treaty between the home country and the People's Republic of China. In 1980, the U.S. and Chinese governments signed an "Investment Incentive Agreement" to trigger the application of insurance and guarantees by the Overseas Private Investment Corporation (OPIC). It provided for settlement of disputes between the U.S. and Chinese governments on matters affecting them and, if unresolved, to be submitted to an arbitration tribunal for resolution. It does not require arbitration for disputes between China and the OPIC or with foreign investors. Thus foreign investors do not have a right to seek or require arbitration of disputes under private law.[7]

Technical specifications covering the product, components, nationally integrated supplies, processes, plant layouts, energy use, materials qualities and inspection, quality assurance, and so forth are matters of considerable discussion, since they will be issues on which the Chinese are inadequately prepared. The technical capabilities of many of the Chinese engineers are quite high; they can *understand* readily. But there are an insufficient number of them to be placed in each enterprise with which the foreigners might be negotiating, or to apply the technology once transferred. The mere transfer of information *about* the specifications is itself a long process.

Training of Chinese is a contribution that is widely desired on the part of the Chinese, especially in the parent company of the foreign partner or an appropriate foreign affiliate. Not only is the cost of such training a matter of negotiation, but also the number of people to be trained, the duration of the training, the location, the content of the programs, and so forth. Given the relatively low cost of such programs, the provision of training is a strong bargaining chip on the part of the foreign company.[8] In fact, some companies are gratuitously training a number of Chinese both in their operations and in university management-development programs, to increase the supply of competent managers and engineers as well as to gain bargaining chips for the future. Although it is not clear how the labor market will develop, or how much independence individuals will have, it is likely that many of the professionally trained will be moved by the government into a variety of companies to diffuse their enhanced abilities. It is virtually impossible to restrict the transfer of those trained through a joint venture into other companies.

Taxes are a matter of negotiation in view of the fact that there are a number of incentives that can be offered to equity joint ventures that are not offered to other forms of business. It appears that the tax rate itself is negotiable, as are tax waivers or exemptions, and reduced taxes are applied on earnings that are reinvested in China for five years. The situation is sufficiently fluid that it is permissible for the joint venture to question an interpretation by tax authorities;

in some instances, the complaint has been resolved in favor of the joint venture. Tax incentives should not be permitted to mask the fundamental economic viability of the joint venture itself. They help to offset the up-front investment by the foreign partner, but they cannot be counted on for the long-term profitability of the venture. Tax incentives are a two-edged sword, and must be used with caution or the foreign investor may find itself abandoning an unprofitable but otherwise operational factory at the end of the incentive period.

The *feasibility study* is a fairly expensive undertaking, since it is really a planning document for operation of the enterprise for the first ten years, which will be approved by various government agencies. The question of who shall conduct the feasibility study and the costs of doing so (usually shared by the two parties) are subject to negotiation. Given the extent of the study and its importance in guiding the operations for the first years, it often is prepared during the negotiation and both affects and is affected by the progress of negotiations. Like corporate long-range plans, the feasibility study can be detailed projections or simply guesstimates. It should be completed with the best data available and both parties' best judgments in regard to the numerous assumptions that must be made. If done this way, it can serve to highlight at an early time differences in the potential partners' opinions and *expectations* in time for friendly negotiations and mutual agreement. In some cases, the feasibility study is viewed by both partners as unneeded governmental paperwork, required by the too-large bureaucratic departments. In this situation, the partners may believe that they have an understanding that the feasibility study is a necessary step in the joint venture agreement, but not something to be referred to or used in the future. In other words, they do not see the need for it because they understand their business and each other, but this is a dangerous assumption.

In regard to format, there is no governmentally dictated presentation for a feasibility study. One would be extremely difficult to design, given the wide array of joint venture operations across many sectors. The critical content of a feasibility study is the *data and assumptions necessary to demonstrate that the expectations of each partner are realistic and obtainable.*

The Chinese interest is in documenting what they are receiving by way of the joint venture—what technology, how much foreign exchange capital, when exports begin, and so forth. The foreign investor needs to document its expectation in terms of repatriatable profits and have the Chinese formally acknowledge it.

Guarantees of loan repayments arise as an issue simply because the Bank of China seeks security for any loans that it may make to the joint venture. The foreign partner (and the Chinese factory as well) want guarantees that the foreign exchange loans will be made available to the joint venture. They are important to the foreign investor in a manufacturing joint venture, in which the foreign exchange is needed to pay for imported parts. It would not be unusual for the foreign exchange requirements of a joint venture to be two to four times the capital supplied to the joint venture, since the Chinese capital contribution normally is in renminbi or buildings. The foreign exchange needed to operate the joint venture can only come from loans from Chinese financial institutions, the World Bank, or the foreign investor parent organization. The foreign investor will want to limit foreign exchange supplied to its capital contribution; using the World Bank's International Finance Corporation will dilute ownership, since the World Bank ownership eventually will be sold to Chinese investors. Thus the foreign investor will want to be certain that all the foreign exchange required is committed.

Termination of the agreement must be prepared for, since the law sets the duration of most agreements at no more than thirty years, with some possibility of extension. The desire of the Chinese to "go it alone" at some time in the future remains strong. Alternatively, policy changes, new legislation, or even political upheaval may make a particular joint venture unprofitable, causing the foreign partner to seek to be relieved of its obligations early. The conditions for termination, the process of valuation of assets—including "going-concern value" and repatriation of the funds—require prior agreement. The financial losses can be reserved for but losing control of the technology may be disastrous.

Force majeure is an acceptable concept even to the Chinese, but there is a tendency to place the blame for external interventions on the foreign partner, regardless of source. For example, a delay in production and sales by a joint venture because of U.S. export controls or Coordinating Committee regulations may cause the Chinese partner to ask for recompense in one way or another. Conversely, the Chinese are perfectly capable of avoiding responsibility for intervening or interrupting events originating from their side. Specification (beyond the usual force majeure clause) of types of events that are the responsibility of neither party is desirable.

XEROX NEGOTIATION IN CHINA

To provide a flavor of the actual sequences of negotiations and the issues involved, the experience of Xerox in forming a joint venture with Shanghai is recorded here in some detail.[9] The events recorded give no information as to the sequence of steps in negotiation among the different levels of Chinese government or within the Chinese partner, but the lack of behind-the-scenes information is the way the foreigner faces the situation. The events are recorded sequentially, with the intervals as they actually occurred.

1979

August: Invitation from China to Xerox scientist to lecture and visit plants, stimulating interest in beginning negotiations for cooperative ventures.

1980–1982

Identification of various potential partners; initiations of in-depth discussions with a copier factory (one of thirty-two in China) belonging to the shipbuilding ministry. Negotiations terminate in June 1982, after foreign exchange requirements are determined. Both sides had expected the other to provide the necessary hard-currency funding required during the start-up period. Xerox-China team is disbanded, but long-term interest in China remains, since Xerox has been selling copiers into China from the Hong Kong company for ten years and has a worldwide network of joint ventures. Xerox realizes that it was paired with a copier factory not under the purview of the First Ministry, Light Industry, which is responsible for copiers, and thus received no central government support.

1983

May: Chairman Peter McCullough and Vice-President Marion Antonine (Worldwide Operations) visit China and sign a ''Memo of Understanding'' with People's Republic First Ministry, indicating a mutual desire to establish a joint venture in copier manufacturing.

1984

January: Xerox technical and legal teams travel to China to visit potential partners in Guangzhou, Guilin, Beijing, Shanghai, and other cities. The People's Republic does not specify a partner for Xerox.

June: Xerox asks SMPIC to consider a partnership for small copier production in China and invites them to visit Xerox in the United States and the Xerox joint venture with Fuji in Japan.

July: Fuji-Xerox complains to Xerox that their Japanese competitors are moving into China more rapidly than Xerox; Xerox commits a team fully dedicated to the China project. It is led by James Shapiro, corporate vice-president from Stamford, Connecticut, with the authority to make decisions in China.

October: SMPIC visits the United States to see Xerox capabilities. Chairman McCullough and President David Kearns host a dinner for SMPIC and express their interest in a long-term joint venture. (Xu Deliang, leader of the delegation and vice-president of SMPIC, admires Kearns' necktie and receives it as a present from Kearns.)

Discussions during this visit are to identify the concerns of each side:

For SMPIC—the then higher cost of Xerox copiers, the low labor content in small copiers, the refusal of Xerox to commit to export, the time required for joint venture to develop a hard-currency surplus, and national integration of components

For Xerox—the small participation in the China market implied by the SMPIC production levels, copier prices in China, and the difficulty of making any profit

November: Xerox Corporate Management Committee meets to agree on the proposed internal principles under which the new effort will go forward, including exporting copiers from China and acknowledging that profitability will take an extended period of time.

China Xerox Review Corporate Management Committee

November 15, 1984

Subject: China Joint Venture
Major Assumptions and Agreements:

- China is a major market opportunity for copiers, telecopiers, electronic printers, personal computers, and typewriters.
- Financially, China must be viewed in the context of an investment, rather than as a marketing opportunity.
- China is a competitive and profit-oriented environment.
- China as a country (and SMPIC) is anxious to move ahead. Xerox or others will fill the need.
- The joint venture requires a steady and stable financial commitment.
- China offers opportunities for lowest-cost worldwide manufacturing.
- Exporting is essential for the long-term success of the joint venture.

RECOMMENDATION: Proceed, if agreement reached on above.

1985

February: SMPIC, after extended discussions, agrees to purchase 10,000 semi–knocked-down copiers to begin occupying the market and halt losing market share against the Japanese. Negotiations break down on technology transfer shortly before the banquet Xerox is hosting to celebrate the initiation of the Xerox-Shanghai relationship. (Many senior Shanghai members are invited. The Chinese, who are never late to banquets, send word that they will be late. Xerox is trying to think of appropriate toasts for a not-so-joyous occasion.)

At dinner, Mr. Tang, manager of China National Machinery & Equipment Import/Export Corporation, says to the Xerox host: "I am older and more willing to be bolder. We will take the risk of going ahead with the purchases of copiers before the joint venture and technology transfer agreements are negotiated."

Negotiations continue on—

schedule for national integration

confidentiality of the technology transfer agreement

identification of the SMPIC feasibility team members

schedule for feasibility study

agreement that members of board of directors appointed by SMPIC and Xerox will be equal in number

license fee percentage and terms

size of joint venture in terms of product and geography

responsibility for hard-currency requirements

handling of pre-joint venture expenses

March: Xerox hosts the next two levels of management above SMPIC in a U.S. visit: Lu Yebo, vice-director, Shanghai Light Industry Bureau, and Xu Qing Xiong, deputy director, Economic Commission, Shanghai Municipal People's Government. Purpose is to display Xerox's wide range of technical and research activities and capabilities.

April: A variety of activities, including a visit of Xerox engineers to a large number of Shanghai factories to assess their capabilities for national integration, and meetings with Shanghai Design Institute on joint venture factory specifications.

May: The following topics are discussed at negotiations with SMPIC in Shanghai:

license fee

pricing

exclusive or nonexclusive product arrangement

salary levels of Chinese joint venture managers compared with expatriates

costs of temporary Xerox personnel assigned to the joint venture

confirmation of equal board representation

valuation of building in Minghang (Special Economic Zone, outside Shanghai) and land-use fee

marketing and service plans

duration of the joint venture

name for the joint venture

plan for earning foreign exchange

Owing to unfortunate circumstances, little is accomplished on this visit. (Mr. Xu Deliang's twelve-year-old daughter unexpectedly undergoes surgery, taking him away at times.) Substitute negotiators cannot really take his place.

A second unexpected event intervenes. During this period, the city of Wuhan requests Xerox to bid (either directly or through Fuji-Xerox) on a copier technology transfer agreement of significant size. This is discussed with Director Xu Qing Xiong, who asserts that even though Wuhan's product would not be geographically competitive with SMPIC's, it would be unwise for Xerox to bid in any form; likewise, he states that Shanghai will not have discussions with any other copier manufacturers. Exclusivity in negotiation partners is agreed on.

July: Xerox team visits Shanghai without Shapiro, senior Xerox corporate officer for China. Xu Deliang attends only a few sessions, and despite an agreed-on composition of the Xerox delegation and agenda, little is accomplished. Most of the time is spent rediscussing the May issues, without any decisions or agreements.

July is the first China mailing of the Xerox *Benchmark* publication, a customer journal oriented to the systems business and new products. Key articles are translated into Chinese.

Throughout February to December 1985, a great deal of work is done to start up the SMPIC semi–knocked-down operation for the 10,000 small copiers to be assembled there.

August–October: A number of trips are made to Shanghai by different Xerox people—some to support the 10,000 copier semi–knocked-down project and a large number to develop the details for the joint venture feasibility study, which requires excruciating detail down to the number of piece parts arriving at each station during the manufacturing process.

An MOU covering the items from the May and July visits is drafted, edited, and exchanged several times. It reflects a number of agreements on items such as license fee rate and base, production plan, percentage of sales in renminbi, salaries of Chinese counterparts in management, board membership, and product exclusivity; but the continued revisions surface new issues. Shanghai wants Xerox to guarantee the balancing of foreign exchange after the first five years.

Smaller problems also arise: Shanghai will not authorize pre–joint venture spending for construction drawings; they use the hard-currency balancing issue to delay signing the MOU, which also confirms the delivery dates for the remainder of the 10,000 semi–knocked-down units; the central authorities restrain overall government (and enterprise) spending in late 1985.

The feasibility study is completed in late October, with fourteen persons from Xerox in Shanghai working with SMPIC. The lawyers for both teams have been drafting, on an ongoing basis, both the joint venture and the technology transfer agreements, reflecting the decisions out of the continuing negotiations.

November–December: Although Shapiro was present at the September–October meeting with Xu Deliang, major issues remain and several new ones develop: Expatriate salaries are still not agreed on. SMPIC wants access to the technology for parts Xerox purchases from various Xerox vendors and argues that start-up costs should be included in the license. Xerox wants assurances that spare parts will be priced at industry levels and agreement that the joint venture can distribute through any trading company, not just the SMPIC-owned trading company.

Out of the feasibility study detail arises the toughest challenge: *the cost of producing the joint venture copier at the end of year 5, with 70 percent national integration, is estimated at 97 percent of the landed cost of the copier in year 1.* The Xerox assumption, until this time, has been that the unit manufacturing cost will be at least 30 percent *less* than industry levels, and specifically those in Japan, South Korea, Singapore, and Taiwan. This new information means that Xerox cannot export profitability in the *second* five-year period, when it assumes the responsibility for balancing foreign exchange.

(Other parties at interest in the negotiations are the local foreign trade commission, the local economic commission, and the local planning commission; each has helped to set the terms of reference for negotiation.)

In planning for the next year, after four years of experience, the Xerox-China team meets to discuss what has happened over the past year, what is required for joint venture success in China, and who (Xerox, Shanghai, or jointly) is responsible. They build on their experience, that of other companies in China, and Xerox's knowledge from its other international joint ventures.

Analysis of Potential for Long-term Joint Venture Success

Enablers/Dependencies Required for Success	Responsibility
Access to full domestic market	China
Concentration of People's Republic production volume (approx. 75 percent in one entity/factory)	China
Profits for reinvestment in future technologies	
Economies of scale	
Concentration of high-quality technical/managerial personnel	
High government priority for:	China
Transportation	
Raw materials and energy	
High government priority for coordination of other factors	China
Cost of production of up-to-date products to be 30 to 40 percent below competitive world basis	Joint
Labor	
Materials	
Overhead/indirect	
Product development for internationally saleable products	Joint
Quality, cost/value, technology features	
Ability to reinvest joint venture profits	
Repatriation of profits	China
Ability to balance foreign exchange at some point in time— import substitution	Joint
Access to complete technology	Xerox
Successful transfer of technology	Joint
Ability to absorb by partner/vendors	China
Successful transfer of management skills and processes	Joint

Openness and trust between partners	Joint
Agreement by each that other's objectives are achievable	
National integration	Joint
Profitable operation—adequate return on investment	Joint
Long-term commitment by both parties	Joint
Availability of Bank of China funding	China
Foreign exchange and renminbi	

1986

January: The unexpected happens. Xerox identifies a small safety problem in the desktop copier SMPIC is assembling and selling in China and Xerox is selling worldwide. Xerox corporate headquarters directs a worldwide modification program requiring a Xerox service representative's personal inspection of each machine. Six thousand machines are installed in China, mostly in Shanghai. Xerox-China group adjusts the corporate program and permits the dealers in China to do the inspection and retrofit. Xerox does not know whether this retrofit will be viewed in China as a Xerox quality problem or as Xerox caring about safety and people. Implementation of the retrofit in China is a different task than elsewhere in the world.

February–May: Start-up costs and salaries of Chinese counterparts of Xerox expatriates are resolved in February. Costs of Xerox-imposed systems and Xerox safety inspections will not be included in shared start-up costs, and Xerox agrees to "top-stop" amount. SMPIC counterpart mangers to Xerox expatriates will receive 80 percent of the Xerox managers' home-country salary. (The total costs of maintaining a U.S. manager is later estimated at $300,000 per year per family. After U.S. managers leave, Chinese salaries will return to local levels; other joint venture managers would remain at local salary levels throughout.)

Balancing of foreign exchange remains an open issue in light of estimated cost of production in year 5 being projected at 246 percent of current cost outside of China. Key factor in estimates is cost of parts purchased from Shanghai suppliers. SMPIC has no control over these, nor can Shanghai Light Industry direct pricing for factories—theirs or others. Western-type cost accounting systems are not used and five-year cost estimates are not a normal part of Chinese business.

Xerox proposes a set of export price levels (based on expected world market prices) for years 6 through 10 of the joint venture operation. SMPIC agrees in concept but proposes a slightly higher set of prices that increases export prices of the joint venture, compared with other sources of supply. *These are only assumptions; getting the cost of production to these levels is a task over which neither the joint venture, Xerox, or SMPIC has full control, but success in exporting depends on it. A basic weakness in manufacturing joint ventures that assemble products primarily from purchased parts is identified.*

Xerox and SMPIC investigate the average return on investment in areas outside of China. For the most recent years available, in the United States it averaged 14.7 percent, in Asia some 30 percent, and in Hong Kong a complete payback usually is achieved in three years. SMPIC and Xerox agree on a return on investment for the feasibility study.

Xerox begins an in-depth analysis of its joint venture situation. The team tries to determine how this joint venture differs from others publicized as successful. It creates a schematic of the joint venture relationship, reflecting the flow of technology, money, and machines. The search for a joint venture model that has solved the problems facing the Xerox-SMPIC joint venture is futile. At this time, there are no joint ventures using imported parts sets that are profitable or close to it, especially on a foreign exchange basis.

June: Foreign exchange available to the joint venture is further reduced by China, forcing a reduction in the production volume anticipated, and return on the Xerox investment drops two percentage points. It is learned that there are supposed to be eight competitive copier technology transfer agreements in eight major cities.

Xerox begins to think that the risks associated with achieving profitability are too great. Achievement of cost reductions are primarily dependent on other factories, sales are dependent on outside trading companies, and pricing is controlled by government bureaus. Xerox suggests some changes to enhance the joint venture's profitability, including increased production levels and the right for Xerox to export other Chinese goods to balance foreign exchange. If these are not acceptable, Xerox proposes that SMPIC and Xerox enter into a technology transfer agreement for three years, after which time costs of production will be better known. Xerox requests a meeting with Shanghai mayor Jiang Zemen to explain its position and to preserve the opportunity of a future joint venture.

To the surprise of many, the mayor meets with Xerox. All managers, deputy directors, directors, and vice-mayors who have anything to do with the Xerox negotiations or foreign investment are present—some called back from holiday. After cordial introductory remarks, the mayor requests Xerox to discuss its views. Xerox states its long-term objectives and its difficulties with the current projection of production costs and the resulting uncertainty in the ability of the joint venture to export profitability. The mayor has been briefed before the meeting, and after a few exploratory questions of Xerox, declares to the entire group, including Xerox, "I believe this joint venture will be good for China, fix the problems." Shapiro asks Mayor Jiang Zemen, "If we reach agreement, will you come to the signing?" He promises to do so.

July: SMPIC proposes that Xerox (which purchases many parts from Asian suppliers) commit to purchase US $15 to $20 million in parts from China over the first five years. SMPIC reduces the projected cost of production to reflect the recent devaluation of the renminbi. Xerox refuses to commit to purchase

Chinese parts, since costs and quality are unknowns, but it indicates that it will strive to do so if cost and quality are competitive. Xerox assigns a procurement person full time to the investigation of suppliers in China.

August: The Bureau of Instrumentation Industries (BII), which is part of the Light Industry Department of the Ministry of Machine Building, asserts that it has full responsibility for establishing the copier industry in China. BII invites Xerox to meet with them as part of their selection process for determining the primary foreign copier manufacturers for China. BII discussions do not change anything. It is not known how these discussions tie into the Shanghai discussions. (Shanghai has, from the beginning, stated that they do not require Beijing approval. In further conflict, representatives of the State Economic Commission (SEC) have stated that the final decision will be made by SEC.)

September: After twenty meetings between SMPIC and Xerox, significant differences remain. Xerox believes that these differences are too great for near-term resolution, and formally notifies Shanghai, BII, and the SEC of its decision not to pursue further a small copier joint venture in Shanghai. Xerox continues its negotiations with China Aero-Technology Corporation (CATC) regarding an engineering copier joint venture and with the Administration of Computer Industries for the establishment of an electronic printing center in Beijing.

BII notifies Xerox that the customs office in China has confirmed that the engineering copier it is discussing with CATC is a copier, not a printer, and therefore is under the jurisdiction of BII. It informs CATC, the Ministry of Aero-Technology, and Xerox that BII is temporarily terminating any contact between Xerox and CATC regarding their project, and that Xerox must follow BII's instructions. Arrangements are being finalized for a CATC trip to Xerox in the United States. CATC, which has been in negotiations with Xerox for more than a year, tells Xerox to ignore the BII directive and describes the conflict as an internal China matter.

The SEC requests a firsthand review of the SMPIC-Xerox issues and tells Xerox that because of the depth of the negotiations, if they cease discussions with SMPIC as a potential partner, it is not possible to select another in China. The SEC division chief for copiers offers to personally participate in future negotiations. (Shanghai has in fact requested SEC assistance.) The SEC works to resolve the internal dispute between BII and CATC to permit the CATC visit. Xerox agrees to coordinate with BII on future negotiations with potential partners for other Xerox products and suggests that a BII representative join the CATC visit to the United States. Xerox stresses its desire to stay out of China's internal matters.

October: Xerox receives an invitation to Shanghai to meet with Lu Guoxian, deputy director, Foreign Investment and Trade, the senior Shanghai official involved with Xerox on an ongoing basis. Queen Elizabeth II is visiting Shanghai, and all of the government officials are involved in official functions; thus it is an unusual time for an invitation to Xerox.

Director Lu Guoxian, at the meeting, reviews the just-published October 11,

1986, joint venture regulations and specific Shanghai plans that Mayor Jiang Zemen has directed for reducing the Xerox-SMPIC joint venture cost of production to levels that assure exports on a profitable basis. Both sides agree to the inclusion in the joint venture plan of sufficient funding for new-product development. This will enable exports of world-class products over the long term. A few items remain open, such as classification of the joint venture as "high-technology" under the October 11 regulations, percentage of hard-currency sales by the joint venture, and foreign exchange credit for export of parts. Mayor Jiang requests that Director Lu Guoxian remain personally involved in the negotiations.

November: Mutual agreements are reached on the remaining issues, and Shanghai requests Xerox to make its final decision regarding the joint venture. The Xerox-China team prepares a proposal for submission to the Xerox Corporation Management Committee.

December: Student strikes in China cause some second thoughts among Xerox corporate staff. Xerox formally informs Shanghai that they would like to form the joint venture.

1987

February–August: Two significant events occur in this period. First, an April visit to Xerox by senior Shanghai officials to meet with Xerox president Paul Allaire, Xerox chairman Kearns, and other senior Xerox managers. Paul Allaire welcomes Shanghai into the Xerox family of international joint ventures. Second is another meeting with Mayor Jiang Zemen during his June visit to Shanghai's sister city, San Francisco.

During preparation for the signing of the agreement, several issues develop. SMPIC would like a guaranteed Xerox commitment to the feasibility study projections and access to third-party technology (Xerox suppliers in other countries, which is an old issue). Xerox wants written assurance that the agreed-upon hard-currency loans will be available. Mayor Jiang meets twice with Shapiro and directs a senior Shanghai official who is traveling with Jiang to contact Shanghai. The issues are mutually resolved, and the signing is back on schedule.

Other activities during these months include the following:

Finalization of the feasibility study

Drafting, translation, and agreement on wording of the joint venture agreement and the technology transfer agreement—documents in both Chinese and English to be equally valid

Addition of Bank of Communications as second Shanghai partner to facilitate funding

Review of agreements and feasibility study by Shanghai Foreign Investment and Trade, Ministry of Light Industry for Shanghai, Bank of Communications, and the various Shanghai bureaus involved in issuing the requisite licenses for joint venture operations

September: Joint venture agreements are signed. Xerox chairman David Kearns attends signing and goes with Shapiro to Beijing to call on Vice-Premier Wan Li. Mayor Jiang attends signing banquet, keeping his promise.

Reprise: Nine and one-half years after initial contact, four years after formal negotiations began, and one year after signing, the Xerox-Shanghai joint venture is in operation. Approaching the end of its second year of production (Fig. 10.1), the joint venture has not experienced any lasting problems, and the outlook remains positive. All agreements, formal and informal, have been met by both parties. The Xerox–Administration of Computer Industries electronic printing center is installed and in operation. Negotiations with CATC slowed after their visit to the United States. Shanghai has expressed interest in the engineering copier previously discussed with CATC.

Additional Xerox Activities in China

- XL direct marketing
  Representative offices in Beijing, Shanghai, and Guangzhou
  Four service stations (agents)
- Shapiro, member of Advisory Board, Dalian Management Center, sponsored by U.S. Department of Commerce and State University of New York—Buffalo (GE, IBM, and Exxon also represented on board)
- Cosponsor of weekly show—*Windows on the World* (with P&G and General Foods); broadcast in English and Chinese as a teaching exercise
- Xerox Foundation Lecture Series (including chief executive officer Shapiro, dean of University of North Carolina Graduate School of Business, and associate dean of Washington University School of Business)
- Two People's Republic interns with Xerox on West Coast
- Xerox senior vice-president of technology (Bill Spencer) headed up China Association of Science & Technology Task Force for Transfer of Technology from U.S. University and Research Institutes
- Xerox representative (full-time) seeking procurement opportunities in People's Republic (some $90 million in procurement through Hong Kong in 1988)
- Shapiro, member Pacific Forum Policy Committee; member of several discussion groups between forum members and People's Republic officials
- Beijing electronic printing center with the National Computer Management Group (ACI)
- Discussions with CATC on possible joint venture

FEASIBILITY STUDY

A feasibility study simulating expected financial performance over a ten-year period is required for all joint venture agreements by the SEC and State Planning Commission of the People's Republic. As mentioned in the Xerox negotiations,

Figure 10.1
Xerox Schematic of Shanghai-Xerox Joint Venture

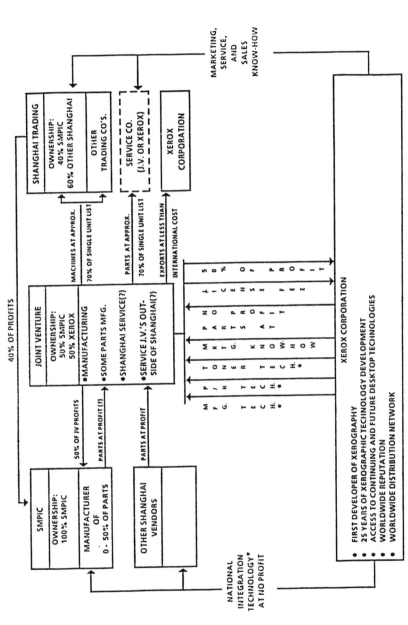

the feasibility study provides a detailed set of planning assumptions that help the partners not only evaluate their investment, but also state their intentions and the conditions under which they expect to operate. Any changes in the actual performance from the expected levels may be explained by changes in the assumptions on which the original projections were based. It should, therefore, detail all of the expected activities, financial responsibilities, and results, including pricing assumptions, staffing, costs of foreign managers, development of local sourcing, means of fulfilling export requirements, and marketing and distribution channels.

The feasibility study will probably be based on Chinese accounting principles and on assumptions as to the rate of domestic inflation and changes in the exchange rate between the renminbi and the home currency of the foreign partner, or U.S. dollars—whichever is most appropriate—plus any other foreign currencies in which the joint venture is conducting significant business. For example, the Xerox-Shanghai joint venture imports parts from Fuji-Xerox and pays for them in Japanese yen.

Contents of Typical Feasibility Study

Sales and production volume	Depreciation/amortization
Marketing and distribution	Operating expenses (detailed)
Revenue taxes	Local labor cost
Market prices of products or parts	Expatriate compensation
License fees	Equalization with local counterparts
National integration process	Inventory projections
Calculation of unit manufacturing cost	Financing
Transfer pricing on intercompany sales	Plan for hard-currency earnings
Start-up costs (detailed)	Sources and uses of hard currency
Vendor development costs	Long-term debt projections
Land and buildings	Reserve funds
Costs of sales	Cash flow
	Profit projections

Final government approvals for the joint venture are the responsibility of the local enterprise, submitting the feasibility study to appropriate authorities. In the case of the Xerox-Shanghai project, officials of the municipal government, the State Planning Commission, the SEC, and MOFERT were involved at appropriate times and, therefore, familiar with the critical aspects of the venture. Any objections that they had to particular terms or conditions were discussed and resolved before formal application for approval.

If the official who has to approve the project has not been brought into the process intimately or early, he may be reluctant to sign off, not knowing the potential success and, therefore, being unwilling to assume any blame for failure. In this event, a Chinese lawyer can be useful in "assuring" validity of the negotiations and the documentation. In fact, Chinese lawyers are becoming more important in the negotiation process, since the form of agreements change case by case and with changes in foreign investment regulations by municipal, provincial, or central government agencies.

The feasibility study is critical in being an instrument to guide the consideration of future managers and members of the board, since not all of them would have been in the negotiations. Even if they were, it is a document that is useful as a base point in resolving differences among the partners as operations proceed. It is not a blueprint for action, but a guide recording the intent and expectations of the partners. It is, therefore, an extensive exercise in "trial marriage," in that the partners have to think through a number of the issues they will face and determine how they expect to handle them. Such an exercise has long been counseled to those entering into joint ventures or even long-term licensing arrangements. Considerable care should be taken in its preparation, involving the future managers, if identified.

A successful feasibility study might be thought of as a safekeeping place for all agreements and assumptions as times change. Using these data and assumptions, results should be projected with ranges of at least ± 20 percent to recognize the inherent inaccuracy of assumptions and to reduce the likelihood of surprises. In summary, its benefit to both partners lies in increasing the probability of similar expectations and avoiding "same bed, different dreams."

LESSONS FROM NEGOTIATING EXPERIENCE

Past experiences in various joint venture negotiations provide some lessons concerning the negotiations themselves and roles of the participants.

Negotiation Process

The process of negotiation can be expected to be lengthy (interrupted with long delays) and to involve the reopening of issues seemingly settled, unexpected interventions, unexpected reversals of government positions or permissions, with government pressure imposed if the joint venture is in a high-priority sector.

To gain as broad a base of support as feasible, it is wise to elevate the project to the highest levels of government at the earliest possible time. It is advisable to involve appropriate government officials at key times in the negotiations, so that they are appraised of the progress and direction, thus increasing their willingness to approve the final documents expeditiously. Government officials may have to be drawn in directly to break bottlenecks between the negotiating partners, and their familiarity with the project and the foreign investor's sincerity will speed the process.

Chinese Parties

The lessons relative to the Chinese participants are several.

1. The Chinese have an adequate appreciation of the role of profit and risk in competitive market situations. They do not have an understanding of opportunity costs, so that profit rates expected by transnationals elsewhere seem to be unreasonably high to the Chinese. Costs of capital are not fully understood, since the Chinese government has provided zero-interest loans to state enterprises and permitted low depreciation charges. However, under the "opening," the situation improved substantially; earlier, foreign negotiators literally had to spend a major portion of their time educating Chinese negotiators as to the nature of business practices. Central planning, long isolation, and the Cultural Revolution created a Dark Age of business knowledge and practice in China.

2. They lack an adequate concept of business dynamics and risk, since they have not faced them in the allocation system under central planning. They do not understand the uncertainty of profit, and consider that profit expectations should be relatively accurate; when more profit is gained than expected, the Chinese consider that they have agreed to pricing or cost terms that were wrong ("zero sum," again). In such cases, they have frequently sought to renegotiate the terms to reduce the profit. Not understanding the function of the entrepreneur in assuming risk, and therefore the uncertainty of profit, sometimes they have offered to guarantee the profit returns or profit rate to show their understanding of the needs of the foreign capitalist.

3. The Chinese, despite their general candor, do not reveal the precise roles of individual negotiators to the foreign party. Sometimes this can lead to confusion.

4. The decision-making processes in China remain bureaucratic and, therefore, highly protective; more experience is needed in making decisions more promptly.

5. There is a lack of incentive on the part of Chinese to agree to the agreements or to make them succeed once implemented. Under current conditions, the career path and rewards will remain the same for each manager, regardless of whether assigned to the state enterprise or to the joint venture; until incentives are changed to induce an assumption of risks in all enterprises negotiating joint ventures, the pressures to cooperate and to generate profitable opportunities will not be strong.

6. The role of information is critical, given the scarcity of adequate information and the reluctance to share it even among departments or agencies involved in the negotiating process. The independence of departments within an enterprise, each of which has a strong reporting relation to a government agency, to which greater loyalty often is given than to the enterprise itself, means that official information frequently is treated as confidential (from others in the enterprise), even though not given in that manner. Given the desire of bureaucrats and

company officials to protect themselves and their personal power, information is held confidentially even though it is not in any sense secret. Even instruction manuals may be kept under lock and key and not provided to those needing them for manufacturing processes. Further, information concerning international practices of foreign companies is difficult to find in China, and though the Chinese are learning about such practices, their interpretations as applied to a joint venture frequently are inadequate to achieve worldwide competitiveness.

7. Analysis of information is not yet done in a market-oriented mode. The facts to be analyzed may be selectively chosen to serve non-market purposes; only "good news" may be reported to government agencies or to top management. Even if the analysis is sound, the conclusions drawn may be warped according to the relations of people involved rather than according to market requirements.

8. Enterprise information frequently is lacking, making assessment of the viability of the Chinese partner difficult. Balance sheets and cost information are not always available, and even if they exist, they are not always gathered together for management's use, since each department considers itself somewhat autonomous within the enterprise.

9. Although the Chinese understand cost-benefit analysis and can apply it directly to a potential project, they do not apply it more broadly, including some indirect effects. For example, the lengthy process of negotiations is itself costly, not only in expenses, but also in lost opportunities; yet this does not seem to be appreciated by Chinese negotiators.

10. A continued lack of coordination within the state enterprises themselves among the various departments of personnel, marketing, production, accounting, and finance means that decision-making is difficult on the Chinese side, and costly delays are introduced.

11. Chinese negotiators are still seeking to draw from the "fundamental principles of socialism and Chinese traditions, while applying Western principles to business affairs." This is a difficult mix even for them, and clearly for the foreigner, to understand.

12. For the Chinese, the "true purpose" of the joint venture is not profit for the joint venture, but technology and foreign exchange earnings through exports.

13. For reasons of culture and the concept of benefits accruing to the weaker party, the Chinese want the rich foreign partner to stick to the contract almost literally but do not require the same response from themselves.

Foreign Companies

The following orientations should characterize Western negotiators in China:

1. Exercise patience—or, as an old aphorism states, "patience must have patience with patience"; never allow time to work to your disadvantage.

2. Choose an appropriately high-ranking manager as chief negotiator and keep him all the way through; this must become virtually his entire responsibility,

since visits will be frequent and travel extensive, leaving little time for other tasks.

3. Recognize the negotiating competence of the Chinese, who cannot be pressured or easily manipulated through a "hard sell." They react to courtesy and candor but can be insulted by unguarded remarks. It is safe to assume that any action that would offend in the United States (such as going over someone's head) will offend in China, but a country concerned with "face" requires additional caution.

4. Select the product to be manufactured or assembled with considerable care, fitting it within the priorities of the government and the resources of China. Select one that can be exported within three to five years.

5. Do ample homework before negotiations start and during them, rather than after the agreement is signed.

6. Understand the real barrier of language and cultural differences, both in negotiation and operation—therefore, spelling out intentions as carefully as possible.

7. Recognize the potential change of policies within China, building appropriate safeguards when feasible.

8. Employ an independent interpreter, only if one is not available from within the company itself. Do not rely on Chinese-supplied interpreters under any circumstances; much of the "intelligence" is lost at the negotiating table by not having a personal translator. It is best to have two persons on the team who are fluent in the foreign language, not just as a contingency or as a means of catching all nuances, but also in recognition of the stress and fatigue that comes from all-day translation.

Expatriates as Negotiators

One of the least advisable tactics in negotiation is the use of an expatriate Chinese, whether from Hong Kong, Taiwan, or California, who does not know your business intimately. The translation from English to Chinese and vice versa is not a word-for-word translation, and a person is needed who knows what the ideas are in the context of your business. Also, the translation of the technical words is critical.

Sometimes a knowledgeable translator can translate for both sides and be accepted by the Chinese because of his technical expertise. It is desirable to have two translators, so that they can check on each other and have time to listen to the flow of the discussions. The time taken for sequential translation can be well used by each party in clarifying their own ideas and positions in their own minds.

---

9. Recognize the value of sincerity and candor, with ample supply of technical information during the negotiations, but do not give anything away before compensation is agreed on.

10. Understand that personal relations are even more important than the unique-

ness of the product and the need of the Chinese for the product, despite the high importance of the latter two qualities.

11. Take time to understand Chinese business practices and social customs; this is even more important than an understanding of Chinese politics or language. Differences in social customs, ideology, or politics are less likely to cause a failure in negotiations than misunderstandings or differences in business practices and negotiating styles. These lead to a breakdown in communications through frustration on the part of the foreigner and sometimes even the Chinese. Although it is important to be sensitive to these differences, the foreign negotiator should not try to "act like the Chinese," for they expect the foreigners also to be themselves, and they are trying to understand Western ways.

12. Recognize the impossibility of precisely calculating the future development of China, economically or politically; this is difficult enough for the Chinese and impossible for the foreigner.

13. Recognize that economic freedom to earn profits, although a departure from traditional Marxism, does not imply a departure from socialism, where the collective good always outweighs the rights of individuals, whether or not the foreign investor agrees with such a view.

14. Remember that human relations are more important than contractual obligations.

15. Attempt to avoid frustrations over misunderstandings and any effort to "get even." A mutual balancing of costs and benefits is more important than personal feelings. The Chinese also can take offense, and personal feelings should not get in the way of successful negotiations. Personal relations are important, but egoistic sensitivities should be set aside.

16. Be aware of and sensitive to symbolic gestures by the Chinese, such as a sudden change of personnel on their negotiating team, the quality of banquets, or the availability and warmth of social contacts.

17. Remember that reciprocity in the Chinese culture does not mean equal exchanges, but obligations according to place in the relationship, with the more advantaged offering more to the less advantaged partner. But their continued pressure to obtain further concessions does not mean a reduction in value of the relationship itself; on the contrary, it is a constant reaffirmation of the relative positions of the two parties.

The guidelines and lessons for negotiation are diverse, but aside from operations themselves, negotiation is the most critical phase of doing business in China. It deserves ample preparation and attention during the process to reduce (the inevitable) misunderstandings.

Rights and Wrongs in Negotiation

Applying the negotiation guidelines to the Xerox experience provides the following assessment of what went right, what could have been done better, and what would enable a more effective negotiation in the future.

What Went Right

- Xerox's organization structure and chief executive officer support
- Early agreement on foreign exchange responsibilities
- Full-time, experienced team members
- Frequent trip schedule—every six weeks—travel and time never became a disadvantage
- Only one lead voice
- Use of experience in joint ventures in other countries
- Continued emphasis on long-term exporting objective
- Establishment of relationship between senior Xerox and Shanghai managers
- Thoroughness of feasibility study
- Good logistics support in China through Xerox's China offices
- Good communications/visibility of Xerox in China

What Needs to Be Done Better

- Targets—capacity, scope, product line, basic requirements—too much "floating"
- Resources and system to generate financial and marketing numbers—inadequate staff
- Technology given in negotiations process—too much provided
- Trust in partner—insufficient by corporate staff
- Too slow in getting cost information for national integration
- Definition of feasibility documentation—needed earlier to limit unneeded detail
- Rules for conduct of feasibility study—none set
- Relationship between Xerox and Shanghai too adversarial at times
- Vendor base in China—not understood or adequately investigated
- Information supplied to SMPIC—too much, too early
- Cost and schedules—Xerox too impatient, leading to unrealistic expectations

Factors to Enable Success

Technical leadership

- Technology transfer strategy well defined
- Management concurrence on technology strategy
- Minimum technology transfer in negotiations and feasibility study; boundaries preestablished

Organization/Management practices

- Goals established before negotiations start
- Modifications to Xerox's goals formally communicated to team as change occurred
- Experienced legal advice early on and periodic
- Negotiating team members and support team members identified, with roles and responsibility clearly defined
- Experienced consultants found and used

- Decision-makers on team in frequent review with corporate management

Design practices

- Xerox translators available for each subteam at all meetings
- Technical translation capability available
- Feasibility study documentation format defined at start
- Support group customers defined and requirements negotiated
- More formal presentation, information transfer style

Planning practices

- Game plan for negotiating, bottom line established
- Plan with realistic expectations for China
- Formally set agenda for each meeting, including desired objectives
- Provide office tools and private work space at remote site

Materials management

- Understand relevant vendor base in China

NOTES

1. See Sally Stewart and Charles F. Keown, "Talking with the Dragon: Negotiating with the People's Republic of China," *Columbia Journal of World Business*, Fall 1989, pp. 68–72, for an account of the experience of fifty Hong Kong Chinese traders negotiating with the People's Republic.

2. Adapted from Howard Myers, "The China Business Puzzle," *Business Horizons*, July-August 1987, p. 26.

3. P. B. Ebrey, ed., *Chinese Civilization and Society: A Source Book* (New York: The Free Press, 1981), p. 137.

4. Lucian W. Pye, "The China Trade: Making the Deal," *Harvard Business Review*, July-August 1986, pp. 74–80. See also his classic study, *Chinese Commercial Negotiating Styles* (Cambridge, Mass.: Oelgeschlager, Gunn & Hain, 1983).

5. John Frankenstein, "Trends in Chinese Business Practice: Changes in the Beijing Wind," *California Management Review* 29, no. 1 (1986): 155.

6. See Denis F. Simon and William A. Fischer, *Technology Transfer to China* (Cambridge, Mass.: Ballinger, 1989).

7. A reorganization of the ministry gave BII the responsibility to streamline the copier industry so as to "import the technology jointly and to form a united front to deal with foreign suppliers." BII announced that, after meetings with interested parties in the copier industry, it would decide on "one or two best suppliers" of technology, based on criteria relating to the level of technology to be supplied, whether the system offered was "complete," the speed of integration of local suppliers, potentials for export of the end-product or other relevant commodities, and competitiveness of prices and technology. For a summary of several aspects of dispute settlement in China concerning the role of courts and arbitration tribunals, see Pitman B. Potter, "Resolving Contract Disputes," *China Business Review*, September-October 1984, p. 21–23.

8. William F. Fischer, "Technology Transfer to the PRC: The Educational Component," *East Asian Executive Reports* 8, no. 1 (1986): 8, 15–17.

9. Another view of the complexities of negotiation is offered in the experience of Thurmond Textiles; see Adan M. Webber, "The Case of the China Diary," *Harvard Business Review*, November-December 1989, pp. 14–40.

11

Implementing the Agreement

A number of joint ventures have been established in China and have been working for several years, but the record of implementation is varied in terms of their success. This record shows the difficulties, for example adverse economic and political conditions, changes in government policies, nonfulfillment (in Western terms) of government commitments, renegotiation in Chinese terms, staffing with expatriates in top management, and the absence of an information-based society. Despite the obstacles, partners of several joint ventures and Chinese government officials remain satisfied even with halting progress because they recognize the continuing difficulties of the transition from a centrally planned economy to one that is more market-oriented. Given the major shifts in economic policies and changes in enterprise orientations, it would be surprising if there were not severe difficulties at times. From the current experiences, more appropriate roles for foreign direct investment and technology transfers into China can be discerned.

RECORD OF SUCCESS

The criteria of success of joint venture arrangements arise from the objectives of the agreements themselves and the intentions of both parties plus the purposes sought by the government, which may not be explicitly written into the agreements. The various criteria can be categorized (in no priority) as follows:

- Profitability
- Effective transfer of technology
- Building of a management team
- Streamlining and motivating the work force

- Developing national integration through local suppliers
- Exports of components or products by the joint venture
- Development of Chinese sources of supply exported to the foreign partner or other companies
- Domestic market development
- Foreign exchange earnings
- New-product development
- Mineral exploration, development, and export
- Duration and termination of the arrangement or project

Profitability

Determination of profitability of joint ventures in China is difficult for an outside analyst because the necessary information is not likely to be made available. The mere assertion by any one of the players that "the enterprise is profitable" can be interpreted variously, depending on whether the source is Chinese or the foreign partner, because the concepts of profitability are different. In addition, earning profits in renminbi is much different than earning profits in foreign exchange. Again, profitability may not have been expected by the joint venture for some years, but progress may be made as expected in the interim, giving rise to statements that the venture is "profitable."

Despite these acknowledged difficulties, the Chinese do claim that foreign investment in China is "profitable." According to Chinese statistics compiled from 2,318 Sino-foreign ventures for the period 1979–1984, total sales from these ventures reached 1.7 billion yuan (about $570 million), of which one-quarter were exports. Net profits of these ventures amounted to about $200 million (or 35 percent of sales, compared with 2 to 10 percent among companies in the United States), of which $76 million were received by foreign investors (but only $7.6 million, or less than 2 percent, was remitted abroad, which is probably a better estimate of profitability from the perspective of the foreign investor).

Average profits by venture were relatively small since average investment was small. The Chinese claim that 90 percent of all Sino-foreign ventures were profitable, but this is highly inflated by Western accounting standards. Averaging out the profits earned by foreign investors in the sample shows less than $33,000 per venture over the entire 1979–1984 period.[1] In some instances, it is unlikely that such small profits did much to offset the high up-front costs of negotiating initial contracts, and thus, in total, the contract was unprofitable. In other instances, small profits are a result of small investments. Indeed, Chu Qiyuan, a vice-president of China International Trade and Investment Corporation (CITIC), has stated that 15 percent of the approximately 7,000 joint ventures operating in China are financially or operationally troubled.[2]

In the late 1980s, reports of substantial venture profits were being made by the Chinese. For example, the China Tianjin Otis Company in 1986 returned profits of $9.7 million on foreign investment of only about $5 million. But in fact these 1986 profits had little to do with the $5 million invested by Otis. Sales until 1988 were of the old (Chinese) models, which sold more quickly because Otis was behind them and also because of the boom in multi-story construction (apartments and hotels) after 1984. New models, using Otis technology and capital funds, were not available for sale until 1987 for 1988 installation.

China Tianjin Otis Elevator

The Otis Elevator Company (U.S.A.) agreed to establish a manufacturing plant in Tianjin in July 1984 after lengthy negotiations. The Chinese partners are CITIC and Tianjin Elevator Company.[3] The equity split is 30 percent Otis U.S.A., 5 percent CITIC, and 65 percent Tianjin Elevator Company, with Otis capital contribution being $5 million. The venture has a contracted life of thirty years, with a technology transfer agreement lasting for ten years.

The major stumbling blocks in the negotiations were foreign exchange balancing and the extent to which technology transfer would occur. The Chinese initially wanted the transfer of a wide range of technology beyond that which the Chinese market could handle, but they eventually settled for less. The foreign exchange question was resolved by a compromise, with Otis agreeing to make "best efforts" to export, without guarantee to purchase a fixed percentage of output. Domestic sales for foreign exchange ultimately, were significant in providing the venture with hard currency.

Since the beginning of operations in 1984, the main difficulties stemmed from frustrations of Otis expatriate managers in Tianjin (developing a management team as well as dealing with employee motivation and compensation, the need to increase local component supply at inflating prices, plus the currency issue). Although both sides seem happy with the venture—Otis U.S.A. is pleased with profits and the access to the Chinese domestic market, and the Chinese acquired desired technology—the longer-term happiness depends on future economic and political conditions

Technology Transfer

Given the importance attached by the Chinese government to the transfer of advanced technology into China, a significant criterion of success would be an "effective" transfer. This requires evidence of the abilities of the licensor to transfer technology and of the licensee to absorb and use it effectively. It is perfectly conceivable that a joint venture can be profitable without any new technology absorbed by China (as the Otis joint venture for elevators was in the first years). The Shanghai–EK Chor Motorcycle Company, Ltd., provides an example of effective technology transfer.

Shanghai–EK Chor Motorcycle Company, Ltd.

The Shanghai–EK Chor Motorcycle Company, Ltd., is a joint venture between the Shanghai Tractor and Automobile Corporation and EK Chor Investment Company, Ltd., of Hong Kong.[4] The main output of the plant is motorcycles, both the upgrade of an existing line as well as a new design for the domestic market. Honda of Japan supplied the technology, but it has no financial stake in the joint venture. It will benefit from the sales of parts and assemblies to the joint venture for some time. Honda will profit without the difficulties and risks of joint venture management.

Begun in 1985, the plant has had great success in the production of motorcycles; profits at the end of the first year of production reached 8.7 million yuan.

Two of several reasons are given for this success. First, the members of the foreign management team are all overseas Chinese. They are able to communicate effectively with domestic managers, and are "understanding" of the Chinese enterprise system with its lingering "iron rice bowl" mentality and "danwei" system.

Second, the technology transfer arrangement reached with Honda alleviated some of the pressures for foreign exchange by leaving decisions as to the substitution of foreign parts for locally sourced products with the Chinese, thus encouraging the rapid shift to the use of local parts and away from dependence on expensive imports. This decision was easier to implement because the Chinese partner already had a good domestic reputation for its motorcycles. The technology agreement was to continue and improve this line. The new line of motorcycles was to serve the domestic market but under the Honda name, offering a competitive advantage.

Success for this venture, according to its manager, stems from its ability to utilize foreign technology in a manner consistent with existing production conditions and management abilities. Early results for the venture back up this view.

Other cases of technology transfer have been less successful. Nike, Inc., for example, has found that poor quality standards have diminished the contribution of advanced technology it has transferred to China, limiting its presence in China and keeping anticipated export sales far below original expectations.

Nike, Inc.

The production of athletic shoes remains a labor-intensive operation. Thus the opening of China's economy at a time when labor in other Asian countries (notably Taiwan and South Korea) was becoming more expensive was seen by Nike, Inc., as opportune. In 1980, Nike proposed a manufacturing contract to the China Light Industrial Products Import and Export Corporation (CLIPIEC).[5] Nike would supply machinery and technology to the Shanghai and Tianjin branches of the CLIPIEC. In return, Nike would receive part of the output as payment plus purchase the remaining output for sale overseas. Prices are negotiated each year but must be lower than those of other suppliers.

The initial amounts involved were quite small, consisting of the shipment of only $75,000 worth of equipment plus production technology to maintain quality control and schedules. Originally, 90 percent of sales were in the United States, although now Nike shoes are available in Chinese department stores at about $22 (one-third of a worker's average monthly wages); sales in China are brisk. Initially, some materials were imported, but the intention is to have them 100 percent locally sourced, thus eliminating the need for exports except for profit repatriation.

Key negotiating points revolved around price, quality control, and the ease of shipping finished goods overseas. It was agreed that China would sell the shoes to Nike at a price comparable to that paid to other Asian countries under similar agreements. Full price is paid for first-quality shoes; "B" grade shoes are brought at 60 percent of the full price, and "C" grade shoes are burned. The Chinese suppliers sought to put seconds of parts, such as soles, on their own brand shoes so as to waste nothing, despite contract terms; Nike had to insist on their destruction; it did so because the soles were identifiable as Nike's.

Quality control has been a difficult problem. In some cases, original suppliers have been dropped, to be replaced by others. In 1984, for example, Nike canceled contracts with four Chinese factories largely because of an inability to meet quality standards. (Cheap labor alone is not enough to assure profitability of labor-intensive products, such as athletic shoes. It requires a combination of automation, raw material supply at low cost, and skillful, cheap labor so as to achieve high quality and low cost through mass production. The success story of Reebok in Korea is a prime example.)

Nike opted not to have third-party quality control supervision (excluding the China National Import and Export Commodities Inspection Corporation), checking quality control themselves and providing on-the-spot assistance. This overseeing role has not extended to any degree of management. Nike accepted the possibility that production efficiency, labor levels and costs, overhead expenses, and so on might not be what they should, but these were concerns for the factory management, since it would reflect in the production cost of the shoes but not in the price to Nike. Through 1986, the cost of producing Nike shoes in China was higher than in any of Nike's other production sites.

Finally, there was the question of shipping the finished goods. The choice of four factories in Tianjin and Shanghai by CLIPIEC was deliberate so as to avoid the infrastructure difficulties involved in shipping from the interior. (An interior source was examined but rejected.) Moreover, the infrastructure problems of Tianjin and Shanghai were to be eased for transporting the Nike shoes through the help of the local municipal authorities in obtaining—though not guaranteeing—good access to local facilities.

Nike's manufacturing contracts are expected to become joint ventures because it can then use foreign exchange earnings to import needed components to improve quality, which will increase sales abroad and raise output and, thus, income.

The policy of having a small initial involvement has given Nike the luxury of getting further involved only after a positive initial experience. For Nike, positive experiences in China come slowly, and it produces in China less than 5 percent of worldwide sales— far below the 25 percent target originally set. Nevertheless, it gradually is expanding output in three Chinese factories, and it seems determined to continue its operations there.

Despite these disappointing results, Nike's step-by-step approach to the Chinese business environment is perhaps a strategy that many more firms are likely to adopt as initial enthusiasm for investment in China cools.

Ironically, Reebok, Nike's chief rival, took a wait-and-see approach to China, beginning production in a Fuzhou plant that had previously been working for Nike. Plant managers already understood the need for higher quality standards, and Reebok's production of athletic shoes in China has grown to match that of Nike in only one-third the time.[6]

Building a Management Team

At an early stage of the joint venture, a significant criterion of success is the building of a well-functioning management team. It has already been noted, for example, that there are serious difficulties in staffing joint ventures with expatriates. Numerous issues, such as the level and role of expatriate employees, expatriate salaries and living conditions, and the status of equivalent Chinese managers, need to be carefully resolved.

Furthermore, problems arise when Chinese managers are functioning in a commercial environment alongside expatriate managers. This became a major concern for McDonnell Douglas, for example, after agreeing to assist China in the development of domestic passenger aircraft production. The development of an effective management team requires much effort and patience; McDonnell Douglas has had sufficient success developing such a team that the initial agreement with China has stimulated a desire to expand its business there.

McDonnell Douglas

The technology transfer agreement signed between McDonnell Douglas, the Shanghai Aviation Industrial Corporation, and the China Aviation Supply Corporation in March 1985 provided for the production of the MD–82 aircraft in Shanghai.[7] In addition, McDonnell Douglas would establish a maintenance and training center as well as provide managerial and technical assistance. This agreement marked the culmination of ten years of negotiations, stalled by bureaucratic delays. It also represented a significant extension of McDonnell Douglas' previously limited involvement in China.

The managerial problems of undertaking such a venture were, admittedly, underestimated. The Chinese managers of the Shanghai plant had no previous commercial production experience. Defining the role that McDonnell Douglas managers would play in the project became difficult. Under the agreement, McDonnell Douglas managers could only advise their Chinese counterparts, having no authority to make final management decisions. These problems led to decision bottlenecks because of an ambitious delivery schedule with its Chinese customer, in terms of both time and quality.

The challenge of these management problems was met in various ways. For example, a Joint Executive Management Board, with all three partners represented, was created. This board helps in dispute resolution, assessment of the progress of the venture, and building the teamwork necessary to its success. McDonnell Douglas also has instituted various innovative training programs among top- and middle-tier Chinese managers. Again, breaking down language barriers between the respective management teams has received much attention: The Shanghai plant employs 300 translators (for technical documents, quality control procedures, and so forth) as well as 80 interpreters.

Work Force

One of the more difficult aspects of creating successful joint ventures is that of obtaining, training, and streamlining the work force. The existence of overemployment in Chinese enterprises presents an obstacle in the removal of workers who are redundant or incompetent. Motivation of the work force also is problematic. The Babcock and Wilcox Beijing Company, Ltd., has confronted these and other issues in its joint venture operations. The increasing freedom in hiring and removing workers will assist in achieving higher levels of productivity, but significant constraints remain, making profitability harder to attain.

Babcock and Wilcox Beijing Company, Ltd.

Faced with severe electricity-generation difficulties, including an inability to produce sufficient large-scale utility boilers domestically, the Chinese government invited Babcock and Wilcox to establish a joint venture in China. Negotiations began in 1983, and in 1985, a $12 million agreement was reached for the formation of an equity joint venture between Babcock and Wilcox and Beijing Boiler Works.[8] The agreement provided for the production of both Chinese-designed industrial boilers and Babcock and Wilcox–designed utility boilers.

Initial indications are that the venture has been a success. Revenues are well ahead of target expectations; Chinese engineers are taking on a larger role than had been previously thought, reducing the engineering work that has to be done in America; and productivity levels in the factory are up 30 per cent since the factory began operations in 1986.

A large portion of the credit for this performance has been given to the expatriate management team that works for the venture. This team occupies key positions in the new venture, running the plant as well as transferring technical and management skills to Chinese counterparts. Their success in this regard is attributed to their cohesiveness as a group (stemming from prior work experience together) and their adaption to the Chinese business environment, with its slow-moving bureaucracy and inadequate infrastructure.

Another important element was the venture's ability to motivate the work force through the widespread implementation of an incentive pay system. Workers now have monetary incentives to meet preset quotas and to operate as a team. Attracting skilled labor also has been a major problem. The venture needs to build housing to attract skilled engineers from outside Beijing—engineers who are in high demand at this stage of China's development. Without these skilled workers, the plant will continue to operate below full capacity.

Although the venture management is happy with the progress made by the work force, other difficulties remain unresolved. Foreign exchange problems loom large. The company should be exporting 20 per cent of its output by the early 1990s. Competition is likely to be fierce and foreign exchange demands (for necessary imports and expatriate employees, for example) remain substantial.

The venture also faces problems obtaining raw materials. Although the high priority attached to the product of the venture accords it some privileges in state allocation of materials, shortages are not uncommon, requiring expensive purchases on the open market. Additionally, the venture has had difficulties accessing transportation facilities, both in guaranteeing delivery dates and in handling the larger-sized components.

Babcock and Wilcox believes that these problems can be overcome and is considering a larger commitment in China.

National Integration

The difficulties of extending technology assistance to a number of enterprises throughout China to increase national integration of local suppliers with joint ventures undoubtedly will produce varied results. However, the need to create a local supply network is vital, given the Chinese restrictions on foreign exchange availability. Those companies that agreed to sell parts for assembly in Chinese factories, as a way into the China market, found themselves in difficulties when foreign exchange became scarce. Like Foxboro Company, they were catalyzed to develop local supply networks for components.

Foxboro Company, which produces electronic control systems in Shanghai, has had success in establishing such networks, but still not enough to eliminate the need for assistance from the Chinese government through infusions of foreign exchange to continue production.[9]

For some companies, such as Shanghai Volkswagen, local supply networks are unable to provide the materials it needs to increase the domestic content of its cars and engines. By the mid-1990s, Shanghai Volkswagen hopes to raise the domestic content from 23.4 percent to 83.3 percent. However, the plants from which it aims to source materials are not only undercapitalized, but also spread over a vast area within China. This hinders materials supply and the extent of on-site quality control by the buyer, and adds to management problems in the Shanghai factory.

For companies such as Shanghai Volkswagen and Fujian-Hitachi TV Company, Ltd., the lower costs achieved through increased national integration are necessary for success in international markets.

Fujian-Hitachi TV Company, Ltd.

Fujian-Hitachi TV Company, Ltd., is a cooperative joint venture established between Hitachi (Japan), Fujian Electronics Import and Export Corporation, and Toei Company, Ltd., in 1982.[10] Located in Fuzhou, the provincial capital of Fujian, the venture is contracted to last for fifteen years.

The venture was set up to produce 200,000 television annually, of which 90 percent would be color. Initially, production would be geared to the domestic market. After three years and as local content increased, attention would be shifted toward the international market. Chinese expectations of exports from this venture were high.

Initial venture results, however, were disappointing. During the first three years, Fujian-Hitachi was compelled to import much of its inputs from Japan, creating serious foreign exchange shortfalls. Furthermore, at the time that output should have been aimed at exports, the company found itself in a disadvantageous competitive position: The factory price of its color sets was more than $100 higher than that of its competitors. Annual export subsidies of $10 million to $13 million would be incurred by Fujian-Hitachi to be competitive in the overseas market.

Local content of the set in 1986 was only 30 percent. It was hoped to raise this to 40 percent through the use of domestic television tubes which would not only reduce demands on foreign exchange, but also cut production costs by $27 (the cost of an imported tube being $67 in comparison to $40 for one that was domestically produced). With high demand for domestically produced tubes from more than 1,500 Chinese television-producing ventures, availability remains uncertain.

Exports remain less than 10 percent of total output, and contribute little foreign exchange to the venture. Most significantly, Fujian-Hitachi has been one of the few ventures to have the privilege of selling domestically for foreign exchange. Furthermore, in July 1986, Fujian-Hitachi received exemption from the industrial and commercial consolidated tax and gained a reduction in the rate of its profits tax. Only through such advantages has the company been able to address its foreign exchange difficulties.

The privilege to sell domestically for foreign exchange has become almost the only way that a high-tech joint venture can meet the foreign exchange requirements. It is virtually impossible for any single joint venture to successfully develop the required domestic vendors. To do so, joint ventures will have to work together and with government support in the development of such suppliers.

Exports

The desire of the Chinese government to increase exports has raised the priority for production agreements that can use China as a base for foreign sourcing of components or final products in their worldwide line. This has meant a high priority for extractive ventures that would automatically find foreign markets for at least some of their production. The ability to export depends on price and quality (as illustrated by the Nike ventures) as well as the ability to deliver on schedule. The success of ventures in raising exports is quite varied.

Beatrice Asia, for example, established a $10 million joint venture in Guangzhou to produce soft drinks, ice cream, and snack foods.[11] The plant was to earn foreign exchange from sales of soft drinks to the nearby Hong Kong market. However, export sales have been disappointing; Chinese-produced soft drinks with unfamiliar brand names have been virtually unable to break into the sophisticated Hong Kong market, dominated by the traditional soft drink giants Coke and Pepsi.

Additionally, production costs are high, making it difficult to be competitive in a very competitive market. The result is that the plant earns profits only in Chinese currency, making impossible the remittance of dividends abroad.

The ability of a joint venture to export profitably is directly related to the degree and type of manufacturing plus the level of technology required for the product to be competitive in the international market. In the labor-intensive apparel industry, Chinese exports are easily profitable, but the Chinese in the apparel industry are not seeking partners for just this reason. Raw materials, coal, and oil also are profitable, and the Chinese are seeking a limited number of partners for technology transfers in these areas. In product manufacturing, in which parts fabrication in China is necessary for profitable exports, the success is slow; as of 1986, there were no profitable joint ventures of this type, and that is probably the case through 1989. They will be profitable eventually, but it will take five to ten years.

Domestic Markets

Virtually all of the foreign investment ventures in China have been attracted to the large domestic market, except for those seeking a branch plant for component manufacture (as in most contractual joint ventures). Despite the large unsatisfied demand for a variety of products and services, the domestic market in China is relatively undeveloped. That is, the brand images and distribution networks are undeveloped, and service facilities for repair and maintenance are scarce. Both networks have to be established and related to the potential markets. There also is a desire on the part of several levels of government to make certain that products are available to the interior regions as well as to the more attractive coastal markets.

Foreign investors who have had success in gaining access to the domestic market, such as the Shenda Telephone Company, have largely been those addressing specific needs identified by the Chinese government.

Shenda Telephone Company

The Chinese have acknowledged that their telecommunications technology is some twenty years behind that of most Western nations. To modernize this sector, China allocated 5.42 billion yuan (c. $1.8 billion) to the modernization of telecommunications systems in the seventh five-year plan (1986–1990)[12] Because its domestic production capability remains backward, much of this modernization would necessarily come through imports. Particular emphasis was placed on the upgrading of inner-city telephone systems (especially in Beijing, Shanghai, Tianjin, and Guangzhou), domestic inner-regional telecommunications (including the realization of fully automatic or semiautomatic communication between provincial capitals, core economic centers, and the eastern coastal region), and international telecommunications services (including the repair of the Sino-Japanese submarine cable).

Cable and Wireless (C&W) is a registered British company with extensive operations in Hong Kong. Its operations in China include a joint venture with the Guangdong Post and Telecommunications Administrative Bureau (GPTAB) and the Shenzhen Telecommunications Development Company to develop public telephone services in the Shenzhen Special Economic Zone. The Shenda Telephone Company has an equity split of 49 percent C&W to 51 percent GPTAB. Capitalization of the venture was $4.35 million. The company employs 400 Chinese workers.

After two years of contract negotiations, C&W entered into a twenty-year agreement with GPTAB for a venture that was to increase the number of telephone lines in Shenzhen from 2,000 to 200,000. An investment program of $180 million from the profits of the venture over the twenty-year contract period was envisaged.

To this point, both sides consider the venture to be successful. Problems such as some foreign exchange shortages, the slow decision-making process, and the high cost of expatriate managers appear to have been resolved. In the expansion of Shenzhen from a small border town to a major economic center, the prospects for the Shenda venture look bright.

Western companies that produce consumer products have certainly come to China in search of its "billion consumers." Yet, in almost all cases, domestic sales are allowed only after exports have been made. The Happiness Soft Drink Company, for example, located in Shenzhen, is a Sino-U.S. joint venture with PepsiCo established in 1982. Seventy percent of Happiness' sales are to other Asian countries and the plant is praised for its export earnings. Although PepsiCo is keen to expand domestic sales, company officials concede that their product is "not the first thing a country like China may need."[13]

This attitude is a realistic one. Although a diversity of consumer goods are now produced in China, most Western companies have realized that the purchasing power of most Chinese consumers is not great. True, some private entrepreneurs are earning relatively large sums, but most consumers are more concerned with higher rents and rising basic food prices and transport costs than with what can still be termed "luxury goods."

Simply put, the domestic market is a renminbi market. One can sell and establish a distribution and repair network, but the billion plus consumers have only renminbi, since it is illegal for them, as individuals, to possess foreign exchange certificates. Without a government-supported plan, the joint venture cannot convert renminbi into foreign exchange certificates to pay for imported parts and to repatriate profits. The government will not provide a renminbi–foreign exchange certificate conversion plan (or supply import licenses) for joint ventures that do not supply some critical technology or reduce the need to import—called "import substitution." There is a one-billion-person market, but reaching it requires more than a competitive product or service.

Foreign Exchange

Foreign exchange problems have plagued many Sino-foreign joint ventures. These problems arise out of the inconvertibility of renminbi, the overvalued nature of renminbi, and strict state controls over foreign exchange availability to the joint ventures. State controls over foreign exchange availability are found in the allocation of foreign exchange to the joint venture in initial negotiations, which has already been touched on in the discussion of Xerox's venture with Shanghai Movie and Photo Industry Company.

For the operating venture, state control over foreign exchange is encapsulated in the foreign exchange "balancing requirement," which essentially calls for balanced foreign exchange receipts and expenditures within joint ventures. This requirement was adopted by the 1983 Joint Venture Law (Article 75) and expanded on (after the 1985 foreign exchange crisis) in the 1986 *Provisions on Balancing Foreign Exchange Accounts of Sino-Foreign Joint Ventures.*

This balancing requirement impacts on any joint venture operation that uses some foreign parts but is unlikely to generate sufficient exports in the early years of operation to earn the required foreign exchange. It is clearly a major concern for those ventures that need to use large quantities of imported materials. Although China continues to emphasize the importance of generating exports to foreign exchange poor ventures, it has become more realistic as to the ability of new ventures to readily enter international markets. Thus it is offering those joint ventures with government certification numerous options for raising foreign exchange as an alternative to exports. Six are outlined here.

The first option is import substitution, that is, selling goods to domestic organizations for foreign exchange instead of renminbi if it is a good that normally would be imported. For the Guangdong Float Glass Company, Ltd., the question of whether it will be allowed to sell domestically for hard currency will be the major determinant of success and failure.

The Guangdong Float Glass Company, Ltd.

This equity joint venture, established to produce high-quality float glass, is one of the most sophisticated ventures in China. The partners in the venture are Pennvasia, Ltd. (which is itself a venture between PP&G Industries [70 percent equity], one of the two major float glass producers in the world, and a private Thai investor [30 percent]) and China Southern Glass (itself formed from four Chinese groups: China Merchants Development Group, Guangdong International Trust and Investment Corporation, China North Industries, and the Shenzhen Construction Material Corporation). The venture has a capitalization of around $100 million, equally split between the two partners. In addition to capital investment, Pennvasia is responsible for licensing technology, management of the project for the first two and one-half years, and selling abroad 50 percent of the eventual annual production, estimated to be 180,000 tons. Expected buyers include Hong Kong, Australia, and New Zealand. Domestic sales are most likely to be concentrated in Guangdong Province to an array of building contractors, mirror manufacturers, glass distributors, and glass cutters.

The need to classify these domestic sales as import substitution sales arises out of the large and varied claims on the venture's foreign exchange resources. First, much of the plant's equipment had to be imported. Second, the plant is located in the Shekou industrial district of Shenzhen, where most good and services have to be paid in foreign exchange. For example, part of the labor costs, land-use fees (HK $3.5 million), and electricity charges are paid in foreign exchange.

The venture has applied to the Guangdong provincial authorities to have their product added to the import substitution list. China has long relied on imports for its supply of high-quality glass, and the venture's management was optimistic about its application, although they admitted that the process would be a long one. The question of foreign exchange balancing has become a make-or-break issue in success of the venture.

The import substitution option has more problems than just the fact that it is difficult to obtain the appropriate certification. For example, if a Chinese enterprise is going to have to use foreign exchange to purchase a domestically produced product, that product will have to be both significantly cheaper than foreign imports and have a comparable quality to imports. Otherwise, there is no incentive for the Chinese enterprise to buy domestically. Furthermore, the prevailing "foreign is better" mentality (especially if the Chinese partner in the venture did not have a prior reputation for product quality) and a lack of coordination of China's foreign exchange spending make it more difficult to push foreign exchange toward assisting such import substitutes.

The second option for the venture without foreign exchange is to sell its product locally for foreign exchange, even though it is not designated as an import substitute. This option is limited to situations in which the joint venture product is of extremely high quality, the renminbi price charged for the product is greater than the foreign exchange price (to cover the cost of converting to foreign exchange certificates), and the vendor has access to foreign exchange conversion (and the cost and quality advantages of buying a domestic product with foreign exchange outweigh advantages offered by similar imports).

The third option is for the foreign exchange–poor joint venture to buy domestically produced goods with renminbi profits and export them for foreign exchange. This is a limited option. The authorized list of products that the joint venture might be able to purchase and, subsequently, export is narrow; it consists mostly of products that would provide incremental exports. It is extremely unlikely that the joint venture could find a product that it could simply "plug into" its own sales and distribution channels. Selling a product outside its market expertise is risky and expensive, requiring the joint venture to establish an export market for the product. It also is likely that this option would encounter substantial bureaucratic hurdles above and beyond those usually faced. Most important, unless directed otherwise, the Chinese enterprise would not sell a product for renminbi if it has export potential; it would earn the foreign exchange for itself.

A fourth option is renminbi conversion into foreign exchange through the Bank of China. Again, this is an extremely limited option, requiring a joint venture to have much "guanxi" with senior political figures, to be a venture using "vital technology," to be a venture with large capital sums already invested, and to be a "high-visibility" venture that the Chinese cannot afford to see struggle. One such case of a struggling high-visibility project was the Beijing Jeep company.

The Beijing Jeep Company

Few Sino-foreign joint ventures have received as much publicity as the American Motor Company (AMC) equity joint venture with the Beijing Automotive Works. Agreed to in 1983, with a contract term of twenty years, the Beijing Jeep plant represented a $16 million (31.4 percent) investment for AMC (half of which was cash) and a $35 million (68.6 percent) investment for its Chinese partner.[14] The plant was to design a new model of the AMC Jeep and, utilizing local parts, export the final product to neighboring countries.

The venture ran into immediate difficulties. First, it quickly became apparent that the plant had severe foreign exchange problems, with AMC assuming (wrongly) that the Chinese would be making foreign exchange available to buy the machinery necessary to produce new engines, axles, and body parts. At one point in 1986, the plant had to close down for two months because it had exhausted its foreign exchange reserves and was unable to import parts.

To overcome this problem, the venture had to persuade the Chinese government to inject foreign exchange into the plant (in addition to arranging currency swaps with other foreign companies, or a joint venture such as the Great Wall Hotel in Beijing, see below), · as well as replace the initial agreement to design a completely new Jeep in China with the assembly of imported Jeep Cherokee kits. Officials became reluctant to make foreign exchange available to the plant because of foreign exchange shortages and a surplus of imported motor vehicles in 1985. (Vehicle imports rose from 25,000 in 1983 to 350,000 in 1985 with the relaxation of exchange controls; they were then limited to 90,000 units in 1987. [Journal of Commerce, December 13, 1988.]) The problem was overcome only after the Beijing Jeep factory became a symbol for foreign investor difficulties in China and Zhu Ronji, vice-chairman of the State Economic Council (later mayor of Shanghai), was given the task of fixing the problem. The plant was designated an "advanced technology" venture, so that it could receive some tax and foreign exchange breaks to keep it alive.

A second problem was that the Beijing Automotive Works had spent twenty years producing a version of a Russian Jeep and knew little of modern automotive techniques. The assembly line was primitive and productivity low: In 1986, the plant produced only 110 vehicles a day, of which only 15 were Jeep Cherokees. Although production of the Cherokee rose to 4,000 by 1988, raising production beyond this level is hampered by lack of basic materials—steel, glass, and rubber.

A third problem was the cost and choice of the Jeep Cherokee, which retailed in China at $22,000. The buyers in China who had foreign exchange certificates were foreigners setting up businesses plus some Chinese enterprises, but they wanted passenger sedans for business, not Jeeps. However, with its designation as an "advanced technology" plant, some of these associated costs were reduced. Worker's welfare payments to the state, for example, were reduced by 3.36 million yuan ($890,000) annually. In addition, the joint venture was permitted to set a domestic price that was a combination of renminbi and foreign exchange certificates.

After initial difficulties and subsequent injections of foreign exchange by the state, the Beijing Jeep plant reported small profits in 1988. Export sales are beginning to grow, but high costs and poor quality remain important barriers to future development. The introduction of the austerity program in 1989 saw Beijing Jeep's domestic sales—like those of other joint auto ventures—slump, requiring more government loans.

A fifth option is currency-swapping. Those ventures that have a foreign exchange surplus—for example, hotels—become sources of foreign exchange for other Sino-foreign ventures with renminbi reserves but little in the way of foreign exchange. Thus, for example, the Great Wall Sheraton became a source of foreign exchange for the Beijing Jeep Company. The decline of tourism after June 1989 sharply reduced the excess foreign exchange from hotels.

The Great Wall Sheraton

Sheraton signed a ten-year contract with the Sino-foreign equity venture partners (E-S Pacific Development and Construction Company Ltd., and China International Travel Service Beijing) to manage the $72 million Great Wall Sheraton Beijing.[15] Sheraton receives a fee based on the percentage of revenue generated, encouraging the management to keep occupancy rates high. The result, after several renegotiations and introduction of cost-sensitive managers, according to Sheraton, "is a big money-maker." The profits of hotels such as the Great Wall Sheraton are predominantly in foreign exchange because hotel bills and services are paid for in foreign exchange whereas expenses are in renminbi.

In 1986, the financially troubled Beijing Jeep Company Corporation was able to exchange renminbi for $2.5 million in foreign exchange from the Great Wall Sheraton. The premium for doing so can be as high as 28 percent, and this can only be regarded as a stopgap measure for a venture while it develops other means of foreign exchange balancing.

A final option is to reinvest the renminbi profits of one venture to establish other ventures that are more export-oriented, and thus balance the foreign exchange requirements among multiple ventures. PepsiCo International, for example, which has a number of contractual joint ventures in Guangzhou, Shenzhen, and Fuzhou engaged in the manufacture of plastic bottles and the bottling of PepsiCo drinks, has recently invested in the Chinese marble export industry, hoping to earn $2 million in foreign exchange from this investment. PepsiCo takes a portion of its Chinese earnings out in mushrooms, which it uses in its Pizza Hut operations outside of China.

Although such options may be attractive, they involve the joint venture in investments in fields outside of its own expertise. Furthermore, investing in other ventures may require the foreign partner of the joint venture to become more involved in the China market than it is really comfortable with. This is especially true for the foreign investor that is simply "testing the water."

Thus, although these options for foreign exchange balancing are certainly a welcome sign of flexibility from the Chinese government to the foreign exchange problem, they are extremely limited. As Gu Ming, head of the Economic Legislation Research Center under the State Council has noted, despite these flexible policies, "the regulations still urge all . . . joint ventures to promote exports [in striving for] a favorable balance in foreign exchange earnings."[16]

New Products

The development of new products both for the domestic market and for specialized export markets also is frequently part of joint venture agreements, and substantial support may be given this activity by the foreign partner in the form of research and development management, capital, and technical assistance. The government has a singular interest in such developments because they provide an outlet for scientific and technical abilities of Chinese personnel and increase the ability to absorb foreign technology.

The success of joint ventures in developing new products is yet to be demonstrated. As illustrated earlier, the AMC Beijing Jeep venture lacked the foreign exchange to purchase the machinery necessary to develop a new line of Jeep as initially agreed, and eventually imported complete kits for assembly in China. New products, however, are essential for the long-term success of joint ventures using imported parts sets. By the time imported parts have been converted to domestic sourcing (a reasonable but still difficult goal would be 70 percent conversion in five years), the product is seven to eight years old, technically, since it was probably one to two years old when the joint venture was formed. This means that with today's rapidly advancing technology, the product is outdated (though still functional) compared with the international marketplace.

Mineral Exploration

The Chinese government has set a high priority on the production of energy resources, petroleum and coal particularly. The discovery of coal resources is relatively easy, but their economical development is not always easy, as illustrated by the Antaibao coal mine. World pricing provides a competitive pressure, but high-cost local resources can reduce competitiveness of Chinese industry relying on these energy sources. The exploration of petroleum is more uncertain, and the joint ventures seeking petroleum resources have not been highly successful, as discussed in Chapter 4.

Island Creek of China Coal, Ltd. (Antaibao)

Island Creek of China Coal, Ltd., represents the largest single U.S. investment in China to date.[17] Occidental, with a 25 percent investment share ($175 million), along with its Chinese partners, Bank of China Trust and Consultancy Corporation (25 percent) and the China National Coal Development Corporation (50 percent), has a thirty-year contract to develop an open-pit coal mine near Pingshuo in coal-rich Shanxi Province, to the west of Beijing.

The mine, opened in late 1987, will tap an estimated 1.4 billion tons of coal reserves, with annual output projected at 15.3 million tons. Production in 1989 was expected to be eight to ten million tons, of which five to six million was destined for export. It represents an important project for China. Not only does the project involve a large-scale investment, but it also includes the kinds of advanced technological skills China is seeking, in an area—resource development—that provides much of its foreign exchange earnings. But it is the large scale of investment that has made the mine a high-visibility venture, with its performance closely watched by both other Western investors and the Chinese leadership.

Several years were spent in difficult negotiations before the ground-breaking on this project in July 1985. One major obstacle to the venture came in 1984, when Occidental's American partner in the Pingshuo project, Peter Kiewit and Sons, Inc., of Omaha, withdrew from its agreement to fund 25 percent of the project. The Bank of China filled the gap.

A further dispute revolved around the wages to be paid to the 1,700 Chinese miners employed in the mine. Chinese negotiators initially demanded U.S. wage rates—at $14 + per hour. Given that the Chinese miners themselves would have been paid only .30 cents an hour, with the remainder going to the local labor bureau, this stood to be an additional "profit" to the Chinese of $45 million per year. Occidental balked at this figure; further negotiation was required to reach agreement to pay wages according to tons produced.

Occidental made other moves to ensure itself against potential losses on the project. For example, its share of output will be delivered before the coal is assigned to the Chinese partners. The Chinese also have agreed to purchase for domestic consumption any portion owing to Occidental that remains unsold. Furthermore, Occidental's financing of the project—through such banks as the Bank of America, Royal Bank of Canada, Industrial Bank of Japan, and Credit Lyonnais of France—has been done through "project financing" rather than through straight commercial loans, ensuring that repayments come from project revenues rather than directly from Occidental.

Adequate transport facilities were a key concern in the Antaibao project. As coal output has begun to increase in China, the real issue has become how to move it to the points of demand. The building of coal-powered power stations near the mines only partly relieves the need to transport coal to power stations on the coast—in addition to making further demands on investment capital for the establishment of power grids.

For the Antaibao project to succeed requires the movement of coal to Qinhuangdao, China's largest coal port, for shipping to other provinces and for export to Japan. While work to upgrade the railway line between Datong (120 kilometers from Antaibao) and Qinhuangdao is completed, the key remains the ability of the Ministry of Coal to persuade the Ministry of Railways to accord priority status to coal shipments from Antaibao. Bureaucratic wrangling between the two ministries—and the final agreement to the project itself—was said to have been resolved by no less a figure than Deng Xiaoping. It is a matter of conjecture as to whether the project would have finally gone ahead without such influence from the top Chinese leadership, and illustrates the kinds of difficulties that other, less well connected and "visible" ventures must face. Plans to open a second mine at Antaibao were stalled in 1989, perhaps indefinitely. Although the deteriorating business climate in the aftermath of the student demonstrations contributed to this decision, the key problem was financing.

Terminations

Initial joint venture contracts were set for a duration of ten years, and the first ten-year period ended in 1989. Few joint ventures were started in 1979, which was the first year of the new joint venture law. It is, therefore, too soon to have terminations through the normal period of the agreements, but some joint ventures have been terminated before their initial period was completed. Even so, the experiences in pursuing the several objectives of joint ventures provide the following "success factors" for consideration by those seeking business in China:

- Realistic expectations of joint venture performance in the Chinese business environment. These are gained through advance preparation and knowledge of the environment, plus a feasibility analysis detailing all infrastructure needs, materials needs and supplies, and labor requirements and how they are going to be satisfied. That is, as far as possible, potential problems should be addressed during negotiations rather than after establishing the venture.

- An accurate assessment of the joint venture's foreign exchange situation, likely foreign exchange needs, and potential sources of foreign exchange

- An accurate assessment of the ability of the local joint venture partner (and its component suppliers) to adapt the foreign technology and expertise that the foreign partner is supplying. Proper partner selection is a key, including capability and compatibility of objectives and styles of operation.

- An ability to work with the joint venture partner, that is, an understanding of enterprise laws, the social responsibilities of a Chinese enterprise, Chinese work habits, close communication, and willingness to be flexible

- A long-term approach to doing business in China. Short-term gains are likely to be minimal, and the Chinese are anticipating a long road to modernization.

- A management team (and families) that understands and can withstand the demands made on expatriates through difficult living and working conditions

- A motivated work force, developed through training, added incentives, and close communication

- Good relations—"guanxi"—built with officials at all levels (state, provincial, and local). Bureaucratic access at all levels can determine the success or failure of a project.

- A project tailored to Chinese needs. It is easier to succeed in a venture that is a high priority than in one that is not.

- Firm limits set on the extent and depth of commitment to the Chinese market. Changes should be made in that commitment only when conditions clearly support or require them. Ventures have turned sour when commitments were made that could not readily be fulfilled or became onerous.

- An accurate and realistic estimate of and commitment for the support needed from local Chinese factories and suppliers for necessary parts and raw materials, plus local government support for the required import licenses and foreign exchange conversions programmed in the feasibility study

SHIFTING ECONOMIC AND COMMERCIAL CONDITIONS

Every joint venture agreement and its accompanying feasibility study (ten-year projections) has to make certain assumptions about macroeconomic events—the rate of inflation and changes in exchange rates—and about the rationalization (competitive structure) of the industry sector in which the joint venture is to operate. Each of these conditions shifted significantly during the 1980s, which is the first decade for the operation of foreign joint ventures.

In several cases, the changes have seriously altered the success of the joint venture. Adjustments have had to be made, and these have been not only costly, but also frustrating—at times threatening to bring the venture to an end. At the end of the 1980s, however, none of the joint ventures had become bankrupt, so that the shifting economic and commercial conditions were met without failures. Illustrations of the significance of these changes are found in several cases.

Inflation

Inflation—the scourge of the Koumintang regime and feared in China as much as in Germany—occurred throughout China as price controls were removed; the rate reached 30 percent unofficially in 1988 (with official reports of 10 percent during the last years of the 1980s) and was reportedly higher in 1989. A two-price system has been unsuccessful, as sharp traders see the opportunity to buy at official prices for sale in the open markets. Food prices in Shanghai and Beijing rose 80 percent in one year (1988), and liberalization of prices had to be stopped in late 1988. Political and social discontent caused the government to adopt damage control measures. (Socialist theory never solved the problem of pricing in open markets so as to make the result socially acceptable while retaining market efficiency.) Much trial and error remain.

Shanghai Yaohua-Pilkington Glass Company

After attempts to develop its own float glass production process ran into quality and process control problems, China decided to look to the West for technological assistance. Pilkington, which developed the float glass process in the late 1950s, was an obvious choice for a joint venture partner.[18] Pilkington preferred simply to enter into licensing agreements with China similar to others it had entered into worldwide. However, it ultimately was persuaded to hold a minority share in an eighteen-year joint venture and to license its technology.

The equity split in the proposed venture was Pilkington 12.5 percent, United Development, Inc. (Hong Kong), 12.5 percent, China National Building Materials Import Export Group 25 percent, Shanghai Yaohua Glass 25 percent, and the Bank of China (Shanghai) 25 percent, with a total capitalization of $120 million. Because it was the first large joint venture producing specifically for the domestic market and the first in the building materials industry, negotiations were difficult and extended over four years.

After the venture was agreed to in 1984, many problems delayed start-up until 1987. Difficulties were experienced with the factory site itself, delaying completion of plant construction; problems arose over the supply of imported equipment, and were resolved only when Pilkington agreed to supply all imported equipment; the Chinese could supply some of the raw materials it had promised only slowly and with difficulty; Pilkington managers involved in plant set-up experienced frustrations with Shanghai city officials, who seemed to have more control over the venture than the venture management; and sensitive issues, such as the proposed wage differential between the joint venture and a neighboring domestic glassworks, were resolved only after protracted negotiations.

Not surprisingly, rising inflation during the course of these further negotiations, as well as the need to source some materials at market prices higher than the projected controlled state prices, meant that original budget specifications had to be scaled up on several occasions. The result has been a significant drop in expected profitability.

Exchange Rates

Exchange rates have presented problems for both the foreign investors and the Chinese government. There has been a significant devaluation of the renminbi (RMB) over the decade of the open door policies. In 1980, the official exchange rate for US $1 was RMB 1.53. This drifted gradually down to RMB 2.33 in 1984 before sagging to RMB 2.94 in 1989. By 1989, the official rate was down to RMB 3.72 per U.S. dollar, a rate that fell further to RMB 4.73 when the Chinese devalued their currency at the end of 1989. To the Shanghai-Volkswagen joint venture, this deterioration presented a serious problem.

Volkswagen in Shanghai

In 1985 Volkswagen established a joint venture in Shanghai.[19] The plant manufactures Santana cars for sale on the domestic market, relying on sales of engines back to Germany to balance its foreign exchange requirements. As of 1987, the factory was beginning to turn a profit after two loss-making years.

One of the most significant problems that the Shanghai-Volkswagen plant had to overcome was the devaluation of the renminbi (yuan). The different exchange rate, combined with the higher prices of domestic materials, meant that the original investment figure of 387 million yuan had soared to 940 million yuan. Months of negotiation were required before an agreement could be reached as to the financing of this additional investment of 553 million yuan. Additionally, both state and local authorities guaranteed the allocation of foreign exchange to the factory during the initial setting-up phase to prevent the burden of foreign exchange shortfalls from falling on Volkswagen.

Current exchange rates also present problems for the Chinese government. Rising domestic prices have meant that the renminbi cost of producing an export item remains above the export price. It is estimated that it costs about 5 RMB per U.S. dollar to produce an export item, which is subsequently exported at the official exchange rate of RMB 3.72:U.S. $1. The government effectively subsidizes the difference. Additionally, this situation encourages multiple exchange rates, with departments and provinces adopting internal exchange rates roughly 1 RMB above the official rate; Shenzhen has a "free" exchange rate that rises as much as 40 percent above the official rate.[20]

CHANGES IN GOVERNMENT POLICIES AND PRACTICES

During the 1980s the policies of the Chinese government and those of provinces and municipalities have changed significantly, with more than 100 laws being passed that have affected foreign direct investment. The changes have principally been in the direction of improving the climate for foreign investment, but the practices in implementing these policies have not been so singularly favorable at one or more of the three levels of government. There is a record of nonfulfillment of some of the commitments made by the governments, for example provision of foreign exchange, freedom in employment practices, and provision of infrastructure and support services. The government also has not always been prompt in making decisions that were necessary for the operation of a joint venture, and in other instances has interfered in ways that made operations less efficient and the venture less profitable. In addition, tax provisions have been changed, and bureaucratic rigidity has remained an obstacle. The impacts of these changes are seen in each of the foregoing illustrations.

Related to government policies and support is the fact that China is not an information-based society, which makes it quite difficult to project joint venture operations and to know how to fulfill those projections. There is a problem in the generation of information out of state enterprises and government agencies; there is a second problem of access to whatever information exists; there is a problem in the generation and access to market-type information; and there is a difficulty in obtaining information on the actual implementation of government policies and even of the locus of decision-making in various government levels. It is not even clear who has certain types of information. If a source is discovered, the ability to acquire the data remains uncertain. This lack of information permeates all aspects of investigation and the negotiation process itself as both sides seek to protect themselves against surprises and uncertainties.

NOTES

1. Baotai Chu, "A Few Things to Know About an Investment in China," *Intertrade*, March 1986, pp. 45–47.

2. *Journal of Commerce*, May 3, 1989.

3. Steven R. Hendryx, "Implementation of a Technology Transfer Joint Venture in the People's Republic of China: A Management Perspective," *Columbia Journal of World Business*, Spring 1986, pp. 57–66.

4. Taken from "Less Haste, Less Waste," *Intertrade*, October 1986, pp. 58–60; see also *Shanghai: Investment Environment, Laws and Regulations* (Shanghai: 1987).

5. Scott D. Seligman, "Nike's Running Start," *China Business Review*, January-February 1982, pp. 42–44; see also "China's Push into Exports Is Turning into a Long March," *Business Week*, September 15, 1986, pp. 66–68.

6. "Setting up Shop in China: Three Paths to Success," *Business Week*, October 19, 1987, p. 74.

7. Drawn from Madelyn C. Ross, "McDonnell Douglas: The Management Challenge," *China Business Review*, September-October 1987, pp. 36–38.

8. Julia S. Sensenbrenner, "Project Notebook: Babcock and Wilcox Beijing Company Ltd.," *China Business Review*, July-August 1988, pp. 10–12.

9. "Setting up Shop in China," p. 74.

10. *China Trader*, February 1987, p. 29.

11. "The China Bubble Bursts," *Fortune*, July 6, 1988, pp. 86–89.

12. Nigel Campbell, *The Challenge of Equity Joint Ventures* (unpublished manuscript, 1989).

13. "Pepsi's Pitch to Quench Chinese Thirsts" *Fortune*, March 17, 1986, pp. 58–64.

14. "China Bubble Bursts," pp. 86–89; *Far Eastern Review*, March 19, 1987, pp. 88–89; *Asian Wall Street Journal Weekly*, December 29, 1986; and *Journal of Commerce*, December 13, 1988.

15. *China Business Review*, November-December 1985; see also *Asian Wall Street Journal Weekly*, December 29, 1986.

16. Liu Dizhong, "New Rules Beat the Currency Problem," *China Daily*, January 21, 1986.

17. "Coal Compensation Trade," *China Business Review*, March-April 1982, pp. 31–33; *New York Times*, July 3, 1985; *Journal of Commerce*, September 11, 1989.

18. *Shanghai: Investment Environment, Laws and Regulations; Shanghai, 1987, passim*; and *Business Week*, October 19, 1987, p. 74.

19. "Shanghai Volkswagen—Progression," *Intertrade*, January 1987, p. 31.

20. "New Freedom to Make a Profit—or Loss," *Far Eastern Economic Review*, May 24, 1988, p. 74.

12

Prospects for Development and Modernization

Doing business in China is likely to lead to quite long-term relations, though there is a contradiction in the Chinese tradition of "relations" as enduring and their desire (albeit changing) to set time limits on joint ventures. It takes time to cultivate a stable and effective relationship, and once cultivated, both sides are expected to continue it so long as mutually beneficial. This means that those involved will be dealing with China as it rises from a relatively underdeveloped status to more modern conditions—without becoming Westernized. But modernity cannot exist in only *one* dimension—such as economic. Other dimensions of the society also are affected and will reflect back on the economic and commercial development. Therefore, it is important to understand the linkages among the several dimensions of development and the impact of Chinese culture on them.

The Chinese have a high culture, developed over millennia, and all "progress" will be peculiarly Chinese—both traditional and socialist. Not to understand the interplays involved in "progress" is to court high frustration. One of the major contradictions in China will be that between freedom and central control—and not just in the planning realm—for central authority is a Chinese tradition. Though the Chinese are diverse peoples with old internal antagonisms, they are responsive to authority, which binds them together. And they are further tied familially, culturally, socially, and religiously to their country (and land). Family and land are still the sentimental centers of Chinese society; the mind-set has not shifted to a modern industrial society.

China has a long history of rural independence (self-reliance) but not of political freedom. The control of the countryside by the Communists since 1949 has required central authority and an elaborate and far-reaching organizational structure to transmit that authority; the commune system was linked in groups down to the production brigade and production team in villages and back up through the counties, prefectures, and provinces to Beijing. But control came at the cost of traditional rural independence, with the subsequent decline of both peasant enthusiasm for rural production and the level of rural productivity.

By way of contrast, the rural reforms of the 1980s have succeeded in stimulating increases in agricultural production and enlivening the rural economy, but only at the expense of central control over the rural populace. This lessening of social control has prompted—in the short term at least—much individual economic activity in the countryside. But modernization of China as a whole will require more than this: It will require the attainment of productivity levels that can only be achieved through strong central guidance of the Chinese people to prevent misuse of scarce resources.

Similarly, to industrialize means to give up living on the land and the independence that accompanies that life-style to take up jobs in industry, where dependence, interdependence, and hierarchies must exist. These are relations that the Chinese are reluctant to adopt voluntarily; they may well need to be imposed from above by a central authority or induced by higher wages (if not by labor allocation). Even then, adherence to these patterns is not guaranteed; for example, placement and promotion within Chinese factories have remained closely linked to familial ties. Thus, for China, industrialization—like control over the rural sector—may not occur without central direction to assure efficiency in market terms and effectiveness in the use of factors of production.

For the West, with its commonly held belief that economic freedom must be accompanied by political freedom and vice versa, the relaxation of central economic control with an absence of political freedom runs counter to its own experience. The difficulty of relaxing economic control while retaining centralized political power was shockingly demonstrated on June 4, 1989, when the Chinese leaders ordered the army to remove the students striking for democracy from Tiananmen Square in Beijing. Before this incident, China was wrestling with the proper use of central control as it seeks to industrialize, in particular as to how to adopt desirable Western technology without acquiring undesirable Western influences that come with this technology. An equally difficult problem is how to decentralize without losing financial control, as China did in 1985–1986 and again in 1988. When a new government and stability are established in China, regardless of the amount of political freedom permitted, the role of central authorities will never be the same. Even if there are economic benefits along the equity dimension, central control will undoubtedly be continually challenged and resented—if not resisted—by those who seek to exercise economic freedom. The several contradictions between the concepts and practices of freedom and control, between agricultural and industrial growth, between urban and rural societies, between central and provincial governments, between the coast and the interior, between the Chinese north and the south, and between Western and Eastern cultures require continued observation by anyone seeking to assess development in China.

A major question is how will China learn to implement its own growth strategy of achieving "Socialism with Chinese characteristics": from the West? From Japan? From the "Four dragons"? Or with major modifications of both capitalism and socialism? In determining how to move into the world economy most effectively, China has a laboratory that has shown itself successful by at least the economic criterion of development—Hong Kong. It has promised not to disrupt the economic life of that city when it takes over from Britain in 1997. As evidence of its intentions, China is involving itself directly in investment and collaborative arrangements for production in Hong Kong and sales into the world market. Hundreds of new enterprises have been set up by the People's Republic of China in Hong Kong, with People's Republic managers. State-owned enterprises reportedly have invested between $8 billion and $10 billion in Hong Kong,[1] making China the largest single investor in Hong Kong (compared with U.S. company totals of $6 billion). In addition, hundreds of People's Republic companies have set up selling and buying shops, bought hotels and office buildings, and invested in the Hong Kong Stock Exchange. China International Trade and Investment Corporation bought 12.5 percent of Cathay Pacific Airways (for $280 million), and Yue Xu Enterprises (Guangzhou's trading company) bought 50 percent of a Hong Kong toy company and then took it public.

Westerners are being hired by People's Republic companies as managers, and People's Republic managers are being hired into Hong Kong companies, so that a cross-fertilization of ideas and orientations is occurring. The movement into Hong Kong is occurring by enterprises from provinces, municipalities, and other governmental units. Such enterprises are permitted to reinvest much of their hard-currency earnings (or they can use them to support foreign joint ventures in the People's Republic). The growth of such enterprises in Hong Kong opens opportunities for foreign companies to widen contacts in the People's Republic and to pick and choose among various projects.

But there are disadvantages. The more liberalized decision-making in China has opened the opportunity for corruption, through "commissions." Complaints have been directed to Beijing, which has seemed powerless to stop corruption. With liberalization has come an adoption of the Hong Kong orientation to quick profits and fast dealing. Beijing is pleased with the learning opportunity, but it is not always pleased with what is learned.

AUSTERITY, 1989–1990

The opening of China is probably irrevocable in the longer run, but the economy ran into trouble early in 1989, as noted in previous chapters. An austerity program was adopted that reduced the attractiveness of China for foreign direct investment. This short-term reversal reflected an understanding by the leadership that progress toward modernization would not always be smooth. In a private interview with a deputy premier of China during the fall of 1988, he was asked how he saw the opening working out. He replied that it was much too soon to tell, but that the country was "committed" and expected to reach the standard of living of the United States by the year 2050; in the meantime, there would be advances and regression and detours, but the direction was certain and irreversible.

Recentralization

The government's response to the difficulties in 1989 was to recentralize the economic system.[2] The government saw unemployment emerging, inflation rising to more than 30 percent in some major cities, state-owned enterprises (SOEs) defaulting on loans, inequities in income, and corruption in both the private and the public sectors. The economic situation was out of control, and China did not have the monetary and fiscal tools that capitalist countries use to guide a freer economy.[3] The techniques it used included controls over investments, foreign exchange, materials allocations, credit, and foreign trade, with local party officials taking control over some factory management. Privileges of coastal provinces were cut back, despite the need for foreign direct investment; the Shenzhen Economic Zone was particularly hard hit, with foreign investors staying away.[4]

The small, emerging enterprises were choked down or out by resource allocations that were directed toward the SOEs. Those that did not go bankrupt had to "toe the party line," producing and selling as instructed. A report a year later stated that

China's leadership, which once hailed [entrepreneurs] as heroes of market-oriented reform, has soured toward entrepreneurs since June. It has closed hundreds of thousands of private firms, stepped up its taxation and control of those that remain, and accused entrepreneurs of evading taxes, selling pornography, and creating vast disparities in income.[5]

Rural factories had increased in number by nearly 30 percent over the decade of the "opening," employing more than 100 million workers (one-fourth of the rural work force) and helping to triple the incomes of China's 800 million peasants.[6] But these industries were hard hit when resources (credit, energy, and raw materials) were shifted to the SOEs to try to keep them afloat, since they provide 75 percent of state revenue. Consequently millions of farmhands became idle in the fields and rural income dropped significantly.

China's trade balance had moved into deficit strongly in 1985 and remained there through the rest of the decade, ranging from US $5 billion to $15 billion annually. This made it virtually impossible to service its increasing international debt. This pressure for imports was enhanced by the government's release of large credits to major SOEs to prevent bankruptcy; wage cuts were made for millions of workers, causing labor unrest. The production of these plants— composed mostly of industrial machinery and goods used in construction projects (rather than consumer products)—largely went into inventory because of the absence of buyers; the result was still greater pressure for imports of consumer items. The government retightened controls over foreign exchange. This action also reduced imports of high-technology goods and machinery needed to increase exports to pay for debts. To maintain export earnings, the government moved to reduce competition among China's exporters so as to keep export prices up.

This return to conservatism was buttressed by arguments of a set of intellectuals, called the "neo-conservatives," who gave the regime a non-Marxist ideological legitimacy but rejected the radical solutions proposed in the Soviet Union and Central Europe.[7] Their objective is to find a "Chinese socialism," which rejects Western democracy and capitalism, for which they assert China is not ready and may never be.[8] This new source of legitimacy is highly important, since Chinese governments have historically sought the council of the "literati," finding them necessary to provide theoretical foundations for policies; without such support, rulers have considered they could lose the "mandate of heaven," which justified authoritarian governments.

In no country has pure pragmatism been sufficient to provide legitimacy to a government, and reliance in China on pragmatism alone was wearing thin, since the absence of an ideology raised questions concerning the legitimacy of party monopoly and governmental control. Without a new vision of its future, the leaders scrapped the encouragement of "getting rich" and returned to admonitions for "hard work and plain living."[9] Thus China has been whipsawed by the attempt to achieve significant economic liberalism with political authoritarianism. This can be done—as in Singapore, Taiwan, and South Korea—but what is achieved is not capitalism; it is a form of guided market economy. These are small countries, whose domestic markets are not significant to foreigners, but that need foreign markets for economic growth. China does not have the same ability to open to the world market while retaining political centralization; it is much too large, diverse, and non-cohesive to be liberalized economically without also being liberalized politically, for the trade-offs required economically—which often are painful—must be approved by the people affected. Further, opening the country to the world economy requires the removal of central planning, weakening the authority of the central government and passing much of the decision-making to the provinces and major cities.

There are no historical models for the guided removal of authoritarian controls. Gradualism holds the problems of a dual-decision system—allocation under controls for some and under markets for others. Radical liberalization holds the prospect of chaotic changes with damaging inflation, bankruptcies, and unemployment. The former approach places security over freedom; the latter, freedom over security. Most workers (agricultural and rural) as well as private farmers would chose the former; intellectuals, the latter.[10] This trade-off is difficult in any society, and in one facing fundamental changes in the society, economy, and polity, it is excruciating. Such pain was itself a cause for dissatisfaction with the government and party, and the potential loss of power by the party was unacceptable to it; it had fought long for possession of China and saw no reason to give it up. Deng wanted economic reform only to achieve efficiency and progress. He probably would not have begun it if he had thought that it would threaten party rule.[11]

Western Business Reaction

The reaction of Western businessmen to the return to central control (plus the events of Tiananmen, discussed below) initially was one of high insecurity and lack of confidence.[12] But with continued assurances that the government did not intend to alter its open door policy, and with assessments that the longer-run conditions would be favorable, companies already there were less pessimistic and projects remained in operation. Yet new projects were slow in developing. The pursuit of the "giant Chinese market" seemed deferred, at least.[13]

There appeared a new understanding of the nature of the Chinese business structure—a two-tiered one, with the major players being the SOEs, to which the government guides foreign venture partners, and the private sector, which is much more dynamic and attractive to the foreigner and for which the government has no means of control save direct controls, which would stifle the economic progress the government seeks. As the bifurcation is recognized, foreign investors are likely to return, finding negotiating with the Chinese as complex, difficult, and frustrating as ever, but also potentially rewarding over the long term.[14]

AFTERMATH OF TIANANMEN

Another regression at the end of the 1980s began with the student opposition to the Chinese government in Tiananmen Square on the anniversary of the Student Uprising of 1919. The students staged protests and hunger strikes, calling for "democracy." But they hardly had an idea of what it was they espoused, having no real experience with freedom of person, thought, or expression, or of individual responsibility associated with it.[15] Certainly they had no idea of pulling down the Communist Party, for their specific complaints were the age-old ones of favoritism and corruption (see Chapter 5) plus inadequate freedom of expression and movement. But the last two were less pressing than the first.

The call was for *reform*, not for *revolution*. But the stridency of the calls, the unwillingness of the students to leave Tiananmen Square, the broad sympathy gained for hunger-strikers, and the eventual calls for resignation of some top officials led to the intransigent response of the rulers. This reaction fits with Chinese historical patterns, for there is no historical tradition of peaceful democratic change in China, and it should not be expected now.

The students suffered from knowing that something better was possible but not knowing how to achieve it. They took Deng's assertion that "practice is the sole criterion of truth," and observed that practices elsewhere were more successful; they then assumed that all leaders would want what was successful, and merely demanded change. The challenge was not widespread, however, for unemployment was already surfacing, and many workers did not like the insecurity of a freer society. Some farmers were becoming rich and did not want to rock the boat. There have been peasant revolts in China, but this time it was the student-intellectuals, who have historically been seen by the peasants or workers as elite and snobbish.

Students have demonstrated on many occasions, historically, causing significant change, though not always what they have sought. The consequences have seldom been what the students intended. This was partly a result of the fact that workers and others did not join in with the "elite" students, so the governments did not take them seriously.

During Tiananmen, however, workers did join in because of inflationary pressures, unemployment, visible inequities, too slow improvement in living standards, and favoritism and corruption by some government officials. Further, the government's willingness to recognize the students and meet with them emboldened both students and workers. The media—both press and television—showed support for the students, reporting "all the news." Initially, even the army refused to remove the strikers from Tiananmen.

The leadership was threatened by what it perceived to be "anarchy," that is, a state of lawlessness by the students and high-level political indecision. It called troops from the West, who were unaware of the events and issues in Beijing; they were told of "a revolt by counterrevolutionaries" in Tiananmen. The result was a regretful event for China, its leadership, and its relations with the rest of the world.

Western Reaction

China faced additional pressure in the international reaction to the massacre at Tiananmen Square and the subsequent violations of human rights in the incarceration of those seen as "traitors" or as acting against the public interest.[16] Many nations stopped selling military materiel or high technology to China, and many diplomatic representations were made on behalf of the students. Some remain harbored in foreign countries, and continue to charge the government with improper behavior.

Under the assumption that "the West needs China more than China needs the West," the government took an arrogant and unresponsive posture, asserting its willingness to "suffer" the rejections but also its eagerness to "punish" foreigners for what the Chinese leaders considered to be unwarranted interventions in internal affairs. Some official positions were that foreigners had actually stimulated and perpetuated the students' challenges and that the United States and others have used human rights as a means of attacking socialism, have sought to inseminate their culture, and are engaged in a conspiracy against the Chinese regime.[17]

Under the view that "China needs us more than we need them," some foreign governments and international institutions imposed sanctions, with processing of most international loans being interdicted. Some foreign companies withdrew executives and sent them back slowly, if at all; others stopped inquiries or projects in midstream, but only a few pulled out completely.[18] A few countries—Japan, Korea, and Taiwan—continued with projects under way and initiated others, but there was a general decline in both foreign direct investment and tourism. Some import contracts were terminated and diverted to other sources, and some technology transfers were ceased or slowed.

The Chinese government responded with a "Great Wall" psychology, and some constraints were imposed on American joint ventures or firms in China, such as blocking access to distribution channels, suddenly imposing price controls, and interdicting raw materials supplies.[19] A number of projects and sourcing contracts, however, continued to function in an orderly manner. Still, the "stability" that the Chinese government promised foreign business has not been guaranteed, as also seen in changes in the joint venture law.[20]

Despite its repulsion by the events in Tiananmen, which it officially protested, the U.S. government took initiatives to keep China within the Western orbit— approving sales of Boeing aircraft, sending top officials (National Security Adviser Brent Scowcroft and Deputy Secretary of State Lawrence Eagleburger) to Beijing for talks, reopening Ex-Im Bank loans, vetoing (at China's bidding) a bill to permit Chinese students to have automatic visas to stay in the United States, and continuing most-favored-nation trading status for China.[21]

In August 1989, the Chinese government offered its own "political-risk" insurance to foreign investors, covering "war, warlike operations, insurrection, strike, and riot." But businesses were not thrilled, since the government was offering insurance against its own acts, and it had asserted that "Tiananmen didn't happen." Collecting damages in Chinese courts was seen as a difficult matter, given party control over them.

Official Chinese Response

Internally, the official Chinese response was to reinstitute the programs of reeducation of students and workers, with some assigned to rural work areas for several years.[22] This was accompanied by propaganda asserting that the killings did not happen and those did were justified, since the victims were common criminals. There also was a partial return to Confucianism to gain legitimacy, with both the government and the opposition using quotations supporting their positions. For example, Jiang Zemin stated at a conference in October on Confucianism that "Confucianism should be used 'selectively' since it does not apply wholly to modern times," but that its strictures urging a "work ethic" should be followed on the part of the people. Others, however, recalled the Confucian saying that "rulers with 'ren' [benevolence, high regard, perfection] should not kill or have others kill for them. If necessary, they should sacrifice themselves for the people." And, "the main duty of the ruler is to serve—not do just anything to stay in power."[23]

Implications of Tiananmen

A number of internal consequences have flowed from the June 1989 events. It is evident that the pressures of modernization will eventually transform the political situation, for the party has fundamentally been rejected by the people in the cities. The army remained split and uncertainly loyal to the party. The people's fear of the government is diminishing in terms of its ability to remain in power long, but their fear of short-term reprisals remains. The real revolution in China—the cultural shift feared by the party—is occurring but not yet fully manifested. Economic reform has temporarily been suspended, but will lead inexorably in the modern world to political reform; economic reform eventually will be demanded by the people, beginning in the coastal cities and moving west. During any given year, however, the direction of movement can be reversed, and has a high probability of happening.

New problems also arose from the Old Guard's attempt to slow down the liberalization. The results ranged from the closing of some projects to the imposition of new regulations, centralization of decision-making, a return to party rule in the courts, the shutdown of new entrepreneurs and some of the media, an increase in corruption, and tensions among the various levels of government.[24] Even Communist Party chief Jiang Zemin admitted the influence of government and party corruption and income disparities in stimulating the events at Tiananmen:[25] "We should admit that corruption and a wide gap in income are the focus of strong resentment on the part of the broad masses of the people. Steep income disparities seriously dampen the enthusiasm and initiative of the large majority of workers."[26] Because many private businesses earned more than ten times the average yearly wage of public employees, additional taxes were imposed on these enterprises, and the existing 14.5 million private enterprises were to be subjected to investigations for possible tax evasion.

But corruption was a significant cause of income disparities and was reportedly pervasive through the government and party. The *Sydney Morning Herald* commented in mid-1989 that "official corruption (*guandao*), its tolerance, and the resultant debilitating effects on the economy are at the root of the student rebellion. The state at its most rotten is institutionalized in the troubled Chinese economy." And "one of China's deepest fears is that the enormous grip forged by conservative Prime Minister Li Peng on the nation merely will extend the network of corruption, nepotism, bribes, and kickbacks that sullies business life in China and helps fuel the economic and political chaos."[27] Jiang Zemin has reportedly made it a priority to reduce the impact of this aspect of officialdom, and another anti-corruption drive was launched in mid-July 1989.[28] But despite the fact that officials have admitted that "a small number of the sons and daughters of senior cadres are indeed corrupt,'' no relative of a top leader has been punished publicly for graft.[29]

Contrarily, the protestors were caught (or at least sought, with rewards as high as a year's wages offered, inducing some families to turn in their own kin), and those of the leaders who did not flee were punished.[30] Indoctrination in ''love of the motherland, of socialism and the party'' was reemphasized from the early grades in school. And ''liberal'' materials and books were confiscated and bookstalls selling them were closed. The party sought to discredit foreign journalists, and the Chinese *World Economic Herald* (renowned for its objectivity) was closed.[31]

The future, therefore, again appears as uncertain, but then it always was; it was just that Western countries and Chinese intellectuals (as always in the past) pushed for a more rapid adjustment of China to the world economy than was acceptable to the leadership. Consequently their expectations and those of many international businesses were frustrated. Greater caution is required, but no less earnestness in pursuit of appropriate ties with the emerging China.

CRITERIA OF DEVELOPMENT

Even if China modernizes, it would not necessarily be developed. All countries are in the process of developing, and some, such as the United States, have retrogressed in a number of characteristics, for example the incidence of crime, degradation of the environment, quality of education, and soundness of the infrastructure. There are different criteria for assessing development, and each of them has a set of qualifications and requisites to achieve acceptable progress. These are artificial criteria, for any stage of development is simply a stage in the process to further development or evolution.

Beyond China's own development, the question arises as to whether China can *begin to lead the world itself to still higher levels of development*, that is, achieve a system of development that is a model for the world in balancing efficiency and equity, growth and conservation, current and future claims, freedom and stability, cooperation and competition.[32] Again, the concept of China as ''the Middle Kingdom'' implies a role of assisting in the translation of the ''will of heaven'' to mankind and an elevation of mankind to a more perfect status. Is China likely to fulfill this role? Even an exercise of assessing the forces at play helps to understand the Chinese dilemmas.

China has set as its objectives the ''four modernizations'' in agriculture, industry, military, and science and technology. But modernization—a replication of what exists in the Western economies—may not in fact be development for China. If economic advancement (modernization) is achieved without human rights and is gained at the cost of social retrogression, what is the net progress? If economic growth (generation and protection of greater wealth) involves increased costs in terms of security, crime prevention, punishment, drug and alcohol rehabilitation, hospitalization, personal stress and anxiety, divorce or separation of families, juvenile delinquency, reduction of educational achieve-ments, increased gaps between the rich and the poor, extensive welfare programs, protection and cleansing of the environment, and ever larger bureaucracies—if progress is accompanied by these additional costs and personal freedoms are forever constrained, what is the net balance of benefits? Perhaps more important, can economic success be achieved by a population that does not have hope of achieving President Roosevelt's Four Freedoms—of speech, of religion, from hunger, and from fear? There are at least seven dimensions (or criteria) of development, the *first* being economic. All seven are pursued by any society, but few of the others seem to have the same high priority as that given to the one of economic growth. Many of them, however, are linked in ways that we do not readily see or identify, especially in a foreign culture.

The *second* dimension is that of science and technology, which strongly sup-port growth in the economic realm. However, not all scientific development leads to, is aimed at, or should result in economic and commercial advance. There are scientific advancements that end up in a better understanding of the world in which we live and how it works, including our relation to it. Some technologies—for example, related to astronomy—may not lead to economic advance, but simply to discovery and the satisfaction of curiosity. Development in this direction may be purely a satisfaction of our desire to know, without any intent to manipulate or direct the use of that knowledge. Yet such knowledge clearly is an addition to our evolution; if nothing else, it illumines our under-standing of why we are here and what we are supposed to be doing. But a predominant part of science and technology, and therefore scientific research, *is* directed at economic advance in each, seeking to guide our growth in a particular way. This buttressing is most clear in the realms of economics, in-dustry, and commerce, but it also is closely linked to the political and military and other criteria of development discussed below.

A *third* criterion of development is that in the political and military arena, leading to military strength and diplomatic techniques aimed at the maintenance of peace rather than the waging of war. The purpose of military strength is not to have to use it; only if that strength is seen as inadequate (materially and strategically) by the opponent is he likely to risk challenging it. On the other hand, continued escalation of military strength is likely to lead to a challenge at some time simply to test the success of the development of military material. Highly advanced science and technology clearly are behind such military de-velopments, and therefore are critical in political development as well. Politics itself is more of an art than a science, but research and experience lead to growth in this realm as well. A politically backward society can hardly grow econom-ically or technologically. The backwardness of the political institutions will constrain growth in other dimensions. For this reason China (and other socialist countries seeking accelerated growth) had determined that a more open political system was required, to free the minds of its people to be exercised along multidimensions of development. However, the quest for a more open political system that is acceptable to all parties remains a difficult one, and late 1989 saw the government moving again to highly centralized political control.

A *fourth* dimension relates to mind and body. For minds to be sufficiently developed to pursue new ideas and directions, they must be educated and they must be housed in healthy bodies. Therefore, education to "health" is an education to a balanced body and a balance between body and mind. To count material economic growth as progress if it destroys the minds and bodies of people within the society is a curious concept of progress and is bought at unknown cost. Similarly, a society whose development has elicited extensive use of debilitating drugs, which leads to juvenile delinquency, gang warfare, and rising rates of crime, is one that has not sufficiently recognized the multi-dimensions of development to balance the different criteria of evolution.

Within the past four decades, China has been critically concerned with a *fifth* dimension of development—that related to equity in the distribution of income and wealth. This is a critical dimension, too often avoided by Western policy-makers; when they do focus on it, they usually treat it as a means of correcting undesired results of the workings of the system rather than as a modification of the system itself. That is, transfers of benefits are made rather than a restructuring of the ways in which the benefits are earned. China has attempted to focus on the process of earning benefits, and has achieved a greater equality (though clearly not as great as commonly perceived) in income distribution than in most other parts of the world. To lose this advancement in terms of equity could mean the purchase of modernization at high costs in terms of popular dissatisfaction and altered motivations. It is clear that individual motivations toward economic progress do not arise strongly in the bureaucratic, centrally controlled economy (the "iron rice bowl") such as China developed; but it is equally clear that the more highly motivated societies in the West have not produced acceptable distributions of income and wealth from a political or community standpoint. There is much development yet to take place along this dimension.

A *sixth* dimension of development is the artistic or creative one. Creativity in any arena is an act of art, that is, not following a prescribed, scientifically known procedure. It is a thrust into the imagination, using the mind to expand beyond itself into completely new concepts or relations. Art is the expression of an idea that is inexpressible in scientific or other language. It is even the use of language in ways that express an idea different from the words themselves, invoking a feeling rather than simply transferring knowledge. It has long been said that development of art and culture leads to the higher evolution of mankind, and it has more recently been argued that the twenty-first century will be the century of development in art. Previously it was said that the seventeenth century saw the development of agriculture, the eighteenth century that of commerce, the nineteenth that of industry, the twentieth that of science and technology, with the twenty-first predicted as that of information. But art does not inform; rather, it touches or enhances the feelings. If the twenty-first century is dominated by art, it will be a true revolution from rationality to emotion. The challenge again is *balance*. In each case, the prior revolutions have continued, rather than being abandoned, and they become increasingly consolidated as progress continues.

The *seventh* criterion of development is spiritual. We have been progressing along this dimension virtually since the dawn of self-consciousness in mankind. Still, the century (or millennium) of its ascension among the dimensions of development is apparently yet to come. Spirituality is at a higher level of understanding than that of art or science; in China, it is identifiable with the concept of "the Middle Kingdom," which translates all of earthly and human development into the spiritual dimension. This dimension infuses all other criteria of development and gives them meaning; otherwise, they are merely thrusts and parries on the world's stage.

Modernization—in China's case the "four modernizations"—is not adequate to describe the process of development that peoples and nations are going through, and China will not be able to—nor should it be required to—achieve modern status by each and every method of the West. It has its own future to create and its own destiny to fulfill—it is hoped with growth in personal freedoms as well. Modernization is neither a stopping point nor a rest stop along the way, or even a state in which the costs and benefits are equable or measurable. Rather, the modernity of the twentieth century is a stage to move out of as rapidly as possible—or better still, avoid—moving into more desirable states of development. But taking the "four modernizations" as the stated objectives of China, the question remains as to whether or not the requisites for their achievement exist or whether in seeking these goals their very definition will change, with new objectives and concepts being conceived. The *I Ching (Book of Changes)* speaks of continuous change resulting from causes that are themselves changing, and not by any known laws of change. China has much to learn from its own sages and much that is positive to teach the rest of the world.

REQUISITES FOR MODERNIZATION

A major question is whether China can traverse five centuries of cumulative Western modernization in the first five decades of the twenty-first century, as it seeks to do. It has only a decade or so to gain the requisite preconditions for "take-off." But it appears clear that mere pragmatism or mere progress is an insufficient goal by which to guide future development. Nations, peoples, and individuals need purpose as well as process, and the setting of a goal or vision determines the processes used. China currently is confused as to both purpose and process. If the purpose is "continuation of the party in power" or "continuation of the leadership in power," then economic reform and modernization will be sacrificed, for the people have lost confidence in their government. As was said many years ago in the myths of the Bantu, "violence and force are sure signs of failure on the part of the ruler. . . . Killing his own people can only increase a ruler's unpopularity."[33]

In the absence of continued use of force, national government authority over the society and economy can succeed only if the people are satisfied with their place and with the degree of equity provided, and if the values of the primary party are consonant with theirs. Even these conditions are insufficient in an open economy, for foreign influences continue to upset both place and equity. Thus modernization for participation in the world economy is the deathknell for planning, as was shown decades ago in the debates on adoption of socialism. Diversity in consumption also is anathema to planning, yet this is the situation worldwide and increasingly as barriers fall.

Modernization will be achieved through the establishment of eleven prerequisites.

1. *Establishment of an agricultural base.* This has been shown by history to be the progenitor of industrial progress. Until food production is efficient (in particular that of basic foodstuffs) and begins to release resources for the extensive cultivation of cash crops, acquisition of industrial raw materials, and urban labor, China will be unable to both feed its people and fuel diverse industrial growth. China's policies in the early 1980s produced significant increases in agricultural production. But in the late 1980s, production dropped as price policies were changed and taxes were imposed to reduce high farm incomes. The single-child policy infringes on human rights, and cannot be viewed by China as the long-term solution to poor food production.

2. *Building of an efficient distribution system for agricultural produce.* A corollary of the first precondition, such a system would include commercial networks, transport infrastructure, and the means of storage and processing. The second precondition is important for two reasons. First, it promotes agricultural efficiency through the development of regional comparative advantage, fitting production to local conditions. Second, it gains income for the rural sector, releasing labor to industry and increasing demand for industrial products. Although China's population constitutes one-fifth of mankind, and there would appear to be many people available for non-agricultural pursuits, 80 percent of the people are still considered farmers, compared to less than 10 percent in the economically advanced countries. It is quite difficult for 20 percent of the population to provide all of the government, ancillary services, industrial products, and infrastructure necessary to raise the standard of living of the remaining 80 percent by a factor of 30, as needed to match U.S. 1985 per capita income. Modernization in an industrial (economic) sense cannot be achieved until the agricultural population is less than half of the total. Thus the surplus agricultural population must be shifted physically to those areas that need infrastructure, ancillary services, and so forth. For this to occur, not only must sufficient foodstuffs be produced, but they must be deliverable, so as to generate farm income and sustain industrialization.

This shift is decades away. Because the cities are overcrowded, the Chinese government is much more concerned with keeping the rural populace in situ, promoting the "industrialization of the countryside." This attitude is another illustration of the dichotomy between control and freedom. A shift in the rural population necessitates a relaxation of the controls on movement that exist in China. These controls limit mass migration and avoid overcrowding in major cities—and the wealthier agricultural regions, for example the central and southern coastal provinces of Jiangsu, Zhejiang, Fujian, and Guangdong). Urban concentration has become the hallmark of many third world countries—a concentration beyond that permitting effective use of labor and causing the state to assume strong control over individual freedom. Furthermore, with such control over movement, tensions and conflicts within these magnet areas escalate as pressures increase on the available land resources. Unless the state is able to find a means to redirect opportunities and redistribute wealth, the urban areas will continue to grow much faster than the rest of China, exacerbating the problems of employment and equity in income distribution.

Although the state wants to restrict the movement of people to the urban areas, this fact alone does not mean that industry will not grow at a satisfactory and significant rate, given that there is already a substantial industrial base. But it does mean that modernization will come to different regions at different times; as indicated above, this will cause problems of equity. Strong governmental guidance—above and beyond controls on the movement of people—will be necessary to achieve an acceptable balance of interior and coastal, rural and urban, and agricultural and industrial growth.

3. *Existence of a middle class that is able to supply the labor skills and to take a political and social position between that of the (rigid socialist) government bureaucracy and the (traditional) peasants.* Such a middle class, based on the urban rather than the rural population, is a necessary foundation for democratic political institutions, since it provides multiple interests within the community, removing the polarization of a feudal society or the centralization of an authoritarian one.

This class arises through commercialization and industrialization of the society, but it can be prevented from developing its political and social role through its exploitation. Permission to become rich has added members to the middle class (with so-called 10,000-yuan families), but income disparities have raised other problems.

The middle class is developing in many parts of China, and will be expanded by current reforms. The transfer of the rural population into cities will accelerate this growth. But the process is slow and will take more than a few decades. The mere building of cities or accommodations within existing cities for an additional 300 million to 400 million people moving from the countryside (plus new births) shows the dimensions of the problem. Japan is just beginning to build entirely new cities centered on technological specialization of research institutes and universities. The mere tacking on to existing metropolitan areas over the past two decades leads only to a degrading of infrastructure, including housing, sanitation, and health facilities.

4. *Development of an ethical basis for individual conduct in commercial and financial dealings.* That is, corruption within the economic and political realms

must be prevented, else the efficiency necessary to raise living standards will not occur, or if it does, the motivation of key people will be diverted to acquiring income rather than producing it.

Income disparities have led to jealousies and apparent injustices: Intellectuals still receive low pay (they were in the "stinking ninth," or lowest, category during the Cultural Revolution); entertainers are well paid; but barbers earn more than surgeons, and tea servers more than nuclear workers. A consequence is scalping of goods and racketeering, with corruption beginning to permeate all aspects of society.

Social morality is deteriorating, as seen in bribery, favoritism, and the return of opium use, prostitution, gambling, alcohol abuse, fraud (fake commodities, such as fertilizer), theft, rape, juvenile delinquency, and greed (made stark by a man's request for money before responding to a call to save a child from drowning in a pond).[34]

Although this process of acquisition could lead to mobilization of funds for investment through large wealth for a few, it provides no assurance that the funds will be invested productively for the growth of the country. There is no clear evidence that corruption has led to modernization of societies. Rather, acceptable patterns of growth require an ethical basis—honesty in dealings, fulfillment of promises, development and dissemination of relevant information, commitments to contract, and protection of the rights of others.

The Chinese government is well aware of these problems, and has shown a concern over the rise of corruption with the emergence of private enterprise and market decisions under approvals by governmental authorities. The existence of pervasive regulations and government controls opens the way for misuse of power and corrupt dealings. But market decisions in times of high scarcity also can lead to corruption of individuals and of the system through decisions taken under extreme circumstances. Whether or not China can hold against the forces of corruption is an important question. Before the Communist revolution, China faced corruption on governmental and private levels. It was corrupted in the nineteenth century by Westerners in many aspects, not the least of which was the introduction of opium and the bribery associated with it. It would be a historical tragedy for the benefits of the Communist revolution to be wasted completely in a return to corruption in the Chinese society, whether at its own hands or those of foreigners. There is no signal that indicates potentials for success or likely failure in this regard. It will remain a question at least into the twenty-first century. In the interim, a strong government hand with a high priority to serve all the people will be necessary. Since the student strikes in mid-1989, greater attention has been paid by Beijing to reducing corruption. Sons and daughters of officials cannot work in some positions in state-owned companies, and even the China International Trade and Investment Corporation has been fined $5 million (equivalent) for not paying taxes.

5. *Economic and political stability*. The necessity for such stability is recognized in Japanese policies. Political stability provides the certainty necessary

for decisions to be made in a market and to be fulfilled in terms of the intentions of both parties. A government that makes radically different decisions within short spaces of time upsets such relations so that they become unproductive and often renegotiated. Economic stability in terms of the money supply, employment levels, and rates of growth is not necessary, but it is certainly a complement to economic progress. It prevents wasting of resources through cycles of depression and excessive rates of growth; it stimulates savings and longer-term investments as needed to put new technologies into commercialization; it provides a motivation for people to prepare for their future through productive investment and savings for retirement; and it is necessary for the attraction of investment funds from foreigners, such as the transnational corporations and the overseas Chinese, who until June 4, 1989, were providing 70 percent of the foreign investment inflows. Both types of stability are being undermined by fiscal irresponsibility through directed investment (supporting inefficient enterprises), premature and excessive consumption, overheated growth, wages and bonuses higher than productivity warrants, bureaucratic perks and corruption, government deficits, plus excessively aggressive military putdowns of peaceful and unaggressive demonstrations. It does not matter to investors that these are internal Chinese affairs; they still directly affect the investment environment.

It clearly is a policy of the Chinese government to achieve both types of stability, but the opening both to free markets and to democracy are destabilizes. Therefore, the Chinese government will not open fully to either economic or political freedom, as has been evidenced. It must now walk a razor's edge for a while until people get used to a China that permits some economic freedom but limits political freedom. Evidence of how this requisite will be fulfilled will probably be slow in coming; paradoxically, its achievement also will require a strong government, but one that is strong in its ability to be sensitive to the people and to the expectations of the international community of which it seeks to become a part.

Given the evidence that the party will kill its own citizens to stay in power, the Chinese people appear willing to "lie low" and wait for reform from within toward a more liberal society. But, to date, the system has eaten its heirs, and there is little time for Deng to prepare a successor. This also is a reason for the buildup of an intellectual justification for a "socialism with Chinese characteristics."[35] Something is needed besides fear to build loyalty, and something besides pragmatism to buttress legitimacy. There is some hope in the fact that not all of the reformers have left the country or gone underground; a few remain and continue to hold the party to account.[36]

But the problem China faces is that it has only one of the four means of achieving stability through social cohesion—fear generated by force ("power comes out of the barrel of a gun" [Mao]). The other three are virtue, zeal, and self-interest. *Virtue* was the foundation for ruling as counseled by Confucius and Lao-T'su, with the ruler epitomizing moral values that the people also should practice; but the Communist Party has permitted pervasive corruption and rec-

ognizes that it has lost legitimacy on this count.[37] *Zeal* arises from adherence to
an ideology, such as communism, or freedom and democracy, or as elicited by
a religion; in the absence of any religion, with the clear failure of communism
(Marxism or Leninism) and with a fear of political and economic freedom, China
is without an ideology. *Self-interest* can bind members of a society through
mutual progress or development, or through mutual support in the face of a
threat to security; but China is little threatened from foreign powers and has
failed under the "opening" to provide security in employment (thereby breaking
the "iron rice bowl") or, under national planning, to provide progress with
security.

This absence of a cohesive force or purpose is crucial, and the reason for the
use of force is clear: There was no alternative identifiable by the party and none
offered by the students or opponents except reform or resign. Something more
positive is required, but the blueprint is not in hand.[38] Still, the ability of the
government to use force to keep China together will atrophy; not only is it costly,
but it also does not solve the longer-run problems of growth. The provinces and
major cities gradually will pull away from central control, and the center will
have to accede for some progress to occur.

Beijing recognized this likelihood and clamped down on the provinces—
especially Guangdong—but it has been partially rebuffed through the direct
access that the major provinces have to resources (other than credit). The central
government can constrain credit, but it can do so only at the risk of further
recession. And Guangdong was in the unique position of not having a major
project financed by Beijing when the clampdown occurred.[39] Further, the major
SOEs, which provide Beijing with its revenue, had to be subsidized to stay
afloat,[40] whereas the multiple private or provincial enterprises continue to appear
more profitable. To put severe brakes on the latter enterprises would raise unemployment even further.[41] In addition, it is difficult to choke off the provinces
by denial of resources, given the ability to bribe officials in the companies set
up by the army to order needed items.[42] Once again, the historical circle of
causation is difficult to break.

6. *Adequate resources—natural and human—to provide necessary inputs for
industrial growth.* China has ample supplies of both, and lacks only the process
of (capital for) their utilization. The natural resources can be developed through
investment, which has already been opened to foreigners. The development of
these resources can be accelerated, but appropriate infrastructure for their use
will need to be added. An adequate infrastructure includes the appropriate preparation of the human resources, both management and labor. Unless the system
of rewards and incentives is changed, there may be a lack of motivation on the
part of the people involved. The fundamental problem is to find a level of
economic reward that will motivate both management and labor to competitive
production, and at the same time not generate such inequities in rewards that
motivation is stifled. This is a neat balance that Japan and Korea are closer to
finding than any other countries.

In the case of Japan, the rewards of management are tied to the structure and level of rewards to labor, rather than being widely separated and untied, as they are in the United States. The differential between top incomes and wages of common labor in both China and Japan is on the order of 30:1, though the usual ratio is 10:1. In the United States, it can go as high as 3,000:1, though the more usual ratio is 300:1.

Motivation is a result of identification of the individual with the purposes pursued by the organization of which he is a member. One strength of the revolutionary regime was to achieve a high degree of loyalty. The China of the future faces a potential return to the Confucian description of China as a "mountain of loose sand," which will separate into individual (or familial) units with the slightest shaking. The emergence of family-dominated farming since the 1978 rural reforms is an example of the desire of the rural populace to organize around familial households rather than the collective units that prevailed in the 1960s and 1970s. As noted earlier, this move has improved rural economic performance, but only at the cost of reduced central control over rural economic and social behavior. Loyalty and commitment, and therefore motivation, are critical issues to watch in Chinese development, and unless the central government plays a strong and just role, the loyalties will quickly be returned to smaller political groups. People will, as they did in the Cultural Revolution, do only what is necessary for personal and family survival.

7. *Generation and dissemination of appropriate, relevant, truthful, timely, and understandable information.* Such information also must be disseminated to appropriate decision units, so that it can be used effectively. This requisite is necessary for an open society, especially one open to the world economy, but China has not developed such an information network. Consequently it is not a society that is significantly information-based, though its relations with and through Hong Kong are emphasizing this necessity and China gradually is responding.

Any set of decision-makers, be they totalitarian or democratic, needs appropriate information. However, closed societies can survive longer with inadequate information than can open societies. A competitor's pressures will simply swamp those who operate in ignorance. This requisite is particularly critical for China, and will require the closest watching and careful attention on the part of those doing business in and with China. Again, the solution found by several countries is the centralization of control over information to assure its accuracy and its dissemination.

8. *Education, especially in science and technology, but also in managerial and labor skills, and for governmental positions.* A very high, if not the highest, priority will need to be given to this requisite. China requires education to master the tasks of modernization. The Chinese are industrious people with a high degree of scientific and theoretical curiosity, displayed also in fine abilities in mathematics and logic. Education requires time and resources, and the large population means that only a small percentage of the people will have opportunities for higher education.

9. *An adequate market.* Rapid economic development requires this. There is

no question of the adequacy of the potential market in China to stimulate high rates of economic growth. There is a large unmet need, and all that must be added is a further opening of local markets to generate numerous opportunities for business of all sizes and types. China has no need to tie into the world economy for the purpose of expanding its market size, as do each of the "four dragons." Even Japan requires penetration into the world market to satisfy its needs for natural resources. China can simply open its domestic market to foreign investment, which would bring the necessary capital to build foreign exchange reserves out of which local companies could finance imports of capital equipment. This would mean the penetration of foreign competition into formerly closed domestic markets, and this is a disturbance that China is as yet unable to withstand. Therefore, the government is far from relinquishing controls, among which is an insistence that foreign investors export to the world market to earn their own foreign exchange; the need remains to limit repatriation of profits of foreign investors.

This may well be an error of policy on the part of the Chinese government because it will slow the rate of economic growth, compared with what could occur if the domestic market were thrown open to foreign investors producing locally but selling in competition with Chinese enterprise. This strategy also would accelerate the efficiency and productivity of local Chinese companies, and stimulate a necessary competitive attitude so as to improve quality and the ability eventually to export.

All Asian countries in which Chinese individuals have prospered in enterprise have maintained a controlled economic and industrial policy, supporting and guiding development; none has been politically democratic. (For example, martial law continued even in Taiwan until the mid-1980s.) For China itself to open to the full exigencies of competition would risk a growth of enterprise cliques and a type of commercial warfare not conducive to development of the country, which is still not unified in the sense of having a national market or a strong national identification that would override personal or family interests in an open-market economy. The Chinese have no history or theory supporting "arm's length" decision-making as through the idealized neoclassic competitive market; rather decisions are made as though with "arms linked." Decisions have long been made for, within, and often by the extended family and friends; treatment of "strangers" has been under different criteria. (This is in fact the pattern for most societies in the world, rather than the British-American pattern of dealing with unrelated buyers and sellers acting on their own behalf.)

Nor is competition sought by foreign investors, particularly in strange environments, since it adds to the risks. As one American negotiator explained: "I am a businessman, and though I must face competition, I prefer not to have to face those risks." The uncertainties and unfamiliarities of the China situation, the necessity to rely on "unreliable" local supplies and vendors, the levels of government approvals, and the eagerness of others to enter the market—all make any investor seek to reduce potential competition. This thrust fits with a deep desire on the part of Chinese officials not to let the situation get out of hand through too many players in any sector. Again, a balance must be struck between free market forces and governmental guidance.

10. *The protection of property and proprietary rights so as to encourage scientific discovery and technological innovation.* This requisite also is needed to protect the property of consumers and to protect parties to business contracts. China has moved in this direction, but not being an information-based society, it will be some time before the various levels of Chinese government will effectively implement such laws.

11. *Ideology to provide the bonds of society and the foundation for the legitimacy of any government.* This requisite will be needed if China is a "mountain of loose sand," in which individuals will fall away easily from consciousness of the larger society and any responsibilities to it. The acceptance of pragmatism for an ideology, as currently is propounded by the Chinese government, will be inadequate to catalyze the loyalty and commitment of the Chinese people to the modernization or development of the nation. Such a commitment requires an identification with a higher purpose than is obtainable by any individual or family. A purpose tied to the wider community, or to the nation or world, and identified with a higher cause than one's own material well-being is the only thing that can bring true happiness to people. When happiness is identified with material advancement, the criterion has no bounds; there is never enough to satisfy the drive for material things. Satisfaction in life is identified with the accomplishment of high purpose, and in many instances, the mere pursuit of its suffices. It is important, therefore, to watch the development of ideology in China and the direction that it takes. It is ideas that shape policy, not the existence of one or another set of resources or external conditions. These latter can be changed through the power of ideas and the will to pursue them.

(In assessing the potential success of China as it proceeds in the next decades along the routes of its development, it would be instructive for any one doing business with China to make comparisons with the processes of development in Japan, among the "four dragons," and even in Latin America. Latin America has been bypassed in terms of the economic and commercial modernization of the twentieth century, and it is doubtful that it can catch up in this dimension. China's development is potentially in a different direction in the twenty-first century, emphasizing the artistic, philosophic, and equity dimensions more than the economic and scientific.)

BEYOND MODERNIZATION: CHINA'S ROLE IN THE WORLD ECONOMY

China has begun late in the process of economic and commercial development, and is even further behind in the dimension of science and technology. It also is lagging in political development toward democracy, so that any prominent (leadership) role that it has to play in the world will be along the other dimensions of development—health, concepts of equity, art, and spiritual growth.

This is not to say that China will not play an important role in economic, scientific, and political development of the world. It will become interdependent with the rest of the world in these realms, and its mere size will give it strength in playing the game.

It is not likely to be a significant rule-setter for the world economy (compared with setting the rules for activities within China) unless it is willing to integrate its economic and scientific activities with other nations and weave its way into the international networks of science and technology, economics, finance, and commerce.

The difference between interdependence and integration is that between mistress and wife. Interdependence is functionally oriented; integration involves all facets of life. The evidence is strong that China wants to keep the foreigner outside of the family circle. For example, the joint ventures have been restricted to fixed (but negotiated) terms of duration—from ten to fifty years —though consideration is being given to permitting some to be "indefinite" to attract certain types of transnational corporations. Also, the Special Economic Zones isolate the foreigners in enclaves. Elsewhere in Asia, and also in Latin America, when Western enterprises band together in joint ventures or do not assimilate readily, such action is derided and criticized. Even the new Jingguang (World Trade) Center in Beijing—a fifty-two-story complex of offices, apartments, hotel rooms, restaurants, shops, and so forth—is all reserved for foreigners. Each of these orientations permits isolation and inhibits assimilation and integration.

China has not shown itself willing to integrate internationally, largely out of a concern to remain "Chinese" by rejecting foreign influence. (The Chinese remember their unpleasant historical periods of being dominated by foreigners commercially, with virtually self-ruled enclaves in cities such as Tianjin and Canton.) It can develop the confidence to integrate only after it develops its own identity. That identity has historically involved being an example, culturally, for the rest of the world—not as conqueror, but as exemplar. As an exemplar, China can either actively help to set the rules of international behavior or merely wait for others to adopt "more appropriate" patterns, as tested by China.

To achieve a prominent role in setting worldwide rules requires assumption of responsibility for making certain that the rules are appropriate, accepted, and applied by all. This requires a willingness to collaborate and negotiate with others in forming the rules. China has historically considered that it has a special role to play and a responsibility in assisting the world to move toward a greater community of interest. But it has not exercised that orientation for several decades, and it will take another decade or so to determine whether it will reassume such responsibility. If it does, it will become the dominant nation in Asia, since Japan—despite its economic strength—has so far refused to accept responsibility for setting rules in the world economy.

Only a few nations are able to play this role, and China can fulfill it if it so wishes. China has special attributes and experiences for leadership, in that it has had to face within its borders many (but not all) of the same issues that plague the world economy: efficiency (which it yet needs to learn), equity (which it has struggled with more than others), participation in policymaking by groups with diverse interests, the generation of creativity and innovation (through science and technology), the maintenance of stability and order in society, and a sufficient autonomy or independence among groups to permit desired diversity in cultures and life-styles.[43] As China resolves problems through meeting these criteria, it can show the way to others.

China can even become a leader in several of the aspects of development. Although it is not likely to be a predominant model for development in the realms of economics and commerce, science and technology, or political institutions, China has long paid attention to the development of medicine, concepts of equity, the integration of art into life, and the life of virtue. These contributions emanate not only from Buddhism and Confucianism, but also from Daoism (Taoism) and the Ancient Wisdom of Tibet. (Indeed, although not recognizing their source, many currents of ancient wisdom were espoused by Mao Zedong in the "Little Red Book.") All of these prescriptions lead to a holistic approach to life, which is the antithesis of the Western concept of reductionism. This approach seeks to gain knowledge through taking things and ideas apart. The Chinese approach, even in traditional medicine and in science, is to consider the whole and how its parts are integrated and appropriately balanced. Imbalances of one sort or another indicate an illness in the body or mind of an individual or, on a community scale, in the body politic or in society in general. The concept of balance is fundamental to the martial arts, such as T'ai Ch'i, and the Western world is sorely lacking in understanding and applying this concept. China, therefore, has a potential leadership role in demonstrating how to apply it throughout all aspects of life—at the individual, community, national, and international levels. Whether it will identify this orientation as a singular contribution that it can make to the development of the world is not clear, since the ideology of communism rejected much of the ancient wisdom of China and it is no longer in the educational curricula. Some of the Chinese leaders have even asserted that it is best to leave the ancient wisdom to ancestors and not to bring it into modern life, for fear of new ideological divisions.

Modernization is not necessarily development, and the development of the world does require a balance among the various dimensions of evolution. One of the rewards of doing business with China is that one can become stimulated to study the people and their culture, and thus to learn from its ancient wisdom about a life of virtue. Whether China will find a way to meld its historical roots in philosophy with the modernization brought from its opening to foreign business, under a system of governmental control, is yet to be seen.

China cannot fully give up centralized control without risking the loss of economic development itself. There are too many separatist pulls and jealousies between groups to let individual decision-making dominate. Individual decisions unmitigated by concern for community turn solely to individual material advances seen in the recent growth of bribery and favoritism, and so a strong ideology of individual virtue is needed, as counselled by Confucius. Such an ideology is one stressing obligation and duty over rights and privileges. To elicit such behavior requires attention to all dimensions of development, not just pursuit of modernization. This constant balancing of the collective good versus individual freedoms is faced by all governments, but it is a more challenging task for China, given its historical development and its ambitious goals. Whether a company invests in China or not, the drama will be exciting and it will strongly affect the patterns and pace of progress in the West.

FUTURE FOREIGN DIRECT INVESTMENT DECISIONS

How should prospective investors in China assess the events during the 1980s, those of the last years, and the anticipated developments? The immediate reactions of companies not yet in China in 1990 have been to adopt a wait-and-see attitude. "The bloom was off the rose," in their view, because of adverse conditions. Raw materials and supplies were short, currency was not readily convertible, and locally manufactured components were difficult to obtain.

From the viewpoint of many Chinese, "the bloom was off the rose" of foreign direct investment also because the impacts of foreign direct investment were not those expected; the anticipated increases in foreign direct investment–driven employment were smaller than expected, many jobs were lost in the establishment of the joint ventures, and economic conditions remained difficult.

Because some in the government believed that the events in Tiananmen Square were caused by too-rapid moves to economic and political liberalism, prospects for foreign direct investment in China during the 1990s are colored by Tiananmen. But although there were different official attitudes toward liberalization domestically and reception of foreign investors, the official position remained one of welcome.

An external long-term assessment of foreign direct investment prospects is required by any prospective investor. Many older China business hands have considered the government position on Tiananmen unrepresentative of China itself currently and over the longer run; some compared the situation with similar events in South Korea in which students had been killed in the quelling of riots pushing for faster political liberalization. And some have noted the generalized disgust of the people from low to high levels with the government's performance, yet an unwillingness to press to the point of generating widespread uncertainty or instability.

The government has since sought to redress the situations that gave rise to the students' protest—corruption and favoritism—without apologizing or admitting a mistake. The government seemed to fear a loss of face in terms of its historical position if it admitted error in Tiananmen; but in attempting to save face domestically, it sacrificed its face and image with the West.

Moves toward an internal relaxation of planning and control as well as the external opening will not meet all of the protestors' demands. Liberalization provides numerous opportunities for favoritism, minor graft, and major bribery, since potential profits will be significant and the desire of government officials to benefit from them will remain. Those in government who see their perquisites being reduced will seek to find new rewards in their declining positions of authority. The eagerness of some foreign investors to cut through the labyrinth of government approvals and regulations will increase the opportunities for insisting on or taking of bribes. A significant increase in corruption can be a serious obstacle to China's modernization.

Given that the government's position toward foreign direct investment is still favorable and it has kept its word and contractual agreements, prospective investors should assess whether this tragic event is unique in a critical sense or the longer-run forces analyzed above are again operative. If it is seen as unlikely to be repeated in *any* form, with repression diminishing and the opening to be continued, the longer-term opportunities in China should be given priority of assessment.

Any such analysis should be done only in comparison with emerging opportunities in the USSR and India. These three countries constitute more than 40 percent of the world's population. A really "international" company will require worldwide sources of materials and labor, as well as markets, to stay competitive—all of which are likely to be highly attractive in these three countries in the future.

Given China's potentials for the future, it is probable that there will be continuing interest by transnational companies, and others with specialized needs or strong initiatives, in building a base for long-term operations in China. However, no company with a high level of risk-aversion should consider China before other international opportunities. China is likely to remain an uncertain quotient, in the sense that it will not easily become wholly comfortable with a large open door to the rest of the world.

Though slow and halting, China's opening is inevitable. The international imperatives have become too strong to resist for any long period. China will seek to become part of the world economy; to do so, it must open up; if it opens, it must liberalize. These results are seen as fearsome by many, forcing a turn inward and yet another attempt to shut out the foreigner. But central planning cannot stand in the face of international liberalization. It can last only as long as the current octogenarians remain in authority, for no new leader arose during the confrontation, and those who appeared to be the successors were removed earlier. It will take some time for new leaders to arise. Then a new opening will occur, building on the record of the decade of the 1980s.

NOTES

1. Ford S. Worthy, "China Tests Its Capitalist Skills," *Fortune*, October 24, 1988, p. 174.

2. See *Christian Science Monitor*, August 3, 1989; and March 21, 1990.

3. A review of the planning structure as it existed in mid-1989, showing how far it had moved away from central control, was given by Madam Hao Jianziu, vice-chairperson of the State Planning Commission (Beijing) before the International Institute for Administrative Sciences' Research Committee on Planning and Forecasting (July 1989, Marrakech, Morocco); see Madam Hao Jianziu, "The Reform of the Planning Structure in China," *Futures Research Quarterly*, Summer 1989, pp. 63–72.

4. See the report in *Washington Post National Weekly*, July 10–16, 1990, p. 17. Practically the only source of foreign direct investment that did not shrink substantially was that from Taiwan. Never having the illusion that the Communists would rush to democracy and capitalism, the Taiwanese have kept a consistent approach to investment in China and have concentrated much of their activity in Fujan Province. Lately they have moved inward and north into Guangdong and Tianjin. Plans were proceeding in mid-1990 for two projects in Fujan, each investment more than $2 billion. (See *Business Week*, June 11, 1990, p. 45.)

5. *Christian Science Monitor*, April 5, 1990, p. 13. See also issue of September 18, 1989, p. 4, for an account of the government's clampdown on new enterprises on Beijing's "Silicon Street," accusing them of mixing in politics.

6. *Christian Science Monitor*, November 29, 1989, pp. 3, 8.

7. In October 1989, a party octogenarian was pulled back into the center—Chen Yun, who has been warning that Deng's reforms would lead to economic instability and that contacts with the Western world would incite political instability. Chen's influence in the party was apparently enhanced by the events of mid-1989. (See *Christian Science Monitor*, October 12, 1990, p. 6.)

8. See the three-part series on "Tiananmen Square Anniversary," in *Christian Science Monitor*, May 14, 15, and 16, 1990.

9. Frank Ching, veteran correspondent, provides an incisive review of the dilemmas facing the government in "The Agonizing Anatomy of Decision Making in Beijing," *Billion*, Inaugural issue, 1989, pp. 57–62. See also the assessment before Tiananmen of the standing of the government by Daniel Southerland, "After a Decade of Reform, Self-Doubt Prevails in China's Leadership," *Washington Post National Weekly Edition*, January 2–8, 1989, p. 16.

10. Note the difficulty students had in recruiting support in one of the poorest of China's provinces reported in *Christian Science Monitor*, November 9, 1989, p. 14.

11. In a review of his new book on *The Search for Modern China* (New York: W. W. Norton, 1990), Jonathan D. Spence is quoted as concluding that "Deng's own legacy to China, it could now be seen, was not to be one in which a united nation marched confidently toward economic and political reform. But insisting to the last that economic reforms could be completely divorced from the immensely complex social and cultural effects that the reforms brought in their train, Deng, the party elders and the younger politicians in their clique threatened jointly to commit the government again to the 19th-century fallacy that China could join the modern world entirely on its own terms, sacrificing nothing of its prevailing ideological purity. The task was even more hopeless in the 1980s than it had been in the 1880s." (*Chapel Hill Newspaper*, May 13, 1990, p. C-8.)

12. See the accounts in *Business Week*, June 19, 1989, pp. 32–33; *Newsweek*, July 3, 1989, p. 30; *Christian Science Monitor*, August 24, 1989; *Wall Street Journal*, August 30, 1989, and "Beijing's Big Squeeze," *Billion*, March 1990, pp. 38–41.

13. A review of Jim Mann's book on *Beijing Jeep: The Short, Unhappy Romance of American Business in China* (New York: Simon & Schuster, 1990) quotes him as concluding that "Western hopes of a stable and increasingly affluent China, buying huge quantities of foreign products, seem more remote today than they did a decade ago. China is likely to remain a relatively poor country for a long time. Moreover, there will always be limits on what foreign businesses may do, and sell, inside China. If there ever is truly a huge, unified China market, it will likely be captured not by the foreigners who have been pursuing this commercial dream for more than a century, but first of all by the Chinese themselves."

14. Several mayors and provincial officials have toured the United States in hope of accelerating investment into key areas, such as the Pudong Development Zone east of Shanghai. But the assessment of U.S. business is that the project is mostly "air castles" until the infrastructure is in place and the ability to earn and return profits is established. (See *Christian Science Monitor*, June 27, 1990, p. 3.)

15. A report on the organization of the student movement showed that it reflected the very communist system that they purportedly wanted to reform: "The students created an overly bureaucratic, highly policed system which like the old, operated on person connections, or guanxi.... Security... was especially tight.... What began as an efficient and necessary security system degenerated into petty abuse of authority." A piece in the May 4 issue of the student newspaper at Beijing University stated: "The tide of democracy allows no obstruction; all must comply with this trend. If not, they will be condemned by history." A student leader was characterized as "having no major errors in his thought," reflecting the intolerance of diversity. (*Washington Post National Weekly*, August 7–13, 1989.)

16. A report on the criminal justice system after Tiananmen concluded that "the party is reviving the political-legal communities through which it directs the police, state prosecutors, and the courts at virtually all levels of the legal system," and quoted a supreme court judge as saying that "the court should follow party policy and party leadership." The system was bent back to the 1950s' "militant discipline" with sanctioned torture and "automatic" sentences for specified acts, such as a year in jail for every two yards of calligraphy expressing dissatisfaction with the government or party. Even so, the civil law has remained liberalized, though many people feel constrained in exercising the rights guaranteed under it. *Christian Science Monitor*, February 22, 1990, p. 12.)

17. See *Christian Science Monitor*, August 17, 1989, p. 3.

18. See *Washington Post National Weekly*, July 17–23, 1989, p. 28.

19. See "China Has Been Giving U.S. Businesses the Cold Shoulder," *Washington Post National Weekly*, November 13–19, 1989, p. 22.

20. Changes in the equity joint venture laws included allowing foreigners to chair a joint venture board of directors, allowing a joint venture to run indefinitely, and guaranteeing that the joint venture will not be nationalized or expropriated except "under special circumstances." (*Journal of Commerce*, October 5, 1990.) Foreign reaction to these changes has not been positive. The protection from nationalization gave little reassurance in the light of Tiananmen, and few thought that a joint venture would want a non-Chinese board chair, given the difficulties of operating with the Byzantine Chinese system.

21. The action to continue unconditionally the most-favored-nation status met with severe criticism in the United States and representations from China that it should not be

penalized in trade for Tiananmen problems. (See *Christian Science Monitor*, May 25, 1990, p. 3, and June 3, 1990, p. 19.)

22. The life of a university student is not so appealing that it contrasts highly favorably with that in the country, except for the boredom and lack of potential advancement. (See "A Slice of the Dismal Life of University Students in China," *Washington Post National Weekly*, July 3–9, 1989, p. 25.)

23. See "Scholars Invoke Confucius to Attack Beijing Leadership," *Christian Science Monitor*, October 12, 1989, p. 6.

24. See "Deng's Great Leap Backward," *Business Week*, June 19, 1989, pp. 26–27; "Who's Minding the Store in China?" *Business Week*, August 14, 1989, pp. 58–59.

25. China has had long experience with corrupt governments, as indicated in the story recounted by Bette Bao Lord (wife of a former U.S. ambassador to China): "Once a sage passed by a cemetery where an old woman was wailing. 'What tragedy has befallen you?' the sage asked. 'In these parts,' she answered, 'there lives a man-eating tiger. Two months ago, it devoured my eldest. A month ago, my second son. This week my last son.' 'Why did you not flee from these hills?' 'Because more ferocious than man-eating tigers is corrupt government.' " (*Newsweek*, June 12, 1990, p. 28.)

26. Quoted in *Christian Science Monitor*, September 8, 1989, p. 8; see also *Washington Post National Weekly Edition*, August 14–20, 1989, p. 16.

27. As reported in *World Press Review*, July 1989, p. 16.

28. *Wall Street Journal*, July 20, 1989, p. A10.

29. *Christian Science Monitor*, August 29, 1989, p. 3.

30. *Christian Science Monitor*, June 23, 1989, p. 1; see also July 18, 1989, p. 4; August 28, 1989, p. 4; and November 14, 1989, p. 6. Also, *Wall Street Journal*, July 20, 1989, p. 1.

31. *Christian Science Monitor*, August 30, 1989, p. 4.

32. In an optimistic assessment, Hazel Henderson argues that it may well do so, having the advantages of a late start, a rejection of ideology, a cohesive society, and a systemic approach to development. (See "China: Key Player in a New World Game," *Futures Research Quarterly*, Fall 1987, pp. 29–42.)

33. Vusamazulu Credo Mutwa, *Indaba My Children* (London: Kahn & Averill, 1966), p. 8.

34. Conversation with Dr. Duan Lian Cheng, former editor of *The Beijing Review*.

35. Premier Li Peng, in a speech in early 1990, emphasized that despite the moves in Central Europe, "socialist China will stand rock firm in the East." This required a step up in ideological education and the promotion of "communism, self-reliance, hard work, [and] revolutionary traditions." (*Christian Science Monitor*, March 23, 1990.)

36. See *Christian Science Monitor*, June 4, 1990, p. 3.

37. See, for example, "In China, Standard Communist Behavior," *Wall Street Journal*, June 23, 1989.

38. For an excellent review of the problems faced by China in gaining political stability, including an assessment of the heavy hand of history and tradition, see Lucian Pye, "China: Erratic State, Frustrated Society," *Foreign Affairs*, Fall 1990, pp. 56ff. In an earlier article, Pye assessed the relationship between economic reform and political change in "Liberalization in China: Can Economics Be the Engine of Political Change?" *Fletcher Forum*, Summer 1988, pp. 221ff.

39. See "China Puts Brakes on Reforms," *Christian Science Monitor*, December 6, 1989, p. 4.

40. A report in late 1989 stated that the SOEs had lost competitive position to the private enterprises, with a consequent drop in the portion of gross national product produced by the SOEs: "Today, state factories employing nearly 100 million workers produce only half of China's industrial output, compared with 80 percent in 1978. Chronically in the red, state-owned firms lost nearly $2 billion in the first half of this year, double the total losses of 1988. Subsidies for enterprises totalled $1.2 billion in 1988, consuming roughly one fifth of the government budget, according to official statistics." (*Christian Science Monitor*, September 19, 1989, p. 1.)

41. An offset is the increase in moonlighting. Second jobs are sought by many for additional income, and they are offered to obtain scarce skills. (See *World Press Review*, March 1990, p. 64.)

42. On the ability of Guangdong to fight the centralization, see "Guangdong Plays the Waiting Game," *Billion*, March 1990, pp. 51–53.

43. The significance of these "criteria of acceptability" of rules for a new international economic order has been shown in J. N. Behrman, *Industrial Policies: International Restructuring and Transnationals* (Lexington, Mass: Lexington Books, 1984).

Selected Bibliography

1986 Almanac of China's Foreign Economic Relations and Trade. Beijing, 1986.

A. T. Kearney (Co.) and the International Trade Research Institute of the PRC. *Manufacturing Equity Joint Ventures in China*. Chicago, Ill.: A. T. Kearney, Inc., 1987.

Administrative Committee. *Hundred Questions and Answers on Investment Rules of the Guangzhou Economic and Technological Development Zone*, Guangzhou: Economic and Technological Development Zone, 1987.

Barnett, A. Doak, and Ralph N. Clough, eds. *Modernizing China: Post-Mao Reform and Development*. Boulder, Colo.: Westview, 1986.

Bernstein, Richard. *From the Center of the Earth: The Search for the Truth About China*. Boston: Little, Brown & Co., 1982.

Blunden, Caroline, and Mark Elvin. *Cultural Atlas of China*. Oxford: Equinox, 1983.

Bond, Michael Harris. *The Psychology of the Chinese People*. London: Oxford University Press, 1986.

Brown, D. G.. *Partnership with China: Sino-Foreign Joint Ventures in Historical Perspective*. Boulder, Colo.: Westview, 1986.

Browning, Graeme. *If Everybody Bought One Shoe: American Capitalism in Communist China*. New York: Hill and Wang, 1989.

Butterfield, Fox. *China Alive in the Bitter Sea*. New York: Bantam Books, 1982.

Campbell, Nigel. *China Strategies: The Inside Story*. Manchester: University of Manchester/University of Hong Kong, 1986.

Cannon, Terry, and Alan Jenkins, eds. *The Geography of Contemporary China: The Impact of Deng Xiaoping's Decade*. New York: Routledge, 1990.

China's Foreign Economic Legislature. Beijing: Foreign Languages Press, 1986.

China's Socialist Economy; An Outline History of China. Beijing: Foreign Languages Press, 1986.

Chiu, Hungdah, and Shao-Chuan Leng, eds. *China: Seventy Years After the 1911 Hsin-Hai Revolution*. Charlottesville: University of Virginia Press, 1984.

Creel, H. G. *Chinese Thought from Confucius to Mao Tse-Tung*. Chicago: University of Chicago Press, 1953.

———. *The Origins of Statecraft in China*. Chicago: University of Chicago Press, 1970.

Editorial Board. *Tianjin Opening to the World*. Reform in China's Cities Series. Tianjin: The Red Flag Publishing House, June 1985.

Fairbank, John K. *The United States and China*. 4th ed. Cambridge, Mass.: Harvard University Press, 1983.

Feuchtwang, S., A. Hussain, and T. Pairault, eds. *Transforming China's Economy in the Eighties*. Boulder, Colo.: Westview, 1988.

Franz, Uli. *Deng Xiaoping*. New York: Harcourt Brace Jovanovich, 1988.

General Office. *Shanghai: Investment Environment, Laws and Regulations*. Shanghai: Municipal People's Government, February 1987.

Ginsburg, N., and B. A. Lalor, eds. *China: The 1980s Era*. Boulder, Colo: Westview, 1984.

Goldstein, S. M., ed. *China Briefing, 1984*. Boulder, Colo.: Westview, 1985.

Harding, Harry. *China's Second Revolution: Reform After Mao*. Washington, D.C.: Brookings Institution, 1987.

Heng, Liang, and Judith Shapiro. *Son of the Revolution*. New York: Random House, Vintage Books, 1983.

Hinton, William. *Fanshen*. New York: Random House, Vintage Books, 1966.

Holbrook, B. *The Stone Monkey: An Alternative, Chinese Scientific, Reality*. New York: William Morrow & Co., 1981.

Holton, Richard H., and Wang Xi, eds. *U.S.-China Economic Relations—Present and Future*. Berkeley: University of California, Institute of East Asia Studies, 1989.

Kemp, Lynette. "Investing in China: Where, How and Why." *Special Report* No. 1071. London: The Economist Publications, Ltd., 1987.

Lacy, Creighton. *Coming Home—to China*. Philadelphia: Westminister Press, 1978.

Li, Victor H. *Law Without Lawyers: A Comparative View of Law in China and the United States*. Boulder, Colo.: Westview, 1978.

Lippit, Victor D. *The Economic Development of China*. Armonk, N.Y.: M. E. Sharpe, 1987.

Lord, Bette Bao. *Leagacies: A Chinese Mosaic*. New York: Alfred A. Knopf, 1990.

Macleod, Roderick. *China Inc.: How to Do Business with the Chinese*. New York: Bantam Books, 1988.

Major, J. S., and A. J. Kane. *China Briefing, 1987*. Boulder, Colo.: Westview, 1987.

Massimino, Sal T. *How to Sell to the People's Republic of China*. New York: International Group Technical Publishing Co., Thomond Press, 1980.

Mathews, Jay, and Linda Mathews. *One Billion: A Chinese Chronicle*. New York: Ballantine, 1983.

Michael, Franz. *China Through the Ages: History of a Civilization*. Boulder, Colo.: Westview, 1986.

Oksenberg, M. *China's Developmental Experience*. New York: Praeger, 1973.

Pye, Lucian. *The Spirit of Chinese Politics: A Psychological Study*. Cambridge, Mass.: MIT Press, 1968.

———. *Chinese Commercial Negotiating Style*. Cambridge, Mass.: Oelgeschlager, Gunn & Hain, 1982.

———. *China: An Introduction*. 3rd ed. Boston: Little, Brown & Co., 1984.

Rabushka, Alvin. *The New China*. Boulder, Colo.: Westview, 1987.

"The Readjustment in the Chinese Economy." *China Quarterly*, no. 100, December 1984. A special issue on Deng Xiaoping's economic reforms.

Richman, Barry M. *Industrial Society in Communist China*. New York: Random House, 1969.

Rossbach, S. *Feng Shui: The Chinese Art of Placement*. New York: E. P. Dutton, 1983.

Schell, Orville. *To Get Rich Is Glorious*. New York: Pantheon, 1984.

Spence, Jonathan. *To Change China: Western Advisers in China, 1620–1960*. New York: Penguin Books, 1969.

Teng, W., and N. T. Wang, eds. *Transnational Corporations and China's Open Door Policy*. Lexington, Mass.: Lexington Books, 1988.

Tung, Rosalie L. *Chinese Industrial Society After Mao*. Lexington, Mass.: Lexington Books, 1982.

The National Council for U.S.-China Trade. *U.S. Joint Ventures in China: A Progress Report*. Washington, D.C.: U.S. Department of Commerce, March 1987.

U.S.-China Business Council. *U.S. Investment in China*. New York, 1990.

Wei, Yung. *Communist China: A System-Functional Reader*. Columbus, Ohio: Merrill, 1972.

Woronoff, Jon. *Asia's "Miracle" Economies*. Armonk, N.Y.: M. E. Sharpe, 1987.

Wright, Arthur F., ed. *Studies in Chinese Thought*. Chicago: University of Chicago Press, 1953.

Index

About the Authors

JAMES E. SHAPIRO recently retired as President and CEO of Dupont-Xerox Imaging in Lionville, Pennsylvania and is currently a consultant in the field of joint ventures. He was formerly Corporate V.P. and President of China and South Pacific Operations for Xerox.

JACK N. BEHRMAN is Luther Hodges Distinguished Professor at the Kenan-Flagler School of Business of the University of North Carolina at Chapel Hill. He teaches international business, business/government relations, ethics, and comparative management. He has published over 100 articles and some 40 books and monographs on international economic and industrial issues.

WILLIAM A. FISCHER is the Dalton L. McMichael, Sr. Professor of Business Administration at the Kenan-Flagler School of Business of the University of North Carolina at Chapel Hill. He is also Professor at the International Institute for Management Development (IMD), Lausanne, Switzerland.

SIMON G. POWELL is a Legislative Analyst with the Maryland General Assembly. He is the author of a forthcoming book *Agricultural Reform in China* as well as numerous articles and book chapters. He received his doctorate in Geography (specializing in China) from the University of Leeds, England and lived in China for a year.